Islamic Fashion and Anti-Fashion

Islamic Fashion and Anti-Fashion

New Perspectives from Europe and North America

Edited by
Emma Tarlo and Annelies Moors

B L O O M S B U R Y
LONDON • NEW DELHI • NEW YORK • SYDNEY

Bloomsbury Academic
An imprint of Bloomsbury Publishing Plc

50 Bedford Square	1385 Broadway
London	New York
WC1B 3DP	NY 10018
UK	USA

www.bloomsbury.com

First published 2013

© Emma Tarlo, Annelies Moors and contributors, 2013

British Library Cataloguing-in-Publication Data
A catalogue record for this book is available from the British Library.

ISBN: HB: 978-0-8578-5334-9
PB: 978-0-8578-5335-6
ePDF: 978-0-8578-5336-3
ePub: 978-0-8578-5337-0

Library of Congress Cataloging-in-Publication Data
A catalog record for this book is available from the Library of Congress.

Typeset by Apex CoVantage, LLC, Madison, WI, USA
Printed and bound in Great Britain

Contents

List of Illustrations

FIGURES

TABLE

PLATES

Acknowledgements

A volume of this kind has many points of origin and accumulates many debts and friendships on the way. As authors and editors we were first brought together by a shared interest in the everyday dress practices of Muslim women situated in diverse circumstances around the world, whether in Britain, India, Palestine or Yemen. Following a workshop organized by Annelies at the University of Amsterdam in 2005, we went on to jointly edit a special double issue of the journal *Fashion Theory* on the topic of Muslim fashions. Although the volume focussed mainly on non-European contexts, and included contributions about Egypt, Turkey, India, West Africa, Iran and Yemen, working on it alerted us to the absence of research about the growing presence of Islamic fashion in Europe and to the potential offered by fashion as a tool for critiquing the limited and repetitive polemical debates commonly invoked in discussions of Muslim dress and of the place of Islam in Europe more generally. Our first debt, then, is to the many Muslim women in different European cities whose clothing choices and experiments commanded our attention and who willingly shared with us intimate details of their sartorial biographies, dilemmas and aspirations, many of which feature in this book.

We would like to thank NORFACE for its generous funding of our research project, *Islamic Fashion: The Emergence of Islam as a Social Force in Europe* (2007–10), which formed part of the wider programme, *Re-emergence of Religion as a Social Force in Europe*. We are also grateful to the Cultural Dynamics Programme at NWO (The Organization for Scientific Research in the Netherlands) for funding some of the costs incurred at later stages of the project. Our thanks also extend to Goldsmiths, University of London, the former ISIM (International Institute for the Study of Islam in the Modern World) in the Netherlands, and the University of Stockholm in Sweden for hosting workshops linked to the project. We have greatly benefitted from the insights of all those who formed part of this initial team of researchers and participated with us in these workshops: Connie Carøe Christiansen, Leila Karin Österlind, Sigrid Nökel, Annika Rabo, Degla Salim, Irene Bregenze and Arzu Ünal. Later, we were joined by scholars who were working on similar themes in Poland, Romania, Italy, France, Germany, Turkey, Britain, Sweden, the United States and Canada, and we thank them all for their contributions. In particular we would like to thank Alessia Gammarota for offering a fashion photographer's view of hijabi street fashion in the United Kingdom which captures some of the visual creativity and playfulness so often left out of discussions about Muslim women. A special thanks also to Zinah Nur Sharif for agreeing to be featured both on the cover of the book and inside, where she lends insight into the life and aspirations of a hijabi fashion blogger.

Finally, a collective volume of this kind with written and visual contributions from a number of researchers, many of whom are not native English speakers, requires a considerable amount of painstaking labour and we would like to thank Page McClean and Seyla Wachlin, both of whom provided invaluable assistance with the preparation of the manuscript. At Bloomsbury we would like to thank Anna Wright and Emily Roessler for their enthusiasm and support, without which the volume could not have come to fruition.

Notes on Contributors

RUSTEM ERTUG ALTINAY is a doctoral candidate in the Department of Performance Studies at New York University. Ertug's primary field of research is gender, sexuality and the politics of subjectivity in Turkey. His articles have been published in many peer-reviewed journals, including *Women's Studies Quarterly, Feminist Media Studies, Journal of Women's History* and *International Journal of Feminist Approaches to Bioethics* as well as various edited volumes. Ertug's dissertation analyzes the role of fashion and embodied practices in regulating the politics of subjectivity and belonging throughout the republican history of Turkey.

BRENDA ANDERSON is Assistant Professor of Women's and Gender Studies and Religious Studies at Luther College, University of Regina, Saskatchewan, Canada. Her dissertation examined feminist Muslim–Christian dialogical activism and she is a co-investigator of a Canadian SSHRC grant researching 'New Muslim public spheres in the digital age: identity, community, diversity and authority in Canada'. Her work focuses on the intersectionality of gender identities and colonialism and includes research on missing and murdered Aboriginal women. The international conference she organised on this theme led to the publication *Torn from our Midst: Voices of Grief, Healing and Action from the Missing Women Conference, 2008* (2010).

SYNNØVE BENDIXSEN is a postdoctoral researcher at IMER Bergen Uni Rokkansenteret, Norway. She holds a joint PhD in Social Anthropology from the Humboldt Universität and Ecole des Hautes Etudes en Sciences Sociales. She has conducted extensive fieldwork on Muslim youth in Germany and is the author of *The Religious Identity of Young Muslim Women in Berlin: An Ethnographic Study* (2013). She has further published a number of articles and book chapters on the religious performance of Islam among young Muslims in Europe. Currently she is working on the living conditions of irregular migrants and their political mobilization in Norway.

CONNIE CARØE CHRISTIANSEN is associate professor in the Department of Society and Globalization, Roskilde University, Denmark. Beyond consumption and Islam, her research interests include migration, gender and development. Currently she is involved in a DANIDA-funded project which collaborates with Sana'a University in Yemen to establish a Masters programme in International Development and Gender. Her recent publications include 'Migrants and Non-migrants in Kücükkale: Consumption and Cultural Differentiation in the Transnational Community', *Journal of Ethnic and Migration Studies* 39.1 (2013) and 'Gender and Social Remittances; Return Migrants from the Horn of Africa to Yemen', *Chroniques Yéménite* 17 (2012).

MARIA CURTIS teaches Anthropology and Cross Cultural Studies at the University of Houston-Clear Lake, Texas. She has conducted research in several cities in Morocco, Turkey, and among American Muslims in the USA, and has written about the ways in which American Muslim immigrant women counter Islamophobia through acts of generosity, renewed piety and religious beliefs that come to life through ritual, clothing, music, new media and public events. Her current work focuses on diversity within the greater American Muslim community, and the ways that they challenge post-9/11 stereotypes and create multi-faith spaces of public dialogue.

ALESSIA GAMMAROTA is a professional photographer with a degree from the Academy of Fine Arts in Florence. For the past ten years she has been taking photographs of fashion and collaborating with leading production agencies. She regularly documents the major fashion weeks (New York, London, Paris and Milan) as well as related events such as Milan Design Week and Pitti Uomo. Her work has appeared in numerous magazines, including *InStyle Russia, Harper's Bazaar* and *Elle* (UK). She has recently been working on an individual project about young Muslim women's relationship to fashion.

FRANZ VOLKER GREIFENHAGEN is Dean of Luther College and Professor of Religious Studies at the University of Regina, Regina, Saskatchewan, Canada. He researches both Islam and the Hebrew Bible, with special interest in contemporary Muslims in Canada and Quranic/Biblical intertextuality. Recently he published articles on the 12th *surah* of the Quran, on Internet polemics utilizing the Quran and the bible, and on the Canadian television comedy *Little Mosque on the Prairie,* and co-authored *An Introduction to the Hebrew Bible: A Thematic Approach* (2008).

BANU GÖKARIKSEL is Associate Professor of Geography at the University of North Carolina, Chapel Hill. Her research analyses the formation of Muslim subjects, spaces and commodities in Turkey. She is currently collaborating with Anna Secor on a National Science Foundation-funded project that examines the production and consumption of veiling-fashion. Her publications have appeared in journals *Area, Global Networks, Social and Cultural Geography, Transactions of the Institute of British Geographers, The Annals of the Association of American Geographers,* and *Gender, Place, & Culture.* She has contributed to several edited books and co-edited a special issue of the *Journal of Middle East Women's Studies*.

KATARZYNA GÓRAK-SOSNOWSKA is assistant professor in the Department of Economic Sociology, Warsaw School of Economics and in the Department of Arabic and Islamic Studies, University of Warsaw, and is vice-dean for Master's Studies at the Warsaw School of Economics. Her research interests include the socio-economic problems of the Middle East and North Africa and Islam in Poland and wider Europe. She has published three monographs in Polish, including *Muzułmańska kultura konsumpcyjna* (2011), and a variety of textbooks on intercultural education, and is editor of *Muslims in Poland and Eastern Europe* (2011).

REINA LEWIS is Artscom Centenary Professor of Cultural Studies at the London College of Fashion, University of the Arts London. Her books are *Re-Fashioning Orientalism: New Trends in Muslim Style* (forthcoming), *Rethinking Orientalism: Women, Travel and the Ottoman Harem* (2004) and *Gendering Orientalism: Race, Femininity and Representation* (1996). She is editor of *Modest Fashion: Styling Bodies, Mediating Faith* (2013) and, with Zeynep Inankur and Mary Roberts, *The Poetics and Politics of Place: Ottoman Istanbul and British Orientalism* (2011); with Nancy Micklewright, *Gender, Modernity and Liberty: Middle Eastern and Western Women's Writings* (2006); with Sara Mills, *Feminist Postcolonial Theory: A Reader* (2003); and with Peter Horne, *Outlooks: Lesbian and Gay Visual Cultures* (1996).

MICHAŁ ŁYSZCZARZ is assistant professor in the Department of Sociology at the University of Warmia and Mazury in Olsztyn and a member of the Common Council of Catholics and Muslims and the *Association of Tatars* of the *Republic of Poland*. His main interest is the sociology of ethnic minorities, in particular the Polish Tatar community. His research focuses on the sociology of culture and religion, especially the process of conversion to Islam and religious dialogue between Christianity and Islam. He is also engaged in research on the assimilation and integration of the Arab emigrant community in Poland, especially in the multicultural borderline area.

PIA KARLSSON MINGANTI is a researcher of ethnology at Stockholm University and guest researcher at the University of Bologna and the Uppsala Religion and Society Research Centre, where she is also a member of the Impact of Religion excellence program. Her research fields include young Muslims in Europe, transnational migration, religious pluralism and cultural transformations of identity and gender relations. Her publications include *Muslima. Islamisk väckelse och unga kvinnors förhandlingar om genus* (2007) and 'Challenging from Within: Youth Associations and Female Leadership in Swedish Mosques' in *Women, Leadership and Mosques: Changes in Contemporary Islamic Authority* (2012).

ANNELIES MOORS is an anthropologist and professor of contemporary Muslim societies at the University of Amsterdam. She has published widely on Muslim family law, wearing gold, postcards of Palestine, migrant domestic labour and Islamic dress and fashion. Her publications include *Women, Property and Islam: Palestinian Experiences 1920–1990* (1995), and she has edited special issues of *Islamic Law and Society* (2003), *Fashion Theory* (2007, with Emma Tarlo), *Social Anthropology* (2009, with Ruba Salih) and *Material Religion* (2012). She is currently writing a book on face-veiling, and will soon start a research project on new forms of Muslim marriages.

LEILA KARIN ÖSTERLIND is a PhD student in the Department of Ethnology, History of Religions and Gender Studies, Stockholm University. Her PhD project focuses on the relation between Muslim fashions and global mainstream fashion.

DEGLA SALIM is a PhD student in the Department of Social Anthropology, Stockholm University. She is now working on her doctoral thesis investigating support group activities directed towards children to guardians with substance misuse problems and/or mental health issues. She has conducted fieldwork in various parts of Sweden and is presently engaged in the theoretical domain of risk and medical anthropology.

ANNA J. SECOR is Professor of Geography at the University of Kentucky. Her research on Islam, state and society in Turkey has been funded by the National Science Foundation. Her most recent work is a collaborative NSF-funded project with Banu Gökarıksel on Islamic fashions. She is author of over thirty articles and book chapters that have appeared in journals such as *Area, Annals of the Association of American Geographers, Antipode, Environment and Planning D: Society and Space, Gender, Place and Culture, Journal of Middle East Women's Studies,* and *Transactions of the Institute of British Geographers.*

DANIELA STOICA is an associate lecturer in the Faculty of European Studies at Babeş-Bolyai University, Cluj-Napoca, Romania. She obtained a PhD in sociology for a thesis on Dutch and Romanian women's experiences of conversion to Islam. Her main research interests are Islamic conversion, Muslims in Europe, citizenship and migration, politics and gender, discourse analysis and online ethnography. She has contributed to *Muslims in Poland and Eastern Europe* (2011), edited by Katarzyna Górak-Sosnowska, and published an article in *Studia Europaea* (2011) concerning Romanian women converts.

EMMA TARLO is Professor of Anthropology at Goldsmiths, University of London. Her research interests include urban anthropology and the anthropology of dress, textiles, material culture, memory and the body. She is author of

Clothing Matters: Dress and Identity in India (1996), *Unsettling Memories; Narratives of the Emergency in Delhi* (2003) and *Visibly Muslim: Fashion, Politics, Faith* (2010). Her new research, which is supported by a Major Research Fellowship from the Leverhulme Trust, focuses on the global trade in human hair with emphasis on the different religious and cultural projects in which hair is entangled.

R. ARZU ÜNAL obtained her BA in social anthropology from Yeditepe University and her MA in sociology from Boğaziçi University in Istanbul. Currently, she is a PhD candidate at the Amsterdam Institute for Social Science Research (AISSR), University of Amsterdam. Her dissertation about *tesettür* wardrobes of Turkish Dutch women focuses on the shifting relationships between Islam, dress and gender. She is the co-author of 'Formats, Fabrics, and Fashions: Muslim Headscarves Revisited', *Material Religion* 8.3 (2012).

Introduction: Islamic Fashion and Anti-fashion: New Perspectives from Europe and North America

Annelies Moors and Emma Tarlo

The past three decades have seen the growth and spread of debates about the visible presence of Islamic dress in the streets of Europe and North America. These debates, which have accelerated and intensified after 9/11, focus on the apparent rights and wrongs of headscarves and face veils, on whether their wearing is forced or chosen and to what extent they might indicate the spread of Islamic fundamentalism or pose security concerns. Such dress practices are also perceived as a threat to multiculturalism and to Euro-American norms and values which are often spoken of as if they are fixed and shared. Such arguments have been used to support bans and restrictions on Islamic dress practices in the name of modernity, secularism or women's emancipation. What is curious about these debates is not only the way in which they have become so entrenched but also how out of tune they are with actual developments in Muslim dress practices which have, over the past decade, been undergoing rapid transformation. They ignore, for example, the development and proliferation of what has become known, both in Muslim circles and beyond, as Islamic fashion and how the emergence of such a phenomenon does not so much signal Muslim alienation from European and American cultural norms as complex forms of critical and creative engagement with them. This book grows then out of awareness of the discrepancy between public discourses about Muslim dress and actual developments in Islamic fashion in the streets of Europe and America, pointing to the need for greater understanding and more nuanced interpretation. Taking critical distance from the popular assumption that fashion is an exclusively Western or secular phenomenon, it points to the complex convergence of ethical and aesthetic concerns expressed through new forms of Islamic fashion whilst simultaneously highlighting the ambivalence some Muslims feel towards such developments. It also suggests that just as Islamic fashion engages with and contributes towards mainstream fashion in various ways, so Muslim critiques

of fashion often share much in common with critiques from secular and feminist sources.

The research on which this book is based was conducted in a variety of cities across Europe and America, enabling us to gain perspective both on the
diversity of Islamic dress practices in different locations and on different regional responses to these. The aim was not to gain statistical representativity but to elucidate how Muslim women in different locations relate to Islam,
dress and fashion through a series of qualitative case studies. Although the
range of countries and cities covered is far from exhaustive, it does provide a
basis for identifying common themes as well as the specificities of particular
sites. Whilst such comparative observations mediate against simplistic ideas
of a single Muslim culture, they also highlight the extent to which so-called
Euro-American values and norms are far from clear cut and that what counts
as European is based on a very particular Western and Northern European experience. By bringing the experiences and clothing preferences of Muslims in
Eastern Europe into the equation, including Polish Tatars, Arab migrants and
Romanian converts, we gain a sense of just how varied the European Muslim
experience and forms of cultural expression are.

One lesson quickly learned by all the researchers who have contributed to
this book is the impossibility of simply reading from appearances. To highlight
this point we include an interview with Zinah, the young fashion blogger represented on the cover of this book whose attitudes towards fashion and matters of appearance only become accessible through dialogue. More generally,
it has been through engaging with Muslim women concerning the motivations
behind their dress that we have been able to gain insight into the complexity
and sensitivity of the issues involved. For example, women wearing similar
outfits may have very different motivations for doing so even within a specific
location. In some cases, the adoption of a particular type of headscarf may
be a first step towards starting to wear covered dress; in other cases, for
those who used to wear more sober forms of covering in the past, the very
same headscarf may be a step towards experimentation with more fashionable styles. Opinions also vary substantially concerning how much a woman
ought to cover and to what extent covering can be considered a religious
virtue. In addition, decisions about what to wear are made in relation to the
attitudes and opinions of relevant others, whether family, peers in school, colleagues at work or even strangers, all of whom may express approval or dis-
approval of particular trends. They are also influenced by popular culture and
political contexts, which may be more or less conducive to developments in
Islamic fashion. In continuity with our earlier research (Tarlo and Moors 2007;
Moors 2009a; Tarlo 2010b, 2013b), we have found it particularly important
to consider dress biographies and the contexts in which they operate, which
include concerns about religion, ethnicity, class, generation and fashion. At
the same time, we have been struck by the variety of styles worn, not only

between women in different regional settings but also amongst women living in the same locations.

In this introduction, we begin by discussing some of the key debates raised by the study of Islamic fashion in Europe and America, addressing the relation between dress and religion, the turn towards materiality in religious studies, women's religious agency and the importance of considering style. We contextualize the emergence of Islamic fashion in Europe and America by reference to the spread of a global Islamic revival and the increased emphasis placed on reflexive forms of Islam. We review how clothing practices have transformed in Muslim majority countries from the 1970s onwards and how these changes relate to recent developments in Islamic fashion in Europe and America. At the same time, we engage with fashion theory, suggesting how Islamic fashion enables us to question many of the assumptions embedded within the world of fashion and fashion scholarship. In particular, we draw attention to the relationship between ethics and aesthetics in Islamic fashion and anti-fashion discourses and practices. We also point to the significance of location and how the Muslim presence in different European and American contexts follows different historical trajectories and engages with different forms of secular governance which shape clothing possibilities for Muslims in particular ways. We end by drawing out some of the key themes that have emerged through comparing Muslim experiences and fashions in diverse locations ranging from a small city in the Canadian prairies to large European cities, including London, Paris, Berlin, Stockholm, Copenhagen, Cluj and Amsterdam. Our key contention is that through their visual material and bodily presence young women who wear Islamic fashion disrupt and challenge public stereotypes about Islam, women, social integration and the veil even if their voices are often drowned out in political and legal debates on these issues.

DRESS AND RELIGION: A TROUBLED RELATIONSHIP?

What does dress have to do with religion? Conventionally, religion has been studied in terms of doctrine and institutions and more recently, especially in the case of Islam, as a sociopolitical movement and threat to secularism. With a focus on Islamic fashion, and the everyday corporeal practices of young Muslim women, the starting point of this book is different. We argue that to better understand the importance of dress to religion, we need to go beyond the modernist concept of religion, grounded in a European protestant tradition, that considers inner belief and faith as the mainstay of religion, with external forms, such as ritual practices and material culture as marginal phenomena (Asad 1993; Keane 2008; Meyer and Houtman 2012). We also need to move beyond the idea that the primary role of religious dress practices is the maintenance of religious boundaries and the reproduction of tradition

(Arthur 1999). Whilst such ideas are relevant, they are inadequate for capturing the dynamic quality of contemporary Islamic fashion with its engagement both with the secular material world and with discursive and reflexive interpretations of Islam. Our focus on particular dress styles and the dynamics of Islamic fashion and anti-fashion tallies, then, with the growing interest in the tangible, material presence of religion in everyday life and with the recognition that for religion to be present in the world, it inevitably requires particular forms of expression. As our previous research has shown, if concerns with modesty encourage the adoption of covered dress, attention needs to be paid not only to the fact of covering but also to the multiple forms it may take, from simple head covering to full body and face covering, from sober to fashionable styles which refer not only to religiosity but also class, ethnicity, generation and fashion as well as membership of particular taste communities which may favour an urban, trendy, sporty, elegant or feminine look (Moors 2009a; Tarlo 2010b).

At the same time, it is important to recognize that some Muslims share a concept of religion that foregrounds faith and spirituality rather than external manifestations of religious belonging. There exists both a historic Islamic tradition that privileges interiority and a more contemporary turn towards such a focus. For some Muslims, modesty is first and foremost perceived as an inner quality that does not require the adoption of covered dress. At the same time, many Muslims consider corporeal practices, including wearing covered dress, to be a religious virtue to which they aspire, even if they are not always able to do so consistently. Wearing fashionable forms of Islamic covering or dressing modestly through the layering of mainstream fashion garments may serve to make religious practice more appealing for some women, whilst for others such fashionable interpretations of Islamic dress are perceived as a distortion or distraction from more weighty theological concerns. In this book, we introduce a wide diversity of perspectives, demonstrating how Muslim women in different European and American contexts position themselves through different levels of engagement and disengagement with fashion. In this sense, Islamic fashion becomes a tangible medium of public debate both amongst Muslim women and in relation to wider publics.

The question of how far external appearances can be read as indicators of internal states has long been an area of both academic and popular debate. On one hand, in everyday interactions people tend to assume that it is possible to read appearances and to know the interior self and inner character from external signs (Finkelstein 1997). Yet it has been suggested that in Europe at least, from the nineteenth century on, there has also been a growing suspicion that appearances are constructed and hence cannot be trusted as 'authentic' (Entwistle 2000: 123). Dress, then, has the potential to both reveal and conceal, and literature and poetry from around the world is replete with examples of its deceptive and seductive potential. In a similar vein, Muslims, including those who wear visibly Muslim dress and consider covering as a religious virtue, often underline that adopting modest dress is not necessarily evidence of a modest, virtuous self. They recognize that some women who cover may not do so out of theological conviction, but, for a whole variety of reasons from pressure from others, a desire to fit in or a preference for a particular look.

TAKING RELIGION SERIOUSLY IN THE STUDY OF ISLAMIC DRESS

If the significance of dress has often been downplayed in studies of religion, the significance of religion has sometimes been underestimated in studies of Muslim dress practices. More than a decade ago, Mahmood (2001) suggested that the literature on veiling only paid scant attention to the religious motivations of many of the women concerned. Instead, covered dress had often been discussed in instrumentalist terms—for instance, as a means for women to acquire greater freedom of movement (MacLeod 1991) or as a form of identity politics or sign of allegiance to Islamist movements (El-Guindi 1981; Ahmed 1992; Göle 1996; Navaro-Yashin 2002). This has also been the case in public debates and policy-making. In a critical reading of the French Stasi report, Asad (2006) argues that this report's definition of Muslim headcoverings as 'conspicuous signs of religious affiliation' did not entertain the possibility that the young women concerned may cover their heads because they considered this a religious duty. Focussing on devoutly practising Muslim women participating in the mosque movement in Cairo, Mahmood (2001, 2005) emphasizes the extent to which adopting covered dress was first and foremost a religiously motivated practice for these women.

Mahmood's work has been important not only for stressing the strong levels of religious intent expressed by some Muslim women who adopt covered dress but also for suggesting how we might rethink debates about gender and agency in relation to religious practice. Writings about Muslim women have often interpreted covered dress as a symbol or tool for women's subordination in Islam (see Ahmed 1992), while those arguing against such an interpretation have considered covering as a form of resistance to domination. In Mahmood's view, both approaches share a definition of agency which assumes that humans have an innate desire for freedom which is defined in terms of individual autonomy. Contesting this view, Mahmood analyses the ethical practices of the women participating in the mosque movement in Cairo as a form of willed submission. Building on Foucault's notion of subjectivation, she proposes an understanding of agentic power as 'a capacity for action that specific relations of subordination create and enable' (2005: 17, 28). In doing so, she moves us beyond the simplistic dichotomy of freedom versus force towards a more complex and less ethnocentric understanding of human motivations and capacities for action.

Finally, Mahmood also takes issue with how the relationship between the interior self and exterior behaviour has conventionally been understood. Whereas wearing covered dress is often considered an expression of a pre-existing inner state of being, she argues that for women of the mosque movement the reverse would appear to be the case. To them, outward behaviour and bodily acts were crucial means by which to realize or bring about a desired inner state of being, for it is through the repeated performance of such practices that a virtuous self is produced (Asad 1993; Mahmood 2005). Covering then works as a technique of the self, as a bodily act that serves not only as the marker of piety but also as 'the *ineluctable means* by which one trains oneself to be pious' (Mahmood 2005: 158). Emphasis on the performative power of dress has similarly been a theme of much recent historic and anthropological work on dress (see, for example, Comaroff 1996; Tarlo 1996, 2005; Woodward 2007; Lemire 2010; Riello and McNeil 2010). Concerning the relationship between dress and subjectivity Miller (2010) argues that clothing is not simply 'a form of representation, a semiotic sign or symbol of the person [but] plays a considerable and active part in constituting the particular experience of the self' (2010: 40). Such an approach then goes beyond the debate concerning the ambiguities of how far dress conceals or reveals inner states towards a focus on the production of subjectivity.

ISLAMIC FASHION: CONSIDERATIONS OF FORM AND STYLE

Whilst Mahmood's work has enabled a rethinking of the relationship between dress and religious subjectivity, it is important to remember that the understandings and levels of piety expressed by women in the mosque movement in Cairo are not representative of all Muslim women. In fact, Mahmood herself acknowledges that other women in Cairo do not consider modesty to be an 'attribute of the body' but rather consider it to be 'a characteristic of the individual's interiority which is then expressed in bodily form' (2005: 160). What the findings of this volume suggest is that not only do different Muslim women hold different views regarding this issue but also that it is not uncommon to find individual women who express both arguments, suggesting that covering is both the means to produce a pious self and an expression of that piety (Deeb 2006; Jouili 2009). Such findings highlight the multifaceted interactive relationship people have with hijab and other forms of covering.

Secondly, this book departs significantly from the work of Mahmood through its focus on issues of fashion and style. It is concerned not just with the act of covering but the numerous forms this may take and in particular the spread of new forms of Islamic fashion and anti-fashion. Once we shift attention to the multiple forms of Islamic dress worn by Muslims, whether in Europe, America or in Muslim majority countries, we become aware that forms of covered dress do not relate simply to matters of religion but also to issues of national and ethnic belonging, class and generation, consumer culture, aesthetic prefer-ence, fashion and style (Moors and Tarlo 2007; Tarlo 2010b). In other words, whilst issues of piety and modesty may be important to many women who wear Islamic dress, developments in Islamic fashion cannot be understood purely by reference to such concepts. Getting dressed is an everyday corpo-real practice that relates to the multiple subject positions a person inhabits and includes aesthetic and stylistic choices which may accentuate or rein-force religious concerns or sit in tension with them. Requirements of modesty may, for example, be respected in terms of degrees of covering but choices of colours, styles, makeup and accessories may result in highly conspicuous and eye-catching ensembles that some Muslims would consider immodest. Many of the contributions in this book point to tensions concerning develop-ments in Islamic fashion, which is both admired and treated with ambivalence by some Muslims. Whilst some embrace an ever-increasing array of fashion-able options and encourage maximum engagement and experimentation with fashion, others are wary that aesthetic and ephemeral concerns may over-ride ethical considerations, divert attention to trivial concerns or detract from what they see as the primary purpose of covering. Some of these concerns are expressed by our cover girl, Zinah, who, in spite of being a keen fashion blogger and aspiring designer, remains ambivalent about the values embed-ded in fashion and the fashion industry. Hers is a love-hate relationship with fashion. Attention to how and why people adopt particular forms of dress in particular contexts and locations is also important for capturing the multi-sensorial character of dress (Banerjee and Miller 2003). This issue has till now received very little attention in studies of Muslim dress practices where attention has focussed more on the significance of visibility (Göle 1996; San-dikçi and Ger 2005) and the question of how people select particular looks in view of Islamic ideas of correct deportment and in light of the high levels of public critical attention accorded to women who dress in visibly Muslim ways (Tarlo 2010b). Contributors to this book continue to place emphasis on the significance of the visual, not least because many young Muslim women express considerable concern about how Islam is represented and how their own appearances might challenge or modify public perceptions of Muslims. However, attention to young women's concerns about dress also reveals the extent to which the selection of what to wear is multi-sensorial, engaging with the haptic or tactile qualities of particular fibres and fabrics as well as the memories associated with these (Tarlo 2004; Ünal and Moors 2012). Such tactile engagement is particularly evident when people are involved in the skil-ful manipulation of cloth as is the case with headscarves, which literally have to be twisted, wrapped and coaxed into particular forms. Wardrobe research has indicated that the ways in which women acquire particular items of dress, whether as gifts, souvenirs or for specific events, also produces particular attachments and links items of clothing to people and places (Woodward 2007; Skov 2011; Tarlo, this book). Items therefore sometimes linger in wardrobes for reasons which relate less to aesthetic considerations or the latest fashion trend than to the social lives in which they are embedded.

ISLAMIC FASHION AND THE GLOBAL ISLAMIC REVIVAL MOVEMENT

Whilst young girls who experiment with Islamic fashion in Europe and America may be more or less conscious of their place within a wider Islamic revival, their discourses and practices cannot be fully understood without some reference to this broader history and context. One thing that is striking is the extent to which many young Muslims employ a strongly reflexive language in talking about their decision to cover. In doing so, they take distance from more habitual taken-for-granted ways of wearing covered dress which they consider to be more cultural than religious. They often highlight how they have made well-informed, conscious decisions to cover and that this is part and parcel of the process of becoming a more committed and practising Muslim. Whereas it may be tempting to consider such an emphasis on reflexivity, choice and conviction to be the result of growing up in Europe or America where traditions of liberal governance foreground the value of individual autonomy and authenticity, it is also important to situate these attitudes within the emergence of a global Islamic revival movement (Amir-Moazami and Salvatore 2003).

During the twentieth century in many Muslim majority countries, elements of a Western lifestyle, including the adoption of European styles of dress, became widespread especially amongst the middle and upper classes. Contesting this trend, the 1970s and 1980s saw the ascendency of an Islamic revival movement which encouraged a growing number of women to adopt recognizably Islamic covered styles of dress (El-Guindi 1981; Göle 1996). Some authors have referred to this as 'the new veiling' (MacLeod 1991) in order to underline that it entailed a new style of covered dress that was worn by young, well-educated women who consciously chose to adopt it. For some, the new veiling expressed and embodied their affinity to Islamist movements which involved a political-religious positioning against Western domination and/or a critical stance vis-à-vis local authoritarian regimes in countries such as Egypt (El-Guindi 1999), Turkey (Göle 1996), Lebanon (Deeb 2006) or Indonesia (Brenner 1996). For others, wearing new covered styles of dress was part of a broader piety movement that had emerged in response to the increased secularization of everyday life (Mahmood 2005). Women inspired by the Islamic revival argued that wearing covered dress would only function to please God if it was done with the right intention, and this attitude has resonance in many of the narratives of young Muslims in Europe and America today.

This new veiling—different from the conventional styles that poorer urban and rural women habitually wore—initially entailed a move towards a uniform and sober style, which many hoped would do away with the sartorial distinctions between the wealthy and the poor (Navaro-Yashin 2002; Sandikçi and Ger 2010). In countries such as Turkey and Egypt, they often wore full-length and loose overcoats in combination with large headscarves that covered all the hair as well as the chest and upper part of the back. Such styles slowly spread to Europe amongst Muslims who similarly felt attracted to the Islamic revival movement, fusing the liberal notion of individual autonomy (which presents covering as a personal choice based on conviction) with the Islamic notion of intentionality, which insists that submission to God should be a voluntary act.

By the 1990s, more fashionable styles of Islamic dress began to appear in Muslim majority countries such as Turkey, giving rise to what has become known as Islamic fashion. In many cases, these fashionable styles of dress replaced the simple, austere and purposely non-fashionable forms of Islamic attire initially favoured in the revival movement. In part, this reflected a shift within the Islamic revival movement from a radical and anti-consumerist position towards a more individualized reformist stance with identities increasingly produced through consumption (Navaro-Yashin 2002). It spawned the emergence of Islamic consumer culture and engendered a greater heterogeneity of Islamic styles of dress which were attractive and appealing for younger, more affluent Islamic women (Kiliçbay and Binark 2002; Sandikçi and Ger 2005, 2007; Abaza 2007). Processes of aesthetization and personalization led to the emergence of highly fashionable Islamic outfits and companies specialized in producing such clothes for religious consumers (Sandikçi and Ger 2010). In some locations, such as southern Beirut, the coming of age of a new generation that had grown up in an Islamic environment further stimulated the emergence of fashionable styles of Islamic dress as part of the development of Islamically licit forms of entertainment (Deeb and Harb 2008). In Iran, where the establishment of the Islamic republic in 1979 transformed voluntary veiling into a state-imposed dress code, the turn to fashionable styles took on different meanings. At one level, Islamic fashion in this context could be perceived as a form of everyday resistance through consumption. At another level, it might be understood as a product of the state's response to the demands of women who had expressed their loyalty to the regime (Moruzzi 2008).

The move towards trendy, fashionable, yet recognizably Islamic dress was also discernible in settings where all-covering outerwear had always remained the norm, such as Yemen, Saudi Arabia and the Gulf states. In such locations, the increased commoditization of dress and the turn to consumer culture stimulated more rapid changes in styles of outerwear (Moors 2007; Al-Qasimi 2010; Lindholm 2010). These were often purchased by migrants, students and visitors from other parts of the world who integrated them into their wardrobes in their home countries. In this way, abayas from the Gulf states became popular amongst Muslims in India, functioning also as status symbols in these new settings (Osella and Osella 2007).

The net result is that a new global market for Islamic fashion came into being. Whereas in the early 1970s women turning to the new veiling still had their clothes made to order (El-Guindi 1999), it did not take long for garment producers, often themselves affiliated with the Islamic revival movement, to enter the field. At first, they mainly produced the uniform full-length, wide coats in muted colours aimed at the lower end of the market, which they advertised using strict Islamic interpretations about representing human forms. But with the turn to more fashionable and expensive styles, the Islamic fashion sector grew increasingly affiliated with the wider commercial field, making use of glossy advertising campaigns, upscale fashion shows and festivals, producing a wide array of recognizably Islamic and highly fashionable clothing and imagery (Sandikçi and Ger 2007).

This raises the question of whether similar processes are taking place in Europe and America. In Europe, a sector is developing that caters to and produces a demand for fashionable styles of Islamic dress, varying from large shawls and headscarves, bonnets, under-scarves and hijab jewellery, to a wide variety of long skirts and dresses. However, this is different from the larger trendsetting Islamic fashion industry present in countries such as Turkey, Egypt, Dubai, Malaysia and Indonesia. Small Islamic shops that also store other Islamic items, such as books, home decorations, prayer rugs and so on, are visible in many European cities, but the garments they sell are often conservative, and most do not stock the more fashionable forms of Islamic wear. More recently, during the last decade, a few stores have started to cater specifically to a public that looks for more fashionable styles of Islamic dress. Subsidiaries of Tekbir, the largest Turkish multinational that is also present elsewhere in the Middle East and in Asia, have been opened in Europe. In the Netherlands, an interesting case is the smaller chain of Manzaram stores, whose owners are also from Turkey. These stores sell a mixture of longish skirts and coats as well as mainstream fashion products such as sleeveless dresses. The most striking item in these stores is, however, the enormous variety of headscarves in every possible colour, which are neither available in the small Islamic stores nor in the large mainstream chains. It is in the United Kingdom, with its longstanding and significant presence of Muslims from different backgrounds, that an Islamic fashion sector is most discernible, with designers and entrepreneurs catering both to British Muslims and to the wider export market (Tarlo 2010b and this book).

Many young Muslim women, however, are not particularly concerned to shop in stores which cater specifically to a Muslim clientele, and some actively avoid such stores which they see as conservative. Instead, they frequent the same shops as other young women of their peer group and generation. We found that well-known high street brands such as H&M and Top Shop were popular amongst young Muslims in a number of different European research settings. Through layering and combining items of dress that are not specifically designed for Muslims, they put together outfits which look both up to date and Islamic and which signal their engagement with both fashion and faith. By combining elements of existing styles to produce new meanings, they exercise their skill as bricoleurs and simultaneously align themselves with the improvisational aesthetics characteristic of contemporary street styles more generally. As the shops they favour offer a rapid turnover of products with short life cycles, they often find themselves making regular repeated visits, which in turn contribute to their heightened fashion consciousness.

In Europe, as in Muslim majority countries, there has in recent years been a proliferation of Islamic Muslim lifestyle journals and magazines catering to an increasingly diversified audience interested in Islamic fashion (Lewis 2010). However, the domain in which Islamic fashion activities have been most prolific in Europe and America, including in areas where only small numbers of Muslims live, is the Internet. From the late 1990s onwards, Web-based stores began to emerge selling Islamic wear online. Today such Web-based stores have become part of a dense web of social media which includes YouTube videos of fashion shows and hijab tutorials, Islamic fashion blogs, discussion fora, Facebook pages and so forth that present a huge variety of fashionable styles of Islamic dress and provide advice and commentary on different ways of dressing fashionably and Islamically (Akou 2007, 2010; Tarlo 2010b, 2013a; Lewis 2013; Moors 2013).

With the spread of Islamic fashion both online and off, a distinctive 'Islamic fashion scape' (Tarlo 2010b) is developing in Europe and America which draws on developments in Islamic fashion elsewhere but is not dependent on them. Before going on to present some of the themes that have emerged from our study of Euro-American Islamic fashion, it is worth first considering how the very concept of Islamic fashion disrupts both conventional understandings of fashion and of the relationship between aesthetics and conviction in the study of religious dress.

RETHINKING FASHION AND ANTI-FASHION THROUGH ISLAMIC FASHION

Many people, including some Muslims, consider the notion of Islamic fashion an oxymoron. Yet, as the contributions to this book confirm, there are numerous people around the world who are engaged in producing, propagating, circulating and wearing highly fashionable styles of Islamic dress. That this is regarded by many as improbable and surprising can be attributed partly to the limited way in which fashion has conventionally been conceptualized as a modern Western secular phenomenon.

The assumption that fashion is a uniquely Western phenomenon that has only recently spread to the rest of the world through globalized networks of capitalist production and distribution has in recent years come under heavy criticism from economic historians, historians of fashion and anthropologists concerned to recognize fashion's global relevance and its complex history in different parts of the world (Jones and Leshkowich 2003; Niessen 2003; Lemire 2010; Riello and McNeil 2010). Niessen, for example, accuses dress scholarship of following a similar model to that of art history, which until recently assumed that only artistic developments in the West were worthy of recognition as art whilst developments in the rest of the world were either ignored or explained by reference to timeless tradition (Niessen 2003). A similar dichotomy has, she argues, been expressed and perpetuated by a long line of fashion scholars who have classified the diverse range of clothing that did not conform to Western fashion as tradition-bound and timeless (Flugel 1930; Sapir 1937; Simmel 1957; Blumer 1968; Polhemus and Proctor 1978). Whereas recognition of non-Western art has led to a radical redefinition of the concept of art in recent years, the same has not occurred in fashion studies. Instead, Niessen argues, fashion scholars have colluded with the hierarchies perpetuated by the fashion world and fashion media by failing to unpack the power relations inherent in popular understandings of fashion and by refusing to redefine the concept of fashion. Whilst some scholars persist in understanding fashion in terms of the distinctive mode of producing, marketing, representing and wearing clothes that emerged in the modern West and that has since spread worldwide, others have taken up the challenge of broadening the definition and provenance of fashion by showing how processes of comparison, emulation and differentiation have occurred in a variety of different historical periods and locations and how these have been conducive to investment in changing tastes and ideas of self-enhancement through dress in different times and places (Cannon 1998; Lemire 2010; Riello and McNeil 2010). Viewed in this light, fashion was not born in the modern West although developments in production, marketing and distributing in the modern West offer an accelerated and extreme example of the dynamics of fashion. Moreover, if one of the key features of fashion is rapid and continual change of styles then the spread of capitalist modes of production and consumption around the world would seem to suggest that what Wilson once said of modern Western societies is applicable worldwide: 'No clothes are outside of fashion' (1985: 3).

The existence and growth of Islamic fashion, then, contributes to the breaking down of systems of classification by which the world is divided into the fashionable West and unfashionable rest whose only access to fashion is by emulation or insertion within a pre-existing frame. Not only does it highlight alternative geographies of fashion (Moors and Tarlo 2007), but it also suggests alternative values by challenging normative assumptions about the assumed secularity of fashion. Whilst some might be tempted to explain away the recent shift to increasingly fashionable styles of Islamic dress as a mere case of the commodification of religion or an example of a more general societal shift away from communities of conviction to communities of style (Maffesoli 1996), what the contributions to this volume suggest is a much more complex set of ideas about the relationship between ethics and aesthetics in contemporary Islamic fashion. As Sandikçi and Ger (2005) have pointed out in the Turkish context, appearing well-groomed and neat and presenting a pleasant and harmonious look can be considered an act which pleases God. Such an interpretation gives Islamic fashion ethical credibility which is further heightened by the idea that wearing aesthetically pleasing forms of Islamic dress can act as a form of *dawa,* encouraging others towards the faith (Moll 2010), persuading others of the beauty of modesty and producing a positive image of Islam in an environment that is hostile towards Islam (Jouili 2009; Tarlo 2010b). Here, Islamic virtue is seen not as external to fashion but potentially integral to it, thereby making the creation and wearing of fashionable styles a form and extension of religious action. Yet, if aesthetics and conviction go hand in hand in some Muslim women's understandings of Islamic fashion, they coexist in a state of tension for others who see fashion as a means by which Islamic values and priorities become diluted, distorted or lost. Anti-fashion discourses therefore coexist in conjunction with the expansion of Islamic fashion.

Just as Islamic fashion is useful for rethinking ideas of fashion, so Islamic anti-fashion discourses are useful for untangling different ideas of anti-fashion. The term *anti-fashion* has served a number of purposes in scholarly writings on dress. It has sometimes been used as a catch-all phrase to describe all types of dress assumed to be outside the Western fashion system. This included both non-Western and religious clothing traditions which were often deemed unfashionable or simply outside of fashion. By such criteria all forms of Islamic dress would be classified as anti-fashion, but such a designation is clearly of little use for thinking about Islamic fashion. What we do find, however, is that alongside a strong attraction to and engagement with Islamic fashion in terms of rapidly changing tastes, enhanced concerns with aesthetics and experimentation with style, we simultaneously find Islamic critiques of fashion. Islamic anti-fashion discourses take a number of forms: some focus on how ideas of modesty, piety and restraint are undermined by fashion; others focus on a wider set of ideas about fashion being wasteful, frivolous, over-sexualized or demeaning to women. These counter-fashion discourses intersect with secular anti-fashion discourses in a variety of ways, highlighting how Islamic anti-fashion discourses bear much in common with Marxist, feminist and ecologist critiques of fashion.

In this book, we do not draw up a distinct dichotomy between fashion and anti-fashion discourses and practices but rather highlight their mutual entanglement, recognizing how any form of anti-fashion necessarily relates to fashion even if this is predominantly by negation. As Wilson pointed out in relation to fashion more generally, even the determinedly unfashionable wear clothes that manifestly represent a reaction against what is in fashion (1985: 3–4). Similarly, we do not see garments as being either in or out of fashion in any obvious way but rather demonstrate how people consider particular garments and styles to be more or less fashionable and accept change within their dress to different degrees and at different rates.

While Islamic fashion is often not recognized as fashion owing partly to the historic hierarchies of fashion mentioned earlier, where it is recognized as fashion it tends to be greeted in one of two ways. Either it is perceived as yet another demonstration of the Islamization of public space—an insidious example of the invasion of an alien religion and the erosion of secularism—or it is welcomed in celebratory tones as proof of the freedom and creativity of Muslim women in spite of what is often assumed. However, as a number of writers on fashion have shown, fashion is as much about emulation as it is about freedom. It involves a combination of individualising and conformist impulses (Simmel 1971). Finkelstein even goes so far as to suggest that fashion is better understood in terms of subjectivation than in terms of individual autonomy or freedom of expression. In Finkelstein's words:

> The historical success of being fashionable has been to provide a sense of individualism within a shared code, since individuals can look acceptably distinctive only within a restricted aesthetic. When they purchase fashionable goods that will distinguish them, they do so only from a range of goods already understood to be valuable. (1997: 6)

Fashion, then, can work as a disciplining and homogenizing force. This is an interesting perspective from which to view the relationship between religion and fashion. If both Islam and fashion can be understood in terms of subjectivation, what happens in the case of Islamic fashion when two different forces of subjectivization intersect?

Mediating against this interpretation of fashion as the selection from a predefined restricted range of goods already valued as fashion is an understanding of how street styles emerge and how goods which may once have been considered unfashionable are transformed into fashion through their juxtaposition, manipulation and use. The improvisational aesthetic visible in many of the Islamic fashion outfits emerging in the streets of Europe and America would seem to suggest that Islamic fashion involves not only conformity to pre-existing possibilities but also, in some cases, high levels of experimentation and invention. Yet, just as happens in other cases of countercultural street style, new creative forms of Islamic fashion soon become conventionalized through the force of fashion and fashion media.

How far Muslim women experiment with fashion depends not only on how ideas of religion, ethnicity, class, generation and taste intersect in processes of self-fashioning but also on how different histories and experiences of secularism have shaped clothing possibilities, priorities and preferences in different locations. In the following section, we trace a brief genealogy of the Muslim presence in Europe and America with a view to highlighting how Muslim women have responded to the history and regulation of visibly Muslim dress in different European and American settings. In doing so, we discuss the partial and provincial nature of discourses about Muslim dress in Europe as well as highlight how Muslim women alter the terms of debate through their engagement with and critique of Islamic fashion.

THE PRESENCE OF MUSLIMS IN EUROPE AND AMERICA: HISTORICAL TRAJECTORIES

Much of the literature on Muslims in Europe privileges north-western Europe and traces the presence of Muslims to post–Second World War labour migration (Larsson and Račius 2010). There is, however, a far more long-standing and diverse presence of Muslims in Europe and America. In Southern Europe (Al-Andalus, comprising parts of Spain, Portugal and France), Muslim rule lasted for over seven centuries, only coming to an end with the fall of Grenada in 1492. In contemporary Spain, some refer to this past to define Moroccan migrants as invaders, while others, including converts, build on this historical presence in an attempt to reinvigorate Islam in Spain (Arighita 2006; Taha 2010). On the Baltic coast and in some Eastern European countries, there is a long-standing presence of Muslim Tatars, in some cases dating back to the tenth century. In the Balkans, the Muslim presence is strongly connected to Ottoman rule, when, on one hand, some Slavic Christians converted to Islam (such as the Pomaks in Bulgaria), and, on the other, some Turkish groups settled in Balkan countries.

But it is not only these earlier Muslim empires that have left an imprint on the shape and presence of Islam in Europe. Equally significant was the role of European colonial powers, which incorporated large populations of Muslims as colonial subjects in North Africa and South Asia, resulting in postcolonial labour migration to countries such as France and Britain respectively. Elsewhere in Northern and Western Europe, labour shortages in the 1960s led to the recruitment of 'guest workers', such as, for instance, Moroccans in Belgium and Turks in Germany, while in more recent years political unrest and warlike conditions in countries such as Lebanon, Palestine, Iraq, Kurdistan, Afghanistan and Somalia have resulted in Muslim refugees settling in different European locations.

In Eastern Europe, the numbers of recent Muslim migrants are numerically small and contain a high proportion of students, partly in continuation of the relation of former Soviet bloc states with Muslim majority countries. Moreover, in the wake of the war in former Yugoslavia, Islamic nongovernmental organizations (NGOs) have become active in the region. There is often considerable social distance between these recent migrants and longer-standing local Muslims, some of whom have been included in leading circles and whose presence has been recognized by the state. Whereas the latter's way of being Muslim has often been influenced by Christianity or Turkish Sufi traditions, the new immigrants, especially those from the Middle East, often bring with them a very different, more literal and strict set of interpretations of Islam, including ideas of appropriate dress (Górak-Sosnowska 2012). Acknowledgement of these different strands of Muslim presence in Europe highlights not only the diversity of Islamic presence and practice in Europe but also how such histories are often ignored in contemporary narratives in which Islam is portrayed as a new alien force which threatens what used to be cohesive European national identities and values.

Similarly, in the United States there is a long-standing Muslim presence, dating back to the slave trade (Aidi 2011). In the 1930s the Nation of Islam emerged with a strong black segregationalist outlook. Today, Islam continues to attract a significant proportion of African American converts. In addition, Turkish and other Muslims that were part of the Ottoman Empire came to settle in the United States and Canada from the late nineteenth century onwards. More recently, when immigration policies relaxed after the 1960s, Asian and Arab Muslims settled in the United States and Canada. In contrast to Europe, where labour migration was mainly working class, in the US case, there is a substantial presence of well-educated Muslims who have become part of the middle and professional classes. Also in the United States, there were clashes in interpretations of Islam with recent migrants from Muslim majority countries often criticising African American ways of living Islam.[1] Not all Muslim groups find representation in the present volume, but our work is informed by awareness of the great variety of historical trajectories that make up the Muslim presence in Europe and America.

CONFRONTING THE POLITICS OF SECULARISM THROUGH FASHION

While the modern secular state claims the separation of state and religion, it simultaneously defines how state and religion should relate to each other, resulting in variations in the ways Islam and Muslims are governed. Differences occur not only between nation-states but also between particular fields of governance whether dress, education, the built environment or commerce. Regulation also varies according to the particular actors involved such as students or teachers or according to particular locations such as schools or public space.

Historically, both Muslim empires and the colonial state expressed concerns about how Muslims should appear in public (Ahmed 1992; Scott 2007; Moors 2011). More recently, controversies about Muslim headscarves, and later face veils, emerged when larger numbers of Muslim girls began to enter public schools in the 1980s and the labour market a decade later. In north-western Europe, this coincided with processes of deconfessionalization, while at the same time, Muslim majority countries were experiencing Islamic revivalism, including the establishment of the Islamic Republic of Iran in 1979. After the fall of the Berlin Wall in 1989 and the so-called Rushdie affair the same year, it was no longer the red (communist) danger that was seen as threatening but the green (Islamic) one. Migrants once welcomed as guest workers became reconceptualized first as ethnic minorities and then as Muslims, which became the new problem category. National identities were increasingly defined in opposition to Islam, whether in terms of strong secularism, an apparently shared Judaeo-Christian heritage or a mixture of both.

In the Balkans and Eastern Europe, relations between religion and ethnicity were influenced by the legacies of both the Ottoman and the Soviet presence. Soviet rule had discouraged religious practices such as wearing recognizably Muslim dress, which was at times restricted to private or folkloric occasions. Following the fall of the Berlin Wall, religion became increasingly important in people's everyday lives in these parts of Eastern Europe. This made the position of those whose religious and ethnic belongings did not overlap more tenuous, as happened, for instance, in former Yugoslavia and in the case of the Pomaks (Slavic Muslims) in Bulgaria (Ghodsee 2007).

In Western Europe, but also elsewhere, the growth of neo-nationalism in the 1990s, further accentuated by the events of 9/11, engendered a broad shift towards assimilationist policies, with Muslims pressured to prove their loyalty to European nation-states and their central values, not simply by adhering to the law but through their everyday behaviour and appearances (Gingrich 2006; Geschiere 2009). In Eastern Europe and the Balkans, distancing oneself from the visible forms of Islam propagated by new immigrants from Arab countries became a means of highlighting one's belonging to Europe. In the United States and Canada (with the exception of francophone Quebec), it was discourses on national security rather than integration that became emphasized, especially after 9/11 and the involvement of the United States in the wars in Afghanistan and Iraq (Fassin 2010).

The effect of these changing discourses on integration and security are evident in the ways many states have tried to regulate Muslim women's headcoverings. In France, for instance, the meaning of laicity has been transformed in the course of the last two decades (Scott 2005, 2007; Asad 2006; Bowen 2007). In its 1990 ruling, the Conseil d'État (Council of State) stated that wearing a headscarf need not necessarily be in conflict with French laicity. Nor was it necessarily a sign of proselytizing. In 2004, however, a new law was passed prohibiting the wearing of conspicuous signs of religious affiliation in public schools.

By contrast, in the United Kingdom, policies of multiculturalism have left space for visible signs of ethnic and religious diversity to find expression in the public domain. Yet here, too, there have been controversies over the regulation of Muslim dress as seen in the 'jilbab case' in 2002 in which a young Muslim girl pursued a legal case against her secondary school for not allowing her to attend school in a jilbab, a loose full-length coat. The school took the position that the uniform option of salwar kameez conformed to Islamic requirements and that it was necessary to protect pupils from Muslim extremists and from the development of a hierarchy of piety in the school (Tarlo 2005).

In Germany, the main focus of headscarf debates has been on teachers in state schools, with the argument that they, as representatives of the state, need to be neutral. However, when in 2003 the federal court in Baden-Württemberg decided to ban the headscarf for teachers in public schools, it used the argument that it was protecting students against exposure to the influence of an 'alien religion' (Vom Bruck 2008: 56).

It is not only headscarves that have been the focus of the politics of secularism. In the past decade, face veils have become a major issue of contestation in Europe and America. In the Netherlands in 2005, a parliamentary majority voted to prohibit the wearing of face veils in all public spaces. When this turned out to be unconstitutional, specific prohibitions were implemented for civil servants and in schools (Moors 2009b). In 2010 and 2011, France and Belgium prohibited wearing face coverings in public space, while a number of other countries have either implemented partial prohibitions or are considering doing so (Grillo and Shah 2012).

Whereas there are differences in how specific nation-states regulate the wearing of Islamic styles of dress, two often-interconnected sets of argumentation stand out. Covered dress has been considered both a sign or instrument of women's oppression and part of the spread of undesirable forms of Islam. Both in colonies such as Egypt (Ahmed 1992) and in the newly formed authoritarian nation-states such as Turkey (Göle 2002), Islamic head coverings were often considered a sign or instrument of women's oppression at the hands of fathers, husbands or the wider ethnic-religious community. The same arguments have been used in contemporary headscarf debates in

France (Bowen 2007: 208ff; Scott 2007: 151ff) and Germany (Amir-Moazami 2005: 273) and to support the prohibition of face-veiling (Moors 2009b: 401). References to gender inequality in Islam are used to construct or prove the apparent incompatibility of Islam with the egalitarian values of European secularism. Showing how such secularism often amounts to a form of 'sexularism', Scott points to how the exposure of women's bodies is valorized in Europe and the unveiling of women presented as a generous and liberating act (2009).

Islamic headcovers and face veils are also considered a sign of adherence to undesirable forms of Islam. They are perceived as signs of a political, fundamentalist, orthodox or segregating form of Islam, constructed in opposition to a positively valued liberal, secular or moderate Islam (Bowen 2007: 182ff; Fernando 2009). In France, bringing one's religious conviction into the public is thought to strengthen communalism and is considered a threat to the republic (Bowen 2007: 155), while in Germany some consider the Islamic headscarf to be a political and missionary statement and a sign of cultural segregation that contributes to the development of parallel societies (Amir-Moazami 2005: 272). Concerns about the potentially segregating effects of face-veiling have also been raised in Britain both by politicians and by members of the public, including Muslims (Tarlo 2010b: 131–60).

How then has this regulation of women's appearances affected the way Muslim women dress in public? What sort of intervention do young Muslim women make through their engagement with Islamic fashion? In this book, we argue that in a context where Islam is increasingly seen and represented as incommensurable with European values and culture, many young Muslim women adopt fashionable styles and combinations of Islamic dress as a means of presenting themselves as contemporary or modern, taking distance from habitual cultural forms of dress favoured by older generations and making clear their engagement both with Islam and with contemporary style trends.

The firmly entrenched perception of hijab as a symbol of women's subordination regardless of what hijab-wearers may feel about the subject often makes it difficult for covered Muslim women to be heard in public debate. In this book, we suggest that it is through their corporeal presence that many young Muslim women find ways of presenting an alternative position to the public. As a medium of communication and expression, dress is open to all, offering opportunities to large numbers to engage in public debate through their visible and material presence. As wearers of fashionable styles of Islamic dress, young Muslim women in Europe and America create a presence which has the potential to destabilize some of the entrenched perceptions of Muslim women. Wearing fashionable styles, blogging about fashion, creating outfits from unexpected combinations and introducing new colours, patterns and silhouettes to the urban landscape works well against the image of Muslim women as dull, downtrodden, oppressed and out of sync with modernity. Precisely because the corporeal aesthetics of fashion have historically been so strongly linked to modernity, they become an ideal means by which women are able to distance themselves from the common stereotypical images of Muslim women.

Covered Muslim women themselves often highlight how they are involved in 'telling through showing' (Mitchel 2002). They are hyperconscious of the fact that as a marked category, they can never escape the burden of representation. Because they are easily recognizable as Muslims, they feel a strong responsibility and urge to counter negative stereotypes about Islam with what they perceive as positive images. This may be especially true of those with a strong public presence through their employment or other public activities including blogging (see interview with Zinah, fashion blogger and cover girl of this volume, in Chapter 11). But it is also true of women whose lives are less visible in the public domain. Even women who wear full-body coverings sometimes choose to adopt lighter colours in an attempt to minimize negative perceptions or perceived barriers to communication.

Our findings suggest that the public visual interventions made by fashionable Muslims *have* affected public debates about hijab in a number of significant ways. On one hand, they have provoked criticism and concern from some Muslims who consider Islam and fashion to be incompatible. On the other hand, they are eliciting new types of attention from the non-Muslim majority public, some of whom are fascinated by developments in Islamic fashion and adopt an almost celebratory tone about some of the more extravagant or revealing styles. In particular, in those settings where women's emancipation is defined with reference to sexual freedom and the public visibility of women's sexuality and where engagement with fashion is perceived as a sign of individual creative expression, the wearing of fashionable styles of Muslim dress is sometimes interpreted as an indication of successful integration. At the same time, women who do not opt to wear such styles and who are often critical of this turn towards fashion find themselves ever more negatively marked, with employers complaining that their style of dress is too dark, sombre or concealing.

ISLAMIC FASHION IN EUROPE AND AMERICA: EMERGING THEMES

Without pre-empting the findings of individual contributions, we would like to end by introducing some of the key themes that emerged from the collective research that makes up this book. One recurrent theme is the extent to which Islamic fashion in Europe and America is a cosmopolitan phenomenon. This cosmopolitanism has many aspects. Not only is the social composition of Muslim populations in these settings highly diverse in terms of history, cultural background and religious tradition, but it also displays high levels of interaction between people of different backgrounds who exchange ideas, including understandings of how to dress and what is fashionable or appropriate. This is true whether in contexts where the Muslim population is small, as in the Canadian prairies (Greifenhagen and Anderson), or in major European cities such as London (Tarlo), Paris (Österlind), Berlin (Bendixsen) or Amsterdam (Moors). Both Islamic fashion and anti-fashion practices take shape in contexts where Muslims from different cultural backgrounds, including converts, interact with each other and the surrounding population to varying degrees, whether in schools, cultural centres or religious buildings or through social activities. Equally, Muslim media, including online activities such as hijabi fashion blogs or online stores, encourage high levels of interaction and dialogue between Muslims from different backgrounds and traditions. Even in cases where interaction may lead to heightened tensions over interpretations of appropriate ways of dressing, as in the case of encounters between Muslim Tatars and Arab migrants in Poland (see Górak-Sosnowska and Łyszczarz), appearances are modified and shaped through transcultural encounters.

One common response to this is the development of a cosmopolitan aesthetic and style which draws on different clothing and fashion repertoires and ideas of covering to create new types of Muslim looks, often by combining ready-to-wear items drawn from popular high street fashions with headscarves wrapped in a variety of ways. In wearing hybrid layered outfits, young Muslim women demonstrate their awareness of and interest in mainstream fashion whilst simultaneously developing distinctive Muslim looks. The ensembles they create often inject new colours and patterns and distinctive silhouettes into the visual landscapes of cities, as can be seen most clearly in Gammarota's photographic reportage of fashionable young hijabi women in London. London, with its particularly diverse Muslim population and its well-developed sense of street fashion, is home to some of the most inventive examples of this cosmopolitan, fashionable Muslim look. But a similar experimental tendency and playfulness is also present in Stockholm (Salim), Copenhagen (Christiansen) and in most of the locations described in this book, to a greater or lesser degree. Wherever they occur, these hybrid but distinctly Muslim visual and material ensembles cannot be interpreted or boiled down to any particular cultural tradition. They are the products of cultural interaction and experimentation.

In addition to the cosmopolitan street fashions visible in a variety of European and American cities, we find Islamic fashion designers emerging, often designing full-length garments to cater for women who wish to wear fuller, more distinctively Islamic forms of dress. Here, too, we find strong cosmopolitanizing tendencies and ambitions as shown in the way some Islamic fashion designers in Britain draw on and make reference to different clothing traditions from around the world through their use of patterns, shapes, textiles and decorative elements and through the names they give to some of the garments they create (Tarlo).

An alternative form of cosmopolitanism is found in the creation and marketing of sartorial propositions aimed at providing some sort of universal Islamic solution to the clothing requirements of Muslims regardless of their regional or cultural background. We include in this category both garments with long-standing Islamic associations such as the abaya, which is widely marketed in Islamic shops and Web-based stores as a quintessential Islamic garment (Moors), and relatively new inventions such as the so-called *burqini*, which proposes a universal Islamic solution to the problem of what to wear for swimming even if such a solution has local variants and is not universally favoured by Muslim women who cover (see Karlsson Minganti). Whereas the abaya gains its credibility as authentic Islamic dress partly through its association with the dress of the first Muslims in the Arab Peninsula, Islamic swimwear was invented less than a decade ago in Australia and is also produced in Turkey and Britain. It is not a foreign import with old historic associations but a modern Western form of Islamic wear. Drawing on early Islamic associations, Eastern origins and contemporary global fashion trends, British inventions such as the 'sports jilbab' are marketed as a new form of Islamically appropriate dress suitable for trendy Muslim youth anywhere in the world (Tarlo). Such universalizing forms of Islamic fashion are less about clothing a pre-existing global Islamic community than about bringing such a community into being through shared religious and aesthetic ideals and material solutions.

Whilst many are drawn towards fashionable cosmopolitan styles of Islamic dress or enjoy mixing and matching ready-to-wear items from department stores, there are smaller groups of Muslim women who have developed a strong anti-fashion stance. Most striking is the public presence of women who wear full-length loose garments, such as abayas and large veils, in dark or subdued colours. The women who adopt such styles often provide theological reasoning for their choice of dress but also point out that they find such styles beautiful (see Moors for the Netherlands). In this book, we also encounter lighter forms of anti-fashion amongst Muslim women in Berlin (Bendixsen) and amongst female converts in Cluj who often choose to follow the styles worn by recent migrants from the Arab world rather than those favoured by other Romanian Muslims (Stoica). Such styles of dress stand in an ambiguous relationship with fashion since the women who wear all-encompassing outer garments often consider themselves free to wear whatever they like underneath.

The fact that Islamic fashion practices in Europe and America have emerged through transcultural interaction does not mean that ethnic or national styles and associations have been eliminated or become irrelevant in contemporary Islamic fashion even if, in some cases, they are muted or downplayed in favour of associations with Islam and fashion. For example, visibly Muslim women from South Asian backgrounds in Britain often avoid wearing ostentatiously Asian styles and fabrics owing to their strong regional associations, although they may retain a liking for particular colours and textures and be particularly adept at manipulating and wearing untailored cloth (Tarlo this volume). By contrast, many young Muslims of Turkish origin favour what have become distinctive Turkish styles of Islamic fashion in which silk scarves and the overcoat known as a *pardesu* have an important place (Gökariksel and Secor; Ünal). A careful tracing of the genealogy of the pardesu gives insight into the significance of generation and place in the clothing preferences and practices of Turkish migrants to the Netherlands (Ünal). Through historical research, Altinay traces the origins of Turkish headscarf fashions to the figure of Şule Yüksel Şenler who featured as an early Islamic fashion icon in the 1960s (Altinay). Today, whether in Istanbul (Gökariksel and Secor), Houston (Curtis), Amsterdam (Ünal) or Berlin (Bendixson; Gökariksel and Secor), Turkish Muslims have further developed distinctive headscarf fashions, sometimes highlighting Ottoman associations (Curtis), sometimes Parisian ones (Gökariksel and Secor). What is interesting is that even Şule Yüksel Şenler, who is credited with having initiated a distinctive modern Turkish Islamic fashion look, claims that her headscarves were initially inspired by those worn by Audrey Hepburn in the film *Roman Holiday* (Altinay). This example reminds us that what are presented as ethnic or national styles are often reinventions that have themselves emerged through cultural interaction. For example, it is in response to the arrival of migrants from the Middle East with their distinctive forms of Islamic covering and reformist discourses that Tatars in Poland have emphasized their national and ethnic roots by increasingly favouring outfits which highlight their Polish and Tatar credentials (Górak-Sosnowska and Łyszczarz). What we have here is a clash of different Muslim interpretations of appropriate dress from women with very different backgrounds, religious interpretations, histories and experiences of migration.

Whilst the contributions to this book highlight the diversity of Muslim perspectives and experiences, they also highlight the extent to which contemporary discourses about Muslims in Europe and America have edited out the historic presence of Muslims in favour of a narrative in which Muslims are foreigners who present a new threat to what were until recently cohesive and coherent Western norms. This narrative disintegrates not only through reference to the historic presence of communities such as the Tatars (Górak-Sosnowska and Łyszczarz) but also through the presence of local converts in different countries who defy the idea of the intrinsic foreignness of Muslims. Their clothing experiences reveal the challenges of juggling different strands of religious and national belonging in circumstances where Muslims are perceived as outsiders and where a change of dress is often interpreted as a change in loyalties (Stoica). It is also through European hostility and intolerance to certain forms of Islamic dress that we find cracks in the notion of shared European norms. Through a detailed analysis of attitudes to covering and nudity in the context of swimming pool changing rooms in Italy and Sweden, Minganti shows how Italian and Swedish attitudes to appropriate forms of dress and undress are culturally variable even if they are presented as culturally cohesive in the face of the perceived threat posed by the burqini. Her contribution provides a useful analysis of how cultural prejudice is built. At the same time, she shows how many of the arguments put forth by burqini wearers share much in common with the anti-fashion discourses favoured by some feminist activists. Here again we find not Muslim exceptionalism but overlapping gendered critiques of fashion which draw on both Islamic and secular arguments (see also Moors).

A final theme that surfaces in all the contributions to this book is the extent to which Islamic fashion in Europe and America operates not as a separate domain but draws on and contributes to developments in global fashion in a variety of ways. Focussing on fashionable Swedish women, Salim demonstrates their literacy in the visual language of fashion imagery, showing how they read different types of images and incorporate ideas into new Muslim looks. She shows how the flow of fashion imagery is multidirectional with some high-end fashion photographers producing arty neo-Orientalist images which some Muslim women in Sweden appreciate on aesthetic grounds. Also focussing on fashion imagery, Gokariksel and Secor show how well-known Turkish headscarf brands frame their products by advertising them against the backdrop of iconic images of European cities that are associated with high fashion such as Paris and Milan.

In her sequences of coloured images for this volume, Italian fashion photographer Alessia Gammarota portrays hijabi fashion through the lens of fashion photography, capturing both its playfulness and the distinctive focus on pattern and form that it offers the fashion world. Her lens does not so much objectify the young hijabi women portrayed as bring out the intensity of their engagement in the activity and aesthetics of fashion. Some of the women in her photographs are well-known hijabi fashion bloggers who spend considerable amounts of time producing and circulating fashion imagery through Facebook, hijab tutorials and other forms of social networking both online and off. One such blogger is Zinah, featured on the cover of this book, who discusses the evolution of her fashion blog with Tarlo.

Such images take on a political force in their capacity to counter stereotypes of Muslim women as old-fashioned, downtrodden and traditional. Tracing different representations of Muslim women in the Danish media, Christiansen contribution shows the self-consciousness with which many Muslim women seek to shape the public image of Muslims through the way they choose to be portrayed, whether this is through classical graceful styles or, as in one unusual case, through creation of a punk hijab replete with spikes. Turning attention to mainstream fashion brands, Lewis's study of hijabi shopworkers in fashion stores in London, Bradford and Manchester reminds us that young Muslim women are not just consumers of high street fashions but are also involved in marketing and selling them. What her contribution highlights is how the bodies of hijabi shopworkers serve to demonstrate possible Islamic ways of wearing the fashions they sell and that this is recognized as an asset by some British employers, especially in shopping areas with a large Muslim consumer base. Focussing by contrast on a major Islamic fair held in France, Österlind demonstrates how Islamic fashion traders produce business narratives and displays which align them much more closely to mainstream business rhetoric than to religious discourses.

What these contributions collectively suggest is that Islamic fashion and anti-fashion in Europe and America are an integral part of what is so often glibly referred to as global fashion. What we hope to have provided are the ethnographic and analytical tools for analysing precisely what such a concept as global fashion might mean in practice.

NOTE

1. For the engagement of African American women in New York with Islamic fashion, see Yasmin Moll's documentary, *Fashioning Faith* (2009).

REFERENCES

Abaza, M. (2007), 'Shifting Landscapes of Fashion in Contemporary Egypt', *Fashion Theory* 11, 2/3: 281–99.

Ahmed, L. (1992), *Women and Gender in Islam: Historical Roots of a Modern Debate,* New Haven, CT: Yale University Press.

Aidi, H. (2011), 'The Grand (Hip-hop) Chessboard. Race, Rap and Raison d'Etat', *Middle East Report* 260: 25–39.

Akou, H. (2007), 'Building a New "World Fashion": Islamic Dress in the Twenty-first Century', *Fashion Theory* 11, 4: 403–21.

Akou, H. (2010), 'Interpreting Islam through the Internet: Making Sense of Hijab', *Contemporary Islam* 4, 3: 331–46.

Al-Qasimi, N. (2010), 'Immodest Modesty: Accommodating Dissent and the "Abaya-as-fashion" in the Arab Gulf States', *Journal of Middle East Women's Studies* 6, 1: 46–74.

Amir-Moazami, S. (2005), 'Muslim Challenges to the Secular Consensus: A German Case Study', *Journal of Contemporary European Studies* 13, 3: 267–86.

Amir-Moazami, S., and A. Salvatore (2003), 'Gender, Generation and the Reform of Tradition. From Muslim Majority Societies to Western Europe', in S. Allievi and J. Nielsen, eds., *Muslim Networks and Transnational Communities in and Across Europe,* Leiden: Brill.

Arighita, E. (2006), 'Representing Islam in Spain: Muslim Identities and the Contestation of Leadership', *The Muslim World* 96: 563–84.

Arthur, L., ed. (1999), *Religion, Dress and the Body,* Oxford: Berg.

Asad, T. (1993), *Genealogies of Religion: Discipline and Power in Christianity and Islam,* Baltimore, MD: Johns Hopkins University Press.

Asad, T. (2006), 'Trying to Understand French Secularism', in H. de Vries and L. Sullivan, eds., *Political Theologies and Global Religions,* New York: Fordham University Press.

Banerjee, M., and D. Miller (2003), *The Sari,* Oxford: Berg.

Blumer, H. (1968), 'Fashion', in D. Sills, ed., *International Encyclopedia of the Social Sciences,* vol. 5, New York: Macmillan.

Bowen, J. (2007), *Why the French Don't Like Headscarves: Islam, the State, and Public Space,* Princeton, NJ: Princeton University Press.

Brenner, S. (1996), 'Reconstructing Self and Society: Javanese Muslim Women and "The Veil"', *American Ethnologist* 23, 4: 673–97.

Cannon, A. (1998), 'The Cultural and Historical Contexts of Fashion', in A. Brydon and S. Niessen, eds., *Consuming Fashion: Adorning the Transnational Body,* Oxford: Berg.

Comaroff, J. (1996), 'The Empire's Old Clothes: Refashioning the Colonial Subject', in D. Howes, ed., *Commodities and Cultural Borders,* London: Routledge.

Deeb, L. (2006), *An Enchanted Modern: Gender and Public Piety in Shi'i Lebanon,* Princeton, NJ: Princeton University Press.

Deeb, L., and M. Harb (2008), 'Sanctioned Pleasures: Youth, Piety and Leisure in Beirut', *Middle East Report* 37, 245: 12–19.

El-Guindi, F. (1981), 'Veiling Infitah with Muslim Ethic: Egypt's Contemporary Islamic Movement', *Social Problems* 28, 4: 465–85.

El-Guindi, F. (1999), *Veil: Modesty, Privacy and Resistance,* Oxford: Berg.

Entwistle, J. (2000), *The Fashioned Body: Fashion, Dress and Modern Social Theory,* Cambridge: Polity Press.

Fassin, E. (2010), 'National Identities and Transnational Intimacies: Sexual Democracy and the Politics of Immigration in Europe', *Public Culture* 22, 3: 507–29.

Fernando, M. (2009), 'Exceptional Citizens: Secular Muslim Women and the Politics of Difference in France', *Social Anthropology* 17, 4: 379–92.

Finkelstein, J. (1997), 'Chic Theory', *Australian Humanities Review,* <http://www.australianhumanitiesreview.org/archive/Issue-March-1997/finkelstein.html> accessed 10 July 2012.

Flugel, J. C. (1930), *The Psychology of Clothes,* London: Hogarth Press.

Geschiere, P. (2009), *The Perils of Belonging. Autochthony, Citizenship, and Exclusion in Africa and Europe,* Chicago, IL: University of Chicago Press.

Ghodsee, K. (2007), 'Religious Freedoms versus Gender Equality: Faith-based Organizations, Muslim Minorities and Islamic Headscarves in Modern Bulgaria', *Social Politics* 14, 4: 526–61.

Gingrich, A. (2006), 'Neo-nationalism and the Reconfiguring of Europe', *Social Anthropology* 14, 2: 195–217.

Göle, N. (1996), *The Forbidden Modern: Civilization and Veiling,* Ann Arbor: University of Michigan Press.

Göle, N. (2002), 'Islam in Public: New Visibilities and New Imaginaries', *Public Culture* 14, 1: 173–90.

Górak-Sosnowska, K. (2012), 'Muslims in Europe: Different Communities, One Discourse? Adding the Central and Eastern European Perspective', in K. Górak-Sosnowska, ed., *Muslims in Poland and Eastern Europe: Widening the European Discourse on Islam,* Warsaw: University of Warsaw, 12–26.

Grillo, R., and P. Shah (2012), 'Reasons to Ban? The Anti-burqa Movement in Western Europe,' Working paper, Max Planck Institute for the Study of Religious and Ethnic Diversity, Gottingen.

Jones, C., and A. Leshkowich (2003), 'Introduction: The Globalization of Asdian Dress: Re-orienting Fashion or Re-orientalizing Asia?', in S. Niessen, A. M. Leshkowich and C. Jones, eds., *Re-orienting Fashion: The Globalization of Asian Dress,* Oxford: Berg.

Jouili, J. (2009), 'Negotiating Secular Boundaries: Pious Micro-practices of Muslim Women in French and German Public Spheres', *Social Anthropology* 17, 4: 455–70.

Keane, W. (2008), 'The Evidence of the Senses and the Materiality of Religion', *Journal of the Royal Anthropological Institute* 14, 1: 110–27.

Kiliçbay, B., and M. Binark (2002), 'Consumer Culture, Islam and the Politics of Lifestyle: Fashion for Veiling in Contemporary Turkey', *European Journal of Communication* 17, 4: 495–511.

Larsson, G., and E. Račius (2010), 'A Different Approach to the History of Islam and Muslims in Europe: A North-eastern Angle, or the Need to Reconsider the Research Field', *Journal of Religion in Europe* 3: 350–73.

Lemire, B. (2010), *The Force of Fashion: Global Perspectives from Early Modern to Contemporary Times,* Ashgate.

Lewis, R. (2010), 'Marketing Muslim Lifestyle: A New Media Genre', *Journal of Middle East Women's Studies* 6, 3: 58–90.

Lewis, R., ed. (2013), *Modest Fashion: Styling Bodies, Mediating Faith,* London: I.B. Tauris.

Lindholm, C. (2010), 'Invisible No More. The Embellished Abaya in Qatar', Textile Society of America Symposium Proceedings, <http://digitalcommons.unl.edu/cgi/viewcontent.cgi?article = 1033&context = tsaconf> accessed 27 September 2012.

MacLeod, A. (1991), *Accommodating Protest: Working Women, the New Veiling, and Change in Cairo,* New York: Columbia University Press.

Maffesoli, M. (1996), *The Time of the Tribes: The Decline of Individualism in Mass Society,* London: Sage.

Mahmood, S. (2001), 'Feminist Theory, Embodiment, and the Docile Agent: Some Reflections on the Egyptian Islamic Revival', *Cultural Anthropology* 16, 2: 202–37.

Mahmood, S. (2005), *Politics of Piety: The Islamic Revival and the Feminist Subject,* Princeton, NJ: Princeton University Press.

Meyer, B., and D. Houtman (2012), 'Introduction: Material Religion—How Things Matter', in D. Houtman and B. Meyer, eds., *Things. Religion and the Question of Materiality,* New York: Fordham University Press.

Miller, D. (2010), *Stuff,* Cambridge: Polity Press.

Mitchell, W.J.T. (2002), 'Showing Seeing: A Critique of Visual Culture,' *Journal of Visual Culture* 1, 2: 165–81.

Moll, Y. (2010), 'Islamic Televangelism: Religion, Media and Visuality in Contemporary Egypt', *Arab Media and Society* 10, <http://www.arabmediasociety.com/articles/downloads/20100407165913_Mollpdf.pdf> accessed 10 July 2012.

Moors, A. (2007), 'Fashionable Muslims: Notions of Self, Religion and Society in San'a', *Fashion Theory* 11, 2/3: 319–47.

Moors, A. (2009a), '"Islamic Fashion" in Europe: Religious Conviction, Aesthetic Style, and Creative Consumption', *Encounters* 1, 1: 175–201.

Moors, A. (2009b), 'The Dutch and the Face Veil: The Politics of Discomfort', *Social Anthropology* 17, 4: 392–407.

Moors, A. (2011), 'Colonial Traces? The (Post-)colonial Governance of Islamic Dress: Gender and the Public Presence of Islam', in M. Maussen, V. Bader and A. Moors, eds., *The Colonial and Post-colonial Governance of Islam,* Amsterdam: Amsterdam University Press.

Moors, A. (2013), '"Discover the Beauty of Modesty": Islamic Fashion Online', in R. Lewis, ed., *Modest Fashion: Styling Bodies, Mediating Faith,* London: I.B. Tauris.

Moors, A., and E. Tarlo (2007), 'Introduction', *Fashion Theory* 11, 2/3: 133–43.

Moruzzi, N. (2008), 'Trying to Look Different: Hijab as the Self-presentation of Social Distinctions', *Comparative Studies of South Asia, Africa and the Middle East* 28, 2: 225–34.

Navaro-Yashin, Y. (2002), 'The Market for Identities: Secularism, Islamism, Commodities', in D. Kandiyoti and A. Saktanber, eds., *Fragments of Culture: The Everyday of Modern Turkey,* New Brunswick, NJ: Rutgers University Press.

Niessen, S. (2003), 'Afterword: Re-orienting Fashion Theory', in S. Niessen, A. Leshkowich and C. Jones C., eds., *Re-orienting Fashion: The Globalization of Asian Dress,* Oxford: Berg.

Niessen, S., A. Leshkowich and C. Jones, eds. (2003), *Re-orienting Fashion: The Globalization of Asian Dress,* Oxford: Berg.

Osella, C., and F. Osella (2007), 'Muslim Style in South India', *Fashion Theory* 11, 2/3: 233–52.

Polhemus, T., and L. Proctor (1978), *Fashion and Anti-fashion,* London: Thames and Hudson.

Riello G., and P. McNeil, eds. (2010), *The Fashion History Reader: Global Perspectives,* London: Routledge.

Sandikçi, Ö., and G. Ger (2005), 'Aesthetics, Ethics and Politics of the Turkish Headscarf', in S. Küechler and D. Miller, eds., *Clothing as Material Culture,* Oxford: Berg.

Sandikçi, Ö., and G. Ger (2007), 'Constructing and Representing the Islamic Consumer in Turkey', *Fashion Theory* 11, 2/3: 189–210.

Sandikçi, Ö., and G. Ger (2010), 'Veiling in Style: How Does a Stigmatized Practice Become Fashionable', *Journal of Consumer Research* 37: 15–36.

Sapir, E. (1937), 'Fashion', in *Encyclopedia of the Social Sciences,* vol. 6, New York: Macmillan.

Scott, J. (2005), 'Symptomatic Politics. The Banning of Islamic Head Scarves in French Public Schools', *French Politics, Culture and Society* 23, 3: 106–27.

Scott, J. (2007), *The Politics of the Veil,* Princeton, NJ: Princeton University Press.

Scott, J. (2009), 'Sexularism', RSCAS distinguished lecture, Florence, European University Institute.

Simmel, G. (1957), 'Fashion', *American Journal of Sociology* 62, 6: 541–58.

Simmel, G. (1971), *On Individuality and Social Forms: Selected Writings,* Chicago, IL: University of Chicago Press.

Skov, L. (2011), 'Entering the Space of the Wardrobe', Creative Encounters Working Paper, no. 58, 2–25.

Taha, M. (2010), 'The Hijab North of Gibraltar: Moroccan Women as Objects of Civil and Social Transformation', *Journal of North African Studies* 15, 4: 465–80.

Tarlo, E. (1996), *Clothing Matters: Dress and Identity in India,* London: Hurst.

Tarlo, E. (2004), 'Weaving Air: The Textile Journey of Rezia Wahid', *Moving Worlds* 4 (2 November): 90–9.

Tarlo, E. (2005), 'Reconsidering Stereotypes: Anthropological Reflections on the Jilbab Controversy', *Anthropology Today* 21, 6: 13–17, front and back covers.

Tarlo, E. (2010a), 'Fashion', in A. Bernard and J. Spencer, eds., *Routledge Encyclopedia of Social and Cultural Anthropology,* London: Routledge, 283–4.

Tarlo, E. (2010b), *Visibly Muslim: Fashion, Politics and Faith,* Oxford: Berg.

Tarlo, E. (2013a), 'Developing Methods for the Study of Dress and Religion', in L. Woodhead, ed., *How to Research Religion: Putting Methods into Practice,* Oxford: Oxford University Press.

Tarlo, E. (2013b), 'Dress and the South Asian Diaspora', in D. Washbrook and J. Chatterjee, eds., *The South Asia Diaspora Handbook,* London: Routledge.

Tarlo, E., and A. Moors, eds. (2007), 'Muslim Fashions', *Fashion Theory* 11, 2/3.

Ünal, A., and A. Moors (2012), 'Formats, Fabrics and Fashions: Muslim Headscarves Revisited', *Material Religion* 8: 308–29.

Vom Bruck, G. (2008), 'Naturalising, Neutralising Women's Bodies: The "Headscarf Affair" and the Politics of Representation', *Identities* 15, 1: 51–79.

Wilson, E. (1985), *Adorned in Dreams: Fashion and Modernity,* London: Virago Press.

Woodward, S. (2007), *Why Women Wear What They Wear,* Oxford: Berg.

SECTION I

LOCATION AND THE DYNAMICS
OF ENCOUNTER

–1–

Burqinis, Bikinis and Bodies: Encounters in Public Pools in Italy and Sweden

Pia Karlsson Minganti

In recent years, a swimsuit which has become known as the *burqini* has attracted immense attention in the European media and from the general public. It is a two-piece costume which offers full-body and hair coverage except for the face, hands and feet. It was launched as a sartorial option for Muslim women who cover to enable them to enjoy swimming at public baths or outdoor locations like anyone else without having to compromise what they consider appropriate levels of modesty.

Muslim women's swimwear is produced in various places. The Turkish company Haşema claims to have been producing 'alternative bathing suits' for women since the early 1990s.[1] The forms and designations of the garment differ, from local terms such as the Turkish *haşema* to general references to Islamic or modest swimwear (Berglund 2008). The actual trademark, Burqini, was registered by designer Aheda Zanetti in 2003. Since then, the term burqini has developed into a generic term and has spread around the globe along with the actual product.[2] Growing up a Muslim/Arab girl who migrated to Australia from Lebanon at the age of one, Zanetti was familiar with the problems faced by women who wished to maintain Islamic dress codes and participate in sports. Introducing the Burqini as a solution, she now distributes her product through her international company Ahiida Pty with the following positive message:

> All eyes are on the appearance of Muslim women in sports. Their appearance should be modest and at the same time it should reflect a professional sporty appearance with pride. By providing the appropriate clothing for the Muslim woman, who complies with religious, cultural and sports obligation, we are helping to bring out the best in Muslim woman, to prove that a Muslim woman is a role model to other women in the world, not an oppressed, no name, and no face being. With Ahiida® sportswear, we can now compete with confidence.[3] (See Figure 1.1.)

On the Web site of Ahiida Pty, the burqini is launched in 'Modest-Fit' and 'Semi-Fit' models, the former consisting of a knee-length top and boot leg

Fig. 1.1 A burqini. The trademark Burqini was registered by designer Aheda Zanetti in 2003. Copyright Ahiida® Pty Ltd

pants, and the latter a thigh-length top and straight leg pants. The company also markets the Hijood sportswear, which has been used by several sports-women, including Olympian Ruqaya al Ghasara from Bahrain. The association of the burqini with swimming and sport is important. In the Ahiida Pty country of origin, Australia, the marketing of the outfit was stimulated by a BBC-produced documentary about young Muslims and their becoming part of the country's special beach and surf culture through their inclusion in lifeguard associations (Fitzpatrick 2009: 3; Suganuma 2010).

In Europe, the opposition to the burqini is to a great extent focussed on it representing some sort of threat to common European norms and values. Real or imagined Islamic norms are presented as fundamentally strange and incompatible with modern European democracy. This notion of

Muslim exceptionality not only reflects intersecting debates about immigration, 'culture clashes' and national identity but is further rooted in normative debates on how to organize gender, the body, sexuality and even beauty (Göle 2009; Moors 2009a; Amir-Moazami 2011).

In Sweden, the burqini has been denounced by segments of the general public, although the media coverage has been positive and public pools allow its use. The criticism focusses on the idea that the burqini is alien to regular practice and a threat both to hygiene and women's freedom. In Italy, some sections of the media have expressed similar critical attitudes and paved the way for local rejections. In the northern Italian town of Varallo Sesia, the mayor, who represents the openly Islamophobic party Lega Nord (Northern League), an influential member of Silvio Berlusconi's coalition government until November 2011 (Guolo 2003; Della Porta and Bosi 2010: 15), has implemented a prohibition against the burqini along with a fine of €500. In nearby Verona, also governed by Lega Nord, a woman dressed in a burqini was asked to leave the pool after some mothers complained she was intimidating their children. The decision was also connected to assumptions made about the potentially unhygienic material of the swimwear.

In this contribution, I will discuss reactions to the burqini and relate these to reactions to the older bikini and to nudity. Drawing on current research on Muslim women and Islamic fashion, along with Mary Douglas's anthropological theory on classificatory order, I will argue against the existence of any clear-cut shared European values concerning degrees of covering in public showers and baths. Likewise, I will argue against the existence of any obvious Islamic norms concerning what to wear for swimming. Rather, I will highlight differences and similarities that vary across national and religious boundaries. The examples are taken from showers and public swimming pools in Sweden and Italy and from my own life experience and fieldwork among Muslims in these two European countries.[4]

WOMEN IN PUBLIC SHOWERS

The burqini is often met with resistance. Muslim women are considered to cover themselves too much. Their habits differ from ours, whether in Sweden and Italy or elsewhere in Europe. One day I experienced how this taken-for-granted assumption on European homogeneity is challenged. During a stay in Italy, I had decided to go swimming at a public swimming bath. While in the shower, washing myself before going into the pool, I noticed an information panel on the wall. It stated the regulations, including the following rule:

> It is obligatory to wear a swimsuit in the shower out of consideration for children and adults who use the bathing establishment.

I immediately felt a sense of shame. Naturally, I had *undressed* before entering the shower; an automatic action fully in line with the moral guidelines that I have been internalizing since childhood. Now this conduct was no longer acceptable. Nor was the binary opposition between Muslim women's veiling and European normality as evident as it may once have appeared. Instead, the situation seemed to indicate a hierarchy of difference based on three variables. According to this formulation, both Muslim veiling and Swedish nudity were inferior to Italian common sense.[5]

The situation evoked difference—to the very skin. But if one views the scenario from a gender perspective, a common element of these three normative dress codes in public showers becomes apparent: all are variations of cultural and religious control over women's bodies and movements. Indeed, all societies seek to systematize human behaviour and create order out of complexity and formlessness, mainly through processes of inclusion and exclusion. To retrieve Mary Douglas's (1984, 1996) anthropological theory on classificatory order, each society has value systems that categorize people and things into the binary oppositions of pure and impure, normal and abnormal, legitimate and illicit. Such cohesive and differentiating systems help us define who and what we *are* just as much as determining who and what we *are not.* Douglas convincingly demonstrated the centrality of the body in the maintenance of group boundaries, and it is especially women who are called upon to fulfil this task of embodying the group's purity and recognized standards of modesty (Delaney 1991; Anthias and Yuval-Davis 1992; Morley 2000; Duits and Van Zoonen 2006). Paradoxically enough, the embodying of purity from one group's viewpoint is likely to evoke notions of dirt and danger for the other. This is quite obvious in the debates on women's bodies, hygiene and decency in public showers and swimming pools.

AN ITALIAN SENSE OF DECENCY

In Italy as well as in Sweden, it is standard practice to wash oneself in the showers before going into public swimming pools, but as we have seen, contrary to Swedes, Italians are urged to complete the washing with their swimwear on. The information panel, which alerted me to this variation, politely referred to the well-being of children. Interestingly, the same argument has been used in Italy when denouncing the burqini. Both the practice of donning the burqini and showering undressed stand out as deviations from the general behaviour of the Italian bathing establishment. Both the exaggerated veiling and the naked body are categorized and excluded as 'matter out of place', to use Douglas's unforgettable phrase, whether representing 'impure' materials, 'strangers', or 'foreign' objects which are seen to defile the symbolic space of the group/nation (Morley 2000: 142–5, 155–6).

The bathhouse staff in the northern Italian town of Varallo Sesia focussed its argument against the burqini on the garment's potentially unhygienic material and advanced a request for its information tag. The woman in question had already cut away the tag, a fact which resulted in the staff successfully removing her from the common bath facility. Considering that the burqini is a synthetic material in line with any other swimwear and that Italians are expected to clean their swimwear in the showers prior to swimming, I cannot but associate the pool staff's reference to 'dirt' with Douglas's theory of sociocultural pollution. Dirt is 'essentially disorder' and eliminating it is 'a positive effort to organize the environment' and make it 'conform to an idea' (1984: 3).

The persons who manifest the two topical deviations from the Italian standard—donning the burqini or showering nude—appear to be strange, indeed strangers, associated with pollution and danger. The children are said to be frightened, spoken for by parents involved in the maintenance of cultural order and identity. Migration and globalization tend to bring about transgressors who blur the lines and are not easily categorized in terms of belonging or not belonging. In fact, the burqini and the visual presence of Muslim women in public are at the core of contemporary debates on citizenship and the place of Islam in contemporary Europe (Göle 2009: 279; Moors 2009b: 175; Salih 2009: 421).

One dominant frame through which Muslims are interpreted in today's Italy is the 'security frame', according to which 'all Muslims are dangerous because they are likely to be terrorists' (Frisina 2010: 560). In 2010, an Italian government report proposed legislation banning face coverings, such as the burqa and niqab. The proposal was presented in a bill from the far-right Lega Nord. The bill aimed at amending a 1975 law that allowed exceptions for 'justified reasons', such as the difficulty of identifying individuals. The Italian Constitutional Affairs Commission is currently considering an Interior Ministry report which claims that the possible law would be implemented not for religious reasons but for security reasons. After hearings with leading Muslims, the burqa was found not to be obligatory in Islam, while the threat of international terrorism and local public disorder was looked upon as imminent (Ministero dell'Interno 2010; see Figure 1.2).

Following the burqa debate, there has also been a backlash against the burqini. The woman in Varallo Sesia is not the only one who has been asked to leave a public bath in Italy or Europe at large. People like me, who have happened to shower undressed in an Italian bath establishment, have not evoked any equivalent public attention in the media. This fact may be interpreted with reference to the concepts of cultural categorization and social hierarchy. Muslims are currently stigmatized as the ultimate Others and collectively ranked low on the social ladder. Contrary to this, the practice of showering undressed is not associated with any supposedly low-ranking and threatening immigrant group.

Fig. 1.2 Billboard announcing the local ban of 'burqa, burqini and niqab' in Varallo Sesia, Italy. Photo: Jon R. Snyder

Yet it is nudity and not the stigmatized burqini that has been targeted in the statutes of Italian public showers and duly publicized on information boards such as the one that caught my eye. A common Italian expression associated with virtuous manners is *il senso del pudore* (the sense of decency). Although naturalized and taken for granted, common sense is always a site of cultural contestation. In this case, it is used to refer to purity in terms of body hygiene but also to the purity of the group as embodied by women's clothing and behaviour.

The dress code for bathing and beach life in Italy has varied over time, spanning from everyday garments and full-cover suits, to two-piece bikinis, tanga and topless outfits. Cultural theorist Stephen Gundle has explored the specific place of female beauty in Italian collective identity. He calls attention to the press, cinema and, not least, beauty contests as vital vehicles in the post-war process of reasserting national ideals of beauty and reconstructing Italian identity on new lines. Strong influence was exercised from the allied Americans, who offered a new image: the pin-up girl, symbolizing vitality with her fresh, yet flirtatious, smile and daring swimsuit (2007: 110–12).

The beauty contests and new ideals brought on 'significant cultural battles between Catholics, bourgeois traditionalists, commercial forces and the left over the nature and meaning of such exposure and its relation to the collective identity of the Italians' (Gundle 2007: 108). The fascists had banned beauty contests in 1938. Their model for 'true' Italian beauty was the peasant woman's assumed simplicity in contrast to the modern, urban femininity associated with cosmetics, fashion and consumption which was denounced as 'un-Italian'. With the post-war boom for beauty contests, the Left resisted galas with girls in swimsuits but arranged alternative events with young women competing for the title *Stellina* (little star) dressed in unpretentious leisurewear (Gundle 2007: 130–1). The bikini was soon introduced, and its size gradually reduced. Today women are competing for the title *Velina*. It is assigned to the lightly dressed pin-up girls serving as decoration to fully dressed middle-aged anchormen in the TV productions associated with media mogul and former prime minister Silvio Berlusconi.

Contestations over the meaning of bodily exposure and its relation to collective identity go beyond beauty contests and TV shows, emerging in the showers of public swimming pools. *Il senso del pudore,* as expressed in the urge to shower with swimwear on, is currently imbued with conservatives' and Catholics' reclamation of fashion and modesty norms. According to anthropologist Ruba Salih, the commonly spread argument about Muslims being a threat to secularized Italian society can be relativized in light of the Catholic Church's striving to reoccupy its position in the public sphere, which has been shrinking since the 1970s.

> The Catholic Church in Italy strives to recreate a bond that revolves around the idea of a homogeneous religious Christian community, defined by a shared ethos, morality and values, that are threatened by the increasing gendered visibility of Islam. Interestingly . . . this ethos places a heavy emphasis on the control of women's bodies and on the preservation of a moral community whose boundaries are defined by the restoration of the nuclear heterosexual family and the reiteration of the Christian nature of the country. (Salih 2009: 421)

Such a Catholic ethos would both compete and overlap with other discourses on gender and morals, such as conservative Muslim views of gender or feminist critiques (Islamic included) of the commodification and exploitation of women's bodies. During the spring of 2011, the campaign 'Basta!' (Enough!) was organized by the movement Se Non Ora, Quando? (SNOQ; If Not Now, When?); for it, Italian women and men of different political and religious orientations protested against the culture of sexism.[6] The protests were triggered by the exposure of Prime Minister Silvio Berlusconi's alleged affairs with escort girls but soon came to include a critique of the image of Italian women represented in the televised Velina.

Much of the critique against sexism in Italy has concentrated on sexism in politics and the media but rarely on how bodies are simultaneously both gendered and racialized and subject to various naturalized axes of power and privilege (Bonfiglioli 2010; Pepicelli 2012). Many grassroots movements and some of the Italian population are, however, developing reflexive and pluralistic perspectives which produce greater understanding and support of women who choose to wear burqinis.

SWEDISH IDEAS OF NUDITY AND DECENCY

The Swedish term for decency, *anständighet,* leaves a certain space for nudity. It is looked upon as healthy for quite old children to bathe naked in lakes and at the seaside. Many parents mix casually with their children at home whilst remaining undressed. In private houses and summer cottages, guests are invited to mixed-gender saunas. A dominant pattern is to wash undressed in public baths and to laugh at others' apparently irrational and outdated fear of nudity and exaggerated sexualization of the human body. If civilized behaviour in Italian showers is generally associated with covering private parts, in Sweden it is associated with the pragmatic cleaning of the natural human body, liberated from any cultural and religious hang-ups.

Yet, in Sweden, as in any society, there are limits to nudity and the interaction between the sexes. Public baths are equipped with separate showers and saunas for men and women, and nudist baths are not allowed except for exceptional events. In my Swedish home town of Uppsala, the regulations of the public baths include the following two sentences:

> Everyone must dress in swimwear intended for bathing (bathing trunks, bikini or swimsuit, without underwear).
>
> Shower and wash yourself with soap without swimwear before you go into the pool or sauna.[7]

The instruction to shower undressed is quite the opposite of that given in Italy. Yet, like my own deviation from the Italian order, in Sweden, too, there are visitors who display alternative practices.[8] There are an increasing number of people, especially youth, who keep their swimwear on in the showers. In the context of Swedish public pools, the burqini is today generally accepted as 'swimwear intended for bathing'. Less accepted, however, are the T-shirts, shorts and trousers worn during the exclusive swimming sessions held for Muslim women. Further rejected is the new trend among some young men of keeping their underwear on under their bathing trunks, exposing just enough to show off brand names.

As in Italy, deviations from the regulations are perceived in Sweden in terms of the dissolution of moral and common sense and, thus, as dissolution of fundamental aspects of national identity. In Sweden, nudity is

viewed as natural and decent within the context of gender-separated saunas and the showers at public baths.[9] When this 'natural' and 'rational' relation to body and hygiene is threatened, so is its link to the very sense of
progressive modernity, which has been shown to be a core feature of Swedish national identity (Ehn, Frykman and Löfgren 1993; Hübinette and Lundström 2011). Many Swedes claim this perceived moral dissolution in public
baths stems from immigrants who are still held back by cultural traditions
and religion. Also accused are American and global popular culture, and
the fashion and pornography industries, which are all believed to reinforce
outdated norms.

RESISTING SEXUALIZATION

The notion of Swedish modernity fuses with international discourses on Western modernity and progress. Critical cultural theorists have called attention to
how governing ideas about modernity and progress have concealed the ongoing marginalization and even exclusion of the Muslim Other (i.e. Abu-Lughod
1998; Mahmood 2005; Ahmed 2010). In her critical analysis of English media
coverage of the burqini, Fitzpatrick exposes the construction of the burqini as
a symbol for the liberation of oppressed Muslim women, making them free
to participate in sport and assimilate into 'Western culture' (2009). These
media and publicity stories seem to ignore the fact that for many women
the covering of their bodies is not understood as a tradition they are forced to
follow but a conscious decision meant to be an individual, cultural, religious,
aesthetical, political or even feminist statement. It is not necessarily in tune
with dominant conceptions of what constitutes progress but is nevertheless
based on women's experience of living Islam in contemporary Europe (Karlsson Minganti 2007; Tarlo 2010).

   Despite the emphasis on liberty, there are women in Sweden and Italy, of
any ethnic or confessional background, who refrain from going to public pools
because of negative body self-perception. Body shape, body hair, sagging skin
and unattainable beauty ideals lead to feelings of failure. They may indeed be
exposed to sanctions for such failures by being greeted with contempt and
mockery. They can be read as objects which are deemed unbeautiful and,
thus, fall into the category of dirt; they are anomalies that do not fit society's
construction of how things should be. Similarly, women who display themselves too much as objects of male desire risk being stigmatized as whores
or bimbos. Women and girls are, paradoxically, expected to be both tempting
and virtuous, sexual and virginal at the same time (Tseëlon 1995).[10]

   The feminist network Bara bröst (Bare Breasts) challenges the expectation
placed on women to manage their own and men's sexual lust with their dress
codes and behaviour, when the same demand is not put on men. It promotes

further desexualization of women's bodies and the right to bathe topless in public pools.[11] With the exception of its promotion of topless bathing, Bara bröst turns out to have something in common with the concerns of many Muslim women activists. Although having different perspectives, goals and solutions, these different groups overlap in their critique of the sexualization, commodification and exploitation of women's bodies.

MODESTLY ACTIVE

In Sweden, Italy and Europe at large, there are Muslim women who argue that their Islamic dress is a protest against the sexism in the media and market forces. Their counter strategy involves not the divestment of clothes as with Bara bröst but rather the full covering of those body parts associated with sexual appeal. They see sexuality as an inevitable force, ever-present in any situation that includes men and women. Contrary to the logic of many secular feminists, but in line with numerous other non-Muslims of various political and religious convictions, they deem pre- and extramarital sexual actions a sin and prioritize the managing of sexuality which, left uncurbed, is considered a potentially destructive force. Full-body covering for women stands out as the preferred means by which to reduce sexual attraction and to signal to the world that this woman is not sexually available. Thus, the burqini acts simultaneously as a critique of sexism and a safeguard against sexual harassment.

Indeed, the women in question perceive their secluding Islamic dress code as a means of achieving recognition as full subjects rather than as objects of male desire. Women's increased participation in mosques and Muslim organizations in recent decades is a well-known fact discussed by a growing body of scholars (Mahmood 2005; Jouili and Amir-Moazami 2006; Karlsson Minganti 2007, 2011b; Bano and Kalmbach 2011). This trend has, among other things, resulted in profound feelings among the women involved of being active agents rather than passive victims of patriarchal customs and Western dominance. Women are becoming recognized as pious subjects with the right and duty to become educated within both religious and secular spheres. They participate in the rereading of religious texts and the search for the true meaning and implementation of Islam in different contexts, including public baths. Intentionality (*niyya*) and free choice are made core moral concepts and pave the way for personal responsibility (Karlsson Minganti 2008: 11; Moors 2009b: 191). The Islamic dress code functions as a signal of such pious intentions. Dressed in hijab on their way to the public baths, and in the burqini once diving into the pool, many women do not see themselves in need of being secluded at home or guided by a male escort. They have strong faith, self-respect and control.

Fig. 1.3 Kausar Sacranie, designer and CEO of Modestly Active. Photo: Emma Tarlo

Living in Europe, belonging to a religious minority and the highly marked category of Muslim, these women are fully aware of their representative position. They express a compelling responsibility to counteract negative images of Islam and Muslims and create an image of normality in which Muslim women are seen as well-spoken, humorous, capable of maintaining a public presence, visible in cinemas and cafés, shopping with friends, talking to young men or even taking part in activities linked to men, such as parachuting and martial arts. The burqini gives its wearers an air of being sporty and cool, 'modestly active'—an appellation that has now turned into an important trademark for Islamic swimwear in Britain and beyond (see Figure 1.3).[12]

Importantly, many Muslims, women included, reject the burqini. The reasons are many. To some, it suggests commercialization and Westernization rather than solidarity with the Muslim ummah. To others, the concern revolves around ideas of Islamic femininity. The burqini is thought to be too revealing of body contours, and swimming is considered an inappropriate activity for Muslim women. Again using Douglas for understanding the acute urge for boundary control within a vulnerable minority, women are seen as potentially staining the reputation of themselves, their families and the Muslim ummah. According to this logic, Muslim women need to personify dignity and should never appear nude or semi-nude in public pools and showers.

However, behind the woman, that is, the elevated symbol of the community's order, dignity and reproduction, there are real women who are in fact acting and negotiating dominant norms in their everyday lives (Sered 2000). Naima in Sweden says her burqini is a perfect invention: 'I exercise regularly in the swimming pool and play in the lakes during the summer.' Cherin enjoys the women-only swimming sessions. With no men present, she wears an ordinary swimsuit rather than the burqini, which is sold and rented out directly at the pool. Hind does not like the feel of the burqini, arguing, 'It sticks to my body, but I still use it when jumping into the pool with my kids.' Dalia says she has 'never tried it and never will. It exposes your body and is not coherent with Islam.' Iman chooses a burqini with 'cute decorations', while Mona goes for a strait, black one, compatible with her notion of *haya* (modesty).

The woman who was asked to leave the public pool in the Italian town of Verona is named Najat Retzki Idrissi. At the time, she was forty-three years of age and had lived in Verona for thirteen years. She works as a cultural mediator and proudly talks about her burqini, which she bought on the Internet. However, she does not like the designation *burqini,* as for her it hints at the face-covering burqa. She usually wears hijab in daily life and uses the Islamic swimwear mainly when bathing with her children (Perbellini 2009).

DIVERSITY AS REALITY

The burqini has been restricted, prohibited and contrasted to 'our European value system' in negative ways. Yet, my simple act of taking a shower in an Italian public bathhouse reveals how European standards are by no means obvious or fixed. In Sweden, washing should be done undressed, while in Italy you should wash wearing a swimsuit, although according to many, not a full-cover burqini. Burqini wearers are regarded by some as the ultimate aliens. Yet, their presence, just like mine, could instead be used to instigate deconstructive self-reflection. In her biographic novel, Italian-born Sumaya Abdel Qader, who is of Jordanian-Palestinian descent, twists the common sense idea of what is normal in the dressing room. Her description of entering the changing room with her female Muslim peers is revealing:

Shock! We do not know where to direct our eyes. Totally embarrassed we search for a free corner and with blank looks we allow ourselves some seconds to recover. The shock comes out of surprise: we have entered a room of nudists. Our education has always prevented us from looking at women and men stark naked, especially without the notorious fig leaf! Anyway, in our little corner we get changed while staring at the wall. We slowly relax, while giggling and joking about the situation. Here we go, ready: gym suit, gym shoes and, obviously, the veil...End of lesson. It is time to return to the nudists' room. Again facing the wall, we force ourselves back to our lockers. Now the problem is the shower. We are disgustingly sweaty and going home to wash is beyond dispute. We move towards the showers. Yet another shock! Transparent cabinets! What the heck! Can't we have a little privacy? Do we really have to share everything? What a communal world! Anyway, we help one another to shield behind the towels. How the other women look at us! Maybe they ask themselves whether we are nuts or what? In fact, after we attend the gym for a while, a young woman approaches us and asks us why we make all this fuss when changing and washing. When we explain our purely demure, moral and religious reasons, she says: 'So, now it is we who are the shameless ones?!' (Abdel Qader 2008: 74–76, author's translation)

Embodying purity from one group's viewpoint is likely to evoke dirt and danger for the other. Abdel Qader's reflections point to the diverse norms for hygiene and decency in public showers. While I have perceived Italian showering norms as prudish in their demand for the wearing of swimsuits, Abdel Qader and her friends experienced another Italian shower room as shockingly shameless. Her example also points to how communities (moral, national, religious) are constructed and renegotiated on the basis of women's embodiment of normative decency.

Typically, the one public example of a non-Muslim woman who chose to don the burqini resulted in her being ridiculed and accused of being a traitor. The world famous British food writer and journalist Nigella Lawson was spotted in 2011 on an Australian beach wearing the full-cover swimsuit. Although she claimed she wore it in order to protect herself from skin cancer, which has allegedly troubled several members of her family, her action was regarded as so transgressive that the Google search combination of 'nigella lawson burqini' triggers thousands of hits, the vast majority expanding on the themes of ridicule and betrayal (i.e. Woods 2011).

There are no reliable statistics about the number of burqinis bought and used in Sweden and Italy. The difficulty with indicating its prevalence is linked to the diversity of Muslim swimwear. Having dealt with the heterogeneous norms for dressing in public baths, I will now offer a closer look into the various regulations for the burqini and into Muslim women's different approaches to this garb.

On a supranational level, the negative stereotyping of the burqini in media and public debate coexists with official policies, such as the European Charter of Women's Rights in Sport.[13] The charter provides measures to reinforce gender equality policies with regard to women's participation in sports and provides specific measures for targeted groups, among them Muslim women. In the town of Turin, the national Unione Italiana Sport Per Tutti (UISP; Italian Union of Sports for All) has adopted the charter and provides sessions for women-only swimming.[14] Besides Turin, only Milan, to my knowledge, provides a similar service in one of its pools. However, Asmaa Gueddouda, a Muslim woman living in Milan, explains that she does not have enough 'passion for swimming' to travel to the other side of this big city where the women-only session is offered. Also, the attraction of the pool is weakened by the negative attention she draws with her burqini: 'Perhaps in the future it will be easier for me having access to public pools in Italy, but for the time being I hold back.'

According to the sociologist Stefano Allievi (2010: 85), Italy still lacks public reflection on multiculturalism as an empirical reality and, thus, a realistic model for cultural relations. Simultaneously, the mayoral ordinances signal considerable fragmentation, both normative and territorial, in a state divided into more than eight thousand municipalities. The situation becomes even more critical as it is often a matter of monolithic regulations characterized by a democratic deficit (Lorenzetti 2010: 363). As a result, few Italian swimming pools comply with the aim of the European Charter of Women's Rights in Sport by explicitly supporting Muslim women's swimming.

Swedish public institutions are required to guarantee equal opportunities with regard to gender, ethnicity, faith or disability (Borevi 2010). The prioritizing of citizens' swimming knowledge, safety and health has led to the allowance of the burqini in public pools, and today it is sold or rented at many bathing establishments (Aytar 2011).[15] Also, many public pools offer separate sessions for women, either for group rental or individual entrance fees.[16] However, such a solution has not become the dominant norm, and this is reflected in women booking outside the ordinary schedule. Affirmative policies aside, there would not be any women-only swimming sessions or burqinis without strong Muslim women initiators prepared to defy the harsh glances and comments from some members of the public.

The one published estimation of the number of burqinis in Sweden I could find was in a newspaper article about Rosengård, a Malmö suburb with a high percentage of inhabitants from Muslim backgrounds. In the article, the manager of the local pool estimated that about one in ten female visitors wear the burqini (Sahlin 2011). Although there are variations between local municipalities, neighbourhoods and public pools, the number is unlikely to be higher elsewhere in Sweden. The single shop in Rosengård selling the burqini claims to have sold a handful during the summer of 2011. In the bath establishment of Skövde a burqini has never been seen. In Flen, two were sold during 2011.

The lady in the shop at Uppsala's main communal bath establishment says many Muslim women take a look at her products, but she only sells the burqini to one in a hundred. She confirms that the price may deter many, although the garment would be more expensive if bought online.[17] Her colleague in Flen is appreciative of the fact that some women ask her for advice on suitable fabrics for homemade swimwear. The general rule favours synthetic material and bans cotton, which allegedly destroys the sewage system. Swedish online resellers such as Tahara.se and Shamsa.se claim to see a growing demand for burqinis. Swedish Web site awpdesign.se sells models from Ahiida Pty online and estimates the number to be a couple of hundred a year.[18]

Italian women turn to international Web sites or to local shops such as Libreria Islamica Iman, a combined bookshop and women's Islamic clothing boutique in central Milan. Peak interest is during the summer season, says Asmaa Gueddouda, the present shopkeeper and daughter of the founder. She demonstrates the one remaining sample, a model of the Turkish brand Haşema. It is a full-cover suit in a fabric that dries quickly and thus avoids exposure of the contours of the body. Yet, stresses Asmaa, who has studied fashion at the Caterina da Siena Institute, fashion is crucial to her customers, and they are predominantly looking for colourful and decorated models (see Figures 1.4 and 1.5).

Fig. 1.4   Asmaa Gueddouda in a shop in Milan demonstrates a model of swimwear designed by the Turkish company Haşema. Photo: Pia Karlsson Minganti

Fig. 1.5 The Asude full-cover swimsuit from the Turkish company Haşema, sold by Asmaa Gueddouda in Milan. Copyright Haşema

The heterogeneous reality of Muslim swimwear in Italy, Sweden and Europe at large is not only a matter of the regulations in public showers and swimming pools or of dominant norms as proclaimed by Islamic religious authorities. Above all, it is a matter of the various practices of individual women. When administrators of public pools try to facilitate Muslim women's participation, they encounter complexity rather than one unequivocal dress code. For some women, swimming is out of the question, since they would never bathe in the presence of women, let alone unfamiliar men. Some may come to the pool but only to supervise their children from the poolside. Then there are women who believe it to be permissible according to Islam to swim during exclusive sessions for women, with curtains covering the windows and female staff at hand. Usually these women feel free to swim in ordinary swimsuits or make do with outfits such as leggings with T-shirts or tops (Tarlo 2010: 226, n9). It seems fair to claim that the burqini is primarily chosen by those who find it legitimate to swim in pools and beaches, which are open to all.

The burqini is, it seems, here to stay. It sells slowly but surely, whether online or in shops. The term *burqini* is disliked by some. Its combination of burqa and bikini may reinforce the dichotomy between Muslim and European women and the former's stereotypical position as aliens and norm-breakers, although some Muslim women appreciate the humour evoked by the term. The women focussed on for this article are all involved in a wider Islamic revival as well as in processes of 'commodification of clothing production and the ensuing more rapid turnover or change of styles as part of a highly self-conscious consumer culture' (Moors 2009b: 197). By defining the burqini and swimming pools as compatible with Islam, they are in fact countering both patriarchal and xenophobic forces which keep them away from public fields of action. By doing this, they participate in the redefining of citizenship, European identity and women's well-being.

NOTES

This work was supported by the Swedish Research Council; the Department of Ethnology, History of Religions and Gender Studies at Stockholm University; and the Department of Politics, Institutions and History at the University of Bologna.

A preliminary discussion of this topic has been published in Swedish (Karlsson Minganti 2011a).

1. See Haşema home page, <http://hasema.com/default_eng.html> accessed 25 March 2013.
2. There are also other trademarks, such as bodykini (www.bodykini.com) and modestkini (www.modestkini.com).
3. See <http://www.ahiida.com/About-Ahiida.html> accessed 22 November 2011.
4. Sweden has a total population of 9.4 million. Approximately 350,000 to 400,000 are Muslims, of which 100,000 to 150,000 belong to officially registered Muslim organizations (Larsson 2009: 56; SST 2011). Italy has 60.6 million inhabitants. An estimated 1.5 million are Muslims, of which only a minority have Italian citizenship (Caritas/Migrantes 2011).
5. Some Italians, with whom I have discussed this issue, do not recognize the common sense of showering in swimsuits. They are not all aware of official regulations and some shower naked. Whilst there are undoubtedly some local variations in practice regarding what is worn in swimming pool

showers, my brief investigation into the regulations presented on the
Web sites of public swimming baths in Italy reveals the prevalence of a
dominant norm. Common sense norms are reinforced through signs and
the verbal correction of norm-breaking practices.

6. See <http://www.senonoraquando.eu/?p=2948> accessed 8 November
2011. See also the influential film *Il corpo delle donne* (Women's
Bodies) by Lorella Zanardi; for the English version, see <http://www.
ilcorpodelledonne.net/?page_id=91> accessed 25 March 2013.

7. See <http://www.fyrishov.se/fyrishov/templates/StandardPage____13704.
aspx> accessed 25 March 2013.

8. Ethnologist Ella Johansson (2011) has examined the negotiations on
body and space in Swedish public pools. Insightfully, she suggests that
the many graphic signboards about how to dress and wash indicate that
the rules are in fact contested.

9. The importance of public baths and saunas in Swedish tradition has
been dealt with by ethnologists such as Jonas Frykman (2004), Ella
Johansson (2011) and Tom O'Dell (2010). David Gunnarsson examines
the fact that the grand mosque of Stockholm comprises a gym and a
sauna—'the only sauna with a mosque attached' as one mosque guide
jokingly said (2004: 20).

10. There is a marginal, yet increasing, demand from non-Muslim women
for gender-separate solutions in the public pools and relaxation departments. Further, some pool staff I spoke to associate such demands, as
well as the wearing of T-shirts and shorts, not only with Muslim women
but also with 'overweight' people.

11. *The Local. Sweden's News in English* (24 June 2009), <http://www.
thelocal.se/20250/20090624/#> accessed 9 November 2011.

12. See <http://www.modestlyactive.com> accessed 22 November 2011.

13. See <http://www.olympiaproject.net/wp-content/uploads/2010/06/
CHART_ENGLISH1.pdf> accessed 8 November 2011.

14. See page 11, <http://www.olympiaproject.net/wp-content/uploads/
2010/06/CHART_ENGLISH1.pdf>. Also see <http://www.facebook.com/
groups/138224270392> accessed 25 March 2013.

15. The policy of allowing alternative swimwear for Muslim women was put to
the test in 2008, when the municipality of Gothenburg had to pay com-
pensation for discrimination on grounds of religion. The case included two
women who were forced to leave a public pool, as they did not obey the
dress code. They were wearing long sleeves, trousers and headscarves,
claiming that they did not intend to swim but were merely watching their
children (Sundkvist 2010: 20–3).

16. An early initiative to develop women-only swimming sessions came from
Muslimska Kvinnors Idrottsförening (MKIF; Muslim Womens Sports
Association), established in Gothenburg in 1997: see <http://www.

mkif.se/index.html> accessed 7 November 2011. The women's need for functional swimwear resulted in the development of the trademark Shamsa (www.shamsa.se), also sold online at Tahara.se and in a shop in Rosengård, Malmö.
17. The prices vary from €35 to over €100. The rental price in Sweden is around €4.
18. See <http://www.awpdesign.se/kollektion/badklader-dam/ahiida-burqini/ahiida-burqini.aspx> accessed 25 March 2013.

REFERENCES

Abdel Qader, S. (2008), *Porto il velo, adoro i Queen: Nuove italiane crescono,* Milan: Sonzogno.
Abu-Lughod, L. (1998), 'Introduction', in L. Abu-Lughod, ed., *Remaking Women: Feminism and Modernity in the Middle East,* Princeton, NJ: Princeton University Press.
Ahmed, S. (2010), *The Promise of Happiness,* London: Duke University Press.
Allievi, S. (2010), 'Immigration and Cultural Pluralism in Italy: Multiculturalism as a Missing Model', *Italian Culture* 28, 2: 85–103.
Amir-Moazami, S. (2011), 'Dialogue as a Governmental Technique: Managing Gendered Islam in Germany', *Feminist Review* 98, 1: 9–27.
Anthias, F., and N. Yuval-Davis (1992), *Racialized Boundaries: Race, Nation, Gender, Colour and Class and the Anti-racist Struggle,* London: Routledge.
Aytar, O. (2011), '"Välkommen till Flen—bäst på bemötande 2011": Berättelsen om en forskningscirkel för bemötandefrågor', in P. Lahdenperä, ed., *Forskningscirkel—Arena för verksamhetsutveckling i mångfald,* Västerås: Mälardalen University, <mdh.diva-portal.org/smash/get/diva2:511191/FULLTEXT01> accessed 25 March 2013.
Bano, M., and H. Kalmbach, eds. (2011), *Women, Leadership, and Mosques: Changes in Contemporary Islamic Authority,* Leiden: Brill.
Berglund, J. (2008), 'Muslim Swim Wear Fashion at Amman Waves on the Internet and Live', *CyberOrient,* 3, 1, <http://www.cyberorient.net/article.do?articleId=3715> accessed 25 March 2013.
Bonfiglioli, C. (2010), 'Intersections of Racism and Sexism in Contemporary Italy: A Critical Cartography of Recent Feminist Debates', *Darkmatter: In the Ruins of Imperial Culture,* 6, <http://www.darkmatter101.org/site/2010/10/10/intersections-of-racism-and-sexism-in-contemporary-italy-a-critical-cartography-of-recent-feminist-debates/> accessed 25 March 2013.
Borevi, K. (2010), 'Dimensions of Citizenship: European Integration Policies from a Scandinavian Perspective', in A. Bay, B. Bengtsson and P. Strömblad, eds., *Diversity, Inclusion and Citizenship in Scandinavia,* Newcastle-upon-Tyne: Cambridge Scholars Publishing.

Caritas/Migrantes (2011), *Dossier Statistico Immigrazione,* Rome.

Delaney, C. (1991), *The Seed and the Soil: Gender and Cosmology in Turkish Village Society,* Berkeley: University of California Press.

Della Porta, D., and L. Bosi (2010), *Young Muslims in Italy, Parma and Verona,* Aarhus: Centre for Studies in Islamism and Radicalisation (CIR).

Douglas, M. (1984), *Purity and Danger: An Analysis of the Concepts of Purity and Taboo,* London: Ark.

Douglas, M. (1996), *Natural Symbols: Explorations in Cosmology with a New Introduction,* London: Routledge.

Duits, L., and L. van Zoonen (2006), 'Headscarves and Porno-chic: Disciplining Girls' Bodies in the European Multicultural Society', *European Journal of Women's Studies* 13, 2: 103–17.

Ehn, B., J. Frykman and O. Löfgren (1993), *Försvenskningen av Sverige: Det nationellas förvandlingar,* Stockholm: Natur & Kultur.

Fitzpatrick, S. (2009), 'Covering Muslim Women at the Beach: Media Representations of the Burkini', Thinking Gender Papers, Los Angeles, UCLA Center for the Study of Women, 1–11, <http://escholarship.org/uc/item/9d0860x7> accessed 25 March 2013.

Frisina, A. (2010), 'Young Muslims' Everyday Tactics and Strategies: Resisting Islamophobia, Negotiating Italianess, Becoming Citizens', *Journal of Intercultural Studies* 31, 5: 557–72.

Frykman, J. (2004), 'I hetluften. Svensk bastu som ideologi och praktik', in C. Westergren, ed., *Tio tvättar sig,* Stockholm: Nordiska museets förlag, 86–107.

Göle, N. (2009), 'Turkish Delight in Vienna: Art, Islam, and European Public Culture', *Cultural Politics* 5, 3: 277–98.

Gundle, S. (2007), *Bellissima. Feminine Beauty and the Idea of Italy,* London: Yale University Press.

Gunnarsson, D. (2004), 'Bastu med tillhörande moské', *Kulturella Perspektiv* 3: 19–25.

Guolo, R. (2003), *Xenofobi e xenofili: Gli italiani e l'islam,* Rome/Bari: Laterza.

Hübinette, T., and C. Lundström (2011), 'Sweden after the Recent Election: The Double-binding Power of Swedish Whiteness through the Mourning of the Loss of "Old Sweden" and the Passing of "Good Sweden"', *NORA— Nordic Journal of Feminist and Gender Research* 19, 1: 42–52.

Johansson, E. (2011), 'I Sverige simmar vi tillsammans. Simkunnighetens etnografi', in H. Tolvhed and D. Cardell, eds., *Kulturstudier, kropp och idrott. Perspektiv på fenomen i gränslandet mellan natur och kultur,* Malmö: idrottsforum.org, 63–82.

Jouili, J., and S. Amir-Moazami (2006), 'Knowledge, Empowerment, and Religious Authority among Pious Muslim Women in France and Germany', *The Muslim World* 96, 4: 617–42.

Karlsson Minganti, P. (2007), *Muslima: Islamisk väckelse och unga kvinnors förhandlingar om genus i det samtida Sverige,* Stockholm: Carlsson Bokförlag.

Karlsson Minganti, P. (2008), 'Becoming a "Practising" Muslim: Reflections on Gender, Racism and Religious Identity among Women in a Swedish Muslim Youth Organisation', *Elore* 15, 1: 1–16, <http://www.elore.fi/arkisto/1_08/kam1_08.pdf> accessed 1 June 2011.

Karlsson Minganti, P. (2011a), 'Minareter, burkini och minibikini: Om religion som syns och värderingar som synas', in S. Olsson and S. Sorgenfrei, eds., *Perspektiv på religion: En vänbok till Christer Hedin,* Stockholm: Dialogos.

Karlsson Minganti, P. (2011b), 'Challenging from Within: Youth Associations and Female Leadership in Swedish Mosques', in M. Bano and H. Kalmbach, eds., *Women, Leadership, and Mosques: Changes in Contemporary Islamic Authority,* Leiden: Brill.

Larsson, G. (2009), 'Sweden', in G. Larsson, ed., *Islam in the Nordic and Baltic Countries,* London: Routledge.

Lorenzetti, A. (2010), 'Il divieto di indossare "burqa" e "burqini": Che "genere" di ordinanze?', *Le Regioni* 38, 1–2: 349–66.

Mahmood, S. (2005), *Politics of Piety: The Islamic Revival and the Feminist Subject,* Princeton, NJ: Princeton University Press.

Ministero dell'Interno (2010), 'Notizie. Portare burqa e niqab non è un obbligo religioso: è il parere del Comitato per l'Islam italiano', <http://www.interno.gov.it/mininterno/export/sites/default/it/sezioni/sala_stampa/notizie/religioni/0056_2010_10_08_islam.html> accessed 25 March 2013.

Moors, A. (2009a), 'The Dutch and the Face-veil: The Politics of Discomfort', *Social Anthropology/Anthropologie Sociale* 17, 4: 393–408.

Moors, A. (2009b), '"Islamic-fashion" in Europe: Religious Conviction, Aesthetic Style, and Creative Consumption', *Encounters* 1, 1: 175–201.

Morley, D. (2000), *Home Territories: Media, Mobility and Identity,* London: Routledge.

O'Dell, T. (2010), *Spas: The Cultural Economy of Hospitality, Magic and the Senses,* Lund: Nordic Academic Press.

Pepicelli, R. (2012), *Il Velo nell'Islam: Storia, Politica, Estetica,* Rome: Carocci.

Perbellini, M. (2009), 'Najat, la donna del burkini "L'etichetta? Una scusa"', *L'Arena.it* (21 August), <http://www.larena.it/stories/Home/79470_najat_la_donna_del_burkini_letichetta_una_scusa/> accessed 25 March 2013.

Sahlin, J. (2011), 'Ingen rusning efter burkini', *Skånskan.se* (7 August), <http://www.skanskan.se/article/20110807/MALMO/110809786/1004/-/ingen-rusning-efter-burkini> accessed 25 March 2013.

Salih, R. (2009), 'Muslim Women: Fragmented Secularism and the Construction of Interconnected "Publics" in Italy', *Social Anthropology/Anthropologie Sociale* 17, 4: 409–23.

Sered, S. (2000), '"Woman" as Symbol and Women as Agents: Gendered Religious Discourses and Practices', in M. Ferree, J. Lorber and B. Hess, eds., *Revisioning Gender,* Oxford: AltaMira Press.

SST Nämnden för statligt stöd till trossamfund (2011), 'Statistik 2011', <http://www.sst.a.se/statistik/statistik2011.4.4bf439da1355ecafdd22 43b.html> accessed 25 March 2013.

Suganuma, K. (2010), 'The (Dis)embodied Swimsuit on the Beach', *Intersections: Gender and Sexuality in Asia and the Pacific* 23, <http://intersections. anu.edu.au/issue23/suganuma.htm> accessed 7 November 2011.

Sundkvist, N. (2010), *The Wearing of Religious Symbols at the Workplace in Sweden,* Lund: Lund University, Faculty of Law, <http://lup.lub.lu.se/luur/ download?func=downloadFile&recordOId=1713352&fileOId=1713371> accessed 25 March 2013.

Tarlo, E. (2010), *Visibly Muslim: Fashion, Politics, Faith,* Oxford: Berg.

Tseëlon, E. (1995), *The Masque of Femininity: The Presentation of Woman in Everyday Life,* London: Sage.

Woods, J. (2011), 'Oh Nigella, from Domestic Goddess to Burqini Betrayal', *The Telegraph* (20 April), <http://www.telegraph.co.uk/lifestyle/8461435/ Oh-Nigella-From-Domestic-Goddess-to-a-burkini-betrayal.html> accessed 25 March 2013.

Covering Up on the Prairies: Perceptions of Muslim Identity, Multiculturalism and Security in Canada

A. Brenda Anderson and F. Volker Greifenhagen

On 11 July 2010, a group of Muslim women, two wearing headscarves (hijabs) and two wearing face covers (niqabs),[1] were videoed on a cell phone at Montreal's Trudeau Airport in Canada boarding an Air Canada flight to England supposedly without having their identity verified. The edited video, with commentary asserting that 'boarding security is required except for Muslims', was posted online and went viral.[2]

Canadian newspapers subsequently reported that women wearing niqabs are routinely allowed to board airplanes without having their photo identification checked.[3] Canada's transport minister at the time said that 'the situation is deeply disturbing and poses a serious threat to the security of the air travelling public', but also urged caution in jumping to conclusions before an investigation into the incident was completed (McCallum 2010a, 2010b; O'Neill 2010). Conservative member of Parliament Shelly Glover pushed for an immediate special meeting of Parliament's public safety committee, claiming that Canadians were afraid to fly and were considering cancelling their holiday plans.[4] Tighter screening regulations, requiring that the 'entire face' of passengers must be checked before boarding, were introduced (Mayeda 2010)—around the same time that France's Parliament adopted a ban on full face cover in public space—and Québec's National Assembly prepared to debate Bill 94, banning niqab-wearers from receiving or delivering public services.

This is but one example of how WMDs—'Women in Muslim Dress' (Khan 2009: 42)—have excited media, public and government concern and spawned a variety of crisscrossing, contentious and contradictory discourses about gender and security that are shaping public perceptions of Muslims in Canada. In this chapter, we examine the discourse of Canadian media tropes on head-covering, and face covering in particular, which centre around the three overarching themes of agency, identities and security concerns. We then go on to examine Muslim women's views on these topics. The focus on these themes is not new. In 1999, Katherine Bullock interviewed Muslim women from the eastern Canadian megacity of Toronto and recorded their reflections on self, their ability to negotiate interstitial identities and the meaning behind their use of headcoverings. In a similar fashion, we present the opinions and concerns of Muslim women in Canada, this time focussing on the very different context of the mid-sized prairie city of Regina with its historical rootedness in prairie survival and neighbourliness. Our interviews also reflect the post-9/11 sense of heightened concern regarding security, with its implicit Islamophobic rhetoric, as well as reflecting Canada's policies of multiculturalism and how these are expressed on the personal and the institutional level.[5]

CANADIAN MEDIA DISCOURSE ON MUSLIMS

The Canadian media[6] tend to portray headcovering as a practice that is forced on women; one can never assume that it is the women's free choice.[7] According to these sources, burkas and niqabs depersonalize, dehumanize and objectify their wearers. The hiding of the mouth in particular seems to suggest a loss of voice and agency. Headcovers inhibit or limit women's participation in certain activities such as sports. Consumers of such media portrayals are emotionally drawn to conclude, in the words of one commentator, 'Many Muslim women say that they elect to cover themselves. But what freeborn human being would do so?...Who would choose garb that limits you to the equivalent of, as someone put it, a "walking coffin"?' (Eyre 2011).

Regarding identities, the Canadian media tend to portray headcovering as a foreign practice introduced by newcomers ('them') who are not assimilating sufficiently into mainstream Canadian society ('us').[8] Burkas and niqabs, it is claimed, are not even really articles of clothing but rather 'tents' or 'sartorial lamination' or the uniform of agents of Islamic fascism, with the distinctly sinister non-clothing purpose of undermining Canadian identity; one letter-writer argued that the niqab and burka signify 'belief in female circumcision, that Islam should be the dominant religion, that polygamy should be legal, that women should be stoned for adultery and many other ideas that would be illegal in Canada. By wearing the burka, women are promoting hatred against other religions, illegal medical procedures and murder' (Usher 2011). This theme of covered women as agents of foreign infiltration clashes with the denial of agency associated with the first theme.

Concerning security, the Canadian media is less vocal. Although sparked by a video questioning airport security measures, most media coverage in the following months focussed on headcoverings as symbols or disclosures of gender oppression and/or anti-Western political views.[9] Face covering, in particular, is portrayed as anti-democratic and subversive, even socially indecent.[10] While security may be mentioned, the real issue is framed as one of conflicting values, especially in the majority of justifications offered for banning niqabs: 'A ban on face cover would protect women under cultural siege and enhance public security, while not impinging on any equality-compatible religious values' (Kay 2010).

The Canadian media's widespread dissemination of the claim that a covered woman is paradoxically both a silenced woman and an agent of barbarism creates an availability bias[11] that may at first glance seem to champion women's liberation. In reality, it does little more than generate the notion of an increasingly expansionist and alien Muslim population. It is not surprising, therefore, that the Canadian public is confused as to what the headcover means both to Muslims and for Canadian identity.

The media tropes described also contrast with the legal foundations of Canadian pluralism (Milot 2009). These include first and foremost the Canadian Charter of Rights and Freedoms, which guarantees Canadian citizens protection from discrimination based on religion (Article 15). Secondly, Canadian pluralism is based on Canada's official policy of multiculturalism, enshrined in the Multiculturalism Act of 1988, which fosters four primary goals: 'the recognition and accommodation of cultural diversity; removing barriers to full participation; promoting interchange between groups; and promoting the acquisition of official languages' (Banting and Kymlicka 2010: 50).[12] Finally, Canadian pluralism is further defined by the decisions of the Supreme Court of Canada, which, for example, ruled in 2002 that 'secular' in Canada is to be understood as being inclusive of religion rather than exclusive of religion (see Benson 2008).

Yet, sparked especially by the growing presence and visibility of Muslim Canadians, and the media portrayals of Muslims described earlier, notions of multiculturalism are increasingly questioned by Canadians. Looking across the Atlantic, some Canadian commentators argue that multiculturalism has demonstrably failed in Europe and that, given what they believe to be multiculturalism's inherent flaws, Canada is following the same trajectory (Banting and Kymlicka 2010: 44–8).[13] The discourse of the covered Muslim woman is called upon to support these arguments by generating a fear that secular democracy is being eroded by a creeping, foreign influence that is actually protected by overly generous notions of multiculturalism. What is missing in these arguments, as in the media coverage in general, are the voices of the women whose image is so easily constructed and then used to justify Islamophobic reactions.[14] It is to those voices that we now turn.

WHEN PRAIRIE MUSLIM WOMEN SPEAK

Saskatchewan is a primarily agrarian province in western Canada comprised of small farming communities and two mid-sized cities, one of which, Regina, is the site of our interviews. Changes in immigration policies to meet labour

Fig. 2.1 *The Antidote* by Maysa Haque, a grade 12 student in Regina who painted the image in response to oppressive representations and stereotypes of Muslim women. Courtesy of Maysa Haque

shortages have created a demographic shift from a population largely of white settlers, First Nations and Métis to one with a greater representation of diverse ethnicities, customs and languages, including significant Muslim populations.[15] The most visual change has been the number of women wearing a variety of styles of headscarves and face covers. The Regina mosque has witnessed a significant increase in its numbers of adherents whose countries of origin range from all over the Middle East, southern Asia and from across the African continent. Predictably, the customs of Muslims from around the world and of those who first formed the mosque in the 1970s vary widely. The Regina discourse on defining authentic and cultural Islams is framed within the larger Canadian discourse on multiculturalism, gender, covering and security concerns. Interviewing ten women ranging in age from fifteen to over fifty, we were able to hear not only their own thoughts on agency, identities and security concerns but also locate these reflections within both local community politics and national sentiment.[16]

The names of the women were changed to protect confidentiality. Countries of origin include Canada (three were Canadian-born), the United States (Yasmin from New York is a post-9/11 convert), Egypt, Dubai, Algeria, India, Pakistan, Bangladesh, Britain, South Africa and Syria. Seven wear the headscarf in varying styles, one wears the face cover, and two wear no headcover at all, although Jamila occasionally wears a headscarf when she worships at the mosque and to public meetings when she wants to entertain questions about Islam.

ADDRESSING AGENCY WITHIN A MULTICULTURAL CONTEXT

While the Canadian media has focussed for the most part on the face cover as a sign of gendered oppression and possible security threats, the various styles of headscarves and modest dress have been left largely unmentioned. For Muslim women, the choice of whether to cover or what style to adopt emerges as a meaningful sartorial dialogue with the general public and within Muslim communities. There was a clear recognition that cultural scripts codify personal decisions and that individuals reflect or react to current events, to pressures between different communities, as women, as immigrants or first-generation Canadians, and as Muslims. They showed awareness of ideas of socially constructed false consciousness and personal agency. Some expressed that individuals could simultaneously understand the agency of the headcover in two ways: as a subversion of hegemonic discourses, whether masculinist discourses within Muslim communities or those of a mono-Canadian culture, and secondly, as an embodied practice constituting the potentiality of faith.

In her book *Politics of Piety: The Islamic Revival and the Feminist Subject,* Saba Mahmood discusses how the secular-liberal feminist notion of agency as *resistance to* or *freedom from* normative culture is limiting to our ability to hear how religious women understand freedom *within* communities. Mahmood's findings in the Egyptian Islamist movement regarding the notion of *al-haya* or shyness (2005: 159) was part of many of our women's narratives as well. Al-haya is considered a learned behaviour that, through the use of the headcover, can teach a woman the internal meaning of her faith.[17] That the piece of cloth worn or unworn can capture seemingly contradictory notions of subversiveness and compliance means that agency is not only about resisting norms but can also be understood in *how* and *why* we inhabit norms and is still, therefore, a matter of personal choice.

Among the women we interviewed, many of the comments about agency were framed within their appreciation of Canada's multiculturalism. As Canadian-born niqabi Dalila said, 'Multiculturalism helps us get our voices out there. The fact that I am both Canadian and Muslim and have the freedom to choose makes me a stronger Muslim.' Much as Bullock's interviewees expressed some years ago, we heard that being a minority can in fact help a Muslim woman embrace the significance of the headcover. Fatima noted that 'being a minority makes you think about what it means, whereas in countries where headcovering is a majority custom, it's just something you do'. Using interesting terminology, hijabi Nadia said, 'I don't dress like a normal person, I dress like a Muslim,' while Khadija, who does not cover, affirmed that 'jeans are the great equalizer in Canadian fashion'. Yasmin, a convert from New York, commented that the Western feature of diversity is what she cherishes, but she still uses the headscarf as a marker distinguishing her from an assumed hegemony that embraces the 'Hannah Montanas' of pop culture. Hijabi Asma also spoke about a multicultural acceptance of a variety of fashions: 'I tend to find clothes that fit into Canadian norms, like shirts except they might be one size bigger and longer.' These comments suggest an appreciation of living comfortably with choice. A notion of a hybridized Canadian Muslim identity is created, with lingering questions of belonging to Canadian norms sitting in tension with their distinctive expressions of faith.

The theme of rebelliousness and conformity was raised numerous times in the interviews. Fatima donned the headscarf in Dubai because it was what all girls her age were doing, and they were 'acting superior to her when she was unveiled'. Dalila was eager to cover in emulation of her Islamic teacher and her 'cool and brave' friends. This doesn't sound so very different from any young person who, during puberty in particular, wants to conform with her peers and act 'grown up'. Muslim girls can choose the socially acceptable, visual symbol of the headcover, which reveals their desire to enter adulthood and discloses to their friends and family that they are ready to make decisions for themselves as young women. For some, convincing their parents they were old enough was part of being a rebellious teenager. Far from conforming to parental expectations, the decision to cover represented resistance.

Convert Yasmin certainly considers herself a nonconformist and uses her understandings of Islam to express a certain social commentary. Adopting the headscarf facilitated her rejection of her family's conservative Christian adherence. Yasmin decided to cover after 9/11 in solidarity with Muslims who, she said, were being portrayed 'really poorly in Fox News'. Media images didn't resonate with the 'everyday Muslims she saw in the streets' of New York. She initially wore the headscarf out of resistance to her family, in solidarity with Muslims and also because, she noted, she wanted the same respect from men that she saw covered Muslim women receiving. 'I wanted a way of defining myself as a certain kind of woman that doesn't want that kind of attention from men. The veil reveals to people to treat me differently.' In time, the meaning of the headscarf worked itself into her heart as an 'inner state of hijab' reflective of al-haya but also reminiscent of how our two non-covering interviewees understand modesty as a matter of intention rather than fashion.

For Yasmin, her headscarf continues to be an external reminder and even 'a protection from myself'. Similarly, Dalila noted that her decision to move from the headscarf to the face cover was because she 'wanted something to struggle with to become closer to God'. It was 'me coming into Islam and it has helped me grow up as a woman'. Other hijabi women agreed that the face cover is a higher level of devotion, a 'further step than hijab'. Some noted that they felt the headscarf was required whereas the face cover was a purely personal choice.

The women seriously engaged questions of how sartorial practices might create a pious subject, and are very aware of how they negotiate between perpetuating masculinist norms or subverting the meaning of headcovering to their own agendas. Their stories, in this sense, are not dissimilar to Bullock's earlier investigations in eastern Canada nor to those from other minority or immigrant communities written about by Emma Tarlo (2007, 2010) or Annelies Moors (2009). What emerges as different is how the stories of our interviewees articulate the distinct context of Canadian multiculturalism and Islamophobia after 9/11.

ADDRESSING MULTIPLE IDENTITIES WITHIN A MULTICULTURAL CONTEXT

Regina's Muslim community is largely comprised of first- and second-generation immigrants coming from many different countries. As women negotiate their gendered identity within these diverse immigrant communities and mosque life, they must also navigate the customs of a prairie city as well as overarching Canadian expectations. Language or accent, colour of skin and economic background play as important a part in creating identity differences as does their choice of clothing. Despite the availability bias in the media and political machinations in Québec, we found women expressing appreciation for Canadian multicultural principles of openness and acceptance of difference, which they experienced through the personal encounters they had with their neighbours. Sometimes, it was the expectations of the Muslim community that most challenged their choices regarding gender and identity. In their comments, we can hear their observations and evaluations of everything from the styles and significance of headcovering to issues of multiple identities to personal encounters that affirm and challenge their choice of sartorial meaning-making.

Nurul described a shift in the ways and reasons that the headscarf is worn today, which she feels is indicative of women asserting and assimilating multiple identities:

> A hijab fashion blog is all about young women trying to wear the hijab more attractively as a fashion item, although they say they're adhering to a certain religious requirement. You can see how they're circumventing some of the rules in trying to fit into society, look stylish and modest. I see older women emailing and saying it's not hijab, it's too bright or your neck is showing. The response is, 'How dare you tell us what we can wear.'

Nurul continued, 'I never saw that response towards the old traditional guard before and now I see more of a defiance. We are just as Muslim as you, we just choose to wear it better than you.'

In the Canadian media, the face cover in particular is portrayed as distancing Muslim women from a Canadian identity. Nurul suggests differently. Not only are covered Muslim women visually changing the scene on Canadian streets, but they are also championing their understandings of Islam in the mosque. Nurul recounts how Muslim women bought a mosque to serve a conservative Somali community in another Canadian prairie city, Winnipeg, and how they are able to ensure no barriers divide male and female worshippers. Without a doubt, they are shaping Canadian Islam by effectively using their multiple identities.

The headcover functions on a communal as well as personal level and is viewed by some Muslims as a way that women contribute visually to the Islamic community. If, then, a woman chooses not to cover, does this signify a lack of communal responsibility? Jamila, who does not cover her face, recounted how recent converts often asked if she needed their help in becoming a good Muslim woman! This 'convertitis'[18] collapses the identity of the Muslim woman into that of the covered woman and suggests that those who do not cover are somehow less pious and faithful. Nurul noted that this attitude usually dissipates eventually and may even evolve to the stage where the convert removes her own headcover as her understanding of Islamic principles changes. The fact remains that in Regina's relatively small Muslim community, those who choose not to cover feel disadvantaged at times in the Muslim community. At the same time, both of our non-covered interviewees wished there was a way for them to express their religiosity to non-Muslims. They were frustrated that people did not ask about their faith as they did not recognize them as Muslim.

Hijabi Nurul expressed frustration from a different angle. Because her headscarf signifies first and foremost her Muslim identity, she believes she needs to put extra effort into engaging non-Muslims so they see her first as a human being.[19] In the mosque, however, Nurul readily admits that her hijab lends her legitimacy and credibility that would be lacking were she to remove it.

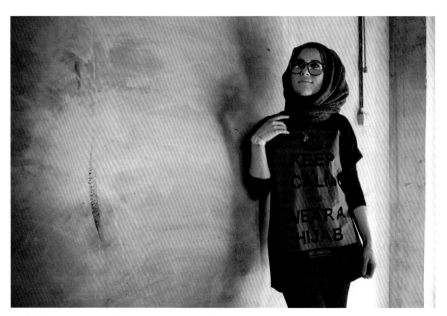
Hijabi street style. Photos: Alessia Gammarota

Yet actions as well as clothing excite comment. One of our youngest hijabis, Nadia, finds herself negotiating her 'Canadianness' in a mosque that, she said, is 'not very friendly towards Canadian customs'. She stands in the main hall instead of in the women's room at prayer time and has heard people mutter 'Haram' and 'Shaytan' as they pass by her family. Nadia commented that some Muslim girls are put off going to the mosque for fear of being chastised over dress. She also spoke of being shunned by other Muslims when she wore a 'Canadian' bathing suit for swimming.

Negotiating multiple identities and loyalties is necessary both within and outside the mosque. Niqabi Dalila is bemused when non-Muslims are surprised she was born in Toronto. She's become accustomed to the reaction of 'why do you wear that when you don't have to? That's not Canadian'—the message being that the face cover represents a foreign, imported identity without relevance to Canada's history or future and that she has been duped. Conversely, Nurul recounted how many Muslims feel uncomfortable with the face cover because 'they already feel under siege and niqabs can't be absorbed (understood) by outsiders. Some Muslims say the niqab is too scary for Canadians and the women shouldn't wear it because there's already leeway with the hijab.' Similar views have been expressed by British Muslims opposed to niqab (see Tarlo 2010)

Nurul argues that Islam in general and Muslim women specifically can adapt quite readily to change because Islam doesn't have a centralized authority, and, 'We don't have time to wait for all the authorities to make decisions. Women want to do things like join sports teams. In fact, Muslim women speed up the rate of assimilation.'

Jamila feels the principles of multiculturalism have not been particularly effective in countering Islamophobia, especially when it comes to portrayals of Muslims in movies and the media. Yet, when it came to examples of personal interactions, the interviewees expressed a surprisingly uniform appreciation for Regina people's efforts in learning about their faith practices. A change in awareness is clear: Fatima related how women wearing headcovers twenty years ago in a Regina mall were asked if they were nuns, whereas today she recounts that her family feels accepted and 'less stared at, safe'. Nadia related a story of how parents of children at a camp where she was working went out of their way to thank her and enquire about her headcovering. She also feels affirmed by her classmates and teachers but noted that the individual's desire to be nice or accommodating does not easily translate into institutional practices or 'infrastructure'. For instance, when her school wanted to express support for their Muslim students by putting on a Pakistani Flood Relief project, the planners forgot to consult with the Muslim students themselves and held the event on a Friday, the day of mosque prayer. Thus, the Muslim students were absent from the very event designed to support them. The disconnection between the life of the mosque and the rest of the world was disappointing to her.

Asma related similar experiences at the high school level. Her teacher held a workshop on how to wear the headcover but taught it as a cultural rather than religious practice. Asma was disappointed that the Muslim students were not able to discuss the deeper meaning the headcover held for them. While Asma said multiculturalism has 'given women a step up to wear hijab', it has maintained the model of a white normative centre with ethnic differences swirling around and outside the norm.[20]

Similarly, Khadija's experience is that the 'hijab is not accepted in retail jobs. How many customer representatives do you see who wear hijab?' While American-born Yasmin may celebrate Canada in its metaphorical glory as the 'underground railway of freedom for slaves', it seems to be difficult for non-Muslim Canadians to accommodate Muslim practices unless Muslims themselves are consulted and brought into the planning stages of implementing multicultural practices.

ADDRESSING SECURITY CONCERNS: ISLAMOPHOBIA WITHIN A MULTICULTURAL CONTEXT

Frequently, when a media report involves Muslims, it raises the spectre of Canada's cherished ideals of secular democracy being swept away under waves of fanatical, misogynistic Muslims. Our interviewees responded passionately to such media portrayals and were also opposed to attempts to regulate their dress practices. Québec's proposed Bill 94, which implies a covered woman is a potential threat to national security, was much criticized.[21] All agreed that to restrict women's choice of clothing, as Bill 94 proposes, is antithetical to the Canadian principles of freedom and equality. A common sentiment was expressed by Khadijah: 'The Québec ban is ridiculous. It's not about banning for security; it's a prejudice against Islam. To ban the niqab sentences women to stay in the home. How does that free them from Islam if that's what they actually think they're doing?' All agreed that the Canadian government had no right to try to regulate women's apparel. Khadijah said Canada needs to be careful not to 'back Muslims into a corner because then, human nature being what it is, we become defensive. We mustn't polarize the issue, we must find a balance to our loyalties. Don't force Muslims to start playing the victim.'

At the same time, the women were uniformly appreciative of Canada's national policies regarding freedom of religious expression. Nurul said:

Canada is much smarter than Europe because it lets us decide how to dress. Those who didn't want to veil stopped and those who did wore it, whereas in Europe the bans created negative resentment and girls who would give it up won't because they feel put upon, so you lose that natural evolution and choice...The

evolution stopped in Europe, it's become very reactionary. Canada is very successful in its multiculturalism model allowing people to be free to choose and do
what they want.

The other women concurred that only with an ideal of balance can Canada
avoid extremism.

Khadijah noted that niqabis must also be willing to accommodate Canadian security needs—for instance, when police need to check identity. Niqabi
Dalila agrees: 'In Islam whenever a need arises you can bend a rule. You're
not doing something sinful.' Dalila has found Canadian airport security, for
instance, to be very accommodating of her, providing female security guards
before she even asked for them. Sixteen-year-old hijabi Nadia, by contrast,
had found herself detained for over two hours at the US border seemingly on
account of her headscarf. Many of our interviewees wanted reassurance from
the Canadian government that their human rights would not be taken away
as they had been in some countries. Simply put, Fatima from Syria said, 'I
can't go back.'

WHEN MUSLIM WOMEN CONSTRUCT
REPRESENTATIONS OF MUSLIMS

One of our interviewees, who agreed to have her identity revealed, is Zarqa
Nawaz. She is a Muslim filmmaker residing in Regina and created the television comedy series *Little Mosque on the Prairie* for the Canadian Broadcasting Company.[22] Breaking ground as the first Muslim television comedy
in North America, the series depicts Muslims and non-Muslims living in the
fictitious western Canadian prairie town of Mercy, going about their prosaic
lives, trying to maintain a sense of community and living as part of the wider
Canadian society. Through this artistic work, Zarqa Nawaz and her collabo-
rators are able to give unique voice to the crisscrossing currents of Canadian and Canadian Muslim identities, including the image of the covered
Muslim woman.

Gender issues come to the fore in many of the episodes of *Little Mosque
on the Prairie,* covering the gamut from 'arranged' marriages and proper Islamic dating protocols to appropriate clothing for males and females. Islamic
views that may be at odds with mainstream Canadian attitudes, such as restrictions on free mixing of men and women or the practice of polygyny, are
presented but usually within a field of contestation that shows diverse Muslim
attitudes rather than a monolithic attitude.

Muslim women's dress appears variously in the series, ranging from an
unknown woman wearing a burka in one episode to Fatima's headscarf worn
with a dress to Rayyan's headscarf and blue jeans to Sarah, who wears a

loose headcover only for prayer. It could be argued that the series inculcates a subtle norm of moderate hijab wearing[23]—the only major Muslim female character who does not regularly cover is Sarah, and she is portrayed as bumbling in her practice of Islam, admitting herself that she is a bad Muslim. However, the wearing of a headcover is nuanced. For example, Baber vacillates when it comes to his daughter Layla wearing a headcover—his concern for her well-being in school mitigates his otherwise unequivocal approach to uncompromising Islamic practice. Baber's strong attraction to a burka-clad woman also brings into question the function of female covering to curb men's sexual desires. Visually, the headcover dominates the dress of Muslim women in the series, albeit fashionably.[24] Perhaps most interesting is the show's normalizing of various forms of dress associated with Islam in a Canadian context. This is especially apparent in the scenes in Fatima's café, where people wearing distinctive Muslim dress and those who don't, whether Muslim or not, regularly interact normally without any special attention being drawn to their clothing.

Dress is lampooned in the episode set during Halloween, when Baber's daughter Layla and Fatima's son Jamal want to go door to door in costume asking for treats like the other children in town. They are required to dress in embarrassing olive and fig costumes because olives and figs are mentioned in the Qur'an. Meanwhile, Baber, their chaperone, who is dressed in his usual salwar kameez, is complimented by those handing out treats for his authentic 'terrorist' costume. But dress is also taken with utmost seriousness. The hijab-wearing women are very concerned to have their hair cut in a private setting, and both Rayyan and Amaar are very upset when the former accidentally sees the latter without her headscarf. In these and many other ways, the series gives voice to multiple perspectives on Muslim dress, and especially Muslim women's dress, in a Canadian context and thus not only reflects a richly layered discourse but also actively participates in the ongoing construction of distinctive Islamic dress, even if not adopted by all Canadian Muslims, as a normal component of Canadian Muslim identity.

CONCLUSION

In spite of their concerns about multiculturalism, Muslims of the prairies feel relatively well-integrated into Canadian society. As Yasmin put it, 'I feel semi-normal here or as close to normal as possible, more so on the prairies than on the east coast.' From our observations, we credit this to at least two phenomena, the first being the unique quality of settler society on the prairies and the second being the direct actions of organizations, such as the churches, university and the police department in facilitating and encouraging face-to-face dialogue.

The prairie ethos has long been built on an atmosphere of collaborative survival. As First Nations peoples knew for centuries and pioneering farmers quickly learned, in order to survive in the harsh climate and scattered population of the prairies, people need to be able to rely on one another. Co-operatives for banks, stores and grain sales, and community pastures for cattle, institutionalized this need, and most of these institutions continue today. Neighbours learn to accept differences because they are neighbours, and this culture of hospitality and warmth has been commented on by numerous immigrants.[25] In our interviews, Dalila recounted friendly conversations in grocery lines enquiring about her and her husband's choice of traditional Islamic clothing. One might say that an accommodation of necessity has contributed to the success of multicultural experiences in the prairie provinces.

At the institutional level, there have been a number of measures that encourage multicultural interaction and dialogue. For example, during the Gulf War of the 1990s, a United Church of Canada minister and a Muslim leader in Regina formed the Regina Multi-Faith Forum, which continues to be a binding influence in the community. A host of events are sponsored, awards received, young people's efforts encouraged, school boards approached, hospital chaplaincies reconfigured to be inclusive, city councils advised and guest speakers sponsored as members from numerous faith communities continue, as their simple motto declares, 'to promote among society at large the understanding, appreciation, and acceptance of the diverse religious communities living in Regina'. In fulfilment of this, following the events of 9/11 the Regina Multi-Faith Forum, the university, the mosque and churches held numerous events that were specifically designed to create face-to-face encounters between Muslims and non-Muslims.

The stories of the women we interviewed reveal the need to move beyond personal multiculturalism to more institutionalized efforts which include Muslims in the planning and execution of events. On a personal level, Canadians tend to be kind, curious and eager to accept others. However, at the level of public discourse their efforts are hampered by media bias and projected fears about Muslims being a threat. The headscarves and face coverings worn by some Muslim women are often used in the media to enforce or confirm this image of Muslims as foreigners and outsiders. Sheema Khan, founder of the Canadian Council on American-Islamic Relations (CAIR-CAN), expresses hope that, while Canadians have historically 'always been unhappy with immigration' and there 'is always the sense that newcomers aren't like us—they're a problem, they're going to be difficult...history also shows the extraordinary assimilative force of Canadian society' (2009: 40). Our findings confirm that, rather than expressing otherness, headscarves and face coverings can be regarded as expressing the ideals of multiculturalism wherein difference is celebrated rather than suppressed.[26]

NOTES

1. We use the general terms *headcover* and *headcovering* to encompass the wide variety of dress practices used by Muslim women to indicate modesty and/or cultural or religious identity (see Çarkoğlu 2009 for a similar use). We use the more specific term *headscarf* to include the variety of styles of scarves worn around or over the hair—what is generally referred to by our interviewees as the hijab—while *face cover* denotes what is generally referred to by our interviewees as the niqab (compare Bullock 2002: xl–xli). We recognize the provisional nature of these terminological choices in the face of shifting 'geographies of vocabulary' (Moors and Tarlo 2007: 136).
2. McCallum (2010a, 2010b); O'Neill (2010); O'Toole (2010); Sidhu (2010).
3. To be fair, some newspaper reports (e.g., McCallum 2010b) questioned the veracity of the video because of its edited nature.
4. Fitzpatrick (2010). Glover's claim was refuted by the travel industry, which said the video incident did not put a dent into record numbers of air travellers that summer (Fitzpatrick and Chai 2010).
5. Headcover seems to function simultaneously to both cover up and reveal (see Tarlo 2010: 9ff., 62) and so seems to be caught up in the particular post-9/11 dynamics of security concerns (read 'war on terror') and identity politics (read 'multiculturalism').
6. Our analysis is restricted to the English-language media and does not include French Canadian publications.
7. For example, 'The majority of women wearing face coverings are not doing so because of free will; they are doing so because some Neanderthal husband or cleric has told them it is necessary' (Martinuk 2011; see also Bramham 2010; Kay 2010).
8. 'The attitudes, beliefs, traditions and practices brought by newcomers to Canada differ ever more significantly from those which prevail amongst those of us who have been here longer... our openness to newcomers from across the world can be perceived as soft, myopic, and exploitable' (Keeping 2010; see also Bramham 2010).
9. For example, the niqab 'messages many things, amongst them anti-Westernism and female depersonalization in the service of fetishistic honour/shame codes' (Kay 2010)—security concerns are not mentioned.
10. 'Apart from ski slopes, the theatre and Halloween Balls, all purposeful adult face cover is by nature antidemocratic and socially subversive' (Kay 2010).
11. Availability bias refers to the repetitive and exclusive use of tropes such as 'the oppressed Muslim woman' and 'violent, foreign Islam', such that the public assumes the truth of such tropes (see Fadel 2011).

12. Canada's constitution also contains a multiculturalism clause (section 27) stating that the Charter of Rights and Freedoms will be 'interpreted in a manner consistent with the preservation and enhancement of the multicultural heritage of Canadians' (Banting and Kymlicka 2010: 51). In the province of Québec, the concept of multiculturalism is rejected as not fitting the province's unique situation of being the francophone minority within Canada; instead, the term *interculturalism* is preferred (Bouchard and Taylor 2008: 40).

13. In contrast, Banting and Kymlicka (2010) argue that multiculturalism empirically promotes citizenship and integration in Canada, and Ghobadzadeh (2010) argues that Canadian multiculturalism actually facilitated the participation of Canadian Muslim women in the Sharia law debates in Canada in the period 2003–5 as compared to the relative silence of Australian Muslim women in comparable debates in Australia.

14. Only one descriptive article on the niqab, written by Norma Greenaway (2010) and published in various papers between 14 and 28 August, stands out as providing a more balanced approach *and* in giving voice to Muslim women.

15. According to the 2001 Census (the last time that statistics on religious belonging were gathered), the Muslim population of Canada was over 500,000 (about 2 per cent of Canada's total population), more than a two-fold increase from 1991 (mainly due to immigration). Canada's Muslim population was estimated at over one million in 2011. Most of this Muslim population is concentrated in the large urban centres of Montreal, Toronto, Calgary and Vancouver. Saskatchewan has a relatively lower population of Muslims; the imam estimates that the Muslim community in Regina numbers up to 5,000.

16. We are both academics affiliated with churches and have worked on interfaith dialogue and with the Regina Muslim community for well over a decade. Each of us acknowledges that our positions of privilege affect the interviews, but we also feel that our presence as partners within the community helped accommodate some genuine reflection on dress practices.

17. Some Muslim men also display modesty as gendered bodies through the use of clothing and facial hair that is thought to be reminiscent of the Prophet Muhammad's style. Interviewee Nurul notes, however, that there is a double standard in mosque life: if a man were to quit wearing robes and a beard, he would suffer less serious repercussions than if a woman decided to remove her headcover. Thus, while clothing may signify *al-haya,* it is clearly done within a particular masculinist notion that shyness or modesty is especially key to the life of female Muslims.

18. A term used by hijabi Nurul.

19. Alia Hogben (2010), past president of the Canadian Council of Muslim Women, concurs: 'When one identity is under attack, we tend to identify with that particular allegiance. This is not a positive attitude.'
20. For similar critiques, see Bannerji (2000) and Thobani (2007).
21. On Bill 94, see Golnaraghi and Mills (2011).
22. The series was launched in January 2007; its fifth and final season ran in 2011–12.
23. While probably the largest category of American Muslim women are those who do not wear a headcover (although they may still dress modestly), the practice of voluntary hijab observance is growing (Ba-Yunus and Kone 2006: 142–3).
24. Rayyan's headcovers, in particular, have inspired admiration and imitation; her outfits are regularly featured on the blog Hijab Chique (http://hijabchique.blogspot.com/).
25. *A New Life in a New Land* (2004).
26. See Beaman's argument (2009, 2011) for a movement in the Canadian context from mere tolerance and accommodation towards 'deep equality'.

REFERENCES

A New Life in a New Land [film] (2004), University of Saskatchewan, Saskatoon, Milo Productions.

Bannerji, H. (2000), *Dark Side of the Nation: Essays on Multiculturalism, Nationalism and Gender,* Toronto: Canadian Scholars' Press.

Banting, K., and W. Kymlicka (2010), 'Canadian Multiculturalism: Global Anxieties and Local Debates', *British Journal of Canadian Studies* 23, 1: 43–72.

Ba-Yunus, I., and K. Kone (2006), *Muslims in the United States,* Westport, CT: Greenwood Press.

Beaman, L. (2009), 'Religious Freedom: From Tolerance and Reasonable Accommodation to Deep Equality', Religious Studies Ideas Lecture Series, University of Regina.

Beaman, L. (2011), '"It Was All Slightly Unreal": What's Wrong with Tolerance and Accommodation in the Adjudication of Religious Freedom?', *Canadian Journal of Women and the Law* 23, 2: 442–63.

Benson, I. (2008), *Taking a Fresh Look at Religion and Public Policy in Canada: The Need for a Paradigm Shift,* Ottawa: Centre for Cultural Renewal, <http://www.millerthomson.com/assets/files/article_attachments/Taking_a_Fresh_Look_at_Religion_and_Public_Policy_in_Canada_The_Need_for_a_Paradigm_Shift> accessed 25 July 2011.

Bouchard, G., and C. Taylor (2008), *Building the Future: A Time for Reconciliation: Abridged Report,* Québec: Commission de consultation sur les pratiques d'accommodement reliées aux differences culturelles,

<http://www.accommodements.qc.ca/documentation/rapports/
rapport-final-integral-en.pdf> accessed 25 July 2011.

Bramham, D. (2010), 'Let's Not Mistake Oppression for Fashion Choices: The French Have It Right', *The Vancouver Sun* (11 August): B5.

Bullock, K. (2002), *Rethinking Muslim Women and the Veil: Challenging Historical and Modern Stereotypes,* Herndon, VA: International Institute of Islamic Thought.

Çarkoğlu, A. (2009), 'Women's Choices of Head Cover in Turkey: An Empirical Assessment', *Comparative Studies of South Asia, Africa and the Middle East* 29, 3: 450–67.

Eyre, B. (2011), 'Face covering Ban Liberates Women', *Star-Phoenix* (30 April): A2.

Fadel, M. (2011), 'Islam, Gender and the Future of Multi-cultural Citizenship', Stapleford lecture, University of Regina, 4 March, <http://www.arts.uregina.ca/drupal/dbfm_send/980> accessed 20 March 2011.

Fitzpatrick, M. (2010), 'Canadians Afraid To Fly: MP', *Leader-Post* (10 August): B7.

Fitzpatrick, M., and C. Chai (2010), 'Public Still Flying Despite MP's Claim', *The Windsor Star* (11 August): A7.

Ghobadzadeh, N. (2010), 'A Multiculturalism-feminism Dispute: Muslim Women and the Sharia Debate in Canada and Australia', *Commonwealth & Comparative Politics* 48, 3: 301–19.

Golnaraghi, G., and A. Mills (2011), ' "Unveiling" Québec's Bill 94 and Implications for Muslim Women—A Postcolonialist Critique', *Proceedings of the 7th International Critical Management Studies Conference,* <http://www.organizzazione.unina.it/cms7/proceedings/proceedings_stream_10/Golnaraghi_and_Mills.pdf> accessed 25 July 2012.

Greenaway, N. (2010), 'Tempest in a Niqab: At Its Simplest, the Niqab is an Unadorned Piece of Dark-coloured Cloth', *The Ottawa Citizen* (15 August): A10.

Hogben, A. (2010), 'We Are Woven Out of Many Coloured Threads', *The Whig Standard* (23 October), <http://www.thewhig.com/ArticleDisplay.aspx?archive=true&e=2813310> accessed 10 October 2010.

Kay, B. (2010), 'Show Me Your Face', *National Post* (4 August): A12.

Keeping, J. (2010), 'Diversity Doesn't Mean Everything "Different" Is Good', *Telegraph Journal* (8 September): A7.

Khan, S. (2009), *Of Hockey and Hijab: Reflections of a Canadian Muslim Woman,* Toronto: TSAR Publications.

McCallum, J. (2010a), 'Veiled Passenger Video Creates Buzz', *Saskatoon Star-Phoenix* (3 August): A5

McCallum, J. (2010b), 'Authenticity of Apparent Breach of Security Questioned; YouTube Shows 2 Women Boarding Plane at Trudeau Airport without Revealing Faces', *Montreal Gazette* (3 August): A6

Mahmood, S. (2005), *Politics of Piety: The Islamic Revival and the Feminist Subject,* Princeton, NJ: Princeton University Press.

Martinuk, S. (2011), 'Burka Ban Will Set Muslim Women Free', *Calgary Herald* (15 April): A14.

Mayeda, A. (2010), 'Faces Must Be Shown at Airports', *Leader-Post* (18 September): A10.

Milot, M. (2009), 'Modus Co-vivendi: Religious Diversity in Canada', in P. Bramadat and M. Koenig, eds., *International Migration and the Governance of Religious Diversity,* Montreal: McGill-Queen's University Press, 105–29.

Moors, A. (2009), '"Islamic Fashion" in Europe: Religious Conviction, Aesthetic Style, and Creative Consumption', *Encounters* 1, 1: 175–201.

Moors, A., and E. Tarlo (2007), 'Introduction', *Fashion Theory* 11, 2/3: 133–42.

O'Neill, J. (2010), 'Baird Moves with Caution on Airport Niqab Claim', *Times–Colonist* (4 August): A5.

O'Toole, M. (2010), '"Concern" Over Veiled Passengers; Airport Video Shot; Travellers in Niqabs Appear to Go Unchecked', *National Post* (3 August): A4.

Sidhu, J. (2010), 'Muslim Groups Fear Backlash from Video; Afraid Uproar over Security Issue May Fuel Racism, Islamophobia', *Toronto Star* (August 4): A14.

Tarlo, E. (2007), 'Hijab in London: Metamorphosis, Resonance and Effects', *Journal of Material Culture* 12, 2: 131–56, <http://mcu.sagepub.com/> accessed 25 July 2012.

Tarlo, E. (2010), *Visibly Muslim: Fashion, Politics, Faith,* Oxford: Berg.

Thobani, S. (2007), *Exalted Subjects: Studies in the Making of Race and Nation in Canada,* Toronto: University of Toronto Press.

Usher, J. (2011), 'The Burka: Part of Our National Fabric?', *National Post* (14 April): A17.

–3–

Landscapes of Attraction and Rejection: South Asian Aesthetics in Islamic Fashion in London

Emma Tarlo

My contribution to this volume begins with a puzzle. Patterns, textiles and styles from the Indian subcontinent have a strong visual and material presence in British cities. Bustling shopping centres in areas with a large South Asian diasporic population offer sumptuous and varied displays of cloth and clothes of Indian provenance or resonance, often highly coloured and patterned or ornamented with embroidery, appliqué and sequins. These distinctive markets are the products of the collective imagination and labour of people from different parts of the Indian subcontinent and cater to their collective needs and desires (Bhachu 2004; Dwyer 2010). But the taste for things South Asian in Britain also stretches well beyond the confines of these ethnically charged neighbourhoods and has a complex history, caught up in long-distance relations of trade and imperialism (Tarlo 1996; Breward, Crang and Crill 2010). Whether in the form of a pashmina shawl, silk scarf or printed summer top, textiles of South Asian resonance or provenance have a well-established place in British wardrobes and feature both explicitly and implicitly in global fashions.[1] The puzzle then, is this: why, when South Asian patterns, fabrics, colours and styles are so popular in Britain do they feature so little in the clothing designs produced and marketed by a new generation of emerging British Islamic fashion designers from South Asian backgrounds? How might one account for the apparent lack of interest or ambivalence to their rich South Asian textile heritage? And on what alternative sartorial heritage, real or imagined, do they draw?

It is sometimes argued that migrants and their descendants develop particularly intimate forms of attachment to the material culture and artefacts associated with their homelands. Such artefacts, it is suggested, are subject to high levels of emotional investment and sensorial engagement, sometimes acting as ritual tools or transitional objects in diasporic contexts.[2] Whilst at first sight appearing to contradict this view, visibly Muslim fashions in Britain problematize these assertions in interesting ways. While British

Asian Muslims often take distance from their South Asian textile heritage, it could be argued that this is less about lack of intimacy with it than about the ambivalent feelings that intimacy with it engenders. Secondly, it is not that they are unconcerned about maintaining diasporic connections but that the material and emotional links they seek to forge through visibly Muslim fashions are about asserting an alternative diasporic identity and heritage, through which they trace associations not to South Asia but to the first generation of Muslims on the Arabian peninsula—the original Muslim ummah. This contribution explores how different aspects of this double diasporic identity are played out through the dress practices of British Asian Muslims, drawing attention to spatial and temporal elements of the diasporic imagination which revolves not only around remembered or imagined pasts and places but also projected futures. It argues that through dress people not only negotiate the tensions of this double diasporic heritage but also bring into being a new material heritage which makes future identities possible and brings them into being. In this sense, a cosmopolitan pan-Islamic Muslim identity is as much anticipatory as retrospective and fashion is one of the means by which it becomes attainable. How and why dress is such an apt medium for negotiating and concretizing ideas of identity and belonging is explored through a discussion of the intimate relationship between dress, body and place.

DRESS, BODY AND PLACE—AN AWKWARD INTIMACY

The most obvious feature of dress is its proximity to the body and the intimacy of our relationship to it. Whilst sociologists of the wardrobe rightly remind us that some clothing remains forever unworn or may be kept only for special occasions, it is nonetheless true that it is through being worn that dress springs into life and attains its primary purpose. This intimate relationship between our bodies and our clothes is not, however, without potential conflict. Bodies animate clothes, but they sometimes let them down, defying their intentions through inappropriate combinations and usage. Similarly, clothes animate bodies, but they also constrain and frame them, modifying the actions of their wearers and inviting particular perceptions and responses from viewers. In fact, clothes and their wearers are often so tightly fused in the perceptions of others that their boundaries become confused and clothes become read not as additional adjuncts to the body but as physical extensions of it—a point beautifully captured by Magritte in his famous painting of a pair of boots with toes and toe nails—a painting which seems to ask, is it bodies that shape clothes or clothes that shape bodies, and how can we distinguish the boundary between the two?

In reality, clothing is of course detachable, and when people refer to it as a 'second skin' they remind us of its difference from our 'first skin', which would require a trained surgeon to remove it and without which we would not survive. Yet, in practice peeling off one set of clothes in favour of another is not as simple as the physical act of undressing might imply. Precisely because of the intimate association between people and what they wear, the removal or replacement of a particular type of dress by another is often perceived as problematic both by the wearer who may feel uncomfortable, conspicuous, unnatural or overexposed without his or her habitual dress and by those connected to the wearer, whether family members, friends or members of smaller or larger group formations such as nations or religious communities who may perceive a person's change of dress as an act of distancing or desertion, on the one hand, or proximity and affiliation, on the other.

At first sight, such observations sit uncomfortably with the suggestion that in a postmodern world people are free to dress as they please and to construct their identities and looks at will from the plethora of sartorial options on offer. Yet anthropological studies of dress practices in Britain show that despite the power of the fashion industry and the postmodern embrace of ideas of individualism and freedom of choice, people often remain relatively conformist in their actual dress practices, partly owing to the relationships and contexts in which these are embedded. In an ethnographic study of the dress practices of women in London and Nottingham, for example, Sophie Woodward suggests that wardrobes can in fact be read as archives of social relationships and contexts (2007). The expectations and tastes of mothers, daughters, siblings, husbands and friends all find sartorial expression in women's wardrobes as do memories of the circumstances and contexts in which clothes were worn—the home, the workplace, the club, the ritual event. In other words, clothes become saturated with personal and social life.

If clothing choices are fraught with the sartorial expectations of others, so too are they fraught with the sartorial expectations linked to place. In an evocative artwork entitled *House near Green Street, E 7* (see Figure 3.1), the artist Helen Scalway explores the complexity of the relationship between people, textiles and place. By projecting and superimposing a richly embroidered, patterned cloth purchased in the popular South Asian shopping centre of Green Street onto the form of a local suburban brick house, she reminds us of how the South Asian presence in certain areas of London has transformed the texture of the urban landscape and how patterns and material preferences migrate, mutate and take on different meanings in new contexts. At the same time, her artwork seems to suggest that the strong South Asian presence in areas such as Green Street creates a particular type of backdrop or frame which, like the relationship between dress and the body, is fraught with ambiguity. 'The distinction between frames and their contents is less stable than may at first appear', writes Scalway, 'they challenge each other, transforming themselves into new entities with new meanings' (2010: 177). So just

Fig. 3.1 *House near Green Street, E7,* by Helen Scalway. Collage, digital photograph juxtaposing a London suburban house with a textile sold in a British Asian shop nearby; working series, 2008–9. Courtesy of Helen Scalway

as we might analyse the complex relationships of attachment and detachment between people and dress, so we might analyse the relationships of attachment and detachment between dress and place. In this sense, it becomes pertinent to explore how the sartorial expectations of place might enable or constrain the clothing choices and perceptions of people and how a South Asian wearing South Asian dress in one part of the city might look 'in place', but the same person in the same clothes might look 'out of place' in other locations (see also Jones and Leshkowich 2003). We can also think about how place of origin might attach so strongly to people that it becomes difficult to shake off.

DIASPORAS OF SOUTH ASIAN PEOPLE AND THINGS

How then do these relationships between people, dress and place play out in the context of the South Asian diaspora in London, and how do South Asian Muslims position themselves within this context? To answer this, it is useful to begin by making a distinction between the migration experiences of South

Asian textiles and those of South Asian peoples. When one uncouples these two things, what becomes apparent is that detached from South Asian bodies, South Asian textiles and designs have long been welcomed into Britain and have circulated with relative ease. For example, in the sixteenth century, well before South Asians arrived in Britain in large numbers, Indian textiles were greatly admired for their superior technological brilliance, complexity of pattern and vibrancy of colour (Crill 2010). Indeed, throughout history we find repeated examples of different segments of the British population incorporating and adapting Indian textiles to their own aesthetic and identity-building projects, whether used to add a sumptuous and bohemian flavour to the image of the British literati in the 1920s and 1930s or to convey ideas of nonconformism, sensuality and exoticism when used extensively by those asserting a hippy identity in the 1960s and 1970s (Ashmore 2010). Once detached from its original referent (the South Asian body), such clothing offered freedoms and the possibility of creativity and experimentation.

However, when South Asian dress and textiles arrived in Britain on the bodies of large numbers of South Asian migrants in the 1950s and 1960s, the clothes acquired very different associations. Instead of being perceived by people in Britain as creative tools for experimentation, they were read as permanent frames which fixed and defined the identity of their wearers as different, foreign, ill adapted to the British environment, 'out of place'. Here clothing seemed to be perceived not as a second skin but as the skin itself—an indelible marker and visible proof of permanent difference, provoking not only curiosity but also ridicule, racism and suspicion (Puwar 2002; Bhachu 2004). In the interests of seeking accommodation and jobs and minimizing racist reactions, many first-generation migrants of South Asian origin found themselves downplaying the more conspicuous South Asian elements of their dress, modifying their appearances in this new environment. It is, I argue, the way in which dress and textiles of South Asian resonance have been used to essentialize people of South Asian origin that in part explains the ambivalence that many second- and third-generation South Asians feel towards wearing conspicuously South Asian patterns and styles in diasporic contexts.

There are a number of studies of South Asian diaspora dress practices that would seem to corroborate this view. Bakirathi Mani, for example, suggests that the juxtaposing of Western and Indian clothing styles popular amongst students of South Asian origin in the United States represents a deliberate attempt to disrupt biologically inscribed racial categories and to challenge the often assumed connection between skin colour and ethnic identity (Mani 2003). In Britain, some South Asian women speak of having hated being obliged to wear the salwar kameez for special occasions in their childhoods. Growing up in the 1960s and 1970s, girls wearing the garment looked and felt alien, foreign, old-fashioned and, above all, at odds with the surrounding fashion and culture to which they wished to assert their belonging (Tarlo 2010a).

Others express feelings of warmth and attachment to the South Asian clothes in their wardrobes but do not necessarily feel comfortable wearing them except in domestic, ritual or social contexts which are predominately Asian. For example, in her study of the clothing preferences of British Asians, Shivani Derrington found people commenting, 'I've never felt right wearing saris to work'; 'I wouldn't say I'm the sort of person who needs to fit in but at the same time I don't necessarily want to stand out either'; and 'I tend to make sure I've got something South Asian on me, like an accessory, but I tend not to wear an entire outfit' (Derrington 2010: 71–6). From other studies we learn how people up- and downplay Indianness in different contexts through the way they compose different elements of their outfits (Woodward 2007). Taken together, such examples seem to suggest a self-conscious play with elements of South Asian dress which demands both processes of engagement and detachment, suggesting that many seek to make reference to their South Asian roots without being defined by them. For some, this may involve a split between personal feelings of attachment and strategic practices of detachment—a split apparent in Nirmal Puwar's description of the contrast between the tactile and emotive intimacy many South Asians feel towards the colourful silky landscape of cloth and clothes they imbibed from mothers and aunts when children and the painful memories of experiences of racism and exclusion many had experienced wearing such clothes in British contexts (Puwar 2002) where they were considered 'out of place'.

How then do these experiences of intimacy and distance towards South Asian textiles play out in the milieu I have identified elsewhere as 'visibly Muslim' (Tarlo 2010b)? By 'visibly Muslim', I refer to the growing numbers of people whose affiliation to Islamic values, identity and faith are marked out through everyday dress practices and who have become a visible presence in the sartorial landscape of cosmopolitan cities in Britain, Europe and elsewhere. Here again, it becomes helpful to distinguish how people from different backgrounds respond to South Asian textiles, enabling us to recognize why some British Muslims appreciate South Asian styles and patterns more than others.

COSMOPOLITANISM AND ETHNICITY IN TENSION

While Muslims from South Asian backgrounds in Britain often assert attachment to Islam in part through a rejection of South Asian textiles and styles, this is not the case with Muslims from other backgrounds. In fact, whether white British, Afro Caribbean or Egyptian, Muslims from other backgrounds often develop positive associations with South Asian textiles and enjoy building fashionable Muslim outfits by incorporating elements of South Asian dress. Some talk with enthusiasm about the wonderful array of cloth and clothes cheaply available in the shops and markets in South Asian shopping areas such as Green Street, Southall, Whitechapel and Wembley (see Figure 3.2). They also describe experimenting with bangles, scarves and jangly Indian skirts or tunics that they purchase in such locations.[3] It is not that they are less concerned than South Asian Muslims with the idea of expressing a cosmopolitan Islamic identity, but for them South Asian textiles, if worn to conform with Islamic ideals of modesty, provide a means of asserting such cosmopolitanism. This points to the significance of the interactions and exchanges that take place between different diasporic populations in cities such as London which are characterized by super diversity (Shukla 2001; Vertovec 2007). However, for Muslims from South Asian backgrounds, this same textile heritage seemed not so much inspiring as restricting. The clothes on offer in areas such as Green Street and Wembley seemed too saturated with

Fig. 3.2   View of Green Street, London E7. Photo: Emma Tarlo

ethnic associations to function as suitable Islamic dress, and to shop in such places seemed only to reaffirm one's ethnic identification rather than provide the means to constructing new cosmopolitan Muslim looks. What was desired by some was distance from the provincialism and intimacy of such areas where one's South Asianness became reinforced through the interpenetration of dress, body and place.

However, Muslims from South Asian backgrounds have been far from inactive in the development of new forms of Islamic fashion in Britain. This is hardly surprising given that over two-thirds of British Muslims are of South Asian origin even if this is not the heritage some of them most want to emphasize. As already suggested, when South Asian Muslims in Britain develop and wear new forms of Islamic fashion, they rely less on the perpetuation of South Asian patterns, prints, colours and styles than on their rejection. Significantly, this also involves differentiating themselves from their mothers whose clothing they increasingly consider insufficiently Islamic. When intergenerational conflict over dress emerges in British Asian Muslim families, mothers tend to accuse their daughters of looking simultaneously 'too Western' (in their jeans or skirts) and 'too Islamic' (in hijab and especially if wearing niqab) to which visibly Muslim daughters retort that their mothers' outfits composed of the salwar kameez or sari are 'cultural' rather than 'Islamic'. Such outfits carry with them the connotations of their parents' places of origin in India, Pakistan or Bangladesh, which make them seem culturally tainted. They tell their mothers that they are ignorant of proper religious dress requirements owing to their insufficient Islamic education. Such arguments offer British Muslim youth a new form of teenage sartorial rebellion in which they claim the moral upper hand over their parents by asserting superior Islamic knowledge. Such iconic intergenerational conflicts have become the stuff of ethnic jokes, but they provide further insight into why stepping away from South Asian styles in favour of Islamic ones may feel emancipating to many young Muslims.

Objections to the many brightly coloured saris, salwar kameezes and *leghacholi* (skirts and short tops) readily available in British Asian shopping centres such as Green Street, Wembley and Southall are voiced in both aesthetic and moral terms. It is said that such clothes are too flashy in colour, limsy in texture, body hugging in style, too exposing of the neck and arms, too eye-catching and glaring, too Bollywood and Barbie-dollish, too ethnic, too Asian and, for some, too Hindu. Such clothes are increasingly defined as 'Islamically inauthentic' by this new generation of young British Asian Muslims attracted to the notion of a pan-Islamic identity. The failure of such clothes to place sufficient emphasis on the covering of the flesh and concealment of the contours of the female body makes them seem immodest as does the preponderance of bright colours and abundant decorative elements, which are perceived as inappropriately eye-catching or flashy. Invoking classic feminist arguments about the objectification of the female body in combination with Islamic arguments about the importance of detracting male attention and protecting female privacy through covering, many visibly Muslim youth from Asian backgrounds now attribute superficial values to South Asian textiles and fashions which seem to objectify, sexualize and glamorize the female body in inappropriate ways.[4]

This rejection of the vibrant and thriving British Asian dress and textile scene by those keen to emphasize their Muslim identity and faith involves not just a negative recoding of certain Asian styles and fabrics but also a positive engagement with a growing Islamic fashionscape which offers new alternative modest possibilities and invites membership of an expanding cosmopolitan Islamic milieu. Whilst critics of religious dress practices tend to perceive Islamic dress as retrograde and restrictive, young women who embrace new forms of Islamic fashion experience not only its disciplining effects (which they see as both challenging and rewarding) but also the opportunity it offers for transcending the local and engaging with a new landscape of material, moral and aesthetic possibilities associated both with the early Islamic community of the past and with an aspirational post-ethnic global Islamic community of the future. Nowhere is this cosmopolitan aspiration more apparent than in the hijabi fashion blogs, YouTube demonstrations and discussion fora, which have emerged on the Internet in recent years. Here, young Muslims located in different parts of the world, but many of them living in Muslim minority contexts, pick up on fashion trends from around the world (including North Africa, Arab countries and Turkey as well as London, New York, Paris and Milan) and represent these for discussion and potential adaptation by visibly Muslim consumers. Also featured on these Web sites are links to Islamic fashion stores and Muslim lifestyle magazines, which offer Muslim customers new ways of looking Muslim and feeling part of a global Islamic community with its emancipating potential to transcend the limitations of ethnicity and locality. Meanwhile, communication between Muslim women of different ethnic backgrounds takes place both through Internet discussion fora and chat rooms as well as in physical locations such as schools and colleges, where young people discuss and exchange clothing ideas and express feelings of solidarity and recognition with Muslims from different backgrounds. The fact that visibly Muslim dress is often treated with suspicion and hostility by outsiders in British, European, American and other Muslim minority contexts serves to reinforce the levels of solidarity and emotional attachment young women feel for such dress.

VISIBLY MUSLIM FASHIONS AS COSMOPOLITAN SOLUTIONS

Unlike in Turkey, where there is a well-established Islamic fashion industry targeted at Muslim women who cover (Navara Yasin 2002; Sandikçi and Ger 2007; Gökariksel and Secor, this volume), visibly Muslim fashions in Britain have grown up in a more piecemeal way through the personal clothing experiments of young

Muslims in search of clothes which might fulfil their desire to put Islamic ideals of modesty into practice whilst at the same time looking fashionable, Muslim and modern. In this final section, I outline some of the solutions they have devised, placing particular emphasis on the cosmopolitan aspirations attached to fashions developed by Muslims from South Asian backgrounds.[5]

Perhaps the most popular solution to the problem of what to wear developed by young Muslims in Britain and Europe has been the wearing of mainstream fashion garments adapted to what are considered 'Islamic requirements of modesty' through processes of bricolage (Moors 2009; Tarlo 2010b). How 'Islamic requirements' are understood varies according to different interpretations of Islamic texts, but for many this is understood to include the covering of the head and skin, leaving only the hands and face exposed. By these criteria, jeans, skirts, blouse and dresses are all suitable candidates for visibly Muslim outfits when worn with a headscarf. So, too, in theory is the popular North Indian and Pakistani outfit of salwar kameez worn with a *dupatta* (loose wrap over the head and upper body). However, as already suggested, for many British Asian Muslims this outfit is too saturated with associations of ethnicity. Its efficacy as a suitable modern Muslim garment is further diminished by its wearing by Hindus and Sikhs as well as by its wearing by some South Asian Muslims who are less concerned with looking and behaving Islamically.

For these reasons, many young British Asian Muslims reject the salwar kameez and choose to build up composite outfits through selecting garments from mainstream fashion stores and adapting them to suit their criteria of suitable covering. Skirts are sometimes lengthened, tight jeans covered by loose tops, and short-sleeved or strappy dresses made acceptable by the insertion of long-sleeved polo necked blouses or jumpers underneath (see Figure 3.3). In practice, many of these outfits are often highly tailored, and there is scope for a detailed and nuanced following of high street trends. In this way, a modern visibly Muslim aesthetic has developed in which emphasis is placed on the covering of the body surface through judicious practices of selecting, layering and coordinating garments which may have been designed with other looks in mind and through a skilful array of techniques of tying, layering and pinning the headscarf which has become a new form of personal art and is often the most conspicuous element of a young visibly Muslim woman's outfit (Tarlo 2010b). Ironically, then, at a time when the salwar has made its way into mainstream fashion to some extent and finds popularity amongst British women from a variety of backgrounds (Bhachu 2004), it tends to be rejected by a new generation of visible Muslims from South Asian backgrounds who prefer to wear clothes less saturated with associations of ethnicity and place.

These outfits described are cosmopolitan through their alignment with global fashion trends which cut across regional and ethnic distinctions to

Fig. 3.3   The art of layering: Rezia Wahid wearing a sundress over a long-sleeved polo neck and trousers. Photo: Emma Tarlo

some extent whilst creating a unifying identifiably Muslim point of reference through the headscarf, which can be worn to signify both fashion savvy and religious conviction. Variations of this fashionable Muslim look are found in many European contexts (see, for example, Salim, Bendixsen and Christiansen, this volume, for examples in Sweden, Germany and Denmark, respectfully) and are further popularized in hijabi fashion blogs, but they also come under criticism from some sections of the Muslim population who criticize certain outfits for being too body-hugging, too sexually provocative, too aligned to consumerist values and insufficiently modest. Some British Muslims who seek to develop a more modest and less conspicuous appearance as part of their endeavour to improve the self take distance from consumerist values and cultivate a more pious way of being turn instead to full-length, long-sleeved outer garments available for purchase in Islamic shops. Such shops are often located in shopping centres specialized in South Asian fashions, but they stand in stark contrast to the latter owing to their more sombre and overtly religious feel. They generally specialize in religious literature, tapes, artefacts and perfumes as well as clothes and usually have recordings of religious lectures or music playing in the background. The garments they sell are mostly imported from North Africa or the Middle East and are usually dark or dull in colour. They include jalabiyas from Egypt and jilbabs and abayas from countries such as Syria and Dubai. Some of these represent forms of regional dress from different parts of the world which have in recent years become recoded as Islamic. For young Muslims with austere interpretations of what constitutes modest dress, such outer garments offer suitable covering worn with headscarves and, in some cases, face covers (niqabs) which are also available in such shops. However, for many young British Asian Muslims who want to dress Islamically, such garments are unappealing owing to their wide voluminous shapes, their thin and dark synthetic fabrics and the perception of them as 'Saudi dress' which gives them a regional rather than cosmopolitan look which some feel is incompatible with British lifestyles and tastes.

A common theme which featured in my interviews with young British Islamic fashion designers from South Asian backgrounds was the extent to which the black jilbabs and abayas available in Islamic shops felt alienating and foreign. Some, like Sophia Kara of Imaan Collections, had tried purchasing and wearing an abaya but found herself feeling alienated and ill at ease and above all embarrassed to face work colleagues in such an outfit which she felt would be viewed as 'old-fashioned' and 'intimidating and off-putting'. Similarly, Junayd Miah, one of the founders of the company Silk Route spoke of 'all this stuff coming in from Dubai, Syria, Asia et cetera' being 'so full of cultural baggage' and therefore inappropriate for British Muslims who wanted to maintain their sense of fashion and style. His comment pointed to the inadequacy of both Asian and Middle Eastern clothing options for British Muslim lifestyles. Not only did these options fail to meet the tastes of many young British Asian Muslims on aesthetic grounds, but they were also saturated with the connotations of foreign places and were therefore perceived as inhibiting and inappropriate for the contexts of their daily interactions with others in British cities. How, then, have young designers from British Asian backgrounds responded to these dilemmas by developing styles of dress which might be considered both fashionable and Islamic and which simultaneously have a cosmopolitan rather than ethnic feel?

The companies I wish to discuss are based in London, Leicester and Nottingham—all cities with a substantial Asian presence, and the entrepreneurs responsible for developing them are from second-generation Indian, Pakistani and Bangladeshi backgrounds. Whilst the designs they have developed are not intended specifically for Muslims from South Asian backgrounds, they are informed by their own experiences of growing up in British Asian families and contexts. In each case, they have tried to develop forms of Islamic dress which have a contemporary feel, blend to some extent with what they perceive as 'Western fashion' but transcend the ethnic associations of Asian dress. In some cases, they place strong emphasis on the significance of the cosmopolitan nature of their designs through reference to the global Muslim community or ummah.

Massoomah is a company based in Nottingham and founded by Sadia Nosheen, who is from a British Pakistani background and was raised in Stoke on Trent. Her designs are an attempt to take the jilbab which she considers 'correct Muslim according to the Shariah' and to modernize it to suit contemporary British tastes and lifestyles (see Figure 3.4). Her designs involve

Fig. 3.4 Masoomah jilbabs in muted shades of purple, lilac and green on sale at the Global Peace and Unity Event in London, 2008. Photo: Emma Tarlo

careful negotiation with what she calls 'Western fashion'. On one hand, she wants them to 'still look like jilbabs' and 'not be slave to fashion'. On the other hand, she incorporates fabrics and design features which show a strong engagement with fashion. Hence, she brings in colours and fabrics that are 'in season' but sticks to a relatively muted palette, referring to her preference for what she calls 'safe and murky colours'. Her designs grow firmly out of her own experiences and those of the young women around her. At university in her twenties, she faced what she called 'the biggest dilemma of her life' when she wanted to dress Islamically but could not face wearing the black Arabic options available locally. Her solution was to make her own jilbabs using contemporary fabrics such as denim and corduroy and adding features like hoods and kangaroo pockets. The popularity of her outfits in young Muslim circles in Stoke on Trent led her to expand to develop her own company. Speaking of some of her younger clients, she comments,

> They are going to have that Western taste. What they like is a product that looks like it's been bought in a shop, is not cheaply made, looks like they've been to H&M, Top Shop or Principles in terms of the workmanship and having labels with washing instructions. We want to be Islamic and dress Islamically but that does not mean we should compromise our standards.

It was clear when talking to Sadia Nosheen that even if she wished to take distance from the fashion industry, she had imbibed some of its norms and follows certain of its trends. For example, she purchases roll ends of popular cotton and linen fabrics from wholesale suppliers in the Midlands so that some of the jilbabs she sells are made from the exact same materials and are the same colours as clothes found in high street shops that season.

While Massomah jilbabs are on the whole rather plain and classical in design, the modern jilbabs developed by the company Silk Route have a more trendy urban feel, incorporating features of sport and street wear such as stretchy fabrics, hoods, piping, combat pockets and rip effects. Alienated by both the Asian and Islamic clothes available, the young people behind the company had approached designers at the London School of Fashion and commissioned them to study urban street fashions and find ways of Islamicizing them, by which they meant making them conform to Islamic ideas about covering. Targeted at Muslim youth, the designs they came up with exuded a cool and sporty urban feel on which they have subsequently expanded (see Figure 3.5). In 2012, the company's Web site introduced the products with the following message: 'The Silk Route Brand shared the modest approach to clothing found in the Islamic-Faith and culture with the trendy sporty urban looks, vibrant colours and high grade materials used by many contemporary brands. The end product has had much praise, support and encouragement

Fig. 3.5 Jilbabs from Silk Route's sporting range as advertised on the Hijabshop.com Web site, in 2009. Courtesy of Wahid Rahman

from the Muslim community especially the many fans and customers we have around the world'.[6] Placing emphasis on the global theme, Junayd Miah told me in 2010, 'We live in a globalized world. Everyone is connected. We want to attract conscious Muslims all over the world and this is the identity we are hoping to create.' He was keen to point out that his jilbabs played a role in catering for and connecting like-minded youth as far afield as Britain, Egypt and Nigeria who were all part of the expanding global ummah.

What is striking about the jilbabs produced and sold online and on the high street by Masoomah and Silk Route is the extent to which they have taken distance from fabrics, styles, patterns, colours and designs which have a South Asian resonance. This is less extreme in the case of fashions marketed by Arabian Nites and Imaan Collections, which are also global in orientation but which draw inspiration from design sources and techniques around the world, including South Asia. The designers behind both companies are British-born women of Indian Gujarati origin.

Arabian Nites is situated in the London Muslim centre just a few doors from the East London Mosque in Whitechapel, an area known as Little Bengal for its large population of Muslims from Bangladesh (see Figure 3.6). Fashion designer Yasmin Safri opened the boutique in 2005, having previously worked in Selfridges and obtained a degree in product development from the London School of Fashion. Working in Selfridges, she had been struck by the glamour and elegance of some of the wealthy customers from the Gulf and by their capacity to look both stylish and Islamic. Travelling to Dubai, she was struck by the contrast between the glamorous covered outfits worn by women there and the comparatively dowdy, conservative 'polyester and parachute' type jilbabs worn by Muslim women who covered in East London. Recognizing a commercial and aesthetic niche, she began to design forms of covered dress that might 'bring a taste of the East to East London'. Whilst the boutique's name emphasizes the Arabic connection, the clothes inside are eclectic, blending what she

Fig. 3.6   Interior of Arabian Nites boutique showing an eclectic mix of influences including Indian, Middle Eastern and Moroccan styles, 2009. Photo: Emma Tarlo

calls 'Middle-Eastern and Indo-Continental traditions' with features from 'Western fashion'. Safri's intention is to show Muslim women who demonstrate that covered dress can be beautiful, stylish, glamorous, elegant and a pleasure to see and wear rather than simply being considered an 'Islamic necessity'. Whilst she does sell quite a number of black abayas to satisfy the conservative tastes of some of her customers, she also makes use of sumptuous colours and fabrics, incorporating embroidered fringes and elegant ruffs. And while she looks to Morocco, Egypt, Syria, India, Pakistan and Dubai for inspiration and employs craftsmen from India and Dubai, the garments she produces are not so much replicas of different styles and fabrics from around the world as reconfigurations of them. Whilst at one level her designs conform to the sartorial expectations of place in this conservative Muslim hub in East London, at another level they subtly subvert them by suggesting the glamorous potential of covered dress, leading some local women to perceive the boutique as an inspiration whilst others criticize it for the glamour and cost of some of the items on sale there. Nonetheless, the boutique attracts a steady flow of women with a preference for long, covered styles, many of whom also wear niqab, as do some of the members of staff who work there.

An alternative way of looking fashionable, Muslim and cosmopolitan has been developed by Sophia Kara of Imaan Collections which is based in Leicester, a city in the British Midlands with a large population of people with South

Asian roots. Significantly, in 2010 Kara began replacing the phrase 'Islamic fashion' with advertising slogans such as 'designer modest wear' and 'faith friendly couture'. Like Sadia Nosheen of Masoomah, she was initially motivated to enter the fashion industry partly through her aversion to the jilbabs available, but unlike Nosheen she is more eclectic and experimental in the styles of covered dress she creates. She cites her inspirations as 'architecture, nature, even trees' and confesses a love of 'buttons, feathers and vintage'. She is keen to make covered dress less intimidating and off-putting as well as less submissive. She also likes to reach out to non-Muslims—hence the reference to 'faith friendly couture'. Whilst steering away from conspicuously Asian styles, she makes ample use of luxury fabrics popularly used in saris and Asian glamour wear such as silk, georgette and metal-wire embroidery,

Fig. 3.7 Selection of clothes from the Web-based store of Imaan Collections, 2012. Clockwise from top left: 1. Africana, 2. Bohemian Princess, 3. Grecian Dame, 4. Egyptian Queen. Courtesy of Sophia Kara

especially in her bridal collection in which she does not hesitate to incorporate bright colours. The daywear she advertises is generally more subdued in colour and made from fabrics such as cotton, linen, felt and suede. Whilst she does not follow fashion trends too rigorously, she is aware of colour forecasts and the need to sell clothes that will go with the costume jewellery, bags and shoes that her customers are buying in high street shops. The global inspiration of her designs is evident from some of the names of the outfits advertised on the Imaan Web site: Egyptian Queen, Arabesque, Kimono Wrap, Bohemian Princess, Silver Roman Empress and Grecian Dame (see Figure 3.7). Whilst South Asian tailors and embroiderers are often employed to make these garments, the ethos and aesthetic is self-consciously cosmopolitan.

CONCLUSION

Through fabricating new types of visibly Muslim dress, a number of British Muslims from South Asian backgrounds are moving away from what they perceive as the constraints and limitations of a South Asian identity and aesthetic and fabricating outfits they consider modern, cosmopolitan and Muslim. Drawing on what they perceive as an older and wider geographic Islamic heritage as well as on contemporary global fashion trends, they contribute to the forging of new forms of contemporary cosmopolitan Islamic fashion with the aspirational intent of transcending the limitations of ethnicity and location.

Fig. 3.8 A certain sensibility and competence with cloth: Zarina tying a headscarf, 2009. Courtesy of Elizabeth Scheder-Bieschin

How far they perceive their designs as contributing to the forging of a global Islamic community or ummah varies. For some, such as Silk Route, this seems to be an explicit aim; for others, it is perhaps more a possible consequence than an intention. Part of this process of developing new forms of Islamic dress has involved moving away from a thriving British Asian fashion scene. But it is worth asking whether this rejection of South Asian aesthetics is as total as it seems. Returning to the artist Helen Scalway's point about how colour, pattern and ornament might travel, split and fuse in unexpected places, I suggest that elements of engagement with South Asian aesthetics remain visible in subtle ways in visibly Muslim dress practices in Britain. A certain love of colour, fine fabric and handcrafted ornament persists in many of the garments designed by Yasmin Safri and Sophia Kara. It is also apparent in the outfits of many young Muslims, particularly in the elaborate hijab-tying techniques they are developing which require skill and competence in the layering and manipulation of cloth and the appreciation of colour and texture (see Figure 3.8). Is this perhaps a case of South Asian aesthetics re-emerging in new contexts?

NOTES

1. While Indian fabrics and prints are the recognizable face of the South Asian presence in British fashion, the labour of workers in sweatshops in India, Bangladesh and Pakistan represents its less visible face.
2. This was the theme of the panel, 'Aestheticisation: Artefacts and Emotions in Diasporic Contexts', organized by Anne Sigfrid Groneth and Maruska Svasek as part of the Twelfth Association of Social Anthropologists (ASA) Conference, on the theme 'Art and Aesthetics in a Globalising World', held at Jawaharlal Nehru University, New Delhi, April 2012.
3. See Tarlo (2010b: Chapter 4) for examples of uses of South Asian textiles by British Muslim converts.
4. For discussion of the range of different interpretations of Islamic criteria of modesty in Britain, see Tarlo (2010b).
5. For more extensive discussion of the religious, political and aesthetic concerns surrounding visibly Muslim dress practices in Britain and the emergence of Islamic fashion companies, see Tarlo (2010b).
6. See <http://www.silkrouteclothing.com/about.html> accessed 11 July 2012.

REFERENCES

Ashmore, S. (2010), 'Hippies, Bohemians and Chintz', in C. Breward, P. Crang and R. Crill, eds., *British Asian Style: Fashion & Textiles Past & Present*, London: V&A.

Bhachu, P. (2004), *Dangerous Designs: Asian Women Fashion the Diaspora Economies,* London: Routledge.

Breward, C., P. Crang and R. Crill (2010), *British Asian Style: Fashion & Textiles Past & Present,* London: V&A.

Crill, R. (2010), 'Trading Materials: Textiles and British Markets', in C. Breward, P. Crang and R. Crill, eds., *British Asian Style: Fashion & Textiles Past & Present,* London: V&A.

Derrington, S. (2010), 'Wardrobe Stories', in C. Breward, P. Crang and R. Crill, eds., *British Asian Style: Fashion & Textiles Past & Present,* London: V&A.

Dwyer, C. (2010), 'From Suitcase to Showroom: British Asian Retail Spaces', in C. Breward, P. Crang and R. Crill, eds., *British Asian Style: Fashion & Textiles Past & Present,* London: V&A.

Jones, C., and A. M. Leshkowich (2003), 'Introduction: The Globalization of Asian Dress: Re-orienting Fashion or Re-orienting Asia?' in S. Niessen, A. M. Leshkowich and C. Jones, eds., *Re-orienting Fashion: The Globalization of Asian Dress*, Oxford: Berg.

Mani, B. (2003), 'Undressing the Diaspora', in N. Puwar and P. Raghuram, eds., *South Asian Women in the Diaspora,* Oxford: Berg.

Moors, A. (2009), 'Islamic Fashion in Europe: Religious Conviction, Aesthetic Style, and Creative Consumption', *Encounters* 1, 1: 175–201.

Moors, A., and E. Tarlo (2007), 'Introduction', *Fashion Theory* 11, 2/3: 133–41.

Navara Yashin, Y. (2002), 'The Market for Identities, Secularism, Islamism and Commodities', in D. Kandiyoti and A. Santanber, eds., *Fragments of Culture: The Everyday of Modern Turkey,* New Brunswick, NJ: Rutgers University Press.

Puwar, N. (2002), 'Multi-cultural Fashion . . . Stirrings of Another Sense of Aesthetics and Memory', *Feminist Review* 71: 63–87.

Sandikci, O., and G. Ger (2007), 'Constructing and Representing the Islamic Consumer in Turkey', *Fashion Theory* 11, 2/3: 189–210.

Scalway, H. (2010), 'South Asian Patterns in Urban Spaces', in C. Breward, P. Crang and R. Crill, eds., *British Asian Style: Fashion & Textiles Past & Present,* London: V&A.

Shukla, S. (2001), 'Locations for South Asian Diasporas', *Annual Review of Anthropology* 30: 551–72.

Tarlo, E. (1996), *Clothing Matters: Dress and Identity in India,* London: Hurst.

Tarlo, E. (2010a), 'The South Asian Twist in British Muslim Fashion', in C. Breward, P. Crang and R. Crill, eds., *British Asian Style: Fashion & Textiles Past & Present,* London: V&A.

Tarlo, E. (2010b), *Visibly Muslim: Fashion, Politics, Faith,* Oxford: Berg.

Vertovec, S. (2007), 'Super-diversity and Its Implications', *Ethnic and Racial Studies* 29, 6: 1024–54.

Woodward, S. (2007), *Why Women Wear What They Wear,* Oxford: Berg.

–4–

Perspectives on Muslim Dress in Poland: A Tatar View

Katarzyna Górak-Sosnowska and Michał Łyszczarz

Compared to that of many EU countries, the Muslim population in Poland is very small, estimated at between 25,000 and 40,000, which is less than 0.1 per cent of the population. This marginal number does not mean that their presence is historically shallow, nor does it suggest their homogeneity. In fact, the Muslim population in Poland is very diverse, comprising not only economic migrants and refugees from Islamic countries but also the Tatars, an ethnic minority that has been living in Poland for over 600 years.

Religion has always been crucial for how the Tatars constructed their identity, along with ethnic (Tatar) and national (Polish) belonging (Warmińska 1999). Thanks to their religious attachment, Tatars managed throughout the centuries to keep their ethnic identity, not giving in to complete assimilation. Co-existence in Polish society and isolation from the main Islamic centres produced a peculiar form of Tatar Islam and religiosity.

Tatar identity is currently at a crossroads, influenced by two independent processes: the divergence from their ethnic traditions and the confrontation with other Muslims (Górak-Sosnowska and Łyszczarz 2010). Both are forcing them to redefine and renegotiate their identity and their relation to other Muslims. Both processes can be analysed through the lens of Tatar sartorial practices. Divergence from ethnic traditions is linked to the process of assimilation—a path which the Tatar community chose consciously in order to become Polish.[1] In terms of sartorial practices, it means getting rid of traditional clothing. Contemporary confrontations with other Muslims involve divergent interpretations of Islam from immigrants from Arab countries trying to impose their understanding of the religion. In sartorial terms, this refers to strategies adopted by Tatar women aimed at confirming that one can be Muslim and not wear hijab.

The aim of this chapter is to present the sartorial practices of Polish Tatars in relation to the emerging and evolving politics of Muslim taste. The research is based on fourteen semi-structured interviews carried out in the period 2008–9, mostly at the homes of respondents, as well as several years of observations. The sample was drawn in order to reflect a variety of opinions according to age, education and gender. Most of our respondents come from the Podlasie region and the rest from other Polish cities.

BECOMING POLISH

Numbering around 3,000–5,000 people, Tatars constitute one of the smallest ethnic groups in Poland. Centuries of living in a mainstream Polish and Catholic society and being isolated from any other Tatar or Muslim population resulted in their losing a lot of their cultural heritage. However, it was not so much the pressure from the outside world as the willingness of Tatars to integrate, or even assimilate, that has informed Tatar clothing choices. Historically, soon after reaching Lithuania and Poland in the fourteenth century, they changed their lifestyle from a nomadic to a settled one. This was followed by linguistic assimilation around the eighteenth century and the adoption of exogamous marriages. Furthermore, their religious practice became 'slavicized' in terms of religious observance (Dziekan 2000, 2005; Drozd 2003) and restricted to the private sphere.

The process of assimilation was also visible in Tatar sartorial practices. Whilst Tatar women did wear headgear, they tended to follow the dominant style popular in Poland. In the cities the practice of covering the hair on a daily basis had more or less died out prior to the Second World War (Łyszczarz 2011), whereas it remains a common practice in the countryside even today. There, the headscarf in the form of a triangle with two corners knotted below the chin is considered part of dressing rather than an Islamic symbol (see Figure 4.1). Both Catholic and Orthodox women also wear such headscarves in the villages of eastern Poland, making the Tatars undistinguishable from those around them. As one woman in her seventies explained:

> Neither young girls nor older women wear hijab. We didn't have such a tradition. That is, there was no such tradition in the cities, where—if anything at all—women wore an elegant hat. Whereas in the countryside all women wore scarves, day in and day out.[2] It made no difference whether it was a Tatar or a Catholic woman.

Tatars understand hijab as covering one's head on religious occasions. The headgear does not have to cover all the hair as it is intended to express one's respect for God rather than hide a woman's hair from the male gaze. In mosques and *mizars* (cemeteries), one can see a wide range of Tatar headgear including elegant hats, caps and scarves tied below the chin or loosely

Fig. 4.1 Eightieth anniversary of the Muslim Religious Union (Tatar Islamic religious community) showing the Tatar style of wearing hijab. Photo: Michał Łyszczarz

wrapped around the head leaving large portions of the hair and neck visible. In the autumn of 2010, I saw only two Tatar women in Białystok (a city of 300,000 in eastern Poland with a significant Tatar population) who were wearing full hijab—that is, one that covered their hair completely.

The understanding of hijab in a symbolic sense is also visible in local mosques. We observed that Tatar women went to mosques more often than men and remained with men in the main prayer hall until *adhan*. Then they went over to *babiniec*—the female part of the mosque—and put their scarves on. After the prayer, they returned to the main hall without their headgear, where the imam offered *sadoga* (from Arab; *sadaqa* for those who took part in the prayer).

Hijab survived as an element of traditional dress, even though it has been limited to the religious sphere and acquired very particular symbolic meaning. One may argue that—even in this vestigial form—it is the only element of traditional Tatar dress that has stood the test of time. Tatars rejected their earlier dresses, as they did not want to stand out from the mainstream population.[3] When in 1999 the Buńczuk Tatar folk group was established (see Figure 4.2), one of the biggest challenges was how to create the appropriate costumes as hardly any remained and people could not recall what they looked like. As the group founder explains: 'The choreography and costumes were Crimean, but that wasn't a problem, because our motifs would not have been present for centuries, and Crimean folklore is very beautiful, and I think to a great extent similar to that of our ancestors.'

Polish Tatars might be aware that they are building on a borrowed (if not invented) tradition, but they are willing to do so and treat it as their own. For centuries, Tatars have been an ethno-religious community in Poland with the two elements of their identity overlapping. Until very recently, Tatars were the only Muslim community in Poland. This meant that being Muslim was synonymous with being Tatar. However, this is changing with the arrival of Muslims from

Fig. 4.2 Buńczuk, a group of young Tatars who sing and dance wearing what is considered traditional Tatar costume. Such styles are 'invented traditions' which have been rediscovered through Crimean Tatars. Photo: Michał Łyszczarz

other parts of the world who bring different interpretations of Islam (Górak-Sosnowska and Łyszczarz 2010).

TATAR ATTITUDES TOWARDS THE HEADSCARF

The influx of new immigrant Muslim populations is undermining the religious legacy of the Tatars. New, Oriental understandings of Islam have been brought to Poland by the first wave of immigrants predominantly from Arab countries (Kubicki 2007). At first, both communities benefitted from each other's presence: the Tatars helped their fellow Muslims to get used to living in Poland, while Arab migrants taught Tatar children Islam and Arabic—a language hitherto unknown to Tatars, making them unable to read the sacred texts.[4] This symbiosis was broken when larger numbers of Arab immigrants arrived in Poland and—what is most important—tried to 'Islamize' the Tatars, turning them into orthodox Muslims. This involved introducing a whole variety of Islamic practices such as eating halal food (what for most Tatars had previously meant not eating pork; Górak-Sosnowska and Łyszczarz 2009), discouraging the placing of pictures of the deceased on gravestones (now interpreted as a form of iconoclasm) and introducing the Islamic headscarf (Figure 4.3).

Fig. 4.3 Tatar dress stylized in an Oriental way. Photo: Michał Łyszczarz

Not covering one's hair or covering it only at religious occasions had, as we have seen, been a long-term Tatar strategy of assimilation to Polish culture. Many Tatars believe that living as a minority requires adjusting to the majority in order to coexist peacefully. The Arab emphasis on hijab seemed inappropriate to these women, as it appeared to have the opposite effect. It has the potential to cause problems between the Christian majority and the Muslim minority, but it also seemed to go against local realities and traditions. As two respondents explained:

> I couldn't wear hijab. I don't like this custom and moreover I am afraid that people on the street would point to me with their fingers if I did [18-year-old female].

> There is no compulsion in religion. If one wants to, then why not? I personally don't feel such need. I believe that wearing hijab is an individual matter. I remember that I used to wear it when I went camping in Germany. We were all alone, just Muslims, so we could wear it without inhibition. Here in Sokółka I have never worn hijab. If we lived in a Muslim state and all women wore scarves then I would also wear one. However, in Sokółka or Białystok it would result in fingers wagging [30-year-old female].

In both cases, the fear of fingers wagging affects attitudes to hijab. Interestingly, one of the respondents pointed to the Quran 2:256 in order to justify her perspective. The respondents make it clear they would feel strange wearing hijab and treated it as something alien that attracts the attention of passers-by. Indeed, except for a few cases in larger cities, the hijab is hardly seen on the streets of Poland. Neither are other visible expressions of cultural differences. Poland is, in fact, one of the most homogenous countries in Europe, both in ethnic and religious terms. That is why women in hijab are considered foreign (see Figures 4.4 and 4.5 for the Tater style), as one of the two Tatar women who decided to wear hijab explained:

> Nobody thinks of me as Tatar because the Tatars don't wear scarves, except at the mosque. And Islam provokes bad associations for many, especially in the last couple of years. Everyone takes me for an Arab or the wife of an Arab. People say to me things like, 'You've learnt to speak Polish so well' or, 'How did you manage to have such a fair complexion?' Nobody could believe that I am Polish! [25-year-old female]

Despite the presence of a well-integrated Tatar Muslim community, Islam provokes rather harsh and negative emotions in Poland, as it is associated with international affairs involving Muslims rather than with Polish Muslim citizens, who, due to their marginal presence, never proved to be a burden or a challenge. Over the years, the Arabs (equated with Muslims in public opinion) are, together with the Roma people, the least liked peoples in Poland (CBOS 2011).

The Tatars' position is far better than that of recent Muslim immigrants because Tatars are considered a local (i.e. autochthonous) ethnic minority, while recent Muslim immigrants are viewed as part of a bigger 'Islamic threat' (Górak-Sosnowska 2010). However, belonging to the category of good Muslims requires keeping religion in the private sphere. The case of the Tatar hijabi clearly reflects this. As soon as she decided to wear hijab, she was considered an Arab.

The Tatars, especially the younger ones, seem to share the general view that the hijab does not belong in Polish society. As one young man explained, 'I cannot imagine a situation where I walk with a girl and she is wearing a headscarf. We live in Europe and one cannot restrict women.' Another man explained, 'The attitude of younger people towards the hijab is [that] most of them completely reject it. Hijab is for them an indication either of the village bigotry of the Sokółka Tatars, or the Arab zeal of the immigrants.'

Interestingly, there were two divergent ways of arguing against the scarf. Village bigotry refers to the elder generation of Tatars—the ones who still wear a scarf as an element of traditional attire. The younger generations of Tatars choose the same urban styles of clothes as their non-Tatar peers. The dressing style of their grandparents' generation simply seems old-fashioned. By referring to 'Arab zeal' and the fact of living in Europe, the respondents clearly suggest that the hijab does not fit into Europe and is linked to the Arab world.

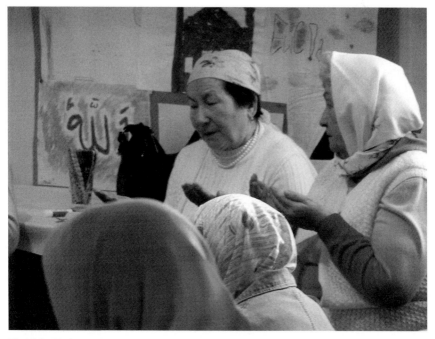

Fig. 4.4 Tatars at prayer in a mosque, wearing small head coverings. Photo: Michał Łyszczarz

Fig. 4.5   Friday prayers. Note how one of the women does not cover her hair and that many people wear shoes, and the space is not gender segregated. Photo: Michał Łyszczarz

Also the comment that 'one cannot restrict women' referred obliquely to the Middle Eastern and Tatar perceptions that hijab-wearing is a tool of oppression. Such attitudes suggest that young Tatars' views do not differ much from the mainstream opinion in Poland. However, associating the hijab with the Middle East does not translate into negative perceptions of women who decide they are going to wear hijab. Our respondents respected such decisions, and many appreciated the inner strength of Polish hijabis. At the same time, they did not intend to follow their example.

Tatars support their position by stating that they are the Polish autochthonous population that has been living in Poland for over 600 years, so they know the situation better than the newcomers. Life in homogenous Poland differs not only from the Middle East but also from areas of Western Europe inhabited by larger Muslim communities. At the same time, the Tatars perceive themselves as Muslims, and the fact that their way of practising Islam deviates from more orthodox traditions does not pose a problem. The imposition of a different, alien type of religiosity is perceived as threatening to their ethno-religious identity.

Arabs and the Middle East seem to be the only reference points cited by Tatars in relation to hijab. Immigrant Arabs are not the only other Muslims that the Tatars have been exposed to, but it was the Arab teachers of Islam who did not manage to convince the Tatars of the need to wear a veil. Two of our respondents mentioned religious instruction that had caused them confusion. The first was a 22-year-old man who recounted:

> I have always wondered why women should wear hijab. Once we were on a trip in Warsaw...We visited...the Islamic Centre at Wiertnicza St. There was some Arab man—reportedly a religious authority...who answered our questions. One was a question about hijab. I remember that this Arab said that women should wear hijab, because men liked their hair a lot, so in order to protect them they were recommended to wear hijabs. It caused us quite a lot of dismay. I mean, what has God got to do with it? Why do these Arabs tell us about hijabs in religious classes when it is just some tribal custom of theirs?

A woman of the same age expounded:

> I don't understand this order. What is wrong if someone can see my neck and hair? In religious classes I was told that it is because only the husband should see the hair of his wife and showing hair on the street is for Arabs the equivalent of walking out naked. I guess that if Arabs want to wear their hijabs, let them. I don't have to because I am safe in Poland—no one gets excited about my hair.

The respondents then try to reduce the significance of hijab by defining it as an Arab tribal custom which evolved in response to the perceived impulsiveness of Arab males, who are unable to refrain from gazing at women's hair. This way hijab loses its religious meaning and does not function as an indication of religiosity. One may wonder whether this really was the explanation provided by the Arab teachers. Judging teachers by what their students recount may be inaccurate. The explanation certainly seems rather literal and inappropriate for Poland. One has to bear in mind that the Islamic teachers from Arab countries were in most cases self-appointed volunteers without any pedagogical or professional religious training. On the other hand, any argument that links wearing hijab to being religious or preserving one's modesty would not be accepted by the Tatars.

Tatars often complain that Arab immigrants do not understand that one has to adjust to mainstream society and that they should not impose their understanding of Islam. Therefore, the Tatars put great emphasis on the cultural context and differentiate between religious doctrine and what is, according to them, the cultural customs of Arabs. These are perceived in stereotypical terms as revealed by the observations of one 26-year-old Tatar woman:

> In Judaism and Christianity in the Middle East, women also wore scarves, so it is their tradition. Moreover, there is desert there, so one has to protect the face against the wind and dust...It is quite dangerous over there. A Bedouin can steal a woman and take her away to the desert. For them a single woman is a sexual

object. Moreover they are crazy about women with fair skin and hair. It is a different culture; they are very impulsive. So the hijabs are justified over there—one, the climate, two, it makes women feel safe.

A 73-year-old man offered the following observation:

With veils it was like with alcohol. In the beginning Muhammad ordered them only for his wives, then Muslims decided that it should become customary and applied it to the whole society. As the wives of Muhammad were travelling by camel or in a sort of sedan chair, everybody wanted to see them. They were famous like the English queen nowadays. Muhammad wasn't happy about that, because he wanted privacy.

In the first case, the respondent points not only to certain psychological characteristics of Arabs but also to the climate, which is thought to make women cover their hair. She also mentions that Jewish and Christian women also covered in the Middle East. Since there are Christians and Jews in Poland who do not cover, the same applies to Muslims in Poland. The notion of Bedouins stealing women in the desert seems to be tainted with Orientalist fantasy and indicates how distant the Tatars are from Arabs, despite sharing adherence to Islam. The second statement confirms the Tatars' detachment from the mainstream Islamic narrative.

CONCLUSION

Religion is still one of the key elements of Tatar identity. However, in the face of growing immigration from Islamic countries, it is being redefined and reinterpreted. Islam in Poland used to be equated with the Tatars. Today, it is increasingly associated with immigrants from the Middle East and burdened with negative stereotypes. The arrival of competing interpretations of Islam has led to a revival of Tatar identity, in which Tatarness and Polishness are presented as opposites to Arabness and immigrant status. Paradoxically, the immigrant Muslim population, while outnumbering the Tatars at least three-fold, has contributed to this rebirth of Tatar cultural identity. In terms of dress, this means, on one hand, delving further into their own (and borrowed) heritage; on the other hand, it means stressing the difference between Arab/Oriental and local dressing patterns.

NOTES

1. The ancestors of todays' Tatars came to the Polish Lithuanian Commonwealth and settled there voluntarily. The Khan family members became

personal bodyguards of the king and, sometimes, even diplomats in charge of negotiation with Islamic countries. Tatar warriors supported the dukes and became solders in the Polish army. Both groups maintained their freedom (including freedom of religion, so they could build mosques; in fact, there was only one case of a burned mosque [in 1609 in Troki], a few anti-Islamic lampoons [with only 'Alfurkan tatarski prawdziwy' of 1616 known to the wider public] but no repressions from the Inquisition, etc.) and enjoyed the numerous rights and privileges of the nobility. They adapted local fashion and customs because they were indicating their high social status (as other members of the Polish nobility). Yet, they did not have political rights (due to their religion) and therefore could not participate in regional and national elections. On the other hand, Tatar prisoners of war, unless bought or brought out, stayed in Poland and were completely assimilated, since they were not allowed to practise their faith. Within several generations, they became ordinary farmhands, and their offspring are not considered part of the contemporary Tatar community but rather melted into Polish mainstream society (see Tysz-kiewicz 1989, 2002, 2008).

2. The original expression, '*piątek czy inny Świątek*', literally means 'Friday or other religious day', so it has a double meaning referring also to Friday in Islamic tradition.

3. An ethnographical description from the late 1930s states that, when it comes to clothing, Tatars did not stand out against the mainstream popu-lation. The only exception were huge scarves wore by women, just like by Cossacks (i.e., not necessarily on their heads). In the second half of the nineteenth century, their dressing patterns became distinctive:

> They wore short, garish and multi-coloured, usually orange or yellow, dress-ing gowns with wide sleeves; on the neck they hang several strings of thick byssus with various coral and silver figures and baubles handed down from generation to generation and apparently originating from the times of bondage (?); in the ears they wear huge silver hoops; heads tie with multi-coloured, light scarves in the shape of a turban with bigger knots over the forehead and long end at the sides; to a great extent they put short shoes on with crescent-shape, red tips (Kryczyński, 2000: 144).

4. The Tatars appreciate and admire the Arabic language as the language in which the Quran was revealed. That is why Tatar religious litera-ture, though written in Polish (or Belarusian), uses the Arabic script adjusted to Slavic languages. Writing religious scriptures with Arabic letters (even though in the Polish language) was a way of showing respect to the Arab script and giving it religious legitimacy (Dziekan 2002: 185–91).

REFERENCES

CBOS (2011), *Stosunek Polaków do innych narodów,* Report BS/13/2011, Warsaw: CBOS.

Drozd, A. (2003), 'Współczesne oblicza kultury Tatarów Rzeczypospolitej', in A. Abbas, ed., *Zagadnienia współczesnego islamu,* Poznań: Uniwersytet im. Adama Mickiewicza.

Dziekan, M. (2000), 'Tradycje ludowe i folklor Tatarów polsko-litewskich', in A. Drozd, M. Dziekan and T. Majda, eds., *Piśmiennictwo i muhiry Tatarów polsko-litewskich,* Warsaw: Res Publica Multiethnica.

Dziekan, M. (2002), 'Einige Bemerkungen über die islamische Literatur der polnisch-litauischen Tataren', in S. Leder, ed., *Studies in Arabic and Islam: Proceedings of the Nineteenth Congress, Union Europeennee der Arabisants et Islamisants,* Paris: Peeters.

Dziekan, M. (2005), 'Historia i tradycje polskiego islamu', in A. Parzymies, ed., *Muzułmanie w Europie,* Warsaw: Wydawnictwo Akademickie Dialog.

Górak-Sosnowska, K. (2010), 'Organizacje muzułmańskie w Polsce', in E. Firlit, ed., *Instytucje religijne w krajach Unii Europejskiej. Wybrane problemy,* Warsaw: Szkoła Główna Handlowa w Warszawie.

Górak-Sosnowska, K. and M. Łyszczarz (2009), '(Un-)Islamic Consumers? The Case of Polish Tatars', in J. Pink, ed., *Muslim Societies in the Age of Mass Consumption: Politics, Culture and Identity between the Local and the Global,* Cambridge: Cambridge Scholars Publishing.

Górak-Sosnowska, K. and M. Łyszczarz (2010), *Znaczenie religii dla zachowania i rozwoju tożsamości mniejszości narodowych i etnicznych–Tatarzy,* Paper for the Commission for National and Ethnic Minorities of Sejm of the Republic of Poland, no. 807/10A, Warsaw.

Kryczyński, S. (2000), *Tatarzy litewscy: Próba monografii historyczno-etnograficznej,* Warsaw and Gdańsk: Wydanie Rady Centralnej Związku Kulturalno-Oświatowego Tatarów Rzeczypospolitej Polskiej.

Kubicki, P. (2007), 'Muzułmanie w Polsce', in *Studia i prace Kolegium Ekonomiczno-Społecznego,* Warsaw: Szkoła Główna Handlowa w Warszawie, 60–80.

Łyszczarz, M. (2011), 'Religia i tożsamość. Socjologiczne studium młodego pokolenia Tatarów w Polsce', PhD diss., Katolicki Uniwersytet Lubelski.

Tyszkiewicz, J. (1989), *Tatarzy na Litwie i w Polsce. Studia z dziejów XIII–XVIII w.,* Warsaw: PWN.

Tyszkiewicz, J. (2002), *Z historii Tatarów polskich 1794–1944,* Pułtusk: Wyższa Szkoła Humanistyczna w Pułtusku.

Tyszkiewicz, J. (2008), *Tatarzy w Polsce i Europie. Fragmenty dziejów,* Pułtusk: Wyższa Szkoła Humanistyczna w Pułtusku.

Warmińska, K. (1999), *Tatarzy polscy: tożsamość religijna i etniczna,* Kraków: Universitas.

SECTION II

HISTORIES, HERITAGE AND NARRATIONS OF ISLAMIC FASHION

–5–

Şule Yüksel Şenler: An Early Style Icon of Urban Islamic Fashion in Turkey

Rustem Ertug Altinay

Turkey, 1967. In the city of Samsun, crowds are gathered to attend a talk by Şule Yüksel Şenler, a 29-year-old journalist. Although it hasn't been long since this young and elegant woman started covering her head, she is already on her way to becoming a leader in the emerging headscarf movement. During her talk, Şenler not only provides arguments for the religious and social need for the headscarf but also serves as a role model for young Muslim women through the stylish Islamic clothes she herself designed and made (Figure 5.1). This talk marked the start of dozens of similar events all over the country. With these popular public performances, Şenler emerged as the country's first Islamic style icon and set the standards for urban Turkish Islamic fashion, characterized by elaborately tied long headscarves that cover all hair as well as the neck—a style that was named by the media as *Şulebaş*

Fig. 5.1   Şule Yüksel Şenler giving a talk. Courtesy of Timaş Yayınları

or *Şulebaşı* (Şulehead)[1]—and used in combination with overcoats, jackets, long-sleeved dresses, trousers, and skirts of various lengths. This style also paved the way for *tesettür*, 'a distinctive form of veiling that developed in the 1980s—an oversized headscarf with matching tailored coat or suit' (White 2005: 124) that is too often (mis)perceived as the first urban Islamic fashion movement in Turkey.

How did Şenler and the fashion style she developed gain popularity in Turkey? What were the concerns behind the development of Şulebaş? How did this style relate to different subject positions that were made available to Turkish women by the dynamics of Islam, secularism, nationalism and modernization, and how did it play a role in the negotiations of identity and belonging? This chapter explores these questions in the light of Şenler's biography to gain insights into the politics and aesthetics of Islamic fashion in Turkey.

THE MAKING OF A MODERN MUSLIM TURKISH WOMAN

The formative years of the Republic of Turkey were characterized by a series of social and legal reforms implemented under the leadership of Mustafa Kemal Atatürk in order to construct a secular (albeit implicitly Sunni Muslim), modern, Western nation-state with an authentic Turkish essence. In Turkey's modernization and nation-building program, women were imagined as the builders of a new life, 'a modern way of living both in the private and the public spaces' (Göle 1997: 51). They were expected to actively participate in the transformation of the country and be symbols of this transformation while also serving as bearers of 'the tradition'—which actually was continuously redefined and reproduced. The symbolic role of women was particularly important because women's bodies were expected to signify national identity as well as the transition from an Islamic empire to a secular Western republic. Hence the female body became a field of contest where the intricate tensions between Orientalisms and Occidentalisms, secularisms and Islams, traditions and modernities played out.

At a time when social and bodily norms were changing at a dazzling speed in relation to invented traditions and imagined modernities, the state elite and public employees were expected to guide the people along the complicated road to Turkish modernity. Beginning in 1923, the year Turkey was established as a republic, a series of laws progressively limited the use of clothing items that connoted the empire and Islam. These laws can also be regarded as an extension of the dress reforms implemented during the Tanzimat Era (1839–76), the impact of which was primarily limited to the urban areas (Jirousek 1997: 206). The republican dress reforms started with regulations about the uniforms of particular groups: students of Istanbul Madrasah, judges, soldiers and policemen (Doğaner 2009: 35). In 1925, a resolution passed requiring civil servants to wear a Western-style hat and dress. In the same regulation, non-clergy men were prohibited from wearing religious dress (Doğaner 2009: 35). The transformation of the bodies of public employees who represented the state aimed not only to create role models for the people but also to mark the transformation of statecraft. These policies were expected to distinguish the Turkish state and society from the Ottoman Empire and the rest of the Middle East, and to undermine the religious sources of power outside state control. Arguably to prevent a public outcry, the Hat Law did not specify anything about female dress (Norton 1997: 162). Nevertheless, politicians and bureaucrats discouraged women from wearing the black veil and the headscarf. Moreover, as writer and teacher Halide Nusret Zorlutuna narrates in her memoirs, female public employees also received official requests to adopt Western fashions and what was perceived to be the modern lifestyle. In Zorlutuna's case, all female teachers in the provincial public school where she was employed were asked to stop covering their hair, attend balls organized by public institutions and dance (Zorlutuna 2009: 236).

Şule Yüksel Şenler's grandfather Mehmet Ali Aycan was a *muhtar,* a village administrator. Hence the sartorial history of her family was deeply influenced by the dress reforms. Aycan received an official request stating that he and his family were expected to serve as role models for the community by adopting the new dress codes. His wife,İkbal, abandoned the veil with a sense of national duty while he started wearing the Western-style hat (Tezcan 2007: 17). Their daughter Mihriban Ümran married her cousin Hasan Tahsin Şenler, who had studied in Russia on a government scholarship to become a chemical technician (Atasoy 2004: 53). Since he was a public employee, the family lived in various cities before settling in Istanbul in 1944. Şule Yüksel, born in 1938, was the third of their six children. In many ways, the family led a very 'modern' lifestyle: they followed Western fashions, consumed alcohol, entertained male guests in the household and the girls took private music lessons from male teachers. However, it is difficult to argue that they were simply Westernized through the Kemalist state apparatuses. Their lives were characterized by the tensions of Orientalist and Occidentalist fantasies which were often manifested through discourses about honour (*namus*).

According to Nükhet Sirman, in Turkey honour defines 'both the identity of the person vis-à-vis others and the sense of worth that a person has of himself or herself; it is the internalized form of a person's social standing' (2004: 44). In that sense, as argued by Sirman, although the concept is intrinsically linked with the codes of sexuality and sexual behaviour, it extends to cover the person's total sense of self. While honour is often too easily associated with tradition and/or Islam, it is neither directly linked to religion nor is it a stagnant concept. On the contrary, the codes of honour are dynamic and constantly negotiated. As a period of rapid social change, the Kemalist era was a time when the importance of the concept of honour persisted while the codes associated with it had become particularly complicated. Caught at the intersection of conflicting discourses, men and women had difficulty deciding on appropriate gendered behaviour.

Following what they perceived as the modern code of honour was of utmost importance for the Şenler family. The girls could attend balls and dance events, but they were allowed to dance only with *mahram* men—that is, kin and affines one is not allowed to marry according to Islamic law. They were allowed to read novels, but the books had to be approved by their mother. Educating the girls was acceptable. However, their presence in public spaces that were not strictly regulated by the state was not. For this reason, Şenler was always accompanied by her parents on the way to and from the school for girls where she studied. Yet, when her mother became ill and her father got a new job, there was no one to take her to school. Hence Şenler's educational life came to an end at the age of fourteen in order to 'protect the family honour'. Later, the theme of honour would play a key role in her invitation to women to adopt the Islamic attire.

Losing the opportunity to continue her studies influenced Şenler's life and intellectual development in complicated ways. First of all, the premature end of her educational life limited Şenler's ideological formation at public schools according to the secular nation-state ideology. Nevertheless, her persistent desire to learn and her love of books exposed her to new ideologies, including ultranationalism, for which she would feel a close affinity for some time. Spending most of her time at home, Şenler also started drawing and writing. At the age of fifteen, she began publishing articles and short stories in magazines. She also worked with a tailor and developed her sartorial abilities. These skills would prove very useful when Şenler got involved in politics and developed the republic's first major urban Islamic fashion style.

Şenler's active involvement in politics started with the Cyprus demonstrations around 1956. Arguably because she was of Turkish Cypriot descent and had deep sympathy for Turkish nationalism, Şenler was involved in the demonstrations supporting the partition of the island. With her body wrapped in a Turkish flag and a green crown with a map of Cyprus on her head, she would recite nationalistic poetry as thousands of people would shout the slogan 'Cyprus is Turkish and it will remain so!' (Tezcan 2007: 35). In these performances, Şenler started exploring the political potentials of fashion and embodiment. These events marked the start of her career as a public speaker, which would develop during her work for the Justice Party.

The Şenler family had initially supported the Democratic Party, which was founded in 1946 to oppose the ruling Republican People's Party established by Atatürk. Employing populist and Islamic discourses in combination with a more liberal economic perspective, the Democratic Party won the majority of the seats in the National Assembly in the 1950 and 1954 elections. In 1960, however, the Democratic government was overthrown in a coup d'état, on the grounds that the party had violated the founding principles of the Turkish Republic. The Şenler family then joined the Justice Party, which was established to replace the Democratic Party. This new party provided the ideal atmosphere for a young and ambitious woman like Şule Yüksel Şenler. She became the chairwoman of the youth branch and the literature and culture branch of the party and was active in fourteen other nongovernmental organizations (Tezcan 2007: 35). At the same time, Şenler launched her career as a columnist for *Kadın Gazetesi* (Women's Newspaper) established by the nationalist feminist İffet Halim Oruz. Contrary to the secular nationalist tendency of the publication, Şenler defended an Islamic strand of Turkish nationalism (Tezcan 2007: 38). However, she was not particularly interested in an Islamic lifestyle until she joined the Nurculuk movement.

Nurculuk is a modern Islamic movement founded by Kurdish Muslim scholar Bediüzzaman Said Nursi (1876 or 1877–1960) who aimed to create an Islamic revival movement at a time of social change in the late Ottoman and early republican period. The movement's appeal lay in the way it drew on Islamic symbols and concepts familiar to people in a way that made sense in the context of modernization and secularization. In many ways, the movement did not emerge as a reaction against modernization. On the contrary, it was very much embedded in the Ottoman and Turkish modernization processes.[2]

When he was in high school, Şule Yüksel Şenler's older brother Özer started attending the meetings of the movement, where high-ranking members would discuss themes from *Risale-i Nur*, the exegesis on the Quran written by Nursi. Once he became a disciple of Nursi, Özer Şenler initially wanted to leave home because the conflict between his newly adopted Islamic values and his family's lifestyle. However, Nursi advised him to stay with his family and try to convert them (Tezcan 2007: 40). These attempts caused serious conflict in the Şenler family. One day, when the family was entertaining guests and consuming alcohol, Özer Şenler spat on the dinner table. Another time, when Şule Yüksel Şenler and other members of the family attended a ball organized by the Justice Party, Özer Şenler slapped his sister in the face and called her a slut. Şenler resisted the pressure from her brother until he got ill with hepatitis. As his 'last wish', Özer Şenler asked Şule Yüksel to attend the Nurculuk meetings. A close witness of the Ottoman and Turkish modernization processes, Nursi had been very much aware of the importance of women's involvement as well as the transformation of the female body for social movements. He wrote a pamphlet called *Hanımlar Rehberi* (Guidebook for Women), where he provided interpretations of the Quranic verses on women and gender and gave advice to women on proper gendered behaviour and on Islamic attire. He also supported meetings organized by women. At one of these meetings, Şule Yüksel Şenler was introduced to Nurculuk and its version of an Islamic lifestyle.

THE BIRTH OF ŞULEBAŞ

At the first Nurculuk meeting Şule Yüksel attended, all of the fifteen attendees, except for one, were elderly women. Şenler went to the meeting wearing short sleeves and a small chiffon headscarf on her big bun. As she kept attending meetings dressed in a similar fashion, the other women started criticizing her dress and her long, manicured nails. Nevertheless, Şenler resisted the pressure and decided not to adopt the Islamic attire until she felt ready. First, she started wearing long sleeves and skirts. Then she added a headscarf covering half of her hair. Her mother and her sister as well as her friends whom she took to the Nurculuk meetings also started wearing the headscarf, often in similar styles. In order to protect other young women from the pressure that kept coming from the elderly women in the group, who wore white full headscarves and long white dresses, Şenler organized separate meetings for young women (Tezcan 2007: 46) and thus facilitated the involvement of younger generations in the movement.

Even after she started wearing the headscarf, it was still difficult for Şenler to tie it in a fashion that would cover all her hair. One reason for her hesitation was that covering all her hair would indicate that she was not wearing the headscarf to make a fashion statement but for religious purposes, which, in the context of Turkey, would also have important political connotations. Özlem Sandıkçı and Güliz Ger argue that 'as the polarization between so-called Islamists and secularists intensified during the mid-1980s, headcovering changed from a traditional and/or spiritual act into a political performance' (Sandıkçı and Ger 2007: 192). Although it is true that the tensions between secularism and political Islam intensified after the 1980s, headcovering already had significant political connotations in the 1960s. Women who wore the headscarf experienced various forms of violence and discrimination in the street and from the state. In fact, the first instance of a student being expelled from a university for wearing the headscarf was the case of Hatice Babacan in 1968. Women also used the performative power of the headscarf to make identity claims and political demands. In a particularly interesting case, a schoolteacher made her students attend a national parade wearing long dresses and headscarves (Tezcan 2007: 150), engaging in a parody of Kemalist identity politics. In this context, Şenler's everyday performances acquired a political dimension that could result in various forms of discrimination and violence.

Şenler was also worried that in the context of Istanbul in the 1960s, the headscarf was primarily associated with the Others of modernity. Thus, when she was experimenting with the full headscarf in front of the mirror in 1965, she became concerned that people would think she was not only a bigot or a radical Islamist but also an elderly woman, a maid or even a *besleme,* a lower-class girl of rural background who is accepted into a more affluent household as unpaid domestic help. When she visited her grandmother İkbal to question her about what she perceived as her family's uneasy relationship with Islam and to share her decision to adopt the headscarf, her grandmother made fun of Şenler, saying that people would think she was Kurdish. Turkey's nation-state building process has also been a process of colonialism against the Kurds. In the popular discourse of Turkish nationalist ideology, Kurds have been framed as the ultimate Others of modernity who need to be modernized by Turks. This discourse has not only served the legitimization of the oppressive policies targeting the Kurdish minority, but also, by positing them as the belated moderns in Turkey, it has helped Turks to overcome the belatedness they experience vis-à-vis the West. Thus, by associating the headscarf with Kurds, İkbal Aycan relegated it to the realm of the ultimate Other of modernity. Nevertheless, Şenler did start wearing the full headscarf and abandoned all her political and nongovernmental organization work to devote her life to the Nurculuk movement and its version of Islam. She also started writing for Islamic newspapers such as *Yeni İstiklal, Babıali'de Sabah* and *Bugün.* Many of her articles were about proper gendered behaviour for Muslim women, inviting the readers to wear the headscarf.

The fashion style developed by Şenler reflected the troubled relationship between modernity and Islamic attire in Turkey and her experiences as a young, urban Turkish woman who decided to follow what she perceived at the time as the Islamic dress code. Because of the Orientalist associations of Islamic attire, it is too often assumed to be completely outside of the realm of Western fashion or even the realm of fashion per se. However, many Islamic styles in Turkey and in Europe not only involve changing trends but are also in constant dialogue with Western (and non-Western) fashions (Sandıkçı and Ger 2005; Gökariksel and Secor 2009; Moors 2009; Tarlo 2010). This dialogue has been of utmost importance in the creation and sustenance of the Şulebaş style.

While developing an Islamic fashion style that would both differentiate her from lower-class, rural, elderly and/or Kurdish women who were perceived to wear the headscarf primarily as a traditional dress item, and also allow her to claim an identity as an urban, middle-class, young and modern woman, Şenler found her main source of inspiration in the scarf worn by Audrey Hepburn in *Roman Holiday* (Karaman 2011). In the movie, Hepburn wore a scarf tied at the back that covered her neck and half of her hair. Şenler developed the model so that it covered all the hair and used it as the basis for developing an urban Islamic fashion style. The power of Şulebaş lay in its regulation of the tensions of individuality and belonging in ways that addressed the concerns of urban Muslim Turkish women, particularly from a younger generation that had difficulties embodying a pious and modern Muslim Turkish female subjectivity. First of all, aesthetically, Şulebaş was considerably different from the headscarf styles that were considered more traditional in Turkey. It thus differentiated the wearers from the Others of Turkish modernity defined along the lines of class, ethnicity and age.[3] Moreover, whilst the more common styles signified class identity and social status rather than religiosity, Şulebaş enabled the performance of a more explicitly religious and political identity. The elaborate style of Şulebaş also implied that the wearer did not use the headscarf simply as a means of protection from adverse weather conditions, as was sometimes done with headscarves tied loosely under the chin, but was a woman who consciously followed a specific understanding of the Islamic dress code. Şulebaş can also be read as a reaction against the elderly women within the Nurculuk movement. By creating a new style instead of wearing white dresses and white headscarves connoting *ihram* clothing (garments worn during the hajj) that they wore, Şenler asserted her difference. This style was also useful for other young women who were interested in wearing the headscarf but had difficulty adjusting to it. Thus Şulebaş became central to the performance of a modern Islamic subjectivity and possibly attracted more young women to Nurculuk and the headscarf movement in general.

Şulebaş also allowed women who identified as modern pious Muslims to form a community and feel a sense of belonging at a time when the headscarf was highly stigmatized in urban Turkey. Thus, this particular Islamic style helped the wearers to overcome the sense of Otherness they experienced. However, some women who wore Şulebaş had mixed opinions about the style. Islamist activist Asiye Dilipak wore the Şulebaş headscarf as part of her uniform when she was attending a Quranic school for girls administered by Şenler. According to Dilipak, the style was not aesthetically suitable for teenagers. Moreover, Şulebaş no longer allowed the students to enjoy the protection of the discourse of tradition. Thus, it intensified the stigma around the headscarf and the abjection the wearers had to bear (Tezcan 2007: 156).

Another important aspect of Şulebaş was its versatility. First of all, even though the term referred to a specific style of headscarf, variations were possible. Thus, women used headscarves in different colours, patterns and material and tied them in different ways. Since the style emphasized the shape of the head, some women also used various materials, including bonnets, sponges, X-ray films and crowns made of wires and nylon stockings to construct their hair, often in ways that would make the headscarf look more shapely and their heads look bigger or taller.[4] The wide range of possibilities in colour, pattern, material and style also allowed different dress combinations albeit within certain limits. As would be the case with later *tesettür* styles, a major item of clothing often preferred by the wearers of Şulebaş was the overcoat. Most overcoats hide the contours of the body while their well-constructed structure around the shoulder area helps the body look fit and straight. The shape of the body is particularly important in the Turkish context, since the Turkish modernization process aimed to create not only secular but also fit and straight bodies (Akın 2004). Moreover, although similar items such as the *ferace* existed in Ottoman costume history, the overcoat was a new item associated with the dress reforms. Thus, the popularity of the overcoat in Şulebaş and later in tesettür can also be read in terms of the embodiment of modernity. Overcoats also hide the clothes underneath and provide a solution to the problem of matching clothes. This is particularly important for women who do not have an extensive wardrobe. Since urban Islamic fashion was still new and not very common in Turkey in the 1960s, many women tried to develop styles that would adhere to the Islamic codes yet did not look radically different from popular fashions in ways that would intensify the stigma they already experienced. Thus, the overcoats worn in the 1960s and 1970s often ended mid-calf as opposed to the full-length overcoats that became popular in the 1980s. As such, the overcoats both played a role in the negotiations of Islamic modernity in Turkey's urban spaces and were shaped through these negotiations (Figure 5.2).

Fig. 5.2 Şenler and her guests at her second wedding. Courtesy of Timaş Yayınları

While the overcoat was a popular element of urban Islamic fashion, it was neither seen as a requirement nor was it preferred by every woman. In the Şulebaş style, women would often wear the headscarf with clothes that reflected the prevailing Western fashions in order to embody a modern Muslim identity. This practice also allowed women to feel that they dressed fashionably while wearing the headscarf. Arguably, this was particularly important for women who adopted the Islamic attire not because they desired to do so but rather because of the pressure they experienced from their families. Although it is extremely problematic to claim that the Islamic dress forms are nothing but tools for women's oppression, and all women who follow them do it only because they are forced to do so, it is also difficult to argue that all women who adopt Islamic dress do it only because they desire to do so. Even in books by headscarf activists, many women narrate how they were forced by their relatives to wear the headscarf (e.g., Erol 2001; Atasoy 2004; Tezcan 2007). For these women, it was a particularly difficult experience to cover because the headscarf was stigmatized not only by other people but also by themselves. The possibility of following the popular fashions made it easier for them to adopt the headscarf. A particularly interesting example of these women is Emine Erdoğan, wife of the current prime minister, Recep Tayyip Erdoğan. Emine Erdoğan was a lower-middle-class teen girl from Istanbul who was forced by her older brothers to wear the headscarf. At some point, she even considered suicide (Özcan 2007: 41). Erdoğan decided to adopt Islamic attire only after she met Şenler in 1970 and realized that 'a Muslim woman can be modern, sophisticated and also wear the headscarf' (Özcan 2007: 42). Having overcome the stigma she attached to the headscarf, Erdoğan started making fashionable clothes and headscarves in the Şulebaş style for herself.

PROMOTING THE ŞULEBAŞ: ŞENLER'S PUBLIC PERFORMANCES

Just as the fashion style she developed enabled the performance of a modern Turkish Islamic female identity, the ways Şenler promoted her designs also reflected this particular subjectivity. Şenler used modern communication technologies and performance forms to convey her message to a wider audience and provide them with a role model as well as the necessary material for the embodiment of an Islamic modernity. Her work as a designer started when she worked as a columnist for the Islamist newspaper *Babıali'de Sabah* (Atasoy 2004: 93). In her columns, Şenler did not only encourage the readers to cover but also prepared and published dress and headscarf patterns. With this material, she educated the readers in the codes of fashionable Islamic dress and provided the tools to help them embody her version of Islamic modernity. Thus, a style that was embedded in the specific experiences of young, urban, middle-class women gained popularity among women of different backgrounds. To promote the style she developed, Şenler also published photographs of Western fashion models she took from fashion magazines, on which she painted her designs. With these realistic collages combining the body of the fashion model, the epitome of Western modernity, and Islamic fashions, Şenler provided the readers with the promise of a modern Muslim femininity (Figures 5.3 and 5.4). Her column was followed not only by women but also by men. A young man who admired the fashion model Şenler presented by the Turkish name Betül wrote her a letter saying that he would like to marry a girl like Betül and asked Şenler to be his matchmaker (Tezcan 2007: 89). As such, Şenler also played a role in defining the body of the desirable pious Muslim woman.

Fig. 5.3 A news story by Şenler about the popularity of 'Turkish peasant girl fashion' in England (*Seher Vakti* 1970)

Fig. 5.4 A collage featuring three Western fashion models wearing headscarves painted by Şenler (*Seher Vakti* 1970)

In 1967, Şenler was invited to Samsun to give a talk on women and Islam. Believing that women's voices should not be heard by marriageable men, Şenler wanted the event to be for a female audience only. The conference venue was packed with women, and there were hundreds of women and men waiting outside. The organizers wanted the talk to be broadcast outside with speakers. Şenler initially refused the request, but she ended up accepting when the organizers obtained authorization from a *mufti,* a Sunni Islamic scholar who is an interpreter of Islamic law. During the talk, Şenler presented her rather conservative opinions about women's place in Islam and encouraged the audience to follow the Islamic lifestyle and dress codes. The content of her talk affirmed the audience's religious beliefs while her body addressed its fantasies about Islamic modernity. Even though Şenler was strongly against feminism, and she articulated messages that contradicted any form of feminist politics, such as her support of domestic violence against women, her criticism of women's participation in the workforce and their demands for equal rights and equal wage (Şenler 1975), the very fact that she was giving those talks and her strong stage persona made Şenler a powerful female figure. In fact, according to Sibel Eraslan, Şenler and her political performances even played a role in transforming the distrustful and overprotective attitudes towards women in Islamic circles (Eraslan 2011: 8). The talk in Samsun was followed by dozens of similar events in Turkey. In these talks, Şenler was dressed in the modern Islamic fashions she developed. It is worth noting that she never had a sponsor, and she never sold her designs. In fact, at the time there were no companies that specialized in Islamic fashion, except for a few that produced scarves. Thus, Şenler had to cover all her wardrobe expenses from her limited income as a journalist. However, being aware that she was a role model for other Muslim women, she tried to dress as well as she could, and she emerged as Turkey's first Islamic style icon.

ISLAM, FASHION AND REGRET: ŞENLER'S DISCONTENT WITH ŞULEBAŞ

Today, remembering the heyday of Şulebaş, Şenler argues that at some point she took issue with the style she created. According to her, because of the versatility of the style, many women combined the headscarf with skirts above the ankle, sheer stockings and overcoats that revealed the contours of the body. Hence in the early 1970s, she wanted to stop wearing and promoting the Şulebaş style. However, according to Şenler, muftis gave her authorization to continue her work because they thought that Şulebaş and her performances were very influential in convincing women to cover, regardless of the style (Tezcan 2007: 158). Thus, even though she did not think it was proper Islamic dress, Şenler continued to dress in the Şulebaş style to help other women adopt some version of the Islamic dress (Figure 5.5).

Nevertheless, things changed after she joined the İsmailağa Community of the Nakshibandi order, a more conservative group than the Nurculuk movement. Upon joining the group, Şenler adopted the black veil. She also changed the social circles she participated in and largely ended her career as

Fig. 5.5 Three girls in Şulebaş in front of Istanbul University. Courtesy of Timaş Yayınları

a journalist and best-selling novelist. At the time, Şenler was married to her second husband, who was also a member of the community. Although she endured it for eleven years, domestic violence finally led to the breakdown of her second marriage, as it had her first. After the divorce, Şenler was ostracized by members of the community. Possibly because her husband's and the community's pressure on her had now ended, she abandoned the black veil and re-established contact with the governing moderate Islamist and neoliberal Justice and Development Party and the now very powerful Islamic bourgeoisie, with whom she shares a common history and whose respect she still enjoys. However, after she abandoned the black veil, Şenler did not go back to Şulebaş. Today at the rare public events in which she participates, Şenler often prefers a modest form of tesettür that is particularly popular among women of her age: black overcoats combined with large headscarves, often in light pastel colours, that cover all hair, ears and the neck. With this style that has become widely available thanks to the rise of political Islam in the country after the 1980s, Şenler dissociates herself from both the black veil and the Şulebaş while embodying a contemporary modern Muslim subjectivity now signified by tesettür.

CONCLUSION

The Şulebaş style emerged in a specific period of Turkish history. At a time when the impact of the Kemalist secular modernization programme was still strongly felt while the Islamic movements were gaining power not only in the provinces but also in the cities, Şulebaş reflected the concerns of a young, urban, middle-class, Muslim Turkish woman. Believing in an interpretation of the Islamic dress code requiring her to cover her head yet afraid to find herself among the Others of Turkish modernity, Şenler developed this style to embody what she imagined as a modern pious Muslim Turkish female subjectivity. As such, the Şulebaş style framed the headscarf not as a traditional item of clothing but as part of a modern Muslim identity.

The versatility of the Şulebaş was both a reason for its widespread popularity and a cause of concern for Şenler. Şulebaş allowed women to embody urban Islamic modernity primarily by combining the headscarf with the prevailing, mostly Western, fashions of the time. Since women dressed in modern Islamic fashions were still rather new to the urban landscape of Turkey, and their numbers were relatively low, many of them used the versatility of the style to seek a balance between modernity and Islam in order to avoid abjection and to satisfy their desires for consumption and fantasies of modernity. Hence, to Şenler's disappointment, many women combined the headscarf with garments such as short overcoats, skirts above the ankle and sheer stockings, which she believed violated the Islamic dress code.

The dynamics of Islamic fashion in Turkey changed as political Islam and urban Islamic movements gained strength in the country, particularly in the aftermath of the coup d'état of 1980. The increase in the number of women dressed in Islamic fashions and the birth of tesettür entailed a market for Islamic fashions (Navaro-Yashin 2002: 82) as well as an increase in the publications, television programmes and, most recently, Web sites targeted at women who cover. In this context, although the practice persists, Islamic fashion no longer depends on its citation or imitation of the prevailing Western fashions to be considered modern or urban. While its dialogue with various Western and non-Western styles continues, tesettür also has its own trends (Navaro-Yashin 2002; Gökariksel and Secor 2009; Sandıkçı and Ger 2010). As a result, Şulebaş as a specific style has gradually disappeared into the history of tesettür and largely been forgotten.

NOTES

1. Although *Şulebaş* was used by the media to refer only to the style of the headscarf, in this chapter I will use the term to refer to the urban Islamic style characterized by this specific headscarf style.
2. For a detailed study of the Nurculuk movement, see Mardin (1989).
3. Ali Çarkoğlu and Ersin Kalaycıoğlu note that in the same period, some middle-aged and elderly urban women who had recently turned religious used the turban in a similar manner to perform modern pious Muslim identities (Çarkoğlu and Kalaycıoğlu 2009: 99–100).
4. For a discussion on the shape of the head and the headscarf in the context of tesettür, see Sandıkçı and Ger (2005).

REFERENCES

Akın, Y. (2004), *Gürbüz ve Yavuz Evlatlar: Erken Cumhuriyet'te Beden Terbiyesi ve Spor,* Istanbul: İletiğim Yayınları.

Atasoy, G. (2004), *Nasıl Örtündüler?,* Istanbul: Nesil Yayınları.

Çarkoğlu, A., and E. Kalaycıoğlu (2009), *The Rising Tide of Conservatism in Turkey,* New York: Macmillan.

Doğaner, Y. (2009), 'The Law on Headdress and Regulations on Dressing in the Turkish Modernization', *bilig* 51: 33–54.

Eraslan, S. (2011), 'Şule Yüksel'in Yazı Masası', in Ş. Y. Şenler, ed., *Bize Ne Oldu: Kırk Yıl Önce, Kırk Yıl Sonra,* 6th ed., Istanbul: Timaş Yayınları.

Erol, E. (2001), *Sen Başımın Tacı: Bir Başörtüsü Günlüğü,* Istanbul: Birun Kültür Sanat Yayıncılık.

Gökariksel, B., and A. J. Secor (2009), 'New Transnational Geographies of Islamism, Capitalism and Subjectivity: The Veiling-fashion Industry in Turkey', *Area* 41, 1: 6–18.

Göle, N. (1997), 'Secularism and Islamism in Turkey: The Making of Elites and Counter-elites', *Middle East Journal* 51, 1: 46–58.

Jirousek, C. A. (1997), 'From "Traditional" to "Mass Fashion System" Dress among Men in a Turkish Village', *Clothing and Textiles Research Journal* 15: 203–15.

Karaman, F. (2011), 'Huzur Sokağı Çok Okunsun Diye Allah'a Dua Ettim', *Star Pazar* (7 August), <http://www.haberciniz.com/haberdetay/237335/> accessed 25 March 2013.

Mardin, Ş. (1989), *Religion and Social Change in Modern Turkey: The Case of Bediuzzaman Said Nursi,* Albany: State University of New York Press.

Moors, A. (2009), '"Islamic Fashion" in Europe: Religious Conviction, Aesthetic Style, and Creative Consumption', *Encounters* 1, 1: 175–201.

Navaro-Yashin, Y. (2002), *Faces of the State: Secularism and Public Life in Turkey,* Princeton, NJ: Princeton University Press.

Norton, J. (1997), 'Faith and Fashion in Turkey', in N. Lindisfarne-Tapper and B. Ingham, eds., *Languages of Dress in the Middle East,* Surrey: Curzon Press.

Özcan, A. (2007), *Emine Erdoğan: İktidara Taşıyan Kadın,* Istanbul: Birharf Yayınları.

Sandıkçı, Ö., and G. Ger (2005), 'Aesthetics, Ethics and Politics of the Turkish Headscarf', in S. Kuechler and D. Miller, eds., *Clothing as Material Culture,* Oxford: Berg.

Sandıkçı, Ö., and G. Ger (2007), 'Constructing and Representing the Islamic Consumer in Turkey', *Fashion Theory* 11, 2/3: 189–210.

Sandıkçı, Ö., and G. Ger (2010), 'Veiling in Style: How Does a Stigmatized Practice Become Fashionable?', *Journal of Consumer Research* 37, 1: 15–36.

Şenler, Ş. Y. (1975), *Islam'da ve Günümüzde Kadın,* Istanbul: Nur Yayınları.

Sirman, N. (2004), 'Kinship, Politics and Love: Honor in Post-colonial Contexts—the Case of Turkey', in S. Mojab and N. Abdo, eds., *Violence in the Name of Honor: Theoretical and Political Challenges,* Istanbul: Istanbul Bilgi University Press.

Tarlo, E. (2010), *Visibly Muslim: Fashion, Politics, Faith,* Oxford: Berg.

Tezcan, D. (2007), *Bir Çığır Öyküsü: Şule Yüksel Şenler,* Istanbul: Timaş Yayınları.

White, J. B. (2005), 'The Paradox of the New Islamic Woman in Turkey', in I. M. Okkenhaug and I. Flaskerud, eds., *Gender, Religion and Change in the Middle East: Two Hundred Years of History,* Oxford: Berg.

Zorlutuna, H. N. (2009), *Bir Devrin Romanı,* 3rd ed., Istanbul: Timaş Yayınları.

The Genealogy of the Turkish *Pardösü* in the Netherlands

R. Arzu Ünal

This chapter focusses on a single item of clothing, the overcoat, and explores what it can tell us about Turkish migrant experiences in the Netherlands. It analyses changing styles of wearing overcoats and overcoat fashions amongst migrant women originally from Turkey and explores what overcoat wearing means to different categories of women at different historical moments and in particular locations. It focusses on how the intersection between the mobility of people and objects within Turkey and the Netherlands enables particular styles and stories of dress. It is, in particular, concerned with transformations in the urban-rural divide and how moving in and out of overcoats and their particular styles expresses the different ways women live Islam in the Netherlands. A focus on the overcoat takes us beyond the dualistic constraints of the categories of covered and uncovered through which Muslim women are so often discussed. A genealogy of the overcoat reveals accounts of continuous engagements with piety and femininity through women's social-spatial mobility in a transnational field.

The research is based on ethnographic fieldwork conducted between 2007 and 2010 in several Dutch cities and in Istanbul with a variety of people engaged with the Turkish Dutch *tesettür*[1] scene, including women who wear religiously recognizable styles of clothing as well as designers, producers and sellers of Islamic dress. This story of the Turkish overcoat is assembled from fragments of wardrobe research and in-depth interviews on tesettür clothing with fifty-six women in the Netherlands. It sketches a genealogy of wearing overcoats from the first journeys of Anatolian women from small villages to the Netherlands in the 1970s through to the large collections of overcoats found in the contemporary wardrobes of Turkish Dutch women. It offers a reading of Muslim women's clothing beyond the practice of headscarf-wearing and addresses an ideological gap between notions of being veiled or unveiled.

THE GUESTWORKER'S OVERCOAT

Three-quarter-length overcoats were the most commonly worn outdoor attire mentioned in the accounts of migrant women coming to the Netherlands in the late 1970s. A few Turkish women came alone as workers; most of them were the wives of guest workers and came as temporary residents. The first generation of migrant women described that particular style of overcoat as the first modern and *şehirli* (urban) item of outdoor clothing they had ever worn. These were relatively close-fitting overcoats, intended to be worn in winter and produced by the mainstream textile industry. Women mostly referred to them as *manto* or *pardösü* (both French names) and used these terms interchangeably in their accounts.[2] Wearing such an overcoat required a transformation of bodily gestures and movements. Closely fitting three-quarter-length overcoats compelled the body to move slower and in a more elegant way. Such a coat produced certain effects both in their wearers and in their viewers, demonstrating different understandings of femininity and modesty in harmony with the stronger division between home and outside experienced in cities where women were no longer labouring in the fields.

Women described their new posture in overcoats as well-mannered and more *hanım hanımcık* (ladylike). This style of dress would not allow women to sit cross-legged on the ground but rather encouraged them to sit on chairs as a sign of having mastered a more civilized and modern way of life. Other urban accessories completed the more elegant style and feminine posture of the body in *manto:* a small and modern headscarf, a handbag and a pair of shoes instead of slippers. Not all women welcomed this change in posture and garments. In some accounts, learning these new forms of feminine visibility was portrayed as an embarrassing experience, which took some time to get used to and feel comfortable with.

'I NEVER WORE MODERN GARMENTS IN MY VILLAGE'

Most first-generation migrant women only had a few sets of clothing in their suitcases when they set out for the Netherlands. Stories of their engagement with the overcoat and its shifting styles are shaped by the specific backgrounds of the women concerned and their patterns of mobility. Some women had emigrated directly from small Anatolian villages; others had already experienced work and life in big cities in Turkey. This rural-urban divide was a major factor in shaping their experiences.

The styles of outerwear they had worn in their villages of origin varied depending on understandings of body covering, modesty and piety as well as the climate of their home region. Mükerrem and Pelda—both in their late sixties now—joined their husbands in the Netherlands in the late 1970s, together with their children. In their sartorial biographies, changes in clothing style were not only strongly linked to the migration process but also intersected with different regional styles, aesthetics and notions of comfort in body covering.

The black *çarşaf* was commonly worn as outdoor dress in the village where Pelda spent her early life, near the city of Elazığ in eastern Anatolia. The çarşaf is a form of outer covering that loosely covers the whole body. It is a combination of a long and loose skirt with an elasticized waist and a wide cape, which is attached to the skirt. Pelda came out of her çarşaf on her way to the Netherlands. At the airport in Istanbul, she took it off and put it in a plastic bag. The next stop on her way to Amsterdam was Frankfurt. When she arrived at the passport control desk in Frankfurt, she was wearing an *entari* (a long, loose-fitting dress) combined with a loose, white cotton scarf and her new leather shoes. She emphasized that she did not have a proper purse because she had never needed one before. She had a small hidden pocket inside her clothes, attached with a cord and safety pin. Her passport was in her husband's pocket. In Frankfurt, one of her relatives bought her a red leather handbag. She kept that bag for almost four decades. It was this outdoor accessory that completed her new elegant posture and look.

Pelda bought her first overcoat from the market in the Netherlands. It was a green, close-fitting, three-quarter-length overcoat. It was the first and last overcoat she bought in the Netherlands. It felt too tight and short for outdoor clothing, especially since she was accustomed to wearing a çarşaf. She felt embarrassed wearing it. For a long time, she continued to wear a çarşaf when visiting her village in Turkey during summer holidays. It took several years before she felt able to wear her outdoor overcoat in the village. The overcoat worn over skirts or trousers and accompanied by shoes and handbags gradually transformed the image of the provincial migrant woman into that of an urban subject. Although worn with headscarves, such styles were not yet labelled as Islamic. To the women who favoured them they were perceived principally as modern garments.

Mükerrem also bought her first overcoat after she came to the Netherlands in the late 1970s. *Şalvar* (baggy trousers) was the most commonly worn garment in her village in the region of Yozgat (a city in central Anatolia), worn with a blouse and vest, which concealed the contours of the upper part of the body. But Mükerrem did not come to the Netherlands in her şalvar. Although she still wears a şalvar when she does the housework, on the day she arrived in the Netherlands, she was wearing a long, loose skirt over loose cotton trousers to cover her legs. Her village clothes had been replaced by urban garments, yet she was trying to stick to her existing understandings of body covering and femininity by combining her new garments in such a way that they still covered her body properly.[3] In the Netherlands, she continued to wear a skirt or long dress over her new Dutch trousers, beneath the new overcoat. As she put it,

'I never wore modern clothes in my village. I never had an overcoat in Turkey. I came here...then, I never took off my pardösü.'

In Kadriye's wardrobe, the overcoat has a longer history compared to other senior women in this research. When she came to the Netherlands, she already had modern urban outfits. As she emphasized, she never really dressed like the other women in her village because she had gone to school and married a young man from a pious family in the city. As one of the few girls attending school, she used to wear a hat as part of her school uniform. She recalls feeling how, through her hat, she could empathize with the girls who wore headscarves in the village. As a little girl, she had tried to hide her hair under the hat as if she were wearing a headscarf.

When she came to the Netherlands in 1978, she had already been wearing an overcoat for years. Her father-in-law had bought her her first overcoat in 1961 as a present. She had married at the age of seventeen and then left her village in the region of Nevşehir for Ankara, the capital of Turkey. There she cultivated positive feelings towards the overcoat. Her description of her arrival in the Netherlands illustrates her feelings of comfort and confidence as a modern şehirli woman in tesettür.

> I did not come to the Netherlands in village dress...My eldest son bought a very nice skirt from *Karamürsel Mağazası* (a popular department store of the period in Turkey) on Mother's Day. I bought a green blouse from a boutique. That matched with the skirt. I had an overcoat and a matching scarf with that. I did not come from the village. I came from Ankara. My outfit was proper.

As the narratives of these women suggest, the adoption of the overcoat in the 1970s both signalled and enabled social and spatial mobility for the first generation of migrant women arriving from Turkey. While not many of them found employment, most did eventually have interactions with Dutch public institutions and encountered members of the Dutch public. However, adopting the overcoat was not restricted to women who migrated to Europe. Overcoats also fashioned an urban look for women who left Anatolian villages for the Turkish cities, playing an important role in the formation of new forms of visibility for women in Turkish public space.

THE OVERCOAT TURNS 'ISLAMIC'

In the 1980s and 1990s, full-length and loose-fitting overcoats combined with large and loosely covering headscarves in plain colours were becoming more and more visible in Turkey and in the Turkish Dutch tesettür scene. The cultural politics of emerging civic religious organizations and movements played a significant role in promoting a particular style of outdoor clothing and knowledge about it among young educated urban women. Students at Quran courses and Imam Hatip schools[4] of the period started to distinguish between habitual forms of covered dress and consciously learned forms of body covering they considered Islamic. Education played a significant role here in transforming women into pious Muslims. Young girls began to learn about proper and *bilinçli* (conscious) forms of tesettür based on religious texts and the interpretations of preachers. New styles, perceived as urban and conscious forms of 'tesettür' marked out differences between women in public spaces.

The *robadan* overcoat was one of these early expressions of urban Islam in women's clothing. It produced the figure of the urban educated Muslim woman as completely covered. It was different from existing long overcoats as it had a seam placed just below the shoulder level, thereby creating a loose shape that hides the contours of the body from top to toe. This style of over "coat" combined with the wearing of a dark-coloured plain scarf on a "daily basis" produced a kind of archetypal uniform style (Sandıkçı and Ger 2010).

In Turkey, such new long and loose forms of pardösü distanced their wearers not only from more provincial styles but also from earlier urban styles of outdoor garments. For instance, the black çarşaf, an equally covering outdoor garment, came at that time to be seen either as a more radical Islamic style or as outdated rural attire. The narratives of women speaking about this period focus on 'the heightened visibility' (Tarlo 2010) of wearing tesettür in public spaces and underline the importance of commitment and strength that was nourished by faith and religious education. Besides shifting understandings of body covering from a habitual to a consciously learned practice, these modest and pious styles differentiated pious women from those who followed the many fashionable styles of outer garment developing at that period. In circles of committed Muslims, the robadan overcoats replaced the closer-fitting, three-quarter overcoats of the 1970s. The former style of overcoat, which had once seemed so modern, gradually became perceived as rural and was identified with poverty.

The 1980s were years of frequent family reunions for Turkish guest workers in the Netherlands. This increasing mobility was not a one-way process. Girls were sent back to Turkey to pursue alternative education in Quran schools or Imam Hatip schools. Returning to Turkey enabled young Turkish Dutch girls to better master the Turkish language, to maintain their ties with the homeland and to receive an Islamic education in addition to their secular one. They also learned about new Islamic fashions that were emerging in Turkey. On their return to the Netherlands, they introduced new styles of outdoor tesettür clothing. They also played an active role in religious organizations and in propagating modern yet correct tesettür fashions, spreading their knowledge about Islamic clothing in the Netherlands. As learned pious women of Imam Hatip and Quran schools, young *tesettürlü* women linked their own sartorial preferences to religious texts and teachings. They disseminated knowledge about tesettür and introduced ideal styles within Turkish religious circles.

Ela Nur, for example, came to the Netherlands in 1980 when she was seven years old. Her father was an imam, employed by the Turkish state in the late 1970s. Ela Nur followed him, studied theology in the Netherlands and now teaches Islam at a college. In 1987, she left the Netherlands to study at an Imam Hatip school for three years. She returned with a change in her style of dress. She had started wearing a headscarf and pardösü, but her first pardösü was chic and elegant by comparison to the robadan style. It revealed both her Islamic education and her understanding of tesettür fashion, as well as her personal taste. Imam Hatip graduates did not only propagate new styles of tesettür and knowledge about them but also new aesthetic preferences and tastes linked to different understandings of femininity and body posture.

> I wore the pardösü...but it was a cool one, I never wore something wide, like the robadan pardösü. I returned to the Netherlands with an overcoat on. I had an İmam Hatip background; people should see what a girl educated in İmam Hatip School dressed like...That was why I wore it. The overcoat gave a different feel to the way you walked and sat, but you needed to be able to carry it off.

Dressing plays a constitutive role among people in diaspora, as it transforms not only their sense of self but also their relationship with others (Tarlo 2007; Moors 2009). Styling does more than signify degrees of religious practice and modernity; it is also lived as an expression of personality and inner self. Young women try to find ways of expressing their individual identity through dress. At the same time, the personal styling and individual search for religious meanings in dress becomes a source of inspiration and motivation for others.

Ela Nur and her elder sister were aware of their responsibility as role models, both as daughters of a well-known imam and as educated tesettürlü women originally from Turkey. They introduced a new aesthetic of tesettür into the Turkish Dutch tesettür scene. Ela Nur's narration powerfully articulates the role of femininity in the formation of the modern pious female subject:

> As the daughters of an imam, we had to be careful all the time...what would others say about our father if we misbehaved? My sister had a beautiful outfit. Everything was matched perfectly. Her style was very different from what people were used to here...she wore a sugar pink overcoat, a matching scarf and pinkish shoes. From head to toe, everything matched. Girls admired her style and so they covered. They went into tesettür not because they admired her understanding of Islam but because of her style.

Producing an elegant and attractive style also involved blending personal understandings of tesettür and taste by matching different garments together to create harmonious outfits. Such stylish combinations of long, loose over-coats with large scarves (90 by 90 cm) covering the shoulders and chest had appeared in major Turkish cities in the 1980s and diversified into an expanding market in the 1990s (White 1999; Kılıçbay and Binark 2002; Navaro-Yashin 2002; Sandıkçı and Ger 2007, 2010; Gökarıksel and Secor 2009). Similarly, Turkish Dutch tesettür wearers began to carve out alternative outdoor tesettür styles to escape being perceived as uniform and fundamentalist. They looked for ways to articulate individual taste within the religious norms and aesthet-ics of tesettür. In this context, robadan pardösü came to be labelled either as rural or a sign of urban poverty, while it also gained heightened visibility as a sign of radicalization and political Islam. As more and more fashionable and stylish overcoats appeared on the market, the robadan overcoat more or less disappeared from the urban tesettür scene (Figure 6.1).

Some women, however, retained their old overcoats for when they visited relatives in Turkish villages over the summer, hiding their preferences for new fashions which would have emphasized emerging differences and inequalities

Fig. 6.1 Women in more form-fitting overcoats/headscarves shopping at a community event

between those remaining in Turkey and those in the Netherlands. Sevda is a 45-year-old tesettürlü woman from Erzurum. When she was in her early twenties, she had one pardösü which she only wore when she went back to her village of origin:

> In the early years of my marriage, I had a pardösü. I put it on when we went to visit his [my husband's] relatives in Turkey. They live in a small village...My appearance would not have been proper; my dresses were showy and were made of thin material. My husband's family wanted me to wear the pardösü. We bought a loose, lilac-coloured stoned-silk overcoat from his acquaintances...After we returned here [the Netherlands], I told my husband, 'You may ask anything of me but don't ask me to wear this.' And he said, 'I would not force you to. Dress as you wish.'

THE *KOT* (DENIM) PARDÖSÜ

The denim overcoat was one of the first alternative styles that combined different aesthetics and knowledge of tesettür clothing with mainstream trends and fashions. Compared to other styles of migrant outdoor tesettür in the

Fig. 6.2 Denim overcoat, made of thin fabric for summer

Netherlands, the denim pardösü was rather unique in the way it integrated the global fabric of denim with tesettür aesthetics and concerns. Both in secular and religious understandings of fashionable dress, being modern requires engagement with the mainstream clothing industry.

Denim had been absent from certain Turkish Muslim milieus for a long time as wearing denim had suggested a particular lifestyle and understanding of religion that was linked to leftist movements in the 1970s (Karabıyık Barbarosoğlu 2006). Denim fabric worked to convert the old-fashioned, austere and fundamentalist image of the Muslim woman in her full-length overcoats into a moderate, urban, trendy and modern figure. This particular design of overcoat brought diverse ideas of femininity, beauty, fashion, modernity and modesty together. *Kot pardösü* (the denim overcoat) and other denim clothes, especially long denim skirts, came to occupy a unique place in the wardrobes of some contemporary tesettür wearers (Figures 6.2 and 6.3).

In their work on denim, Miller and Woodward (2007, 2011) discuss the ubiquitous character of denim fabric as a global phenomenon. Denim is the

Fig. 6.3 Denim overcoat

single most common form of everyday fabric around the world. The growing tesettür market embraced the ease and pleasant feel of this particular globally worn fabric and combined it with particular understandings of femininity and piety. Denim garments were styled and patterned with motifs and embroidery that fitted Turkish tesettür taste. The ubiquitous nature of denim fabric allows tesettürlü women not only to solve the dilemma of everyday clothing but also to reduce the heightened visibility of the full-length Islamic overcoat. Through denim, a marginal and radical style often perceived as *irticacı* (fundamentalist) loses some of its negative connotations through the association with this global fabric.

CONTEMPORARY OVERCOAT TRENDS

In the course of the past decade, the contemporary tesettür scene has seen two distinct trends, both of which could be considered retro. On the one hand, there has been the development from full-length increasingly fashionable styles of tesettür to three-quarter-length, tighter overcoats (now called *kap*). On the other hand, a contrasting development has been the return to full-length, loose outer garments, somewhat similar to those of the 1980s, yet displaying a more cosmopolitan Islamic style, for which the Arabic term *jilbab* and Ottoman term *ferace* are used.

The three-quarter-length, close-fitting kap style is reminiscent of a 1960s and 1970s winter coat in terms of form and shape. However, these new kaps are made from a much wider variety of fabrics, variable according to different seasons and occasions. They are largely adapted to mainstream fashion trends; moreover, they are mainly produced by well-known tesettür companies and marketed with other items and accessories of tesettür clothing such as headscarves, purses, skirts and tunics. Like the robadan overcoat, the name of this new style originated from its tailoring. The waist part of the overcoat is tightly fitted with additional stitches along the front of the chest and back. These extra stitches highlight the slimness of the waist.

Kaps are worn together with fashionable, trendy accessories. Footwear ranges from high-heeled shoes and knee-high leather boots to Converse All Star sneakers and sandals. Original as well as imitation bags, showy watches and big sunglasses from well-known luxury brands, worn with fashionably patterned silk scarves from seasonal collections, stylishly tied around the neck with a swinging short edge at the back, complete the look of the fashionable kap wearer. Young Muslim women in the Netherlands call this new trend the Istanbul style. It is urban, modern, classy and hip. Young tesettürlü Dutch Turkish women claim that the introduction of kaps to tesettür clothing led to two different trends. On one hand, some young women who wore full-length overcoats shifted to this less-covered style, while, on the other hand, some who had previously found it difficult to wear a pardösü at all now felt able to do so.

Dicle is a shop assistant in a Turkish clothing store who came to the Netherlands in 2004. She grew up in a very small village in central Anatolia and later moved to a small town. She is twenty-six years old and also an Imam Hatip graduate. Her taste and preferences in clothing changed as she moved and made new friends in the Netherlands. Her style continues to change, and she has become a trendsetter and source of inspiration for tesettürlü girls and customers in her neighbourhood. Kaps are new items in Dicle's wardrobe. Through the kap she is gradually adopting the practice of outdoor tesettür. Although she thinks that wearing an outer garment is an important element of tesettür, she had not previously been able to find a suitable style of overcoat to wear. However, the new kap highlights the dynamic figure of the body and can easily be adapted to mainstream fashion trends. Most of the young women who wear it now associate former tesettür overcoats with elderly women. Asked if she ever wore a pardösü, she replied:

> No, I never wore pardösü. I sell them here and I have tried them on a few times. It is not suitable for my age...But I want to wear proper tesettür. I do not want to pretend to be tesettürlü; I actually want to be so. Tesettür is not only about putting on a headscarf. I want to pay more attention to my appearance than that. I bought this recently from Istanbul [she points out an Armine kap hanging behind us]...It is from Armine. [It had an asymmetrical cut at the front, with a thin leather belt] [Figure 6.4]...I wear it a hot day...I feel naked if I go out without it. I do not feel comfortable. Besides, I like the style.

Some fashionable kaps can hardly be considered as covering outer garments owing to the way they highlight the figure. Some are very eye-catching, especially when worn with accessories and ornaments. Wearing such new styles can sometimes lead to contestations between young women, their parents and *hocas* (religious teachers). The question of which style of outer tesettür garment to choose also becomes more pressing with the proliferation of new styles.

Zeynep is a 25-year-old college-educated woman from Amsterdam. She decided to put on the headscarf five years ago. Her tesettür decision was not unexpected, yet it was difficult for her parents to accept. Her story reflects how wearing kap mediates questions of style and piety in new ways. The kap allows her to practise outdoor tesettür; furthermore, it rescues her tesettür from her parents' criticism, as they had not wanted her to wear a full-length pardösü. Zeynep does not think that her current style reflects her understanding of tesettür entirely. She has tried to find a middle way in order to diminish the tension caused by her decision to cover. She sees her

Fig. 6.4 Dicle's kap in the Armine catalogue. Courtesy of Armine.

current style as transitional, with the kap enabling her to practise outdoor tesettür. With a rather loose kap and a shawl covering her shoulders and chest, she fashions a style that her parents do not find too radically religious or old-fashioned. As Dicle emphasizes, the kap style is modern and does not evoke the same meanings as the older tesettür pardösü (Figure 6.5). Zeynep explains:

> When I first covered, I wanted to wear a long pardösü so much. Yet my mother did not let me. 'Well, you can cover but you cannot wear the pardösü' she told me...For her that style is *sofu* [puritan, fanatical]...but what I wear now is not my ideal style. I envisage a particular look with a pardösü and a big shawl. It will be my real statement in the future *inşallah*...It does not have to be all black. I can make it individual through the colours I choose.

Fig. 6.5   A form-fitting long black overcoat

Young Turkish Dutch tesettürlü women strive to fashion distinct styles of outdoor attire, even in cases where they would rather wear long overcoats. Personal preferences are not always in line with mainstream fashion trends. As Göle (2002) points out, the search for authenticity can for some individuals create a critical distance from the assimilative strategies and potentially homogenizing practices of modernity. Different understandings of tesettür are often marked by personal styling. Knowledge about combining certain colours and kinds of fabric and a thorough understanding of the aesthetic principles of different publics informs choices of outdoor tesettür and constructs an ideal tesettür for pious young women. Contemporary styles reflect not only new ideas of femininity and piety but also taste, social status and distinction (Bourdieu 1984). In this sense, sartorial practices become a 'performance of difference' (Göle 2002: 185). Searching for an individual, innovative look in a larger field of sensorial interaction, women manage the heightened visibility that wearing certain types of garments produces (Tarlo 2010: 11).

NEW LOOSE-FITTING AND LONG OVERCOATS: FROM GRANDMA'S PARDÖSÜ TO A COSMOPOLITAN AESTHETIC

Old-fashioned, loose-fitting, full-length and dark-coloured overcoats are fast disappearing. Yet a few young women purposely adopt this elderly, unfashionable look. In doing so, they make a personal statement about their constant attention to working on the inner self and their high levels of devotion. Both the producers of such styles and young wearers label this style the 'grandma's overcoat'.

Nermin is a former çarşaf wearer. She is thirty-five years old and works as a hoca in a particular religious community. She teaches the Quran and several different courses on Islam and organizes *sohbet* (religious meetings) amongst women. Her outdoor tesettür has been black and very simple since she first put on a çarşaf in the 1990s. Her present style consists of a black, loose-fitting, long overcoat and a large, black headscarf that covers her shoulders and chest. Her conversation with the shop assistant in a tesettür store illustrates how difficult it is to choose this style:

> You go into a store and you describe what you want and they say it is *babaanne* [the grandma's] style. Eventually, you have to say yes! They frankly say we do not sell babaanne fashion. They call it grandma's overcoat when you ask for a loose-fitting overcoat.

There is no doubt that many elderly women still prefer this particular style of overcoat, which is comfortable and concealing. Yet for younger women, this style usually denotes a different understanding of tesettür. As its name illustrates, it shows a person's willingness to distance herself from mainstream ideals of beauty. By choosing this elderly style, she cultivates a particular understanding of modesty. Thus, the choice of the 'grandma's' overcoat on the part of a young woman designates a devoted and modest self, especially in the current era with its emphasis on youth fashion.

While some young women adopt the grandma's overcoat as a personal tesettür style, other young Turkish Dutch women try to combine a religious understanding of bodily covering with cosmopolitan aesthetics. In the final section, I will illustrate how women bring together diverse elements of outer garment fashions from various localities in a transnational field and how they combine them innovatively according to their understanding of Islam and in relation to different publics in the Netherlands. New cosmopolitan styles an aesthetics of displacement are a means for Muslim women to carve out their visibility in the Dutch public sphere. Rüzgar is a 22-year-old university student who works as a tour guide at the natural history museum. She was born in the Netherlands. She is one of the few young women who have adopted loose long outer garments. She makes a very sharp distinction between indoor and outdoor clothing. Rüzgar takes off her pardösü indoors when there are only women present. She fashions her outdoor appearance in an Islamically inspired and informed way. She chooses the simplest overcoat and the plainest headscarf possible. She thinks of ornaments (pockets, buttons, patterns, etc.) as additional elements that attract the wrong type of attention. Rüzgar prefers her outdoor clothes to be plain and modest to represent her understanding of tesettür, which is based on notions of piety and modesty. However, at the museum where she works, she favours what she considers a more professional look. Recently she has been wearing long, loose dresses (*ferace*), which she buys from a Moroccan store. To make these look more professional, she combines them with formal jackets. This is a relatively new indoor trend among young Dutch Turkish women who work with members of the public. It represents an accommodation to circumstance which involves managing the heightened visibility of Islamic garments through an engagement with fashion and aesthetics in contexts where Muslims are faced with questions about the legitimacy of their presence (Moors 2009; Tarlo 2010) (Figures 6.6 and 6.7).

Fig. 6.6 A 'grandma's overcoat' from Rüzgar's wardrobe

Fig. 6.7 Rüzgar's combination for work: ferace and jacket

A young Turkish Dutch tesettür wearer who adopts Egyptian-, Gulf- or Moroccan-inspired styles distances her individual style from mainstream tesettür fashion trends amongst the Turkish community in the Netherlands. This style communicates well with a larger diverse public in Dutch public spaces. Fashioning a new style with diverse trends and aesthetics denotes the multiple belongings of young tesettürlü women in the Netherlands and beyond.

Yusra is another young woman who synthesizes different aesthetics and diverse styles, through which she communicates with a wider public. Her understanding of bodily covering and outdoor tesettür style is similar to that of Nermin and Rüzgar. She is studying Islam and spiritual guidance at university and actively works for a particular Turkish religious community. She was born in the Netherlands and is the only woman in her family to wear tesettür, which she adopted eight years ago when she was fourteen years old. Yusra decided to add an outer garment to her tesettür during a trip to Egypt, and she returned to the Netherlands in what she calls a *jilbab*. This is the Arabic word that refers to a woman's outer garment in the Quran. Her outer garment is a long, black, loose overcoat made from thin, silky fabric. It is light, airy and comfortable to wear both outside and indoors. This particular style is relatively new in the Turkish tesettür scene both in the Netherlands and in Turkey. However, it is a style that is becoming increasingly popular among young women. In the tesettür market of Turkey, this new style of outer garment is called a *ferace*.

The term *ferace* recalls Ottoman women's outdoor clothing, even if the actual designs are varied and different from other Ottoman styles. The label *ferace* fits well with the promotion of an Ottoman revival in Turkey and beyond (Walton 2010). New outdoor feraces are generally black in colour and have ornaments around the sleeves. They are made from a thin and shiny fabric called 'Medina silk'. They are cheaper than fashionable, long pardösüs (the price of a fashionable overcoat is around €100 whereas that of a ferace is about €35). Feraces have become an alternative for tesettürlü women like Yusra who like neither the fashionable, close-fitting pardösü nor the old-fashioned, long and loose pardösü which has become known as the grandma's overcoat. Speaking of her ferace, Yusra comments:

> I feel free in this, I feel so comfortable. I do not care about my body. I feel free to mix among men...This is a jilbab. You can find these in Moroccan stores. This one is from Egypt.

Three years after we first met, Yusra still wears the ferace. She has different ones from Syria, Jerusalem and Istanbul. Although they are made from very thin fabric, she wears them during the winter with layers underneath. Meanwhile, both in Turkey and in the Netherlands, the number of ferace wearers is increasing. Furthermore, new styles of ferace have already become tight and fashionably ornamented as well as expensive. To some extent, feraces solve the dilemma of the distinction between indoor and outdoor tesettür clothes, blurring the boundaries between the two and highlighting changes in practices of both.

CONCLUSION

This chapter has aimed to address the complex set of dynamics that play a significant role in the changing meanings, styles and practices of the overcoat among Turkish Dutch tesettürlü women. Initially the guest worker's overcoat as a status symbol indicated its wearer's spatial and social mobility, from small villages to urban areas and finally to Europe. The urban outdoor garments of provincial women concealed the stigmas of rural poverty an ethnic background as women entered modern public spaces. Later in the 1980s, wearing an overcoat was transformed into a religiously inspired and informed practice. The accounts of the women that I have presented illustrate vividly how the fashionable, loose and long overcoat style worn in the 1990s became the grandma's style, even before the promoters of the style became grandmothers themselves.

The mobility of both garments and individuals has transformed the practice of wearing overcoats in tesettür clothing. The proliferation and dissemination of styles enables actors to develop their unique presence through diverse aesthetics addressed to different publics. Connections between actors and styles across countries constitute new tesettür preferences, aesthetics and personal styles in a cosmopolitan transnational field.

NOTES

I am grateful to Gül Özyeğin, Ferhunde Özbay, Jeremy Walton and R. Gökhan Koçer for their helpful comments and suggestions on earlier drafts of this chapter. I would especially like to thank Annelies Moors for her insights, constructive comments and support. This publication is the result of research (partially) funded by the Cultural Dynamics Programme of the Netherlands Organisation for Scientific Research.

1. In the Turkish context, *tesettür* is an umbrella term that includes various styles of recognizably Islamic clothing among women.
2. Overcoat producers have promoted the label of *pardösü* for covered and religiously inspired styles of overcoats since the 1980s. Contemporary *tesettür* companies continue to release fashionable, long overcoat collections with the label pardösü.
3. In some wardrobes, *şalvar* and loose trousers made of colourful, flower-patterned cotton fabric were replaced by the flared trousers that were popular in those days. They were often worn in combination with the long dresses or short skirts of the period.
4. Imam Hatip schools are Turkish state schools originally established for the education of mosque functionaries that function as secondary schools. Their popularity declined when in 1999 Imam Hatip graduates were no longer granted access to all faculties of Turkish universities but only to faculties of divinity.

REFERENCES

Bourdieu, P. (1984), *Distinction: A Social Critique of the Judgment of Taste,* Cambridge: Cambridge University Press.

Gökarıksel, B., and A.J.A. Secor (2009), 'New Transnational Geographies of Islamism, Capitalism and Subjectivity: The Veiling-fashion Industry in Turkey', *Area* 41, 1: 6–18.

Göle, N. (2002), 'Islam in Public: New Visibilities and New Imaginaries', *Public Culture* 14, 1: 173–90.

Karabıyık Barbarosoğlu, F. (2006), *Şov ve Mahrem,* Istanbul: Timaş Yayınları.

Kılıçbay, B., and M. Binark (2002), 'Consumer Culture, Islam and the Politics of Lifestyle: Fashion for Veiling in Contemporary Turkey', *European Journal of Communication* 17, 4: 495–511.

Miller, D., and S. Woodward (2007), 'Manifesto for a Study of Denim', *Social Anthropology* 15, 3: 335–51.

Miller, D., and S. Woodward (2011), 'Introduction', in D. Miller and S. Woodward, eds., *Global Denim,* Oxford: Berg.

Moors, A. (2009), 'Islamic Fashion in Europe: Religious Conviction, Aesthetic Style and Creative Consumption', *Encounters* 1, 1: 175–200.

Navaro-Yashin, Y. (2002), 'The Market for Identities: Secularism, Islamism, Commodities', in D. Kandiyoti and A. Saktanber, eds., *Fragments of Culture: The Everyday of Modern Turkey,* New Brunswick, NJ: Rutgers University Press.

Sandıkçı, Ö., and G. Ger (2007), 'Constructing and Representing the Islamic Consumer in Turkey', *Fashion Theory* 11, 2–3: 189–210.

Sandıkçı, Ö., and G. Ger (2010), 'Veiling in Style: How Does a Stigmatized Practice Become Fashionable?', *Journal of Consumer Research* 37: 15–35.

Tarlo, E. (2007), 'Hijab in London: Metamorphosis, Resonance and Effects', *Journal of Material Culture* 12, 2: 131–56.

Tarlo, E. (2010), *Visibly Muslim: Fashion, Politics, Faith,* Oxford: Berg.

Walton, J. F. (2010), 'Neo-Ottomanism and the Pious Aesthetics of Publicness: Making Place and Space Virtuous in Istanbul', in D. Göktürk, L. Soysal and İ. Türel, eds., *Orienting Istanbul: Cultural Capital of Europe?* London and New York: Routledge.

White, J. (1999), 'Islamic Chic', in Ç. Keyder, ed., *Istanbul: Between the Global and the Local,* Oxford: Rowman and Littlefield.

–7–

Closet Tales from a Turkish Cultural Center in the 'Petro Metro', Houston, Texas

Maria Curtis

Recent studies on American Muslim communities show that they constitute the single most diverse religious group in the United States today (Younis 2009). Despite a sense of crisis amongst American Muslims and the increase in hate crimes committed against them after 9/11, in some cities Muslims feel a sense of belonging even if they experience a degree of discrimination. One such place is Houston, Texas, the fourth largest city in the United States, also known as 'the Petro Metro', where most of the oil for American consumption is produced.

Houston is a sprawling city with a patchwork of Muslim communities.[1] According to the Islamic Society of Greater Houston the Islamic Society of Greater Houston, Houston is home to some 250,000 Muslim Americans (Stephens 2011). In 2010, a congregation of 50,000 attending a gathering marking the end of Ramadan's Feast of Sacrifice festivities constituted the largest single Muslim gathering in the United States (Stephens 2011). The degree to which Muslims in Houston have built neighbourhoods and businesses, climbed the social ladder, created public spaces frequented by Muslims and non-Muslims alike and responded to discrimination through positive activism is remarkable. Well-established Muslim neighbourhoods with thriving commercial sectors including specialty ethnic and halal food markets, clothing shops and restaurants serve as small worlds unto themselves and are experienced as Muslim comfort zones. As a city without a white majority, with a long-standing presence of religion in everyday life and where women in other communities also wear covered styles of dress, Houston seems to be both home to Muslims and at home with Muslims (Figure 7.1).

Among Houston's newest Muslims are Turks, Central and Eastern Europeans and Central Asians who identify as broadly 'Turkic'. Little has been written on Muslims in Houston and still less on Turks in the United States (see Kaya 2009). In contrast to Turkish migrants in Europe and some Turkish communities on the East Coast of the United States, which are mainly working class, Turkish Americans in Houston have a high level of education and more often belong to the middle class, to which their large walk-in closets testify. Turkish Islam in Houston has been strongly influenced by the work of Turkish

Fig. 7.1 CAIR billboard, Houston, Texas, 2011. Courtesy CAIR Houston

Islamic scholar Mohammed Fethullah Gülen. Gülen brings together orthodox Sunni Islam and the writings of Said Nursi, modern Sufi thought with Mevlevi and Nakshibendi influences, and Turkish nationalism. The Gülen community's worldview emphasizes the importance of education, interreligious dialogue and charity work, and it is often supported by Turkish entrepreneurs. These blends of Islamic thought and Turkey's concern for modernity become visible in the sartorial practices of women in the Gülen community. Among them are American converts who identify with the way 'Turkish Islam' is taught through various programmes and study circles (Aktay 2003: 146; Yavuz and Esposito 2003: vii).

In this chapter, I will discuss how Turkish American women build their sartorial practices while honouring religious convictions and navigating what Cainkar calls 'cultural sniping that comes through in gendered forms of nativism' (2009: 229–30), and how non-Turkish women build on Turkish dress ideals. How do these women 'feel good' about what they wear (Woodward 2005)? How does their 'emotional labour' and their moments alone before the mirror 'anticipate the sartorial judgments of others' (Syed, Ali and Winstanley 2005: 151; Woodward 2005: 23)? The insights I present are drawn from interviews with thirty-five women who are part of the newly forming Turkish American community in Houston and who frequent its newly built houses of worship and cultural centres.[2]

OTTOMAN AND TURKIC CULTURE IN HOUSTON: NOSTALGIA MATERIALIZED

The Turquoise Center, or the Turkish Cultural Center as it is commonly called, consists of the Raindrop Turkish House and the Istanbul Conference Center (Figure 7.2). It reaches out to Turkish Americans, American converts and anyone interested in learning about Turkey. Raindrop Turkish House estimates Turks constitute 6,000 of Houston's 250,000 Muslims. Whereas some of them came decades ago and have lived mainly secular lifestyles, younger practising women have often come to Houston with a well-developed and very stylish modest wardrobe, broadly referred to as *tesettür* (covering dress), comprising styles that were not available to their mothers and grandmothers.

Fig. 7.2 The Turquoise Center in Houston, Texas. Photo: Maria Curtis

In 2010, some twenty thousand people attended the Turkic Cultures and Children's Festival. Turkish American women transformed the green lawn of Houston's town hall into a nostalgic zone (Karaosmanoğlu 2010; TurkicFest 2009), where 'food from home' was central for organizers and attendees. One could dress in Ottoman costumes for photos, pose beside a Turkmen yurt and purchase religious books and evil-eye jewellery. These entangled cultural and economic circuits testify to 'the myriad ways in which individual, collective, and commercial choices are contingent and constrained' (Lewis 2010: 84). The commercialization of Islamic products in Turkey is well-documented, and these processes are now occurring in the United States.[3]

This festival did not only cater to Turkish Americans but built on the notion of 'Turkicness', also featuring booths from former Central Asian Soviet Republic states as well as the Balkans. Here Turkicness weaves together Atatürk's vision of ancient Turkic Central Asia, elements from greater Soviet Turkistan and remnants of Ottoman culture in the Balkans, and includes proto-Turks who may have travelled from the Turkic-speaking tribal areas of what is now called Central Asia to North America during the last ice age as the ancestors of contemporary Native Americans.[4]

In the spring of 2007, the Raindrop Turkish House served as the site for a Nevruz celebration, which brings together these various ethnic and national groups, including Sunni and Shia Muslims, who gather, break bread and celebrate together.[5] Visitors to the Raindrop Turkish House were welcomed by women mannequins dressed in Ottoman-inspired attire that recalls a 'past time' (Navaro-Yashin 2002: 223).[6] The second floor has a large reception area with 'neo-Ottoman' style furniture and windows overlooking the prayer space reminiscent of the women's areas in Turkish mosques (White 2003: 30). Here, *ablalar,* or big sisters, who have spiritual training in Gülen's teachings, offer guidance for the community. Adjacent is the Istanbul Conference Center, whose largest room contains replicas of the Ottoman Topkapı Palace and Central Asian Turkic tribal flags, which are mounted in glass frames.

Gender segregation is subtly negotiated as men and women share these spaces. Women say they dress more conservatively to ensure comfort for all. When Akbar Ahmed, the author of *Journey into America: The Challenge of Islam,* visited the centre, he mentioned the 'clean-shaven [men], attired in gray business suits with white shirts and ties, and invariably smiling...the modern face of mystic Islam' (2010: 225). Indeed, there is a conspicuous lack of dark, long robes, both amongst men and women. All who take part in the activities of the Turkish Cultural Center share the belief that it is a religious duty to look one's best in a way appropriate to Muslim norms of modesty.

Near the Turkish Cultural Center, one encounters alternate modest sartorial practices, which may make it easier to dress as a Muslim in this neighbourhood of Houston compared to other places. Orthodox Jewish women with their modest clothing, wigs and scarves live alongside South Asian Hindus and Muslims in long, flowing saris. Mexican Mormons and Catholics wear longish skirts, while Nigerian, Somali and African American women articulate different versions of African Islamic styles. Turkish women contribute another parallel conception of modesty, tesettür. Not only do Turkish, Turkish American, American and Central Asian communities who frequent the centre bring with them their own understandings of modesty, they select clothing appropriate for local ideals of modesty:

> In environments where Muslims are in a minority, the situation is equally varied .... The result is the emergence of a variety of hybrid styles that blend concerns with religion, modesty, politics, and identity with a creative engagement with both Western and Eastern fashions. (Moors and Tarlo 2007: 138)

While the term *tesettür* refers generally to principles of modesty, in the Turkish setting it implies a European fashion chic, or *şık,* that encourages the wearer to be out in public, engaged and, most importantly, seen, rather than withdrawn. Here I will discuss three forms of modest dress that emerge through the clothing biographies of the women concerned. Tarlo's term *clothing biography* underscores that women's styles fluctuate, indicating that 'clothing choices are a direct product of their cosmopolitan lifestyles and attitudes' (2010: 17). Turkish women take this as a given and avoid judgement of others' style and modesty because they believe that only God should judge the behaviour of others.

WEARING *PARDESÜ* IN HOUSTON

Pious women in Turkey often wear pardesü, a long overcoat resembling a stylish trench coat. According to Jenny White, pardesü coats are costly, appealing to a new middle- and upper-class consumer, whom she has called 'Islamist yuppies' (2003: 47). In Houston, the pardesü version of tesettür is one of the three loosely overlapping styles of dress worn by the women attendees, both Turkish and non-Turkish, at the Turkish Cultural Center.

When someone wears the pardesü version of tesettür at the Turkish Center, this generally signals that she is a regular attendant and an active participant in weekly spiritual discussions. These women will dress modestly in stylish tuniks and long skirts but rarely if ever go out into public without an overcoat as a finishing item. They are also the most likely to observe stricter gender segregation norms, even if many work in mixed-gender settings.

Among the women I interviewed, only Turkish women fell into this category; I very rarely saw any non-Turks wearing the pardesü. Some may wear it at very formal occasions, but few if any regularly wear it as a daily clothing item. While many Muslim clothing stores exist in Houston, there are no specifically Turkish-owned clothing stores. The closest equivalent is the American clothing chain Burlington Coat Factory, which sells coats for men, women and children. Some women were able to find overcoats and jackets here, but rarely were they lightweight and comfortable like the pardesü, which is made to be worn over at least one more layer of clothing. The women interviewed for this study said that they usually updated their pardesü collection and other tesettür clothing essentials when travelling to Turkey during holidays.

Women of all ages may wear the pardesü, and the range of styles is very wide, from simple conservative dark colours to bright patterns and colours, with some lengths nearly reaching the ground and others stopping at the hips or knees. Whereas education and socioeconomic levels fluctuate greatly in this group, a greater level of sobriety in dress tended to correlate with a greater level of piety observed. Some women who studied in Turkey without their scarves and overcoats have taken to wearing them in the United States. Most of the women in this category agreed that dressing modestly in the United States is easier than in Turkey and that doing so in Houston is easier than it was in the other American cities where they had lived previously. All women who wore the pardesü reported being complimented by non-Muslims. The pardesü version of modesty was not only a functional form of covering but a beautiful one the women felt good in, and they felt it was a point of national pride (Figure 7.3).

Fig. 7.3   The Arboretum and Botanical Garden, Dallas, Texas, just before Halloween 2011. Photo: Adele Altynbaeva

BETWEEN PARDESÜ AND TUNIK

The second form of modest dress that was spoken of in interviews consisted of wearing the headscarf and varieties of tuniks, or minidresses worn as tuniks, with some layering underneath for fuller coverage. Such combinations of scarves and tuniks of various lengths were by and large the most common category of dress seen at the Turkish Center in Houston. Some women in this second category may have opted for wearing pardesü on certain occasions, particularly when attending the Turkish Cultural Center, but would adapt their level of modesty in other contexts. Others, American converts as well as women of Turkish background, claimed that they would never wear an over-coat. They did not enjoy it as a style of covering, sometimes stating, 'I do not like Islamic fashion'.

Women who routinely wore the scarf and a long tunik seemed more will-ing to experiment, combining minidresses with layered tops underneath. They would wear both trousers and skirts. Women in this category were also much more likely to purchase items online and to experiment across ethnic styles and revelled in the many ethnic boutiques and discount stores found in Houston. They seemed to take greater fashion leaps in mixing and matching brighter colours and adopting different ethnic fashions for different occasions.

Almost universally, women considered the skirt as a marker of a greater degree of modesty. The most coveted item were long skirts from Turkey, which had the most to offer in terms of styles, fabrics and colours. Women often commented that they had a very difficult time finding long skirts in the United States and that they attempted to either get skirts from Turkey themselves or ask a friend or relative to deliver some.

Women and young girls who alternated between pardesü and tunik often had mothers and grandmothers who wore the pardesü or long cardigans with skirts that fell at the mid-to-lower shin, as that had been the style until the longer pardesü overcoats appeared on the fashion scene. Some mothers objected to the modified styles of modesty their daughters adopted. They especially disliked the look that was, at the time, popular amongst older teenagers and girls in their early twenties, which included skinny pencil jeans and a longish top that looked more androgynous than the tuniks, which were often highly embroidered or sequined. These young girls may also have worn a wide, tight-fitting belt reminiscent of 1980s US styles, with large colourful plastic beads and colourful bangles that picked up the colour of their scarves, which were neatly tucked in at the neck of the shirt rather than flowing over the shoulders as their mothers might prefer. One mother who wore the longer pardesü outside (but removed it when in all-female company) over well-coordinated tunik-based outfits did not consider tight pants with tuniks a form of tesettür. She did not forbid her daughters to wear the tight pants with tuniks but hoped that they would make different choices in the future. She was most content when her daughters adopted a long or mid-shin-length pardesü outdoors with a very stylish and well-coordinated outfit underneath, which they would show off in female company. More generally, levels of covering differed according to generation. Whereas a mother may wear a long pardesü, her teen-aged daughter would fluctuate between tunik and pardesü, while the youngest ones would observe modesty by wearing long sleeves and longish skirts but not a scarf.

Women in this second category were much less likely to wear the gold jewellery that those who wear a pardesü often do. They considered wearing gold impractical, and most preferred costume jewellery that they could match with their clothing. A substantial wardrobe had in fact become part of the *mahir* (the dower, presented by the husband to the wife at marriage). One Latina convert described herself as 'transitioning' to a more mature wardrobe as she was graduating from college, getting married and considering living with her future husband in Turkey. She had grown up as a conservative Christian and had always intended on adopting a more conservative dress style after marriage.

Some non-Turks in this fluid second category commented on what they perceived as materialism regarding clothing in Turkish culture. Not entirely at home with the Islamic consumer mode and not happy with a Turkish secular mode of dress, they felt lost somewhere in an uncomfortable middle. An Azeri woman married to a Turk claimed that she did not wear the scarf because it was uncommon in her country but liked the pardesüs and tuniks that were mid-thigh length. A woman who identified as Çerkez from the Caucasus had not yet 'found her style' in Houston. She generally wore loose jeans with a dark blue, long tunik jacket and alternated her scarves in blues that matched her striking eyes. Her style, 'tesettür sport' as she called it, was 'practical clothes for covering appropriately'. A young Tatar Russian woman held that she was only able to decide to wear the scarf and modest dress in the United States. She had hesitated in Russia, Turkey and the United Kingdom, where she had lived as a student. After wearing the scarf and modest dress in Houston, she became highly experimental in style, moving between levels of modesty depending on the occasion. A recent find for her had been Lycra-cotton blend, elbow-to-wrist-length detachable sleeves worn under a variety of tops. Her mother was a photographer in Russia, and she had grown up with an eye towards design. She had become a graphic designer producing brochures and advertising for the Turkish community.

MODESTY BEYOND THE SCARF: FINDING A MIDDLE GROUND

The third category of modest attire included women who wore no headscarf but went to great lengths to build modest wardrobes. Much less has been written about Muslim women who adhere to ideals of modesty without veiling (Delaney 1994; Read and Bartkowski 2000; Killian 2003; Fadil 2011). These women may have had more simple hairstyles than their Muslim sisters who wore a scarf. They often cut their hair relatively short (shoulder length or shorter) or tied it pulled back away from the face. Whereas women with scarves may have coloured or highlighted their hair to show at home with family and friends, this was much less common among modestly dressed women who did not wear the scarf. Thus, hairstyles, whether seen outdoors or not, had as much to say about modesty as scarves. Amongst the women who attended weekly spiritual *sohbet* lessons in English, non-Turkish women generally did not cover their heads; most of the Azeri, Chinese Huigur, Kirgiz, Ahiska (Turks who lived for an extended period in Russia and Uzbekistan) and Bosnian women did not wear the scarf. An Azeri woman recalled a Soviet-era statue[7] in Baku of a woman removing her scarf: 'This was our national symbol for womanhood—women lifting their veils to go out to help build their society'.

Some Turkish women explained that they were not yet ready to cover their heads. A Turkish woman involved in interfaith activities explained she had worn the scarf when she was younger but realized that she was not ready for it. Her definition of modesty meant that she should 'feel secure'. Sometimes that meant wearing longer clothing; at other times, it meant dressing in a short-sleeved T-shirt. She had been to an academic conference in the United States and had felt badly about the attention she received from other Turkish women present. She wore light makeup and sported a stylish haircut, but her choice of modest professional business clothing had signalled conservativism to the other more secular Turkish academic women.

Another Turkish woman reported similar experiences as a graduate student in Turkey. She did not wear the scarf but purchased clothing one size larger than she needed for a looser fit. A male professor had made harsh comments, and she had considered quitting. She later studied at a prestigious American Ivy League university and avoided these issues altogether. She did believe that wearing the scarf was a religious requirement and had worn it before but claimed she was not ready for it. Her father had done business in Kyrgyzstan, and she had spent time there. She loved everything about her experience and was intrigued by the local women's sense of style, which she thought very beautiful. She wore long tuniks and jackets of cotton and linen blends with fine embroidery, which could be called modern peasant style. Her definition of modesty was telling: 'For me modesty is a part of how one sits, how one speaks, how one helps others. Modesty comes from within, not only seen on the outside.'

Another woman, half Turkish and half American, did not wear the scarf but displayed a pronounced sense of modesty. She preferred darker colours and longer tuniks and jackets, and she only wore American designers. She dressed modestly because it suited her personality, not to create a Turkish style. When she found an item that met her needs, she bought it regardless of cost. Not an accumulator of clothing, she kept her wardrobe tidy to ensure expediency when putting together outfits. She had never been the object of discrimination but had been asked why she dressed in dark colours and long sleeves in the summer heat while out in public in Houston. Her husband was Kurdish, and she often adopted his family's styles, including the scarf, on important Islamic holidays.

THE TEXAS-SIZED WALK-IN CLOSET

In drawing conclusions on how women who visit the Turkish Cultural Center build their wardrobes, I briefly turn to the walk-in closets generally found in Texas homes. Overall, women found wearing modest clothing easier in Houston in terms of social acceptance than in other places. To say it was *easier* is not to say it was *easy*. Some women had encountered extreme resistance to wearing modest clothing in previous places. In many former republics of the Soviet Union, the women reported that their grandmothers were strongly encouraged to remove their veils to work outside the home. In Turkey, women have had access to a wide array of clothing, but some could not afford it, while others could not wear it in certain career paths or did not feel attracted to tesettür. In the Balkans, women needed to come to terms with difficult pasts, with Albanians discovering what it meant to be religious after official atheism and Bosnian women trying to rebuild a sense of Muslimness after the atrocities of war. American converts in turn who were drawn to Turkish/Turkic Islam often did not recreate tesettür but blended styles. What brought these women together seemed to be a collective process of coming to terms with previous opposition to visible expressions of Muslim identity and a co-creation of a safe space for building new Muslim imaginaries. These women seemed to share a sense of marginalization, which was processed through the idiom of 'Turkicness' that has contributed to an ease in dressing Muslim in Houston.

When asked how the physical space of their closets impacted their sartorial practices, women offered a variety of responses. One said she adored her walk-in closet because it offered space for all parts of her identity to coexist. Another thought of her walk-in closet as a workshop where she could arrange clothing by colour to create daily artistic expressions. Another woman wanted to wear the scarf but hesitated; her scarves were visible and hanging so that she could touch and see them when walking by. Another woman loved the extra space of the closet because it allowed her to collect and store modest attire from all over the world which she was able to find in the many boutiques in Houston. Her closet was like a museum of which she was the curator. Another woman liked her closet because it offered space for blankets and pillows for frequent guests. Another spoke of the gold jewellery from her marriage, saying the one constant was the gift her husband had given her, which remained tucked away neatly in the heart of her closet. For the women interviewed for this research, their Texas-sized walk-in closets were their workshops, the place to recreate their Muslim public identities, the palettes from which to draw contrasting elements of modesty and the journals in which to write the next pages of their personal clothing biographies (Figure 7.4).

Fig. 7.4 A young woman seated on the Harşena rock tombs of the Pontus kings in Amasya, Turkey, on the Black Sea coast. Photo: Adele Altynbaeva

NOTES

1. Its diverse neighbourhoods have been documented in the Houston Oral History Project (Klineberg 2005).
2. These interviews took place in Houston, Texas, between March and August 2011. Some were done in groups with several women at a time, others were one on one. Initially questionnaires were sent to a few contacts in Houston, and those women forwarded them to women in Turkey and in Europe. For the purposes of this chapter, I incorporated comments from women actually living in Houston, with the exception of an Albanian woman who had lived in Houston previously but was residing in Turkey in 2011 and a Turkish woman who had moved from Houston to Boston.
3. For more on this topic, see Kandiyoti and Saktanber (2002), Kılıçbaş and Binark (2002), and Gökarıksel and Secor (2009).
4. For more on the many lives and half-lives of the term *Turkic,* see Cağatay and Kuban (2006).
5. See *Cihan Haber Ajansı* (2007). Nevruz is an ancient celebration of spring with Zoroastrian roots that has been reappearing in Turkey since the 1990s. For more on this topic, see Demirer (2004) and Yanik (2006).
6. See also Robertson (1990), White (2003) and Karaosmanoğlu (2010).
7. The 'Azad Qadın Heykəli' (Liberated Woman) statue located in Baku, Azerbaijan.

REFERENCES

Ahmed, A. (2010), *Journey into America: The Challenge of Islam,* Washington, DC: Brookings Institution Press.

Aktay, Y. (2003), 'Diaspora and Stability: Constitutive Elements in a Body of Knowledge', in H. Yavuz and J. Esposito, eds., *Turkish Islam and the Secular State: The Gülen Movement,* Syracuse, NY: Syracuse University Press.

Cağatay, E., and D. Kuban (2006), *The Turkic Speaking Peoples: 2,000 Years of Art and Culture from Inner Asia to the Balkans,* New York: Prestel.

Cainkar, L. (2009), *Homeland Insecurity: The Arab American and Muslim American Experience after 9/11,* New York: Russell Sage Foundation.

Cihan Haber Ajansı (2007), 'Texas'ta ilk defa Nevruz kutlandı' (3 April), <http://www.haberler.com/texas-ta-ilk-defa-nevruz-kutlandi-haberi/> accessed 26 March 2013.

Delaney, C. (1994), 'Untangling the Meanings of Hair in Turkish Society', *Anthropological Quarterly* 67: 159–72.

Demirer, Y. (2004), 'Tradition and Politics: New Year Festivals in Turkey', PhD diss., Ohio State University, Columbus.

Fadil, N. (2011), 'Not-/Unveiling as an Ethical Practice', *Feminist Review* 98: 83–109.

Gökarıksel, B., and A. Secor (2009), 'New Transnational Geographies of Islamism, Capitalism and Subjectivity: The Veiling-fashion Industry in Turkey', *Area* 41: 6–18.

Kandiyoti, D., and A. Saktanber, eds. (2002), *Fragments of Culture: The Everyday of Modern Turkey,* New Brunswick, NJ: Rutgers University Press.

Karaosmanoğlu, D. (2010), 'Nostalgia Spaces of Consumption and Heterotopia', *Culture Unbound: Journal of Current Cultural Research* 2: 283–302.

Kaya, I. (2009), 'Identity across Generations: A Turkish American Case Study', *Middle East Journal* 63: 617–32.

Kılıçbaş, B., and M. Binark (2002), 'Consumer Culture, Islam and the Politics of Lifestyle', *European Journal of Communication* 17: 495–511.

Killian, C. (2003), 'The Other Side of the Veil: North African Women in France Respond to the Headscarf Affair', *Gender and Society* 17: 557–90.

Klineberg, S. (2005), 'Public Perceptions in Remarkable Times: Tracking Change Through 24 Years of Houston Surveys', *Houston Chronicle,* <http://houstonareasurvey.org/REPORT-2005.pdf> accessed 26 March 2013.

Lewis, R. (2010), 'Marketing Muslim Lifestyle: A New Media Genre', *Middle East Women's Studies* 6: 58–90.

Moors, A., and E. Tarlo (2007), 'Introduction', *Fashion Theory: The Journal of Dress, Body & Culture* 11: 133–42.

Navaro-Yashin, Y. (2002), 'The Market for Identities: Secularism, Islamism, Commodities', in D. Kandiyoti and A. Saktanber, eds., *Fragments of Culture: The Everyday of Modern Turkey,* New Brunswick, NJ: Rutgers University Press.

Read, G. H., and J. Bartkowski (2000), 'To Veil or Not to Veil? A Case Study of Identity Negotiation among Muslim Women in Austin, Texas', *Gender and Society* 14: 395–417.

Robertson, R. (1990), 'After Nostalgia: Willful Nostalgia and the Phrases of Globalization', in B. S. Turner, ed., *Theories of Modernity and Postmodernity,* London: Sage.

Stephens, M. (2011), 'Muslim Population Grows, Mosque Plans Center', *Your Woodland News.com/The Woodlands Villager* (15 April), <http://www.yourhoustonnews.com/woodlands/living/article_0e25ed31-fc9c-5acd-b959-da77f6d15fed.html> accessed 26 March 2013.

Syed, J., F. Ali and D. Winstanley (2005), 'In Pursuit of Modesty: Contextual Emotional Labour and the Dilemma for Working Women in Islamic Societies', *International Journal of Work Organisation and Emotion* 1: 150–67.

Tarlo, E. (2010), *Visibly Muslim: Fashion, Politics, Faith,* Oxford: Berg.

TurkicFest: Houston's Turkic Cultures and Children's Festival (2009), 'TurkicFest 2009 Participants Survey Results', <http://www.turkicfest.org/newsroom/73-turkicfest-2009-participants-survey-results Staat er ook niet in> accessed 26 March 2013.

White, J. (2003), *Islamist Mobilization in Turkey: A Study in Vernacular Politics,* Seattle: University of Washington Press.

Woodward, S. (2005), 'Looking Good: Feeling Right—Aesthetics of the Self', in S. Küchler and D. Miller, eds., *Clothing as Material Culture,* Oxford: Berg.

Yanik, L. K. (2006), '"Nevruz" or "Newroz"? Deconstructing the "Invention" of a Contested Tradition in Contemporary Turkey', *Middle Eastern Studies* 42: 285–302.

Yavuz, H., and J. Esposito, eds. (2003), *Turkish Islam and the Secular State: The Gülen Movement,* Syracuse, NY: Syracuse University Press.

Younis, M. (2009), 'Muslim Americans Exemplify Diversity, Potential Key Findings from a New Report by the Gallup Center for Muslim Studies', Gallup, <http://www.gallup.com/poll/116260/Muslim-Americans-Exemplify-Diversity-Potential.aspx> accessed 28 April 2009.

SECTION III

MARKETS FOR ISLAMIC FASHION

8

Transnational Networks of Veiling-fashion between Turkey and Western Europe

Banu Gökarıksel and Anna Secor

In the autumn of 2008, following a conference on Muslim consumption in Germany, we decided to visit the Berlin branch of Tekbir (God is great), the leading designer and manufacturer of Islamic fashion in Turkey. We had previously interviewed Tekbir's CEO, Mustafa Karaduman, who spoke glowingly of the company's international presence, its retail branches in over twenty countries and its European-inflected style. Address in hand, we set off for Wedding, a working-class neighbourhood in central Berlin with a high concentration of Turkish-origin residents. Yet when we found the address under the familiar Tekbir logo, the modest-sized store was empty and looked as though it had long been closed (Figure 8.1). In contrast to the elegant promenades where Tekbir stores are found in Turkey, this defunct franchise was next to a corner grocery piled with fresh fruits and vegetables. We learned later from Mustafa Karaduman that the store had been mismanaged by its owner. Karaduman explained that he had gotten suspicious of the low sales figures of the store and discovered, upon inspection, that instead of selling Tekbir products, the owner had started to produce and sell Tekbir counterfeits. This is why this Tekbir franchise had closed down in the midst of the company's booming sales to Western Europe.

Not willing to leave Berlin empty handed, we started to ask passers-by about where we might find a shop selling Islamic dress. We were directed to a store called Hilal not far away. In the shop window, modest dress for women was displayed alongside circumcision outfits for boys. Inside, the clothes were conservative, mostly in muted colours, with loose-cut overcoats (*pardesü*) and ankle-length skirts. The styles resembled Islamic dress found in Turkey in the 1980s, before veiling had become fashionable at the hands of Tekbir's designers (Kılıçbay and Binark 2002; Navaro-Yashin 2002). Waiting to speak to the manager, we observed customers coming and going. The store appeared to serve Muslim immigrants of many different origins from Africa and the Middle East. When we did speak to the manager, who was of Turkish origin, she made it clear that she was sceptical of researchers and resentful of the attention the headscarf was getting in Germany. Dismissing both fashion and politics, she explained that for her veiling was a way to connect to her Turkish

Fig. 8.1 Defunct Tekbir franchise store in Wedding, Berlin. Photo: Banu Gökarıksel and Anna Secor.

origins and mark her membership to a Muslim community. Veiling, she insisted, was about heritage and Islam, nothing more. Her remarks contrasted with the emphasis on trendiness, modernity and class distinction that the producers and retailers in Turkey associate with Islamic fashion.

Our search for Tekbir in Berlin was motivated by curiosity piqued by our extensive research on veiling-fashion[1] in Turkey, where women's Islamic dress has developed into a fashion industry with its own trends, fashion shows, catalogues, television show tie-ins and vibrant retail districts. Today, there are more than 200 firms in Turkey that design, produce and sell what we call *veiling-fashion* (Gökarıksel and Secor 2009, 2010a). While in the 1980s and early 1990s these commodities were limited to oversized headscarves, long overcoats and modest dress (much like what was on display at the Hilal shop in Berlin), over time the growth of the industry, its insertion into global fashion networks and the demand for innovation have led to the wide diversification of veiling-fashion. Today, it is the combination of the headscarf and an outer layer (a *pardesü*, a tunic or a jacket) which remain the distinguishing elements of veiling-fashion. The shape, size, colour and style of these as well as how they are assembled change seasonally. Veiling-fashion is an inseparable part of the taste and lifestyle of a growing Islamic bourgeoisie in Turkey.

Although the almost simultaneous emergence of new veiling styles in various geographical contexts has been noted (Jones 2007, 2010; Lewis 2007, 2010; Moors 2007, 2009; Schulz 2007; Tarlo 2007, 2010), the efforts to trace the connections between these contexts have been limited. In this chapter, we trace these networks of veiling-fashion production and consumption from Turkey to Western Europe and back again. Based on our 2008 survey of 174 Turkish veiling-fashion firms, our case studies of three such firms and our visual analysis of catalogues, this chapter demonstrates that, in the relationship between the Turkish industry and Western Europe, material and symbolic elements are intermeshed in complex and uneven ways. For example, locations such as Paris and Milan serve both as central nodes for design and as reference points for anchoring the image of veiling-fashion as part of a cosmopolitan Muslim identity for producers and consumers. Western European locations where there are high concentrations of Turkish-origin migrants are important export destinations. Yet, as the case of the defunct Tekbir franchise store shows, the transnational networks that connect the Turkish veiling-fashion industry to Western Europe are not always seamless and predictable but are contingent on the agency and practices of a variety of actors. We begin by giving an overview of the transnational linkages formed in the veiling-fashion industry, including patterns of exports and sales. We then turn to the question of what role Europe plays in the design and marketing of veiling-fashion. We thus find that we cannot think of Islamic fashion as another realm, existing somehow outside of the global circuits of fashion that take Western Europe as their central node (see also Tarlo 2010). Rather, our analysis shows that the multifaceted transnational linkages of the Turkish veiling-fashion industry insert Islamic fashion into dense networks—albeit at times patchy—of material and symbolic interconnection with Europe.

GEOGRAPHY OF EXPORTS AND SALES

The Turkish veiling-fashion industry, while paralleling many of the broader trends in apparel production in Turkey, nonetheless has a unique profile. In the autumn of 2008, we conducted a detailed survey with 174 veiling-fashion firms (that is, firms with 10 per cent or more of their production in Islamic dress for women), which we identified through the membership lists of textile associations, advertising and industry fairs. We estimate that there are a total of 200 to 225 such firms in the country (see also Sandıkçı and Ger 2001, 2002). Of the 174 firms that participated in our study, over 80 per cent have half or more of their production in veiling-fashion, and half of them report that veiling-fashion comprises 90 per cent or more of their production. Half of the companies were founded after 1996, and a third were founded in 2000 or later. Like the Turkish apparel industry more broadly, Istanbul serves as a major hub (61 per cent), though a quarter of the firms are located in Konya, the central Anatolian city that has emerged as an important node in networks of Islamic entrepreneurship (Demir-polat 2008; Gumuscu 2010). And like most other apparel firms in Turkey (ITKIB 2009), the firms in our sample are small to medium-sized operations, employ-ing on average 42 workers. Tekbir is by far the largest company by any measure, boasting 1,450 employees, 33 branches and a reported annual earnings over $10 million. The next largest veiling-fashion firm in terms of earnings, SETRMS, employs only 212 people and has 9 branches (Table 8.1).

Veiling-fashion firms, like the rest of the Turkish apparel industry, are in-tegrated into networks of international trade. In line with global trends in textiles, companies reported using fabrics imported from East Asia (espe-cially China). Veiling-fashion firms are also active participants in the export economy. Forty per cent of the firms we surveyed reported being engaged in export, double the rate for the Turkish apparel industry more broadly (ITKIB 2009). Germany, the top destination for Turkish apparel exports according to the Istanbul Apparel and Textile Exporters' Bureau (ITKIB), also figures promi-nently as an export destination for veiling-fashion firms. Most exporting firms reported Germany as their largest market and primary export destination.[2] However, the Middle East, North Africa and Central Asia were also frequently cited export destinations. ITKIB points towards the Middle East as a grow-ing area of concentration for the expansion of Turkish apparel exports, and indeed it appears that the firms in our sample are among those seeking out these markets. After Germany, the next most frequently mentioned destina-tions for exports were Iran and Syria.

Veiling-fashion firms have various approaches to accessing European mar-kets. On one hand, Tekbir retails in Germany, the Netherlands, Belgium, Austria, Britain, the United States, Canada, Australia, Bosnia-Herzegovina, Switzerland, Macedonia, Azerbaijan, Lebanon, Libya, Egypt, Jordan, Syria, Sudan, Algeria and Palestine (Tekbir 2011). Tekbir currently has a twofold approach to international

Table 8.1 Basic Data on the Firms Mentioned By Name in This Chapter

Name	Year founded	Location of head-quarters	Number of branches	Number of employees	Annual pro-duction (in millions of US dollars)	Per cent of production in veiling	Per cent export
Armine	1982	Istanbul	4	48	3–7	75–90%	30
Butik Dayı	1974	Istanbul	7	113	No answer	26–50%	70
SETRMS	1974	Ankara	9	215	7–10	51–75%	10
Şelale	1993	Ankara	0	73	3–7	26–50%	0
Tekbir	1982	Istanbul	33	1,450	> 10	> 90%	15

sales. Either it franchises the store itself in places such as Germany, a strategy with management challenges as discussed earlier, or it supplies its brand-name products to independent boutiques. By contrast, smaller businesses often do not have direct sales access to customers in Europe and instead rely on individual consumers and their networks in order to seek out and distribute their products. These networks, shaped by patterns of Turkish migration to Europe, are embodied by individuals who travel between Turkey and Europe and have established relationships with Istanbul shops. For example, in our interview with staff at Armine, an up-and-coming veiling-fashion firm that has recently expanded from scarves to stylish apparel, the company representatives (a designer/owner, a marketing director and a retail manager) emphasized that customers played an important role in carrying their brand to Germany, France and the Netherlands. Armine has only had stores in Istanbul since 2011 but serves an international clientele mostly through customers' personal connections and word-of-mouth relations. In the words of the retail manager:

> We send an unbelievable amount of product [to Europe]. Every week a delivery truck goes out. Customers call me and place an order without even having seen the product or having tried it on... I have clients who are like unpaid marketers, spreading the word about Armine products. If I were to open a store today in Hamburg Germany I know that I would have at least twenty-five customers right away. And they would bring others.

Finally, one of our case-study firms, Butik Dayı, had moved into veiling-fashion production for the domestic market only after having established itself as an exporter. Demonstrating the diversity of the veiling-fashion industry, Butik Dayı produces a range of styles, including a line of decidedly immodest dress targeted at the Russian market. The sales manager emphasized that Islam did not interfere with the business of Butik Dayı. In response to a question about the role of Islamic principles in Butik Dayı's business practices, she took pains to distance her company from Tekbir, with its public image as an Islamic business:

> If Islam had a role in Dayı's business all we'd produce would be veiling-fashion. I mean, we would be Tekbir. But we are not like Tekbir. The owners of Dayı are practicing Muslims. But because they never let their religion influence their business, we have a wholesale outlet in Laleli [where exports to Russia are concentrated in Istanbul]. We produce specifically for the Russian market. This is a very different thing.

The manager went on to explain that Butik Dayı advertises not only on Islamic television channels in Turkey but also on Show TV, which broadcasts from Turkey to Europe, and on European television. Butik Dayı thus has a very different relationship to European markets than either Tekbir or Armine. Its insertion into the transnational networks that connect Europe to Turkey is not exclusively defined by Muslim identity but instead by a diverse set of business opportunities and market imperatives.

In short, we find that the Turkish veiling-fashion industry may be even more oriented towards international markets in Europe and the Middle East than the apparel sector more broadly. At the same time, these firms link to transnational markets in a variety of ways. While Tekbir is working to establish its brand internationally through a mix of formalized retail relations and plans to embark on direct retail in the near future,[3] upcoming companies like Armine rely on more informal networks to penetrate the European market, at least for the moment. Finally, the case of Butik Dayı, whose target consumer in Europe may not be a veiled Muslim consumer, illustrates the contingent role of Islam for both consumers and producers. Thus, the material transnational networks that connect the Turkish veiling-fashion industry to Europe are far from seamless and unidirectional. Instead, these networks are shaped by histories of migration, patterns of tourism and of apparel exports and the practices of diverse customers, retailers and franchisers in Turkey and abroad.

THE PLACE OF EUROPE

Veiling-fashion is part of a much broader reorganization of society in Turkey: the rise of a new Islamic bourgeoisie, an aspiring middle class with tastes, styles and modes of social interaction notably distinct from the secular, Western-oriented lifestyles of the republican elite (Göle 1996, 1999; White 1999; Sandıkçı and Ger 2001, 2002, 2007; Navaro-Yashin 2002; Saktanber 2002). At the same time, Western Europe plays a significant symbolic role in the construction of what White (1999) has called 'Islamic chic'. The leading companies of the industry attend fairs and fashion shows in Paris and Milan. The design team of Tekbir, for example, goes to Paris up to six times a year, observing new trends in colour, cut, fabric and details such as the size and placement of buttons. Tekbir uses these observations to create seasonal lines that are ahead of the trends on the streets of Istanbul. The company's PR manager explained that Tekbir does not simply replicate the global trends: 'Everyone knows where the fashion centres are and we all [veiling-fashion companies] feed on them. But Tekbir reinterprets these trends in its own distinct style.' Others such as Armine and Butik Dayı that do not travel regularly to Europe similarly follow global fashion trends, keeping up by responding quickly to customer demand and changes in the Turkish apparel market. Thus, while veiling-fashion is part of a new middle-class Islamic habitus, it is very much bound up with international fashion industry with a focus on European centres.

The Tekbir PR manager gave the example of the şalvar, loose-fit trousers that are especially baggy at the top, to illustrate how acceptance within European markets can legitimize styles that have originated elsewhere. She sees the şalvar as an indigenous Turkish garment even though the version that has become fashionable in Europe more closely resembles the South Asian style şalvar worn together with a kameez. She says:

> Can you imagine? Şalvar became a fashion! We think of şalvar as a local costume. But now the whole world is wearing it. You can see şalvar even on the most famous designers of the world. Şalvar is not something foreign to us so when the customers demanded şalvar, we could easily make it. Şalvar is our custom, it came from our culture, and therefore we can present it to our customers. And there's nothing about şalvar that conflicts with veiling.

The şalvar, brought to Europe by South Asian migrants, starts cropping up in mainstream European fashion, makes its way to Turkey and finally to Tekbir. The şalvar's circulation through the European networks of fashion adds value to a costume that was formerly seen as rural and traditional. And, of course, the baggy şalvar is easily integrated into Islamic fashion.

Tekbir would not have started producing şalvars if they had not first become fashionable in Europe. The veiling-fashion industry has explicitly marketed its clothes as modern and distinct from rural and traditional styles. The Armine store manager emphasizes how his company's mission is to produce styles that are urban and modern:

> Our goal is to provide women who have chosen the Islamic path with comfortable clothes … A covered woman can go shopping but what she finds in the stores are styles that are not stylish, that have not kept up with the trends, that have fallen behind, that are more in the Anatolian style. This is what we want to break from. A covered woman can still be very chic. Our goal is to combine fashion and veiling and to clothe veiled women in the latest and most modern styles. This is our mission.

Thus, Armine contributes to the cultivation of a new middle-class Islamic lifestyle in which taste is defined with reference to modernity and international trends. Anatolia, Turkey's heartland, comes to signify that which has fallen behind and that which veiling-fashion seeks to surpass.

If Anatolia is rejected as a referent for fashion, Europe is glorified. Images of Europe appear in the advertising campaigns and catalogues of veiling-fashion firms. The leaders of the veiling-fashion industry increasingly use high-end professional services in the production of catalogues. Most of these catalogues seem to be produced for customers and retailers in Turkey while advertisements target the Western European markets as well. In line with popular tastes in beauty in Turkey, the models are generally light-skinned and often green- or blue-eyed. The colours of the clothes are often bright, though white and gray are also popular.

The overall effect of these images is typical of clothing catalogues more generally: what is on display and being marketed is not just an outfit but a complex set of aspirations about lifestyle, taste and beauty (see also Gökarıksel and Secor 2010b). Models are often posed within luxurious interiors, holiday scenes or European-looking urban environments. The 2008 spring-summer catalogue of one of the larger veiling-fashion firms based in Ankara, SETRMS, provides an example of this latter motif. The catalogue is stylized as a scrapbook of a definitively urban, cosmopolitan woman. Pictures of the model are superimposed on abstract images of cityscapes and recognizable images of historic sites in Paris and Rome. The spring-summer 2009 Armine catalogue takes the customers not to these sites but to a summer holiday on the Mediterranean, with its beautiful beaches and whitewashed buildings on whose walls bougainvillea climbs. Instead of a quick trip to Turkey's Aegean coast where one could find similar scenes, the model is seen on a cruise ship, suggesting that she is going farther away, most likely to the Greek islands. The composite images of both the SETRMS and Armine catalogues underline the idealized mobility of the veiling-fashion consumer, her ability to travel, to experience the goods of the world and to participate in the lifestyle of the cosmopolitan elite.

An alternative narrative of cosmopolitanism is constructed in the pages of the catalogue for Iklim, a label produced by a mid-sized firm, Şelale. The catalogue features models posed in outerwear (ankle-length coats, headscarves and handbags) within an opulent interior. The scene evokes an Ottoman heritage, signified by historical maps of the Dardanelles, Greece and Italy, and miniature portraits of Ottoman figures. Prominently displayed on bookshelves behind the model is a collection of books with English and Turkish titles such as *Vienna, Renaissance* and *Troia* (Troy). Both SETRMS's and Şelale's representations evoke European sites as referents for desirable lifestyles but in different ways. While SETRMS places its models as tourists in Paris, şelale's catalogue blurs the boundaries between 'Europe' and Turkey by positioning its styles within a neo-Ottoman narrative of cosmopolitanism. Şelale's images thus reposition the symbolic capital of Europe within the historical power of the Ottoman past. While the SETRMS consumer is expected to dream of visiting Paris, the Şelale consumer can find Europeanness at home. Yet both representations of veiling-fashion reclaim Europe and its undisputed cosmopolitanism for the newly ascendant Muslim elite of Turkey.

CONCLUSION

Despite the failure of the Tekbir franchise and the unfashionable styles of Hilal, we did not fail to find veiling-fashion in Berlin. Just a few blocks away from Hilal, we found mannequins wearing layers of clothes in the windows of H&M (see also Moors 2009). These outfits closely resembled those that young veiled women in Turkey assemble. In clothing boutiques in hip peripheries of central Berlin, headscarves were displayed alongside fishnet stockings, leather jackets and edgy ensembles. The combination of veiling and fashion was visible on the streets of Berlin, embodied by mostly young women wearing headscarves as part of ensembles that resembled H&M displays, similar to what their counterparts wore in Turkey, combining items from the hip Miss Poem stores (which do not display any scarves on mannequins' heads) and veiling-fashion retailers. What was not so apparent in Berlin was the particular formation of middle-class Muslim taste and lifestyle that has arisen in the Turkish context and is the foundation for a designer-driven veiling-fashion industry.

Veiling-fashion in Turkey is central to the fierce contestation between secular and Islamic versions of cosmopolitanism, modernity and class distinction. Europe becomes important because of the role it plays in this struggle. Europe acts as the central referent for bourgeois identity whether secular or Islamic. Just like the broader Turkish fashion industry, the veiling-fashion sector looks to Europe not only as an export destination but also for identifying new trends and producing taste (What is in fashion now? What will be in fashion next year?). Veiling-fashion companies thus work within existing circuits of fashion, transnational migration, tourism and consumer markets that position European sites as material and symbolic nodal points. At the same time, Turkish companies do not simply replicate European trends. Europe is certainly neither the only export destination for this industry, which is increasingly oriented towards Middle Eastern markets, nor the only source of design ideas. Veiling-fashion companies both reinterpret the latest styles and produce multiple narratives of cosmopolitanism, including ones that understand Turkey's connection to Europe and the Middle East through a neo-Ottoman lens. For the Turkish veiling-fashion industry, the place of Europe is thus neither singular nor unambiguous but is instead constructed within a broader network of symbolic and material relations that not only condition the symbolic capital of Europeanness but also the cut of a sleeve, the size of a button or the sheen of a scarf.

NOTES

1. We use the term *veiling-fashion* to describe the ever-shifting dress styles that combine headscarves with skirts, pants and coats. While veiling indicates an Islamic system of modesty in dress (*hijab* in Arabic or *tesettür* in Turkish), this practice in general may range from just covering the hair with a headscarf to full covering of the body. In the context of our work, the women we talked to described themselves as covered (*kapalı* as opposed to non-covered or open, *açık*) and wore headscarves paired with outfits that, to varying degrees, attempted to conform to an idea of women's modesty in Islam. Like most veiled women in Turkey, they did not cover their faces, and they did not wear enveloping outer garments

(such as the abaya, or in Turkish, the *çarşaf*). Rather they often wore over-coats (*pardesü*) or tunics over long skirts or pants. The colours, fabrics and designs of each piece of clothing, as well as the headscarf, changed seasonally following fashion trends.

2. ITKIP provides aggregate data for apparel exports of Turkish companies as a whole and does not break down the data by any subcategory. Therefore, it is not possible to find any data about the veiling-fashion industry other than that reported by the companies in our survey. Self-reporting may lead to exaggeration, especially when exports are important to the image of the company.

3. Interview with CEO, 2011.

REFERENCES

Demirpolat, A. (2008), 'Selçuklu kulesinden kule site'ye: Konya'da din, ser-maye ve dönüşüm', *Ekev Akademi Dergisi* 12: 483–502.

Gökarıksel, B., and A. Secor (2009), 'New Transnational Geographies of Islamism, Capitalism, and Subjectivity: The Veiling-fashion Industry in Turkey', *Area* 41, 1: 6–18.

Gökarıksel, B., and A. Secor (2010a), 'Between Fashion and Tesettür: Marketing and Consuming Women's Islamic Dress', *Journal of Middle East Women's Studies* 6, 3: 118–48.

Gökarıksel, B., and A. Secor (2010b), 'Islamic-ness in the Life of a Commodity: Veiling-fashion in Turkey', *Transactions of the Institute of British Geographers* 35, 3: 313–33.

Göle, N. (1996), *The Forbidden Modern: Civilization and Veiling,* Ann Arbor: University of Michigan Press.

Göle, N. (1999), *İslamın yeni kamusal yüzleri,* Istanbul: Metis.

Gumuscu, S. (2010), 'Class, Status, and Party: The Changing Face of Political Islam in Turkey and Egypt', *Comparative Political Studies* 43, 7: 835–61.

ITKIB (İstanbul Tekstil ve Konfeksiyon İhracatçı Birlikleri) (2009), *Hazır giyim ve konfeksiyon sektörü 2009 Ocak-Haziran ihracat performans değerlendirmesi,* <http://www.itkib.org.tr/ihracat/DisTicaretBilgileri/raporlar/dosyalar/2009/konfeksiyon_performans_raporu_haziran2009.pdf> accessed 24 May 2011.

Jones, C. (2007), 'Fashion and Faith in Urban Indonesia', *Fashion Theory* 11: 211–31.

Jones, C. (2010), 'Images of Desire: Creating Virtue and Value in an Indonesian Islamic Lifestyle Magazine', *Journal of Middle East Women's Studies* 6, 3: 91–117.

Kılıçbay, B., and M. Binark (2002), 'Consumer Culture, Islam and the Politics of Lifestyle: Fashion for Veiling in Contemporary Turkey', *European Journal of Communication* 17: 495–511.

Lewis, R. (2007), 'Veils and Sales: Muslims and the Spaces of Postcolonial Fashion Retail', *Fashion Theory* 11: 423–42.

Lewis, R. (2010), 'Marketing Muslim Lifestyle: A New Media Genre', *Journal of Middle East Women's Studies* 6, 3: 58–90.

Moors, A. (2007), 'Fashionable Muslims: Notions of Self, Religion, and Society in San'a', *Fashion Theory* 11: 319–46.

Moors, A. (2009), '"Islamic Fashion" in Europe: Religious Conviction, Aesthetic Style, and Creative Consumption', *Encounters* 1: 175–201.

Navaro-Yashin, Y. (2002), *Faces of the State: Secularism and Public Life in Turkey,* Princeton, NJ: Princeton University Press.

Saktanber, A. (2002), *Living Islam,* London: I.B. Tauris.

Sandıkçı, Ö., and G. Ger (2001), 'Fundamental Fashions: The Cultural Politics of the Turban the Levi's', *Advances in Consumer Research* 28: 146–50.

Sandıkçı, Ö., and G. Ger (2002), 'In-between Modernities and Postmodernities: Theorizing Turkish Consumptionscape', *Advances in Consumer Research* 29: 465–70.

Sandıkçı, Ö., and G. Ger (2007), 'Constructing and Representing the Islamic Consumer in Turkey', *Fashion Theory* 11: 189–210.

Schulz, D. (2007), 'Competing Sartorial Assertions of Femininity and Muslim Identity in Mali', *Fashion Theory* 11: 253–80.

Tarlo, E. (2007), 'Islamic Cosmopolitanism: The Sartorial Biographies of Three Muslim Women in London', *Fashion Theory* 11: 143–72.

Tarlo, E. (2010), *Visibly Muslim: Fashion, Politics, Faith,* Oxford: Berg.

Tekbir (2011), <http://www.tekbirgiyim.com.tr/> accessed 24 May 2011.

White, J. (1999), 'Islamic Chic', in Ç. Keyder, ed., *Istanbul between the Global and the Local,* Lanham, MD: Rowman and Littlefield, 77–91.

9

Made in France: Islamic Fashion Companies on Display

Leila Karin Österlind

Muslim fashion entrepreneurs and designers often wish to reverse negative stereotypes by promoting clothes that suggest that fashion and faith are compatible (Tarlo 2010: 11). Amongst European wearers, designers and retailers of Islamic fashion, locally developed styles and looks have emerged during the past decade. Whether oppositional to, differentiating from or imitating dominant cultural forms, such styles and looks should be understood in relation to the surrounding local context (Mercer 1994: 111). France has the largest Muslim community in Europe, yet it is a country where visible displays of Muslim identity in public places are restricted and greatly criticized (Bowen 2006; Scott 2007). That public manifestations of Islam are often deemed problematic in France may explain how the large annual Muslim fair known as RAMF,[1] which has been held in the outskirts of Paris for more than twenty-five years, has been largely ignored by French media (Bowen 2006: 103). This event is, however, significant for many Muslims living in France as well as for businesses targeting French Muslims. It is an unusual public event in the French context since it constitutes a specific space and moment where Muslim identities are out on display, public, multiple, visible and majoritarian. Le Bourget is a place to be French, Muslim and proud.

When I headed out to the RAMF at Le Bourget, north-east of Paris, on the first day of the event in 2008, at the Gare du Nord train station there were many families, groups and individuals heading to the fair who were recognizable by their 'visibly Muslim' clothes.[2] Some clearly had had difficulty finding the right train and many were queuing in front of information stalls in the underground passages. Through loudspeakers, the RATP (Paris public transport) staff made repeated announcements: 'A message for travellers heading to the annual gathering for French Muslims. Please take the northbound RER B towards Charles de Gaulle or Mitry Claye and descend at Le Bourget where coaches will be waiting.' That Le Bourget is an official manifestation of significant size means that going there gives the visitors a chance to feel part of a large French Muslim community.[3] It is a site to which you bring your family

Fig. 9.1 May 2008, Paris. Swedish fashion designer Iman Aldebe waiting for the bus at Le Bourget after attending the annual meeting for French Muslims. Photo: Leila Karin Österlind

and friends, a site where you can go to shop, listen to lectures, pray or just look at people, but it is also a site for pride, a site where being both French and Muslim is the norm. Whilst French Muslims sometimes find themselves having to underplay expressions of being Muslim in public, this is a time and place where their situation is temporarily reversed. It is one of the largest Muslim public events in Europe. The gathering at Le Bourget lives up to the organizers' goal of making a significant 'rendez-vous' and 'pleasant setting' for French Muslims to congregate.[4] During the four days I visited the fair, it was filled with friendly and enthusiastic visitors.

The bazaar or marketplace was situated in a large separate hall, the largest of the three exhibition halls hosting the RAMF.[5] The actual building was rectangular, high and hangar-like and accessible through several gates on two sides. Inside, all types of different products, ranging from books, halal candy, soap, SpongeBob SquarePants balloons and high-heeled shoes to Muslim toilets were on display.[6] Along one side of the hall, a restaurant area was situated, and although it was not easy to differentiate between the stands, a smaller part of the hall was reserved for charity projects and exhibitions. This part of the bazaar was facing the yard where halls were used for praying, lectures and concerts. Stands displaying women's wear dominated the bazaar, but it was not until the evening of the first day, when many of the thousands of visitors started to leave, that I managed to get a proper overview of the scene. Since I had been avoiding the largest crowds in the interest of being able to move around, I had not until then seen what the most popular stands had on display.

The large stands of Amal-mode, Knz-couture and Saouli stood out from the other Islamic fashion stands in the bazaar. Their stands were more shop-like and better organized than those of most other retailers present in the bazaar. This chapter explores the business narratives and sales strategies of these three Islamic fashion retail companies, looking primarily at their display of goods and their use of founding stories. What strategies of narrative and display do the three businesses use? Do they adjust their strategies to the high levels of intolerance shown towards visible manifestations of religious dress in the French context?

To start with, the three businesses are actors on the French Islamic fashion market. Fashion retailers have to differentiate themselves vis-à-vis other actors in the same market and produce convincing narratives in order to become credible in the eyes of the targeted groups of consumers (Czarniawska 1997; Thanning Vendelø 1998). The choice of whether to highlight business rather than faith can be significant in altering the way Muslim women are perceived by the wider public. In the descriptive presentation of the three businesses that follows, I will discuss the types of goods displayed and marketed as Islamic in the bazaar of Le Bourget, a context where being Muslim is the norm rather than the exception. It was not the first time Amal-mode, Knz-couture and Saouli were present at Le Bourget, so they were well aware of the types of crowds that flock to the exhibition halls for this four-day event.

Amal-mode

The fashion retailing company Amal-mode has two shops in the outskirts of Paris.[7] In the bazaar, it had chosen to separate its goods into three categories, each with their own stand. At one of these stands, only festive dress was sold. Items of more modest dress such as jilbabs, abayas,[8] khimars[9] and accessories such as gloves were sold on a second stand, while clothes from the Amal brand were sold on a third stand. I have chosen to discuss this last stand in this chapter since it is more comparable with the Knz-couture and Saouli stands. It was a rectangular, easily accessible space open towards the paths on three sides but closed with a temporary wall constructed with wooden tiles on a metal frame along one long side. The Amal summer collection was displayed on hangers in straight lines arranged according to colour. On the wall separating the Amal stand from the neighbouring stand, mannequins with suggestions of clothing combinations were hung up. The mannequins were plain, headless torsos, which are common in mainstream fashion.

The garments central to the collection on display were patterned, knee- or hip-length, long-sleeved tunics[10] and dresses, matching ranges of plain skirts and harem trousers. The harem trousers were a great success, and I saw many women coming back wearing them during the following days of the fair. They were tight-fitting from waist to thigh with widening legs gathered and sewn up at the ankle. Most of the Amal dresses and tunics were vividly patterned with abstract geometric shapes, yet a few simpler, single-coloured ones were also on display. Items were sold as single pieces but also combined and displayed as ensembles of two pieces.[11] The prices ranged from around €25 to €45 for single items, and buying an ensemble was cheaper than buying two single items. Towards the end of the event, the original special offer of €65 for the ensembles had fallen to €55. Selling as much as possible at this important event was the main focus at Amal-mode, and the company aimed at targeting female consumers of different ages and tastes. Even though the company had three separate stands, each of the stands was crammed with garments, especially at the beginning of the four-day event.

Most of the saleswomen who worked for Amal at the fair were non-hijabis. They were all young North African–looking women in their early twenties. When interviewed, the saleswomen were not cautious about what was said, when, how or by whom. The founder's sister was one of the few to wear the hijab. She told me that Amal is a family-run company that her sister founded with support from their father. The founder had decided to start her own business because she thought that there was a lack of places where nice garments for hijab-wearing women could be found. When Amal was first founded, the idea was to sell garments imported from the Middle East; only much later did the company decide to also start producing collections of its own. The designs for the Amal collections were made by a hired tailor in cooperation with the company's founder. All the garments labelled Amal were also labelled 'Made in France'.

Knz-couture

Knz-couture is a family business based in Lille, where it runs two shops.[12] The designer Karima Jabbar founded the brand Knz (or Kenza as it was then called) as a nineteen-year-old after having finished a degree in design in 2001. She wore the hijab herself and designed garments based on her own needs, items she wanted to wear but could not find. Until 2008, Karima Jabbar designed all Knz collections, but after she had a child, her brother Brahim took over more of her work. Knz has found its niche in trendy tunics, but the company also produces trousers, skirts and headscarves. When marketing the women's line, both hijab-wearing and non-hijab-wearing models are used. That the company targets both these groups is a fact that Brahim underlined when

I interviewed him at Le Bourget. All materials used for Knz's collections are bought in France, where production also takes place. Several of the young hijabis I talked to during Le Bourget stated that Knz was their big favourite amongst what was available on the French Islamic fashion market. Salima, a 23-year-old from Paris, even said Knz was the only stand in the whole bazaar worth entering. She did, however, also tell me she had liked what the company had brought the year before much more. While most other Islamic fashion stores with their own brands in France target differentiated consumer segments, Knz, with its up-to-date collections, including retro-looking items, primarily targets consumers in their twenties or younger.

The Knz stand was identical to the Amal-mode stand in size but arranged more like a shop, and hangers were not reachable from the paths. The stand was framed with huge posters—displaying fashion shots from the company's Web store—where some of the models posing were wearing headscarves and some not. The stand only had one single opening, and the walls were constructed of shiny cream-coloured tarpaulin covering metal frames. Knz also displayed outfits on headless mannequins that hung next to the posters. Inside, the hangers were placed along three sides, helping to constitute walls. A big table with headscarves was placed along one short side so that customers could buy a scarf and get a peek inside the stand without entering. Only members of the Jabbar family were working in the stand. The prices for Knz items ranged between €25 and €40.

Knz is short for the company's original name, Kenza. The company changed names to avoid mix-ups after another Islamic fashion shop called Kenza[13] opened in Paris. Knz mainly sells women's wear but introduced a small menswear collection in 2008. When I first interviewed Brahim Jabbar at Le Bourget, I got few useful answers, and his mother stood close by, ready to interrupt at any moment. In order to get to know more about Knz-couture, I went to Lille in November 2008 and visited the Roubaix shop, where I met the mother, Fatima Jabbar, again. That time, the interview lasted several hours and while loud rap music and customers shopping for the Eid al-Kabir filled the shop,[14] I learned how almost everyone in the family was involved in the business. Amongst the many other things Fatima Jabbar explained to me was one of the reasons why they were so cautious when talking to strangers: they had been to court to (successfully) defend their designs after some had been copied.

Saouli

Designer Karima Saouli and her sister founded the Belgian company Saouli together. Karima claims to have been the first in the French-speaking world to establish a brand targeting Muslim women. Saouli first produced collections that were sold by other Islamic fashion retailers worldwide. The sisters opened their first shop in Brussels in 2003 and claim that 40 per cent of their customers are non-Muslims. Karima Saouli is from a Moroccan background and many of her relatives in Morocco are active in the textile industry. Although she has strong links to the Moroccan fashion production industry, she explained how she insists on producing the Saouli collections in France and how this was a strategic as well as a symbolic choice.[15] The 'Made in France' label is a well-established guarantor for good-quality French fashion, and hence producing Islamic fashion items carrying this label not only adds value to the garments but also states that the garments (as well as plenty of the future wearers) are indeed French.

The Saouli collections are sold not only in the company's own shop and Web store[16] but also in other Islamic fashion stores around the world—for example, in the United States, in the Arab world and in Malaysia. In order to market her brand, Karima Saouli has travelled extensively, and Saouli garments have appeared on many Islamic fashion catwalks worldwide.[17] When I interviewed Karima, I received an impressive, shiny press folder that included information and images that could also be found on the Web site. Her answers to my questions constituted parts of a story she knew by heart and included parts of her own life script.[18] While narrating her company's founding story, she also told me about her relation to dress and her experiences of growing up in Belgium with Moroccan parents. When explaining about the difficulties she used to face trying to find outfits suitable when wearing the hijab to work, she generalized and turned her (and her co-founder/sister's) story into the story of all the working hijab-wearers of her generation in Europe some years back:

> Today, Muslim women work, not like our mothers when they first came to Europe. The mother, she did not work, she did not go to school so she did not need a fashionable garment, the djellaba was enough. But we realized that the Muslim woman could not find clothes that suited her, especially in the context in which she lives . . . I have always been immersed in a fashion design ambience and when I made my own clothes Muslim women liked them. So I started out like that, little by little, with our business.

Saouli has been coming back yearly to market its collections at the RAMF bazaar for many years. It was the only company to have constructed a completely secluded room where decorated shop windows framed the entrances both at the front and rear. In the shop windows made of transparent tarpaulin, full Saouli outfits were presented next to flower arrangements with small pink lanterns and draperies hung behind them. The Saouli collection on display included all sorts of different women's wear garments. Hired, skilled, non-hijabi saleswomen dressed in the same outfits shown in the shop windows served the customers in the Saouli shop. During the RAMF, it was busy at all times.

SIMILARITY AND DIFFERENCE ON DISPLAY

When looking at each one of the three collections discussed and how they were displayed, concerns about modesty, Muslim-ness, profit *and* fashionability are perceivable. There is nothing obvious about what constitutes a Muslim garment as such (Tarlo 2010: 5), so this leaves companies with plenty of leeway for developing and displaying their collections. Islamic fashion retailers need to differentiate themselves vis-à-vis mainstream fashion while simultaneously working within it. In the spring of 2008, for example, garments inspired by 'the oriental' were all the rage in mainstream fashion, with lots of headscarves, kaftans and harem pants in high fashion and looks such as 'the Afghan look' gaining popularity.

Amal, consequently, had produced harem trousers and Saouli presented Asian-inspired outfits, such as white wrap-over tops combined with large, black belts and wide black trousers.[19] Most of the tops and tunics included in the collections were, however, long-sleeved, high-necked models that were more modest than that spring's mainstream fashion suggested. This way of combining adaptation to mainstream fashion and diversification (reworking subfield-specific ideas about Muslim aesthetics and looks) within one and the same collection is typical for European Islamic fashion design. While branding themselves, Saouli, Knz-couture and Amal-mode are also reinterpreting Muslim-ness fused with fashion. They are negotiating similarity and difference through commodities (see also Dwyer and Crang 2002, 2003, on ethnic business niches) when aiming both at being recognizable as Muslim businesses and as fashion businesses.

Visual identity and image (corporate name, logo, publicity, etc.) are particularly important in the fashion retail sector. Store image and interior design are also crucial. If choices of visual identity are to work as differentiation strategies and have the desired effects in terms of attracting consumers they have to be communicated to and perceived by targeted groups in the intended way (Cheng, Hines and Grime 2008). When displaying their collections both in the stands at Le Bourget and on their respective Web sites, the three companies strategically handled what some stricter Muslims might find offensive.[20] Knz were the only of the three to display full-figure pictures of both hijabis and non-hijabis at Le Bourget. Amal and Saouli had, on the other hand, chosen to have mainly non-hijabi saleswomen working in their respective stands. Still, Amal was the most careful of the three, completely avoiding faces or heads or the use of full-figure mannequins. On their Web site, headscarves are wrapped around empty holes, something one rarely sees in the context of European Islamic fashion. To depict female bodies without showing faces or heads is, however, relatively common in the mainstream women's fashion imagery, and therefore doing it for religious reasons can pass unnoticed. On their Web sites, Saouli and Knz-couture show both faces and full-body images of models with and without the hijab. The companies have all chosen labels that are personal names, which are neither unique to their businesses nor explicitly Islamic. The fact that they have chosen logos and brands that do not signal Muslim identity is significant in the French context. Amal and Kenza (Knz for short) are popular girl's names in France. These names are also used for businesses selling other things than fashion. Knz's choice of logo—bright pink text written against a black background—connotes notions of punk styles, do-it-yourself and feminist movements rather than Muslim-ness.[21] Saouli's logo in black, gold and white is more sophisticated than what is common in the context of French Islamic fashion. However, both Saouli's and Knz's visual identities are in line with how they want to be perceived by consumers amongst their respective target groups, Knz aiming at being perceived as cool and attractive by the youngest French hijabis and Saouli at primarily attracting working Muslim women on a global Islamic fashion market. Amal does not have a pronounced visual identity; the logo can be found written in different manners.

MOTIVATING AND LEGITIMIZING FOUNDING STORIES

Using founding stories and controlling how and when they are told is an essential part of the marketing strategy for designers founding small fashion brands.[22] At the RAMF, what was told, when and by whom seemed more important to Knz and Saouli staff than to Amal staff. The hired young saleswomen working in the Amal stands all told different and partly contradictory things about the company while at Saouli only the designer herself and her sister/co-founder answered questions. Brahim Jabbar of Knz-couture was even more careful than the Saouli sisters.

Younger European hijab-wearers' narratives about dress choices can by no means be generalized into one, but after having conducted many interviews on the issue, it is possible to detect certain recurring key themes[23]:

1. An emphasis on generational differences when it comes to choices of dress.
2. An emphasis on difficulties experienced in finding suitable clothes and on the earlier lack of suitable things available in the market.
3. An emphasis on a turning point in personal style with a before and an after, often culminating in an increasingly individualized style as the outcome.

Identifiable key patterns of meaning such as the aforementioned similarities between stories of different hijab-wearers also appear in the founding stories narrated by the producers and retailers of Islamic fashion interviewed here.

Karima Saouli uses a polished and well-rehearsed founding story for marketing purposes. The company's founding story includes parts of her own life script and through shifting back and forth from I to we, she successfully connects her story to the experiences of other young Muslim women. Through generalizing her own experiences she even establishes her story as *the* second-generation hijab-wearing narrative. While presenting her business as part of the answer to the needs of young hijabis, she also stresses that young hijabis are *modern, fashionable European, working women* with *the same needs* for nice things to wear as other European women of their generation. Hence, when telling her company's founding story, Karima Saouli aims at reversing negative stereotypes in a manner common amongst designers and entrepreneurs promoting visibly Muslim fashion (Tarlo 2010: 11). The Saouli founding story is both an exceptionally well-turned narrative and a story that works. Even if Amal-mode and Knz-couture do not make use of stories in the same way, their business narratives also include personal hijabi experiences; for example, the experience of a lack of nice things to wear. Stories about being a hijabi, looking for suitable fashionable clothes, founding a business (and striving for profit) while supplying goods earlier experienced as difficult to find play a legitimizing role. However, even when the stories include recognizable and particular hijabi experiences (for example, parts of the founders' life scripts), they are primarily stories constructed for marketing purposes, stories about finding a business niche and about the intent to supply what the market demands. While others have found that Muslim fashion entrepreneurs often refer to *da'wa* (calling others to Islam; see, for example, Tarlo 2010) when talking about their work, there was no mention of this, or of any other religious duties, in relation to the business activities of any of the many shop owners and shop assistants I talked to during the 2008 RAMF.

DISCUSSION

The three companies, Amal-mode, Knz-couture and Saouli, are actors in a highly competitive market where business and profit is in focus at all times. They are first and foremost fashion retailers who present themselves as actors in a diversified market rather than as members of a homogenous faith-based community. The RAMF event at Le Bourget is strikingly commercial and the attitudes of all persons interviewed within the companies were strictly business. To be present at Le Bourget is essential for businesses targeting French Muslims, and the Islamic fashion entrepreneurs interviewed described it as their major yearly marketing event. In the bazaar at Le Bourget, differentiation is partly and temporarily toned down in favour of expressions of unity amongst Muslims. To be associated with Muslim consumer groups and clearly signal Muslim belonging becomes more important during the annual fair.

The three companies' respective choices of display and marketing were different but corresponded with the consumer groups targeted. While Knz targeted the young and trendy and Saouli displayed more professional looks for working women, Amal-mode promoted the idea of having something for everyone. Even though unity can be said to have been in focus in the bazaar Amal-mode, Knz-couture and Saouli all managed to communicate a coherent image for their respective companies. As actors in the field of Islamic fashion, the three companies are involved in ongoing negotiations about fashionability and respectability. Through their specific business strategies, as shown in their respective choices of business name, logo, products and techniques of display, they continuously renegotiate the limits and possibilities of Islamic fashion. When they decide what goods to produce and how to market them, they help to set the frame for European and French Islamic fashion. The defining of what Islamic fashion is and can be, of what can be produced and marketed as such and also *how* such goods should be marketed, both within a specific Muslim context like Le Bourget and towards larger consumer groups, is an ongoing process. The businesses simultaneously contribute to negotiations on what Muslims should wear, developing local Muslim subcultural aesthetics.

Key patterns of meaning that partly resemble stories told by different wearers and consumers of Islamic fashion can be identified in the companies' narratives. Through establishing themselves within a recognizably European hijab story, the female entrepreneurs accentuate their relations to their target groups. The stories function as both explanatory and legitimizing. Narratives including notions of a gap in the market that needs to be filled are commonly used to legitimize the creation of a niche market, and when the entrepreneurs use such narratives, they ally themselves with commercial discourses. I do not think the adoption of such classic commercial narratives and capitalist logic should necessarily be read as attempts by the entrepreneurs to be understood as well-integrated in the national context. But, since secularism is valorized and hegemonic in the French context, this might be a possible positive outcome for the entrepreneurs.[24] Amongst young Muslims in France (and elsewhere in Europe), I have noticed a strong tendency to idealize entrepreneurship. I argue that being a good Muslim, which for many equals being a role model, and being a successful entrepreneur in the context examined here can be seen as complementary and mutually enforcing.[25]

Even if I do not see the general business-mindedness included in the strategies of the three companies as specifically adjusted to the French national context but rather as an adjustment to international Muslim contexts where businesses selling Islamic products primarily to other Muslims are common (Haenni 2005), other parts of their strategies relate specifically to the French context. Choosing to mainly produce certain garments, namely tunics and trousers, is motivated by the, in the French context, relative acceptance of the hijab when worn in combination with such garments. The label 'Made in

France' is a bearer of strong symbolic value and a quality marker, both in the French and in the global market. The decision to produce in France is a means to add value to the collections while also placing them within the prestigious context of fashion made in France. To succeed on the French Islamic fashion market you need to be able to combine not only faith and fashion but, more importantly, similarity (to other fashion actors) and difference (as Muslim), and you need to be present at Le Bourget.

NOTES

1. The Rencontre Anuelle des Musulmans de France (RAMF) is held in May at Le Bourget outside Paris and is commonly referred to simply as Le Bourget.
2. See Tarlo (2010) for discussion of different articulations of the 'visibly Muslim'.
3. According to the organizers, the UOIF (Union of French Islamic Organisations), the number of visitors during the four days of the event was more than two hundred thousand in 2008.
4. *Rencontre annuelle des musulmans de France,* 'Un cadre agréable', <http://www.uoif-ramf.fr/> accessed 15 November 2011.
5. Although called the bazaar by most visitors, the marketplace at the yearly event is officially called 'Le salon du Bourget'.
6. For a short description of the event in preceding years, see Bowen (2007: 101).
7. The two shops are situated in Saint-Denis and Sarcelles.
8. Jilbabs and abayas are both full-length outer garments, somewhat similar to kaftans.
9. Long, modest headscarf model that covers the shoulders and sometimes even the hips; it is also worn for prayer.
10. Tunics (in French *tuniques*) were not only central to many French Islamic fashion collections in 2008 but also what all the young hijabis I interviewed in France during 2007 and 2008 would mostly wear and hence shop for.
11. *Ensemble* means suit of matching garments sold together; here, tunics or dresses combined with trousers or skirts.
12. One in central Lille and one in Roubaix, in the north-eastern part of Lille.
13. This store also has a small brand of its own called Kenza and is located on Rue Jean Pierre Timbaud in Paris 11th.
14. Eid Al Kabir (the greater feast) or the Eid al-Adha (the feast of sacrifice) is the feast at the end of the hajj.
15. This is something she has repeatedly told when interviewed (see also Haenni 2005).

16. *Saouli,* <www.saouli.eu> accessed 20 November 2008.
17. For example, in Chicago, Dubai and Kuala Lumpur.
18. For further discussions on life scripts and women's narratives see Fivush (2010: 93–5) and Sangster (1994: 15–21).
19. The taste for ethnic fashions amongst Islamic fashion producers does not necessarily imply direct relation to so-called traditional clothes or dress from the designer's eventual country of origin. See Skov (2002, 2003) for further discussions on self-Orientalizing business strategies.
20. For example, showing women's hair and faces or playing music. The Web sites are <www.knz-creation.eu>, <www.saouli.eu>, <www.amalmode.com>.
21. Compare, for example, the NPNS (Neither Whores Nor Submissive) logo: <http://www.niputesnisoumises.com/>.
22. Compare smaller designer-founded fashion brands such as, for example, the Swedish brands Dagmar (<http://www.houseofdagmar.se/>) and Swedish Hasbeens (<http://www.swedishhasbeens.com/>).
23. Some of these themes are also present in the sartorial narratives of Muslim women recounted by other researchers such as Tarlo (2010) and Karlsson Minganti (2007).
24. Entrepreneurship can be rewarding in many ways. For example, in 2007 Karima Saouli was honoured by the Belgian monarch for being a successful Belgian entrepreneur.
25. The ways in which self-employment and enterprising spirit are idealized and the focus on consumption during fairs like Le Bourget resemble charismatic Protestant contexts. The amount of goods on display is much more varied but the ways in which goods are marketed as particularly suitable for Muslims is similar (see Coleman 1998).

REFERENCES

Bowen, J. R. (2006), *Why the French Don't Like Headscarves: Islam, the State, and Public Space,* Princeton, NJ: Princeton University Press.

Cheng, R., T. Hines and I. Grime (2008), 'Desired and Perceived Identities of Fashion Retailers', *European Journal of Marketing* 42, 5–6: 682–701.

Coleman, S. (1998), 'Charismatic Christianity and the Dilemmas of Globalization', *Religion* 28: 245–56.

Czarniawska, B. (1997), *Narrating the Organization: Dramas of Institutional Identity*, Chicago, IL: University of Chicago Press.

Dwyer, C., and P. Crang (2002), 'Fashioning Ethnicities: The Commercial Spaces of Multiculture', *Ethnicities* 2: 410.

Dwyer, C., and P. Crang (2003), 'Commodifying Difference: Selling EASTern Fashion', *Society and Space* 21: 269–91.

Fivush, R. (2010), 'Speaking Silence: The Social Construction of Silence in Autobiographical and Cultural Narratives', *Memory* 18, 2: 88–98.

Haenni, P. (2005), *L'Islam de Marché: L'autre Révolution Conservatrice,* Paris: Broché.

Karlsson Minganti, P. (2007), *Muslima: Islamisk väckelse och unga muslimska kvinnors förhandlingar om genus i det samtida Sverige,* Stockholm: Stockholms Universitet.

Mercer, K. (1994), *Welcome to the Jungle: New Positions in Black Cultural Studies,* London: Routledge.

Sangster, J. (1994), 'Telling Our Stories: Feminist Debates and the Use of Oral History', *Women's History Review* 3, 1: 5–28.

Scott, J. (2007), *The Politics of the Veil,* Princeton, NJ: Princeton University Press.

Skov, L. (2002), 'Hong Kong Fashion Designers as Cultural Intermediaries: Out of Global Garment Production', *Cultural Studies* 16, 4: 553–69.

Skov, L. (2003), 'Fashion-nation: A Japanese Globalization Experience and a Hong Kong Dilemma', in C. Jones, A. Leshkowich and S. Niessen, eds., *Reorienting Fashion: The Globalization of Asian Fashion,* Oxford: Berg.

Tarlo, E. (2010), *Visibly Muslim: Fashion, Politics, Faith,* Oxford: Berg.

Thanning Vendelø, M. (1998), 'Narrating Corporate Reputation: Becoming Legitimate through Storytelling', *International Studies of Marketing & Organisation* 28, 3: 120–37.

–10–

Hijab on the Shop Floor: Muslims in Fashion Retail in Britain

Reina Lewis

In the United Kingdom, a discernible cohort of young Muslim women is at the vanguard of new styles of modest fashion, working mainstream trends with creative combinations of layers and inventive forms of hijab (Tarlo 2010). But unlike other celebrated instances of British street style, these style innovations are rarely recognized as such by the mainstream fashion media. In popular discourse, the veil is usually seen as a controversial symbol, rarely as a piece of clothing. Scholarly interest in Muslim fashions tends to focus on Muslims as consumers rather than as participants in the mainstream fashion industry from which most of the garments they wear are derived. Yet a quick stroll around London's Oxford Street, home to the flagship stores of many of Britain's high street fashion chains, reveals visibly Muslim young women working front of house—a picture echoed in high streets and malls across Britain. In most high street fashion stores (and in all those discussed here), staff are required to dress according to company criteria. Most often this involves wearing a selection of clothes from the store's seasonal collection. Sometimes, especially in stores aimed at the youth market, staff is provided with a branded T-shirt which can be worn with bottoms in a set colour—mostly sourced from the employee's own wardrobe. Focussing on young women who wear hijab and who work in high street fashion retail aimed at young women, this chapter asks, what is the impact of sartorially Muslim women behind as well as in front of the shop counter?

THE LEGAL CONTEXT

UK employment law has shifted in recent years from equal opportunities legislation which outlawed discrimination on the grounds of race and ethnicity to new policies concerned more broadly with diversity. In 2003, the UK Employment Equality (Religion or Belief) Regulations brought the United Kingdom in line with the European Employment Equality Directive of 2000, extending legal protection to cover discrimination 'on the grounds of perceived as well as actual religion or belief'.[1] Previous legislation had offered protection only in terms of race or ethnicity and could therefore only cover those faith groups recognized in law as an ethnic group, such as Jews and Sikhs. Now, anyone can seek protection against discrimination at work or in vocational training. Applying equally to minority and majority religious populations, the new legislation requires employers to permit and facilitate the expression of faith or philosophical belief as defined by the employee. Like all the other categories of employee incorporated into the Equality Act of 2010—which includes disability, marital status, sexual orientation, as well as gender and ethnicity—employees' rights are limited by provision for generic and unspecified limitations that could include, for example, health and safety restrictions on operating machinery in loose robes, and so on. In each case, employers are required to make 'reasonable adjustments', with disputes and court cases revolving around definitions of *reasonable* in each context.

Challenges to British and EU legislation concerning the expression of faith and belief at work have focussed public attention on the comportment and adornment of the dressed body with controversies emerging over a diverse range of items from the niqab worn by a teaching assistant at school to the crucifixes worn by medical and airline staff and the chastity rings worn by school pupils (Perfect 2011). These cases centred on a variety of issues from health and safety, the ability to perform physical tasks, and compliance with uniform codes. Only in one case so far has a legal dispute centred on an employee's ability to embody the company's aesthetic ethos through her appearance. This was the case of the hijabi Muslim hairdresser, Bushra Noah, who in 2008 was turned down for a stylist position at an independent small North London salon by the employer who claimed that the visible hairstyles of employees were essential for advertising the salon. The industrial tribunal did not uphold Noah's claim of direct religious discrimination because the employer's decision would have applied equally to any person who covered their hair whatever the reason. But she did win on indirect discrimination because other Muslim women who covered would similarly have been disadvantaged. Noah was awarded £4,000 for injury to feeling. Unlike other high-profile cases taken against public sector or large private sector employers, this case was against a small independent company unlikely to have employment procedures overseen by HR professionals.

In conceptualizing the research on which this chapter is based, I was interested in investigating how these regulations were working out in fashion retail. To my surprise, I found that hijab wearing, far from being considered problematic by employers, was sometimes actually perceived as an asset for mediating between retail companies and their consumers.[2]

THE RETAIL CONTEXT

Studies in consumption have come increasingly to regard all elements of the production-distribution-consumption relationship as important, analysing how products come to consumers and how consumers make sense of themselves through commodities (Wrigley and Lowe 2002; Entwistle 2009). Challenging previous approaches that had focussed mainly on industrial labour, studies of retail have been animated by recognition of its crucial role in mediating the links between commodities and consumers.

In the context of fashion retail, women, and especially young women, make up a significant majority of the workforce. Always heavily dependent on labour, retail has long sought to reduce costs: an initially higher status, male-dominated and better-paid workforce has been feminized and casualized since the early twentieth century, with a shift towards customer self-service (Winship 2000). Jobs became more often part time, favouring the cheaper labour of those (women and young people) perceived not to be the main family wage earner. Today, retail in the United Kingdom and United States is characterized by a higher percentage of staff working not only part time but for fewer hours per week (Wrigley and Lowe 2002). The implementation since the 1980s of innovative electronic distribution technologies has facilitated the shift to a retail-led rather than producer-led globalized supply chain, further reducing or replacing previous retail jobs.

Nonetheless, retail remains notoriously labour intensive and, as Susan Christopherson (1996) argues, the various forms of labour involved in retail (from owner/managers to warehouse staff to sales assistants) do not simply shift product from one place to another but actively create value that adds to the meanings of products. In the journeys of fashion products from distributor/manufacturer to consumer, the bodies of shop staff modelling the products on sale have a special prominence (Leslie 2002). Clothes and accessories that mark the wearer as Muslim, or as belonging to any religious community, are especially significant in fashion retail where front of house staff literally represent the company or the brand with their bodies.

The public comportment of employees has been rendered even more important by the widespread take up of corporate branding, as marketing shifted from differentiating products to fostering distinctive identities for companies and corporations. This is especially significant in fashion retail where, in both luxury and mass-market sectors, one corporation may own several apparently separate companies presented and marketed as distinct and competing brands. This has reduced the number of independent stores. In the United Kingdom especially, the high street multiples (including department stores and supermarkets) enjoy a larger percentage of overall apparel retail sales (near 75 per cent) than is the case elsewhere in the European Union (Woodward 2009: 89).

However, customer service returned to some sectors of retail in the mid-1980s as part of the ongoing transition from a supplier-driven to a buyer-driven commodity chain. Many employers moved towards '"customized service provision" and "customized workers" to match' (Crang and Martin 1991; Lowe

1991: 42). From the early 1990s, mid- and higher-end stores began to emphasize customer care as a competitive strategy whilst the budget sector downgraded staff roles with self-service shopping systems (Lowe and Crewe 1996). The requirement on staff to engage in scripted performances of emotional authenticity further privileged those workers most able to embody the values of the brand. The American company Gap 'transformed the British High Street and importantly the British shop assistant beyond all recognition' (Lowe and Crewe 1996: 207), using point-of-sales technology to free up staff time to deliver a highly developed script that ensured constant customer interaction. Embodied performances of staff have become commodified to the point where 'the sales assistants...increasingly comprise the actual product on sale' (Wrigley and Lowe 1996: 24). As front-of-house staff became more important in communicating the value of the brand in the mid-1990s, clothing retail was characterized by 'a homogenization of staffing' and 'increased competition for similar and possibly smaller labour segments...particularly true for youth-oriented chains which employ young people (many part time) as a marketing strategy' (Christopherson 1996: 168). The need for staff to be imbricated in the habits of appropriate consumption still structures recruitment today and has particular relevance to the marketing of Islamic fashion.

The high street (or its corollary, the mall) is not simply an inert space in which shopping happens. Marked by social and aesthetic relations, the high street is a space in which styles are actively made, moderated, disseminated and adopted. To shop, to work in a shop, to be simply perambulating in the stores is to be part of a consumption-scape in which one sees and is seen as part of the fashion spectacle that surrounds and fosters the mechanisms of acquisition. Window displays, visual merchandising in-store, adverts that surround the shopper in the street or the mall all provide tips on ways to wear current trends. So do the dressed bodies of other consumers and the bodies (and sometimes the advice) of shop staff. Not surprisingly, the young women who populate this study are immersed in a high street fashion culture as both consumers and workers. Like many of the Muslim and non-Muslim customers they serve, their wardrobes consist to a considerable extent of a mix of high street purchases carefully combined with items sourced elsewhere to create their own minutely differentiated look that is both 'unique' to them and on trend with the dominant fashion story of the day (Woodward 2009).

Nearly all the women I spoke to were motivated to seek shop work because they were interested in fashion, often choosing where to apply on the basis of liking the store's merchandise and wanting the staff discount. In the context of low-paid fashion retail, the discount can 'constitute a portion of the wage...realized through consumption' (Leslie 2002: 72). But the ability to look 'right' can also allow staff to accrue forms of distinction conferred by working in fashionable brands (Crang 1994; Wright 2005), whilst further diminishing the servile associations of service work by breaking down the set script with the theatrical development of personalized 'improvisational performances' (Crang 1994: 693).

In fashion retail, the clothed bodies of shop staff have especial importance in signalling the aesthetic vision and values of the company. Employees at all levels need to demonstrate cultural competency with the codes of fashion relevant to their sector. As Joanne Entwistle has demonstrated in her study of the women's fashion buying team at London department store Selfridges, these senior decision-makers at the top of the fashion retail hierarchy, not usually on display on the shop floor, acutely feel the need to look right in order to demonstrate 'through bodily enactments and expression' their aesthetic capital to designers and competitors: 'Critically in this market the knowledge is worn on the body' (2009: 41).

The same requirement to have and display embodied fashion capital applies to front-of-house shop staff. Despite shop work's generically low status and low pay, staff members need to use their fashion savvy to advise customers and gain sales. The rapidly changing cycles of style that characterize the industry go beyond clothes to the bodies that wear them. A new ad campaign may produce a look only achievable on certain sorts of staff bodies. This can pose an element of 'employment risk' to staff, given that the different body 'types' demanded by stores are constantly changing (Leslie 2002: 69). The question posed here is, what happens when the body that represents the brand is wearing hijab?

SHOP STAFF

A selection of young women who wore hijab and worked in high street fashion shops told me about their experiences at work and their relations with managers, co-workers and customers. Their places of employment covered a range of high street multiples including River Island, Peacocks and, from the Arcadia group, global brands such as Topshop and Dorothy Perkins, plus department stores such as Debenhams and Selfridges.

Respondents (referred to by pseudonyms) came predominantly from London, Manchester and Bradford and were all of British South Asian, mostly Pakistani, family backgrounds. Whilst one was a first-generation migrant, the others were second- and third-generation, heirs to the mass migration of South Asians to Britain in the 1960s (Peach 2006; Gillat-Ray 2010). For young women growing up in the former textile and industrial towns of Manchester and Bradford, the neighbourhood often contains not just other Muslims but other members of their family and kinship or *biradari* (clan) networks. This tendency to co-ethnic/national clustering is also found in London to some extent where there is relatively little intra-ethnic marrying given the diversity of the Muslim population (Lewis 2007). For Muslims who migrated to work in the textiles industries in the North, and manufacture elsewhere, the decline of British manufacture has been of tremendous impact; Muslims nationally report lower-than-average incomes and many live in areas of multiple deprivation, often relying on municipal housing that is not large enough for traditional three-generation families with several children (Gillat-Ray 2010) and often (especially when minority ethnic) experience workplace disadvantage (Kariapper 2009).

There is, however, a growing Muslim middle class that now lives in the affluent suburbs of towns of Muslim residential density, such as Manchester (Werbner 2002). The London Muslim population also includes people of East African Asian, Middle Eastern and Arab origins who, unlike the South Asian migrants who were mostly from peasant backgrounds, arrived in Britain with educational and financial capital. There are also wealthy Gulf Arabs who use London as a base for their transnational, luxury, peripatetic lifestyle. The elite Muslim demographic is further extended by the Gulf nationals who visit London most summers and whose legendary shopping excess is anticipated and catered for by many central London retailers.

The Muslim population has, however, been characterized by a spectacularly low rate of female participation in the formal wage economy, and it is only more recently that Muslim women are entering paid employment in greater numbers and in a greater range of occupations. The generation of young women I spoke to are therefore emblematic in a number of ways. They are all fluent in English and au fait with British cultural forms (including fashion and fashion media) as well as having varying degrees of fluency in other community languages. They typify the educational achievements of the second and third generation encouraged to outstrip the often-limited educational opportunities available to previous generations: all of my respondents are high school graduates and are either currently at or about to start university or have graduated. Some are doing or about to start master's programmes. Whilst one young woman was making a career in fashion buying, all the others were working part time in retail whilst studying or in college holidays.[3] Their occupations outside the home counter the commonly held presumption that Muslim parents won't let their girls go to college or work for fear of tainting family honour and indicates that these young women and their families have negotiated ways of containing potential perceived risks and gossip, such as attending local universities so that they can continue living at home and wearing hijab which may act to make their public presence more acceptable (Basit 1997; Dwyer and Shah 2009). The disciplinary visuality of the retail space developed by stores to regulate staff labour (and maximize sales) can also be appropriated into the panoptical regime of the local community. Whilst some jobs such as taxi driving involve encounters with strangers in the closed and mobile space of the car, the open space of the store means that a woman's comportment with others is subject to 'the disciplinary gaze of the store and the public as a whole, including parents, who can make an inspection of their daughter's performance anytime' (Mohammad 2005: 195).

As well as spatially making work 'safe' in community terms, the geographical location of the retail workplace is also a major factor in how easy it is to be hijabi when at work. In areas with a large Muslim population and/or a cosmopolitan mix, the existing familiarity of managers, co-workers and customers with Muslims created forms of cultural competency that rendered individual Muslim shop assistants less of a novelty and easier to accommodate. In Bradford, eighteen-year-old, third-generation British Pakistani A. Y. was not even looking for work but was recruited when shopping in a branch of Dorothy Perkins because her cool ensemble, including hijab, was exactly the image the non-Muslim store manager wanted to project:

> It was just one of them things. I just went into the shop, literally, and the lady said to me, oh you look like the perfect sort of person we need to be working in this branch, and they were just admiring the way I looked and the way I dressed...[they liked that I looked] slightly different I think.

Looking 'different' in this instance did not mean looking Muslim; it meant looking trendily Muslim. The manager's ability to recognise A. Y.'s hijab as *part of* her overall fashion savvy self-stylization normalizes the hijab within a discourse of fashion innovation. This transcends an affirmative action approach in which the hijab would have registered primarily as a religious symbol. In Bradford, with a large and youthful Pakistani Muslim population, A. Y.'s modish modesty counts as cultural capital. As a cool school-leaver (having just completed her A levels with a place secured at a local university), A. Y.'s personal fashion knowledge continued to be valued by staff and customers: soon she was promoted with extra responsibility for visual merchandising, styling the store mannequins, and was frequently asked advice by customers who, she told me, 'say I represent the shop quite well, in the sort of clothes that I wear and the way I present myself'.

The capacity of the hijabi body to be a cool brand ambassador is understood by workers to be reliant on cultural competencies that are socially and spatially specific. Twenty-two-year-old graduate Naila, who worked part time (before starting her master's) at the mid-market apparel store of Next in Bradford, argued that this was

> something that's quite specific to Bradford...if somebody from out of Bradford came they wouldn't expect to see it, but I think in Bradford it's just normal to see a Muslim girl wearing headscarf. People [are used to seeing] the wide range of how Muslim girls dress.

The presence of visibly Muslim staff is understood in this context as a bonus for the shop, especially when faith combines with ethnicity and multilingual

Muslim staff like Naila, a second-generation British Pakistani, who can assist non-English speaking customers. That said, hijabi shopworkers demonstrated considerable delicacy in how they negotiated processes of mutual recognition with Muslim customers. Naila is sometimes greeted with 'As-Salaamu Aleikum' by 'older ladies and older guys', and whilst she responds in kind, she doesn't herself initiate the salutation, sticking to the generic store script (here presented as entirely naturalized behaviour):

> I think it's just a habit of saying 'hi', 'hello' to whoever it is...I think it's just an automatic thing that I say to whoever approaches a till. But, even though I can tell someone is Muslim....I never say it [As-Salaamu Aleikum] first.

Not inaugurating the departure from store protocol, Naila can nonetheless accurately interpret the unspoken concerns about modesty that underlie some customer enquiries:

> Sometimes you might get other girls in headscarves coming up to me and saying, 'Oh, does this look okay?' Or they might have a dress or something in their hand, [and they] might say, 'Oh, do you think this is alright?' Or they might say, 'Oh, is this too see-through? What do you think? Would I need to wear something underneath it?'

In contrast to Naila's reticence, Laila Shah, at budget brand Peacocks in Manchester, will often initiate the Islamic salutation. Currently a first year undergraduate at a local university and herself a first-generation Pakistani migrant, arriving in Britain with her family via Saudi Arabia, Laila links the declaration of religious identity closely to her linguistic community affiliations:

> If it's a Muslim customer I would be like Islamic, I would say, you know...if they're speaking Urdu, I will speak Urdu with them because that's my own language as well, so they feel comfortable. People like it I think, and my manager [said] it is a positive thing.

At Dorothy Perkins, A. Y. is also seen by management as a language resource for Punjabi speaking customers. Some of the customers also say 'Salaam' to her, but she is careful not to initiate:

> I'll wait for it to come from them...it's not even because I think it's rude, it's just I think it's more professional [to] wait for them to come to you, [also, it makes it fairer] so that other staff don't think that I'm undermining anyone else or saying anything bad about another customer.

Her hesitation is a sophisticated mix of respect for customers about whose preferences she doesn't want to presume and sensitivity to how her Islamic interactions might be perceived by co-workers unable to participate in this linguistically and religiously specialized communication.

BUT WHAT ABOUT MANAGEMENT?

It was not easy to find brand HR directors willing to participate in this research. Their job is to protect the brand, and most requested that their participation be kept confidential. Whilst my interviews with United Kingdom and London regional HR directors for brands and consortia cover most but not all of the brands at which the shop assistants worked, when brands or companies are referred to in quotations or material deriving from interviews with HR professionals, they are identified only by generic descriptors agreed with the HR respondents.

Few of the brand representatives I approached agreed to talk to me about their experiences of diversity regulations and their HR policy. Among those that did, it was notable that their HR and ER (employee relations) managers/directors were almost unanimous in presenting the company as already in accordance with the spirit of the new regulations. Keen, as one might expect, to present a positive rendition of company employee relations, this narrative is also in keeping with the UK retail sector's history of anticipating government regulatory regimes in order to maintain autonomy where possible via compliance with private (voluntary) rather than public (legally enforceable) regulatory codes (Wrigley and Lowe 2002).

HR policy in many stores exemplified the shift across the sector from policies based on equal opportunities to those conceptualized in terms of diversity. Company policy on religious expression was often presented as part of wider 'dignity at work' package, in keeping with the emergent inclusive diversity frame. This was often associated with codes of conduct concerned with social and environmental sustainability—a major preoccupation of popular consumer discourse in the United Kingdom. Employee relations were seen as part of a wider corporate responsibility programme that needed to be promoted not only externally but also internally to all sectors of the company.

In relation specifically to store uniform codes, none of the HR professionals I spoke to saw any reason why wearing hijab should be a problem, often expecting that hijabis would be self-selecting about where they applied, just as was the case elsewhere in the fashion retail sector. Jackie, now HR director for a major UK department store chain, pointed out in relation to her previous post in the United States with a high-end designer store that he (the unnameable American designer) would only have beautiful bodies, male and female in his shops: 'If R walked out into the store and somebody wasn't gorgeous, then heaven help you'. It was quite typical in retail, she noted, for bodies not considered appropriate to be 'selected out' during different stages of the recruitment process, with the luxury sector and cosmetics the most notorious on this count. In the UK department store sector where she now worked, the company needs staff to communicate a corporate image rather than fashion-forward bodily gorgeousness. The black uniform includes a choice of trousers or skirt, and staff who choose to wear a veil

> will be able to do so but will be expected to conform with some of the business-like requirements with regards to colour, et cetera...[so] veils are normally in black...in the same way [as they and all their colleagues] coordinate their shoes.

As one individual element within the restricted uniform options, the hijab can be normalized as one among other accessory choices.

The overt and covert regulation of the dressed body of the shopworker is a well-established retail industry standard. But how this is implemented varies according to sector and location, with less employment protection in the US retail sector, for example, than in the United Kingdom and European Union. My research in the United Kingdom showed compliance with store dress codes to be regulated in a number of ways, but to my surprise, Ruth, the HR manager of the London flagship store of brand X, a major high street retailer with high-profile designer tie-ins, told me that the modest dressers were the least of her worries. Shop staff members had to wear a short-sleeved T-shirt with the company name on it and plain bottoms of their own choice. If someone wanted to add a hijab,

> that's fine; we don't have any problem with it. The key thing is that they wear the branded T-shirt, so if they want to wear that under, or over their clothing, or with part of the T-shirt showing through their religious attire, then that's fine. [The T-shirt is short sleeved], but often people wear a long sleeve under it or they wear a cardigan over it... As long as the [company] name is visible to customers, [so] they can find someone to help.
>
> The only problems we had with the T-shirt is people customising them, but it's not for religious reasons. They'll just slash them and tie them in the middle and make them into bikini tops, and all sorts.

This company, like many others in the youth sector, has a staff base that closely mirrors its customer demographic, so the visibility of the branded T-shirt is crucial for distinguishing staff from customers. It is not religiously motivated dressers that cause problems but young secular staff members desperate to customize the top. In scenes reminiscent of my schooldays, these uniform insurrections, says Ruth, have to be constantly monitored:

> It's up to the managers to police that in their own teams. You have team briefs at the start of the day, and at the start of each shift, [and if] someone's not complying with the standards then they'll be challenged and asked to change.

The fashion-forward store's dress code policy deliberately allows for individual interpretation but finds itself needing to guide the limits with regard to dress and comportment; Ruth states further:

> We're a creative industry; we like people to express their individuality; we don't want everyone to be clones. The only uniformity is those branded T-shirts, everything else [is open to interpretation].

In the light of this regulation, religious employees were considered a good option owing to their self-disciplined modes of comportment by comparison to other young people:

> I would actually prefer to have *more* Muslim employees...Younger employees who *don't* follow any particular religion and are out drinking and taking drugs every night tend to be the ones who take up most of our time in HR. So I would much rather have more religious diversity for that reason.

MUSLIM BODIES AT WORK—CONTENTION AND COOPERATION

Conversations with both employers and employees seem to suggest that clothing is not emerging as a key problem area in fashion retail work. At least, clothing requirements seemed to be easily accommodated. More challenging in terms of resources and management were requests for prayer rooms and time off for festivals. Prayer rooms were difficult in shops, especially smaller branches, where nearly all available space is devoted to front-of-house functions, with staff facilities often minimal. For festivals, many companies have been proactive in developing 'diversity calendars' so that managers can anticipate staff demands for shift changes and leave.

Time off for religious festivals is not usually a problem in the fashion retail sector, employee relations manager Helen claimed, because 'staff working in retail know that it will involve unsociable hours' and because retail employers 'favour part-time as opposed to fulltime contracts'. It is commonplace for company recruitment policy to ensure that retailers have a highly flexible workforce with which to respond to seasonal sales variations. In relation to diversity demands, this can allow managers to use staff flexibly not just within a given store but across the region if needed. As Helen explained, in a large flagship store with over a thousand staff,

> we can easily accommodate a number of requests, but if you're in a store where you've only got twenty staff and ten of them want the same days off for Eid or Diwali...then it's going to affect the service and being able to actually operate the store. So you have to look at, you know, in advance if you're going to give all those people the same time off, do you need to call in support staff from other stores or whatever that may be.

In the one instance, I heard of someone being denied leave for a festival; Taslima in River Island in Manchester encountered problems when her manager didn't understand that she needed an extra meal break for *iftar* to break her fast during Ramadam. Fed up with protracted negotiations and with a manager who couldn't believe that she didn't just eat at work and pretend to her parents that she was fasting, this 22-year-old, second-generation Indian undergraduate left the job.

In contrast, in Bradford, A. Y.'s non-Muslim manager and colleagues were well-informed and overtly solicitous; says A. Y.:

> [We don't have to tell them]; they already know—and a few weeks before, they're warning us, 'Ramadan's coming up, are you ready? Make sure you're fit and healthy.'
>
> They don't give us heavy jobs, so it'll just be basically, A.Y., would you like to stand on the till today for a few hours instead of [doing heavier stockroom work]?

Muslim staff sometimes have to define and legitimate their forms of religious practice. In the case of disputes that actually go to arbitration—that is, unlike Taslima, who simply quit—the religious rights covered by the new legislation create opportunities for the development and exercise of new forms of religious authority as those representing employers and employees seek interpretations of doctrine to support their cases. In retail, most faith-related disputes that have made it beyond local discussion have been in the supermarket sector (mostly concerning time off for festivals or handling non-halal food products) where the shopworkers' union USDAW has more members than in fashion retail.[4]

In the visually loaded climate of fashion retail, any significant style change can make one feel conspicuous. But for Muslim women who decide to transform their appearance by starting to wear the hijab, the workplace can feel especially daunting. Maleeha, a 27-year-old, second-generation British Pakistani business studies graduate was happy in her job as assistant lingerie buyer at Selfridges, but had considered leaving and taking a new job in order to avoid staging this transformation in her current workplace. In the end she decided she couldn't wait and initiated a careful and assertive public relations exercise with her colleagues:

> I was very nervous...because I feel the way I dress is kind of a reflection of my personality so, you know, I like to dress nicely, I like clothes, I like fashion and like to spend my time looking at fashion magazines and going shopping and things. So—and I kind of almost felt like, you know, changing the way that I look, people will think she's changed, or whatever...I'm also the kind of person that doesn't like the attention on me, I don't like people making big hoo-ha, so I just sent a quick email round [to my immediate team] to say that I'm going to start wearing

a veil so don't be alarmed when you come in on Monday morning and see me sitting there.

And I did actually say in the email, I don't want a big fuss...And I think I also mentioned that it was quite a big thing for me and I was feeling a bit nervous. So walking in, gosh it was just, it was just a really strange feeling walking in on Monday morning. My manager quietly said, 'Oh my God, Wow! You look amazing, you look lovely,' which was really nice. The rest of the team just carried on doing their work and I think because of that email didn't really say much...Overall everyone was amazing, everyone was like, 'It suits you, you look lovely.' I was asked why I did it of course, to which I was just honest and just told them that it was because of my religion. I am commanded to do it.

I've been called a princess, been called romantic, a queen...it's quite strange but if people say things like that it's really nice, very sweet and it does make you feel better.

Although Maleeha does not work primarily on the shop floor (the buying team makes regular observational visits), her location in the open plan buying office does not reduce the significance of how she looks. Whist open plan offices generically bring into view the bodies of everyone that works there, the scrutiny of personal style and appearance that inevitably ensues (Freeman 1993) is of particular significance in a fashion workplace. Here, Entwistle argues (coincidentally, regarding the same Selfridges buying office), 'high fashion style circulates visually in the fertile environment of the open plan office as a form of embodied knowledge' emphasising the extent to which 'dressing fashionably constitutes something of the "aesthetic labour" in this employment market' (2009: 115).

For Maleeha, in the lingerie buyers' section, the need to achieve current norms of high fashion may be less pressing, but her understanding of the prevalence and power of visual scrutiny is spot on. Her assertive email to colleagues proved helpful in anticipating some of the questions that might arise in relation to her spiritually driven visual transformation. But underneath this specificity lies her tacit understanding—as a participant—of the importance of appearance in her workplace social relations. Announcing her intended change of dress makes overt the practices of visual surveillance and evaluation, gossip, rumour, and discussion that govern the sociality of the open plan office. Whilst all staff may feel similarly subject to the collective gaze, to announce, for example, a radical new haircut would be perceived as inappropriately attention-seeking. In contrast, Maleeha's decision to wear hijab, whilst a private personal spiritual choice, is of such visual magnitude that it cannot be ignored and so enters a different category of communication within the visuality of the office. Here, the aesthetic labour of fashion melds with the intended spectacle of religious observance: hijab renders adherents immediately conspicuous to a mixture of observers. Whilst Maleeha's highly visible change in her appearance at work did as expected prompt discussions with co-workers, it is also entirely common for Muslim shopworkers who have always appeared in hijab to find their religiously inspired attire a topic of conversation and question.

The display of Muslim identities through dress factors into relations with co-workers in two key ways: generically, it prompts questions about Islam, and specifically it prompts implicit and explicit comparisons with other workers who are Muslim, raising questions about different types of Muslim self-presentation.[5] Most often, hijabi shop assistants are asked to explain why they cover and why other Muslim co-workers don't; although to their informed eyes, it might be perfectly obvious that their colleague is dressing with modesty in mind (long-sleeved tops, no short skirts), the majoritarian shop team is rarely equipped to recognize this. In these discussions and in interactions with other Muslim staff, hijabi shopworkers tread carefully not to criticize the choices of other Muslims whose interpretation is different to their own.

CONCLUSION

It remains to be seen how the neoliberal desire to incorporate minority identities into new forms of consumer citizenship will play out in relation to religion in fashion arenas around the world. With few notable exceptions (such as Walmart's Toronto-based Bollywood range and their UK Asda Asian clothing collection in 2009), most mainstream fashion retailers don't see ethnic or Muslim consumers as a niche market. Yet local store managers in parts of Britain can recognize the benefits and value of having bodies on the shop floor whose self-presentation marks them as Muslim. The ability of hijabi shop staff to act as mannequins not just for the store's products but also for modest fashion adds to their generic value as in-store style mediators. Just as ethnic marketing has become 'an industry in its own right' (Halter 2000: 49), so too has Muslim marketing emerged as a new growth area (Sandıkçı and Rice 2011). The enhanced value that ethnic corporate branding strategies place on staff who can 'meld local and subcultural behaviours' (Schultz and Hatch 2006: 15) may now transfer to Muslims, as is seen in the ways that shop customers use young women as cultural and linguistic translators.

There were lots of stories in London a few years ago that Russian-speaking staff members were being recruited in Knightsbridge at Harvey Nichols and in luxury boutiques to serve the incoming Russian plutocracy. If special knowledge for selling to Russians was based in language, will more stores start to recognize the specialist knowledge that stylish hijabis offer both through language and appearance? Whilst the globalization of fashion retail means that many of the same stores appear in malls or high streets across the world, hijabi shop staff, and customers, are not similarly accommodated in each territory. Just as local planning and employment regulations determine the commercial and industrial relations available to supranational brands in all sectors, so too will local and regional norms and legislation about the expression of religious identity determine how hijabi shop staff are valued and employed (Floor 2006: 17). With the international increase in hijab-wearing as part of a fashion ensemble, the embodied aesthetic knowledge of cool young hijabis could become a form of desirable economic and cultural capital for brands wanting to break into newly discernible markets.

NOTES

This research was made possible by a British Academy Small Grant. I am grateful to Clive Bane, Chrissy Mckean and Yvette Genn for their advice on HR and employment tribunals.

1. <http://www.dti.gov.uk/er/equality> accessed 1 December 2003.
2. This chapter draws on a series of individual semi-structured interviews with shopworkers and HR directors that I carried out in the UK in 2009–10.
3. The retail industry is structured on the use of part-time labour, therefore providing job opportunities for many students in the United Kingdom, but its core workforce does not tend to be college educated with few students continuing in shop floor positions after graduation (global recession notwithstanding).
4. Personal conversation, 18 September 2009, with Jo Bird, national equality research officer USDAW.
5. For wider discussion of different interpretations of appropriate Muslim dress in Britain and sensitivities over how different forms of visibly Muslim dress are interpreted, see Tarlo (2010).

REFERENCES

Basit, T. N. (1997), '"I want more freedom, but not too much": British Muslim Girls and the Dynamism of Family Values', *Gender and Education* 9, 4: 425–40.

Crang, P. (1994), 'It's Showtime: On the Workplace Geographies of Display in a Restaurant in Southeast England', *Environment and Planning D: Society and Space* 12: 675–704.

Crang P., and R. L. Martin (1991), 'Mrs Thatcher's Vision of the "New Britain" and the Other Side of the "Cambridge Phenomenon"', *Environment and Planning D: Society and Space* 9: 91–116.

Christopherson, S. (1996), 'The Production of Consumption: Retail Restructuring and Labour Demand in the USA', in N. Wrigley and M. Lowe, eds.,

Retailing Consumption and Capital: Towards the New Retail Geography, London: Longman.

Dwyer, C., and B. Shah (2009), 'Rethinking the Identities of Young British Pakistani Muslim Women: Educational Experiences and Aspirations', in P. Hopkins and R. Gale, eds., *Muslims in Britain: Race, Place and Identities,* Edinburgh: Edinburgh University Press.

Entwistle, J. (2009), *The Aesthetic Economy of Fashion: Markets and Values in Clothing and Modelling,* Oxford: Berg.

Floor, K. (2006), *Branding a Store: How to Build Successful Retail Brands in a Changing Marketplace,* London: Kegan Page.

Freeman, C. (1993), 'Designing Women: Corporate Discipline and Barbados's Off-shore Pink-collar Sector', *Cultural Anthropology* 8, 2: 169–86.

Gillat-Ray, S. (2010), *Muslims in Britain: An Introduction,* Cambridge: Cambridge University Press.

Halter, M. (2000), *Shopping for Identity: The Marketing of Ethnicity,* New York: Schocken Books.

Kariapper, A. S. (2009), *Walking a Tightrope: Women and Veiling in the United Kingdom,* London: Women Living Under Muslim Law.

Leslie, D. (2002), 'Gender, Retail Employment and the Clothing Commodity Chain', *Gender, Place and Culture* 9, 1: 61–7.

Lewis, P. (2007), *Young, British and Muslim,* London: Continuum.

Lowe, M. (1991), 'Trading Places: Retailing and Local Economic Development at Merry Hill, West Midlands', *East Midlands Geographer* 14: 31–49.

Lowe, M., and L. Crewe (1996), 'Shop Work: Image, Customer Care and the Restructuring of Retail Employment', in N. Wrigley and M. Lowe, eds., *Retailing, Consumption and Capital: Towards a New Retail Geography,* Harlow: Longman.

Mohammad, K. (2005), 'Negotiating Spaces of the Home, the Education System, and the Labour Market: The Case of Young, Working-class, British Pakistani Muslim Women', in G.-W. Falah and C. Nagel, eds., *Geographies of Muslim Women: Gender, Religion and Space,* New York: Guilford Press.

Peach, C. (2006), 'Muslims in the 2001 Census of England and Wales: Gender and Economic Disadvantage', *Ethnic and Racial Studies* 29, 4: 629–55.

Perfect, D. (2011), 'Religion and Belief', briefing paper, Manchester: Equalities and Human Rights Commission.

Sandıkçı, Ö., and G. Rice (2011), *Handbook of Islamic Marketing,* Cheltenham: Edward Elgar.

Schultz, M., and M. J. Hatch (2006), 'A Cultural Perspective on Corporate Branding: The Case of LEGO Group', in J. Schroeder and M. Salzer-Mörling, eds., *Brand Culture,* New York: Routledge.

Tarlo, E., 2010, *Visibly Muslim: Fashion, Politics, Faith,* Oxford: Berg.

Werbner, P. (2002), *Imagined Diasporas Among Manchester Muslims,* Oxford: James Curry.

Winship, J. (2000), 'Culture of Restraint: The British Chain Store 1920–39', in P. Jackson, M. Lowe, D. Miller and F. Mort, eds., *Commercial Cultures: Economics, Practices, Spaces,* Oxford: Berg.

Woodward, S. (2009), 'The Myth of Street Style', *Fashion Theory* 13, 1: 83–102.

Wright, D. (2005), 'Commodifying Respectability: Distinction at Work in the Bookshop', *Journal of Consumer Culture* 5, 3: 295–314.

Wrigley, N., and M. Lowe, eds. (1996), *Retailing, Consumption and Capital: Towards a New Retail Geography,* Harlow: Longman.

Wrigley, N., and M. Lowe (2002), *Reading Retail: A Geographical Perspective on Retailing and Consumption Spaces,* London: Arnold.

SECTION IV

ISLAMIC FASHION IN THE MEDIA

–11–

'Fashion Is the Biggest Oxymoron in My Life': Fashion Blogger, Designer and Cover Girl Zinah Nur Sharif in Conversation with Emma Tarlo

Can you tell us a bit about your background?

I was born in Somalia, but my family originated from Yemen. I was brought up in three different countries (Yemen, Switzerland and the UK) and currently live in London with my family. I come from a large family of six sisters and four brothers, most of them older. I recently graduated from the University of Westminster with a degree in graphic design, and I'm now in pursuit of a career in fashion.

What attracted you to blogging about fashion?

I started blogging on the 24th of July 2010. It wasn't initially a fashion blog but more of a creative lifestyle blog. Strangely enough, I was not inspired by other blogs. In fact, I did not have any idea about the blogging world until I watched the film *Julie & Julia*. It has nothing to do with fashion, but I was really inspired by seeing how the main character started a blog to share her true passion for cooking and journalism. She was doing it as a hobby at first, but then it all picked up and turned into the professional job of blogging and writing cookbooks. That's where I got the idea of starting a blog—to share my own creative ideas with the rest of the world. I had just completed my first year of graphic design and was regretting not having studied fashion academically. I had a GCSE in art and design and A levels in photography, fine art, fashion design and media studies and felt I didn't want to throw it all away. After a year of blogging, I discovered my true obsession with fashion and started blogging more and more. I see the blog as a platform to show my talent in fashion, photography and creativity and as a ladder for slowly climbing up in the fashion industry as a designer.

Was there anything in your background that made you particularly interested in fashion and clothes?

Creativity runs in my family. I've been doing art for as long as I can remember and was encouraged by my siblings and teachers in Yemen. They convinced me I had talent! This made me look into other creative fields, and I was introduced to knitting and tailoring in year four in Switzerland. This grew into a love of not only making clothes but also wearing, designing and styling them. I hardly had any access to mass media such as magazines, Internet, TV or any kind of medium that promoted fashion. In the village where I lived, no one could care less about fashion and style; that always made me wonder and think about fashion even more. Fashion certainly was not mainstream or popular there and then, and what's not mainstream naturally captures my interest and sparks my curiosity.

Do you follow other fashion blogs?

Yes. Nowadays I follow several blogs that inspire me and resemble my style or the style I would like to reach. My absolute favourite is From Me to You, but I also like Trendland, Gary Pepper Vintage, The Cherry Blossom Girl, HijabScarf, Hijabs & Co and many others.

Can you tell us how your style has evolved since you became a hijab-wearer?

I have been wearing the hijab since I was eleven, in year four in Swiss school. It was more of a turban style than the hijab style I wear today. I wore the same clothes as other teenagers—jeans and tops, even short-sleeved tops—and only covered my hair, not the neck. I knew little about the true meaning of hijab at the time and believed modesty was only about covering the hair. Also, I was the only one in my class and entire school wearing the hijab, which meant I did not see how it should be worn. I was worried about the questions, teasing and bullying from other kids. There were some boys and girls who would pull my hijab off or laugh at me or just make horrible racist jokes about it. It was already difficult being the only coloured person in the entire school and being teased for that, but the hijab on top just made things more difficult. I was upset and kept myself to myself most of the time. But once I got to year five, I stopped caring what anyone thought and let them accept me for who I was. I simply ignored all the horrible words and even the kids who were bullies. They started to realise I wasn't reacting to their words and actions and so finally gave up on it. With or without the hijab, I stood out back then, being of a different race and colour, so I felt that wearing the hijab did not make that much difference. I only developed a style consciousness when I started secondary school in Switzerland. I began experimenting with different types of clothes, but I carried on wearing the hijab in the same turban style.

My fashion and style consciousness grew stronger when I moved to London. I saw so many fashion-conscious people, hijabis and non-hijabis alike. This is when I started experimenting with layering, wearing the hijab differently and just trying to be more fashionable. Each year, my style would change; it was eclectic. I started looking at clothes and fashion differently, tried to find ways of wearing regular clothes, from regular high street stores, and turning them modest. I never bought or even considered buying clothes from Islamic stores, as I do not consider them stylish or suitable to my personal style. I was more enthusiastic about turning regular clothes, or Western clothes as some may call them, into modest outfits. Each year I would learn and discover so many ways of wearing one specific item of clothing—what to pair it with, which textures and colours to combine, what cuts, et cetera. I started to consider myself a style guru, and friends would start asking for tips and tricks, which is another reason why I post fashion outfits on the blog. Also, I really enjoyed it all and still do.

Would you say you find fashion inspiring?

Not entirely; no. Most of the time, fashion is inspiring solely for doing stuff that relates to fashion or that just is fashion. I don't think I have ever looked at fashion and then suddenly thought, Oh how inspiring; I want to help the orphans now! Fashion only inspires me to do more fashion design, styling and making clothes. Other stuff such as photography and graphic design inspires me to do other things as well as fashion-related things.

Do you ever find fashion oppressive?

Yes, I think so. I think the fashion world is exclusive to certain types of people in terms of class, race, location and appearance. Although many people believe that fashion is open to everyone, actually, it is not. Creatively speaking, yes, it's open to everyone everywhere. However, career-wise and as far as being in the fashion industry itself is concerned, it's limited, restrictive and to some extent it even seems controlled. I don't think Karl Lagerfeld will ever welcome people of a bigger size with open arms, and I don't think a man can be a successful designer or in the fashion industry without being either camp or gay: Christian Dior, Prabal Gurung, Jason Wu, Marc Jacobs, Tom Ford, Zac Posen, Yves Saint Laurent, et cetera. I believe that the fashion industry puts a burden on men to be more feminine. I mean, why do we have to know anyone's sexuality? Why does the media give out the message that if you're a man, best be gay or camp to fit into this fabulous feminine fashion world?

Another obvious thing is that the size of women matters. If you're slim, you'll be welcomed and embraced. If not, best work extra hard and prove that you fit in. The same thing goes for religion. I don't think the fashion industry gives much respect to any faith; at least that's the impression I always get. I also believe that people with hijab aren't too welcomed in the larger fashion industry. Yes, there are many Muslim and hijabi fashion designers, but they are successful amongst themselves and mainly known in the community of fellow hijabis—and yes, of course, a few non-hijabis. When I went to London Fashion Week this September, I was rather shocked to see that I was the only hijabi there. I was there three to four hours each day for three days, and no one except me wore the hijab. It's 2012, but it didn't feel like it. I don't think

Vogue would print a page with hijabi models. *Marie Claire* did that for their December 2006 issue, and there were some online debates about it. How ridiculous it is that people can't accept each other.

Wealth and class is another thing, but that's what fashion is known for, right? I think everyone who does not fit into the typical fashion categories—that do not exist as concrete rules but are mentally there—needs to work extra hard and really prove that they have what it needs to get into the industry.

Do you ever feel under pressure to be in fashion?

Yes, I do. I don't think that I particularly fit into the fashion industry as a person. My work does, yes, but I don't. People will naturally connect my work to me. At times it's an unconscious thing they do. During my A levels, I was the only hijabi in my fashion class—yes, even in London—and people gave me a surprised look at the beginning, a sort of, 'Are you sure you want to pursue a career in this shallow and ignorant fashion world?' look. I sometimes feel the pressure to change things about myself, so people will perceive me differently and accept me, but then I always remind myself that regardless of what I do, there will always be someone to pressure me or judge me. I can't please everyone, and I need to stand my ground concerning what I believe—not only about faith but also lifestyle.

I once had an interview at Vivienne Westwood, and a friend of my sister gave me the advice to wear my hijab as a turban and to show a bit of hair at the front, so it would look like I was rocking the turban style rather than being a hijabi. She then later added that once I got the job, I could wear my hijab as I normally do. I was disgusted by the idea of altering my hijab—and therefore showing lack of respect towards my faith—just to get a position in a fashion house! Not only would that have been cheating myself but also showing lack of self-esteem, weakness, and would have been just plain wrong.

I could try to create more distance between myself and my work, but that of course is impossible. Regardless of what kind of clothes I make or design, I will always be seen as the hijabi designer. It's not just pressure from the fashion industry but also pressure coming from fellow hijabis. Now, most of my readers or anyone who is familiar with my work will automatically assume and expect me to design modest clothes. If not, then the criticisms will storm in, and I of course may be seen as a bad influence for younger hijabis. To be frank, at times I couldn't care less what people want me to be or make. I see it like this: Do you like my work? Great! Or, You don't like my work? Move on!

Do you find other people understand your interest in fashion and your style, or do you feel you need to explain or justify it?

I don't have to justify myself most of the time, but when I have to, it's to friends who aren't hijabis or Muslim. It's not my style but my interest in fashion that

I have to justify. My university friends always wondered why I would want to go into an industry that wasn't always accepting. When I told a fellow graphic designer I worked with that I no longer wanted to work as a freelance graphic designer as I want to pursue a career in fashion and needed to be able to work to tight deadlines, he responded, 'So you're running away from clients from hell to run into hell itself?!'

But I want to be able to do what I enjoy and love in the hope that my love for it will lead to some good. London has also given me a world of possibilities and of course the hijabi community is much larger here than in the rest of Europe, so people nowadays understand that fashion doesn't necessarily mean working with people like Anna Wintour, but that there are other fashion communities. Smaller, yes, but still present.

How would you describe your personal style?

I would describe my style as simple, comfortable, elegant and sophisticated. I love clothes that have texture rather than patterns. I love wearing natural fabrics rather than synthetics. I love loose and comfortable clothes and don't like clothes that hug my figure. I try not to over-layer my clothes and keep them simple yet modest.

What have been key inspirations to you concerning your style?

I'd like to think that the online world of pretty things may have inspired me with my current style. Websites such as Tumblr and Pinterest, where people not only post about fashion but also great graphic and interior design, amazing photography and food and much more. Also, as I learned from my graphic design course, simplicity is the key to great design. I enjoy things that are designed simply yet show elegance and sophistication, even when it comes to serving food on a plate. It all looks effortless, but I know a great deal of mind-mapping and work has gone behind those great designs. So I try to let that influence my style in clothes as well. Not to mention, I have built an obsession with Erdem and Prabal Gurung's collections, the way they dress women and highlight femininity with such elegance.

Why do you think style matters?

I think it matters to a certain extent. Without appearing shallow, I think style defines who you are. What you wear is what you are. I think style is different from fashion. Fashion is what you get; style is what you make of it. There are occasions where it's acceptable to be stylish, overdressed and make an effort, and there are occasions where it just makes you look bad and shallow. Imagine turning up with a dress, high heels and a perfectly done manicure to play golf like Mariah Carey did? Now that is when you have crossed the line and being stylish has become your primary motivation and way of life. Style should be a secondary concern and should not take over your life.

Where are your favourite places to shop?

Zara, H&M, occasionally Mango and Primark, but 95 per cent of the time, Zara. I think that Zara perfectly designs my style and the style I am aiming for.

Do you feel that modesty and fashion are always compatible?

Yes, I'd like to think so; perhaps not always, but most of the time. Personally, I didn't experience much restriction in being stylish and modest at the same time. Clothes can be worn and altered to appear modest; they can be paired with other clothes, and there really aren't any limitations besides avoiding the obvious clothes such as miniskirts and shorts. If by fashion you mean the fashion industry itself, then no. I don't think modesty and fashion are always compatible for all the obvious reasons stated above and because fashion exploits women's bodies.

How do you understand or interpret modesty?

To cover your body except your face, hands and feet, to not wear figure-hugging clothes, to avoid clothes that are too loud in colour and pattern and to avoid attracting the eyes of others intentionally. Even if covered from head to toe, don't dress like Lady Gaga, metaphorically speaking! That is not modest in my opinion. That's my personal understanding.

Do you ever experience tension between your religious beliefs and values and your love of fashion?

At times, yes, mainly regarding the fact that I should not be wearing figure-hugging clothes, and I sometimes wear skinny jeans. That's only one small thing, considering that I can wear everything else and just simply change whenever I feel guilty. The other things are more about moral issues, such as doing things for the sake of helping others. In my religion and belief, it is highly encouraged to work to not only help yourself but also others. For example, professions in the medical field help the ill or are researching the next cure for a disease; a teacher or lecturer provides knowledge for the next generation; even drivers help people by taking them from one place to the other; or cleaners, by keeping everything clean and hygienic. Psychologists help people with mental distress; journalists provide information to the mass population—even though some may be biased. I don't see what help fashion offers people. Yes, making clothes is useful, but does fashion help people? It helps fulfil their creative needs, makes people feel good and special—but that's it really. Much as I love it, it does not give me the satisfaction of knowing I have helped someone. Yet I try to convince myself that maybe someone out there feels inspired by my blog or the things I do.

Do you feel fashion is a good way of communicating? If so, what do you hope to communicate?

I'm still not too sure what I hope to communicate through the use of fashion. I think I just want to show that there is diversity in the fashion world; it may not have reached the mainstream yet, but that day may come if people work hard. I hope to build awareness through the use of fashion, but at the moment my blog is simply inspiring those who want be stylish, which isn't doing much, to be honest. I'm hoping to work in fashion as a designer, not to start creating and selling my own fashion label but to simply work as part of a company and perhaps one day have the power to bring a more diverse image into the fashion world. For now, all I know is that this world doesn't need any more designers to spend billions of pounds of money on creating more clothes that we don't need. We focus way too much on buying things we don't need, to please people we don't even like—a vicious cycle that needs to be broken.

How much time do you spend blogging?

I used to spend much more time on blogging during the first year. It was live blogging, which meant writing and posting things up on the same day—quantity over quality. However, after the first six months, I started to focus much more on quality and the content of the blog rather than how many times I blogged. I created a pattern of scheduling blog posts one to two months prior to the posting days on Tuesdays, Thursdays and Sundays. I now spend much more time picking the content of my blog, making sure it's all high- and good-quality material, as it is no longer just a hobby but also about building a good online portfolio with solid content. I leave all the raw and low-quality material to my Instagram and Twitter accounts.

Who are your main followers/readers?

I'm sure that over 90 per cent of my followers/readers are young girls, aged seventeen to twenty-five, mainly hijabis and Muslims, but I also have some non-hijabis and non-Muslims.

According to my Google stats, 27.4 per cent from South East Asia—Malaysia, Indonesia and Singapore—21.8 per cent from the UK and 10.3 per cent from the USA. Two countries that surprised me are Australia [9.1 per cent] and France [6.8 per cent]. With France, I thought that with their ludicrous law banning the hijab, I wouldn't have readers from there, but clearly that's not the case.

If you could change something in the fashion industry, what would it be?

Well, in my wildest dreams, I would very much love to build fair trade into fashion. Yes, some companies say they already do, but I don't believe that; I don't think Mango or Zara are paying Indian workers a minimum of £2 an hour. It's more likely to be £2 or less for an entire day! They're selling a dress for £100, knowing that it only costs them £6 to make. Zara even lowers the price of a garment from £100 to £10, knowing that at the end of the day, they're not making any loss. Why not just sell it for £50 from the beginning? I can't only point my fingers at high street stores when designers are charging a monstrous £10,000 for a piece of fabric! I understand that it's all about brand, buying the name, et cetera, et cetera, but I'm sure these greedy and hungry people in the fashion industry could help solve world problems such as world hunger, poverty and other serious matters. I watched *The September Issue,* and when Anne Wintour asked the art director to reshoot a fashion editorial that had cost $15,000, I asked, 'For what?!' So they were going to spend another $15,000 on something that was perfectly fine in the first place!?

I would hope to close the income gap, starting with fashion. As I said, this is only in my wildest dreams. I have a love/hate thing for fashion; it's the biggest oxymoron in my life. I enjoy it, yet feel guilty about it but hope to do it for a good cause rather than selfish and obnoxious reasons. I enjoy graphic design for the reason that during my degree course, we focussed on building and creating visual awareness of global crises through graphic design, whether it was the negative effects of compulsive consumerism, global warming, poverty or serious diseases such as cancer. So I would like and hope to do the same thing through fashion. Even though I have seen some bad aspects of the fashion industry, I still hold on to the good and still love fashion because people like Dame Vivienne Westwood and Prabal Gurung inspire me to believe that you can still have morals and use fashion for good, that you can have a vivid personality and still fit in to the shallow world of fashion.

NOTE

Edited version of an interview conducted over email by Emma Tarlo in October 2012.

–12–

Mediating Islamic Looks

Degla Salim

Fig. 12.1 Picture taken by the fashion photographer Jimmy Backius for *BON* in 2002.

As we are sitting having a coffee at a cafeteria in downtown Stockholm in the spring of 2008, Mejsa's cell phone rings, and she picks it up. It seems to be an important call. While looking for a piece of paper to take notes on, she smoothly fastens the cell phone by her ear with the help of a tightly tied hijab which frees her hands, enabling her to both pick up a paper and move her cup a couple of centimetres to the left. Sitting there, I couldn't help noticing how swiftly this garment became quite functional. A couple of minutes later the phone conversation was over, and I was told that Mejsa was being booked for a workshop in Gothenburg that spring. Her designs had been appreciated both by Muslims and people interested in this 'new' take on Islamic fashion as something elaborate and beautiful. Nowadays she is quite often contacted regarding articles, workshops and TV appearances on the subject of the hijab and its place in fashion. As we moved on to go and look for clothes in the shop Mejsa most often visits (H&M), we continued a discussion about how she would go about her future workshop in Gothenburg. At the store, I noticed a shirt that actually had a neck long enough to constitute somewhat of a hood. Spontaneously I turned to Mejsa and asked her how she felt about these types of shirts; they must be very functional I went on. With a smile and a very decisive tone she responded, 'But Degla, we don't want functionality!' It turned out that what she wanted was anything but functional:

> I want to surprise people and provoke them by seeing something that is not commonly used as a hijab made into exactly that, a hijab.

While following Mejsa through the store, I found her picking up scarves from the men's section, accessories that usually are said to be punk in style, and she finished off the look with a very 'ladylike' hat in a dark colour. All in all, I found it very hard to follow the stylistic creation taking place before me.

In this chapter, I shed light on understandings of 'Islamic fashion' through focussing on how young hijab-wearing women in Sweden understand diverse types of fashion imagery, including popular and art-fashion images as well as images which exoticize headscarves for a Western audience. I ask what sorts of mediations are involved in different modes of looking at such imagery. How are they understood from the 'Islamic fashion' perspective of these viewers? I approach this field through the use of semiotics as an initial analytical tool which can help us understand how people make sense of images in general and fashion photography in particular. To understand the contested concepts of Islamic and fashion and the relationship between the two, I make use of Mazarella's (2004) notion of 'nodes of mediation' which enables the production of social meaning in time and space. My key argument is that young hijab-wearing women are fashion literate and have interesting ways of making a wide range of fashion images relevant to themselves even in cases where the images might at first seem far removed from their lives or even demeaning. In discussing these issues, I also consider the hierarchies embedded in the fashion system and how young hijabi women try to subvert these hierarchies.

IMAGINING FASHION

The field of fashion is an industry of images (McRobbie 1998: 172). Imagery dominates the industry to such a degree that the distinction between what is really being sold, the garment or the image of the garment, has become increasingly blurry (cf. Baudrillard 1975).[1] When it comes to understanding the visual world of fashion, Barthes's elaboration of the distinction between denotative and connotative systems is helpful (1993). The first level to be comprehended, the denotative system, is supposedly the self-evident message. In linguistics, it is simply that which is literally alleged in a specific context. In photography, it is the trace of the physical and chemical features that constituted the reality at the time the photograph was taken. When speaking in terms of fashion, the denotation in the appearance of a garment is its physicality as an object. If, for example, we take the loose, baggy jeans of hip hop fashion, the denotation of such jeans would be precisely that, a pair of baggy jeans. The connotation of wearing such jeans would be the affiliation of this particular style to hip hop. The concept of denotation allows limited understanding of the context of the object viewed. This is where the connotative system comes into play. Rarely do we understand sights completely based on the information provided through denotation. Furthermore, an image in one context generates different meanings when placed in another context. The sight of loose, baggy trousers probably means something different when seen in a glossy fashion magazine in Sweden than it does on the streets of Los Angeles.

What Muslim dress and particularly the hijab connote for many people who do not live in Muslim-majority areas, is Islam, and by extension, difference. Regardless of how overcharged the sign of hijab is for Europe, the hijab, as many writers have made clear, is still just a piece of cloth that only bears meaning when put into a social context. El Guindi (1999) has, for example, through her work demonstrated how, within the same geographical space, the symbolism of that piece of cloth has shifted over time, operating as marker of authority sometimes for men and sometimes for women. Thus the movement of this sign has been considerable. The significant matters here are, firstly, the sign's dependence on social context in order to bear meaning and, secondly, the extent of agility that signs such as the hijab have. However, the fact remains that in the social context of present day Europe the agility of the sign has become restricted by the often limited interpretations of and reactions to it by non-Muslims. This strictness in the interpreted meaning of hijab is what makes fashion especially charged for the women who choose to wear it. On the one hand, the choice of hijab might be motivated by religious beliefs, aesthetic preferences or a whole variety of different motivations (see other contributions to this book), yet, on the other hand, these motives are not necessarily accepted or understood by the majority in the European context.

The Italian philosopher Agamben (2009: 47–50) has contributed some interesting reflections on how fashion is related to ideas of time. He argues that the very search for what is most recent distracts us from seeing the present. He points to the impossibility of ever 'being in fashion'. This observation to some extent deflates fashion's claim to modernity. He shows how, on the one hand, modernity is invested with the idea of being better than that which was before; on the other hand, it simply refers to what is most recent. These two ideas are related. Those most knowledgeable of the most up-to-date and preferably future trends are considered the most modern which puts them in a position of power. Although an illusion, this idea of modernity has nonetheless very real consequences.

There is also a spatial aspect to this concept of being in fashion. It is not only connected to a certain time (the present) but also to certain spaces. New York, Paris and certain localities in the metropolitan cities of the world are all examples of spaces viewed as modern or more modern than others, especially when it comes to fashion. Hierarchies of time and hierarchies of place therefore reinforce each other. Although this discourse of modernity being bound in space is contested in today's eclectic world, it is nonetheless reproduced in fashion imagery and by individual and collective interpretations of that imagery.

How is this relevant to the ways Islamically fashioned bodies are viewed? While fashion in the West has always been regarded as offering the most contemporary ideas and ideals (Niessen, Leshkowich and Jones 2003), Islam and the Other have been understood as the opposite (Said 2000). This places Islamic dress in the category of the traditional in relation to the modernity of fashion. In the case of Muslims in Sweden, these Muslims are often perceived as oppressed traditionalists and their clothes are viewed through this lens. Given that this is the case, it becomes interesting to try to understand how the very women who are viewed in this light perceive fashion imagery. To what extent do they imbibe and reproduce the temporal and spatial hierarchies embedded in fashion discourses, and to what extent do they contest these? What modes of looking do they employ when looking at images that are highly connoted as contemporary when their own fashion is often regarded as the very opposite of contemporary? Finally, how can we better understand their search for a positive iconography?

This contribution focuses in particular on the medium of photography, which is simultaneously reflexive and reifying. The principal research method used was photo elicitation. A range of fashion imagery was discussed with two young hijabi Muslim women in particular, providing insight into how they make sense of such images from what we might call an Islamic fashion perspective.

THE FIELD IN FASHION PHOTOGRAPHY: RECOGNIZING THE ISLAMIC

Fashion and fashion photography is often criticized for not being adequately representative of reality and of real bodies. Debates about models' body size and the fact that they are predominately thin, young and white is illuminating for revealing the expectations placed upon the world of fashion photography. The realist expectations of photography more generally have historical roots that are discussed extensively in the works of, amongst others, Banks (2001),

Fig. 12.2 Picture taken by the fashion photographer Jimmy Backius for *BON* in 2002.

Barthes (2000) and Berger (1972). Whether the photographers or the fashion world have realist representational intents and claims seems irrelevant in the public's eye. The notion of representing 'real' women and 'real' men is thus a well-established and expected requirement of fashion imagery. But the expectation of realism is not equally distributed. It is expected and required less of high-fashion photography (which is often recognized as abstract and not really wearable) than of photography representing the ready-to-wear catwalk fashion of high street shops such as H&M, where realism is more expected.

The deployment of a realist mode of interpretation of fashion imagery is particularly expected when it comes to decoding representations of minorities such as Muslims in Europe. At the same time, looking at fashion photography is an act saturated with matters of identification (Göthlund 1997; Lewis 1995). When women look at fashion images, they are invested in a dual play of seeing which involves both the physical act of seeing and the imaginative act of seeing oneself in the pose, clothes and bodies represented. If this self-identification is activated, then the images are deemed relevant or useful to the spectator through processes of mediation. The concept of mediation as understood by Mazeralla (2004) enables the recognition that social meaning is an everyday practice only comprehendible as socially shared once it is mediated through both the semi-conscious and the externally structured (2004: 347).

Furthermore, the mere recognition of something as belonging to one discourse or another testifies to the specific knowledge that is put to use when reading (seeing) fashion magazines and fashion photography in general.

High-fashion imagery is frequently quite illusive and makes ample use of connotative tactics rather than denotative ones. In certain magazines such as the Egyptian *Hejab Fashion* and at times in the Dutch exhibition magazine *MSLM,* the images included clearly denote the hijab and current Islamic fashions, although in differing geographical spaces. But what happens with the interpretive process when a Muslim woman reads fashion images oriented towards non-Muslims in which headscarves and various forms of loose, covered dress are incorporated as fashion, as happened, for example, in H&M's spring 2008 catalogue 'Exotica' and continues to happened periodically in mainstream and high art fashion media? For many readers, the implied reference and connotation of such images is not only the bohemian and exotic but also the Islamic. The discrepancy between what is to be read when Islamic fashion is either denoted or connoted in fashion photography is thus at the core of my interlocutor's mediation of an Islamic look in 2008.

THE OVERTLY ISLAMIC

Islamic dress has in recent decades been regarded by many as just that, namely 'dress' that lacks the active movement of a fashion system. This perspective is expressed not only by non-Muslims but also by some Muslims. Within Muslim groups, there has been considerable discussion of the compatibility or incompatibility of fashion with Islamic beliefs. Those taking an anti-fashion perspective often suggest that Islam should take distance from the idiosyncratic and whimsical trends of consumerism. However, more recently, this stand has been challenged by many young Muslim women who have a closer relationship to the European media of fashion, as many of the contributions to this book show. This generation has been exposed to and is able to relate to the codes and valorizations of fashion imagery. Showing fashion-ability or fashion competence (cf. Tarlo 2010), these women are sufficiently literate in fashion imagery to be able to employ a variety of modes of looking at fashion representations.

Mejsa, the woman I introduced earlier, for example, has developed an elaborate personal style. By designing headscarves and being more or less a poster girl for 'Islamic and Veil Fashion' in the print media in Sweden,[2] she has taken an explicit stand in the debate on the relationship between fashion and Islam. She is convinced that 'being beautiful, fashionable and taking care of yourself' does not contradict an Islamic way of life. While she states that avoidance of the over-attentive male gaze is desirable, she also points out that a hijabi in Sweden can never escape being looked at:

People's gazes will be there whether you are wearing a beautiful scarf or an ugly one. 'So why not wear something beautiful?' Besides the veil makes me feel special!

The hijabs she designs, she defines as being very feminine. She makes use of accessories that were not originally intended for headscarves. Necklaces, earrings and pins are used to help decorate and stabilize the layers of cloth. Pins, she tells me, are 'a must' when wanting to make a chic and exclusive hijab design. These pins may be simultaneously functional, decorative and indicative of other things. For example, she claims that she is able to see if a pin was bought during hajj (the journey of pilgrimage to Mecca) due to her knowledge of the market there. This competence in and knowledge of trends and markets in the Middle East is one of the working tools she makes use of when styling hijabs to suit customer specifications.

When asked about what inspires her in her designs, she refers to fashion magazines such as *Sayidaty* (an Arabic equivalent of *Elle*) and a historical TV series on the prophet's time available on Arabic satellite channels. A moment later, she hands me something I would never have expected her to regard as a source of inspiration—an Arabic book containing colonial images of women in headscarves, some of which are naked; others fully dressed. The purpose of the book was clearly to display the Orientalist attitudes of colonial powers when it came to viewing and representing Middle Eastern women as sexually flamboyant objects. Mejsa commented:

> Well, the basic idea behind this book is of course unpleasant but, I don't know . . . I find the pictures beautiful!

Looking at the images in the book, I could not help seeing similarities with the images produced for the TV series on the time of the prophet, which has both a religious and pro-Arab agenda. There are, of course, historical and structural reasons for that similarity. As many have pointed out, the Orientalist gaze has been exported back to the former colonies, creating visualities of self-exotification (Hutnyk 2000).[3] Although Mejsa seemed to be aware of this journey that particular visions of the Orient had undertaken, she nonetheless still considered them a source of inspiration.

An overtly Islamic look today entails historical traces both to specific geographical localities and to the historical and cultural processes of colonialization and 'Orientalization' (Said 2000). Any stylistic look is hard to analytically detach from historical and social contexts, and it is particularly hard to disentangle Islamic fashion from the history of colonialism. What kind of social marks does this transnational and historical expedition of signs leave in the intimate dress practices and tastes of Muslims like Mejsa in Sweden?

Mejsa sees the pins and other markers of ethnic belonging used in her creations as a positive expression of individuality; it is also what she relies on when styling hijabs for her clients according to their wishes and the social context in which outfits will be worn.

> I like contrast, like really sexy red lipstick or nail polish together with a discrete hijab or a traditional African colourful scarf with something very Western or modern. I like to play off these kinds of contrasts.

These contrasts are part and parcel of the same illusive dichotomy of modern/ traditional that also became a big hit in Sweden in the fashion year of 2008 and continues to resurface with regularity. It is furthermore very clear which spaces and localities are evoked in this dichotomy. One only needed to look at the shop windows of Stockholm that summer to get an idea of how the continent of Africa was evoked not in a literal way but through the circular movement of signs. The tradition/modernity dichotomy enables the exotification and simplification of complex social belongings and renders a colourful shawl consumable as a specifically African shawl.

THE WOMAN BEHIND THE VEIL

When I showed these images (Figures 12.3, 12.4, 12.5) to Mejsa, she immediately liked them.

> This is what I mean [she said, pointing to the images above]; I think these images help show us hijab-wearing women as beautiful and at times, why not, even sexy. The photographer has really captured the woman behind the veil. I mean, we are all born naked. We are sexual beings. How do they think we [Muslims] reproduce? By telepathy? These images can help portray us as ordinary humans.

Fig. 12.3   Picture taken by the fashion photographer Jimmy Backius for *BON* in 2002.

Fig. 12.4 Picture taken by the fashion photographer Jimmy Backius for *BON* in 2002.

Fig. 12.5 Picture taken by the fashion photographer Jimmy Backius for *BON* in 2002.

Jimmy Backius's images correspond more or less to familiar contemporary representations of female beauty. They contain sexually charged iconic signals such as half-open lips glittering with lip gloss, the 'come on' look that challenges the presumably excited heterosexual male and the angel-like, subdued, non-threatening pose of a female ready to be conquered. All these connotations must be deciphered, at least at some level, in order for them to be understood as sexy images according to the prevailing logic of the day. Furthermore, these poses and connotations could be considered as exoticizing and eroticizing the Other by denoting the hijab in provocative contrast in sexually tantalizing images.

Seen within that context, Mejsa's comment on the 'woman behind the veil' confused me. I asked her to develop her thoughts. She talked further about the political importance of being seen as 'ordinary people' by non-Muslims. Taking into consideration the context of the images, she emphasized that they were clearly not directed towards Muslims but towards fashion-conscious Swedes. She did not find the exotification damaging. She preferred to see the images as complex and abstract depictions that were not to be read through a realist lens. She chose to regard the images as relevant to her and even to some extent representative of her because they helped portray Muslims as multifaceted and sexual humans.

It is not that Mejsa is unaware of how 'the women behind the veil' corresponds to long-term stereotypes of the Muslim women in 'the Orient' (Lewis 1996; Said 2000; Massad 2007), but she is more interested in what is new in the images: 'These are modern images, not at all what one is used to seeing!'

She approved the images partly because they go against the grain of mainstream media images of hijab-wearing Muslims. She explained that she feels as if people often presume that a woman wearing a headscarf must be either oppressed or completely asexual. Displaying a sexualized model in hijab is consequently seen by her as an act that combats this particular prejudice. It thus appears as a form of politicized affirmative action. Her responses revealed high levels of competence concerning the 'economy of looking' (McRobbie 1998). While aware of the hierarchical valorizations at hand in distinctions between art and craft (Aspers 2001), she sides with art with the symbolic capital this implies (Bourdieu 1984). By showing her recognition of what is 'modern', she proves herself to be a modern subject. On the other hand, Mejsa employs more literal modes of reading some mainstream fashion imagery found on billboards and in popular fashion magazines. Of these, she comments:

> Nowadays we see so much nakedness, so much skin that I think people have gone numb. I notice that a lot of men find it more attractive to be with a woman that is more covered...in a beautiful manner though. The woman behind the veil becomes more interesting and mystical then.

The relationship between the denoted and the connoted signs in comparable images is subsequently brought to the surface, dissected and judged by Mejsa, who suggests that an 'Islamic view' of beauty, that is covered beauty, is preferred and is gaining in popularity.

In general, Mejsa seemed very aware of the targeted audiences for images.[4] She often spoke of her own style in terms of provocation. For example, she had for a while been looking for a scarf in a particular green colour that she referred to as 'Islamic green'. She was very specific about the tone of green, that it was not pistachio, nor military green, nor neon green. It was the colour found on the flag of Saudi Arabia. Her explanation for being unable to find scarves in this colour was that they would be too provocative in connoting Islam. The coming together of the connotations of green and hijab would make the scarf, previously barely recognized as Islamic, seem 'over-Islamic'.

Dressing provocatively when maintaining a strictly Muslim appearance was for Mejsa an act of resistance against the waves of post-9/11 anti-Muslim feeling. In fact, she often referred to political events in discussing her own style. But then again, her dress could be read as a form of 'a positive divergence' (Göthlund 1997);[5] that is, a semi-conscious identity forming process that is done with the purpose of diverging in style from what you consider mainstream fashion in order to develop a sense of a unique self. In Göthlund's study, this act mediates between phases in self-formation. In the case of Mejsa and other respondents, their Islamic 'look' has become a node of mediation when it comes to their interaction with both the neo-liberal demands of individuality and the political atmosphere of anti-Islamism in Swedish society.

SEEING 'LAYER-ABILITY' AND THE CONNOTATION OF ISLAMIC

When interviewing Maha, an eighteen-year-old woman, I had been interested in her choice of style. It was not that she was extravagant in dress nor was her way of tying the hijab particularly special. In fact, it was the exact opposite. Her headscarf was grey, tied around her head, covering her neck in the most classical of ways, and colour coordinated with the pattern on the dress that she was wearing on top of a pair of black jeans. Black and grey shades dominated her appearance while her dress was of a thicker fabric that was in style that year. There was something very 'correctly fashionable' in her style. It was 'correct' to the point that her hijab was barely noticeable despite the fact that she was the only one wearing a headscarf in the cafeteria where we were seated. All in all, her dress denoted a Muslim, and her neutral look, the patterns, fabrics of the dress, were all connoting 'fashion-ability'. This connotation of 'being in fashion' brought to mind the reasoning of Barthes (2006) on the materiality of the colour blue. At some point, certain signs or details, cease to denote their materiality and instead start to simply connote fashion. If anything, this was the case for this choice of wardrobe at this precise time.

I presented Maha images of headscarves and fashion in differing contexts. We started with the 2007 spring fashion issue of *Elle*. Allowing her to spontaneously react to the imagery she was attracted to, I managed to withhold the questions for later. She clearly was drawn to 'wearable' representations of fashion as opposed to 'haute couture' images which she simply denounced as 'not real', too abstract and thus irrelevant to her. These wearable outfits fulfilled certain criteria such as simple cuts, subtle colours and clearly comfortable fabrics. Her reaction of the non-realness of specific images similar to the ones taken by Backius contrasted strongly with Mejsa's comments on their 'modernity'.

Early on in the interview, she explained to me that she rarely thought about Islamic fashion in terms of specific garments or as a whole concept when going through magazines. When she occasionally flipped through a glossy magazine, she was much more aware of her own personal style and what she usually looked for in dress regardless of religious boundaries:

> Most western styles can be compatible with Islamic fashion today, thanks to the fact that certain key garments have become trendy to layer with other clothes. Sleeveless dresses can easily be donned on top of a long-sleeved T-shirt. Even tight jeans are trendy to wear beneath both dresses and longer shirts. Everything can be combined in a covering manner. It's really about other details and personal tastes.

If everything is about personal taste, then can we distinguish anything in particular about these women's relationship to fashion imagery?

One visual ability that reoccurred in almost all photo elicitation sessions I had with a good number of interviewees was the act of imagining the photographed clothes on top of or beneath other garments. Simply put, they could immediately imagine the clothes' potential look when layered. This ability was naturalized to such a degree that people barely recognized it. This seeing of layer-ability in clothes might not restrict or limit their interest in pictures, but it did subtly permeate the act of viewing fashion images.

I argue that images of women in dress that is not thought to be compatible with Islamic regulations are not an impediment to acts of self-identification. The poses, the make-up, the gaze are all pictorial features that in the end help to constitute the desire to be 'her', the model, holding the desiring gazes of the spectator. As a result, mechanisms of gendered identification continue to be triggered, as they do with other women.

Here, self-identification is often dependent upon the capacity to co-opt images in order to make them valued as relevant. Maha, Mejsa and others had become proficient at isolating, evaluating and categorizing pictorial features as either identifiable or irrelevant, not on the basis of how much skin was revealed but on the recognition of the possibilities of layering that different garments offered.[6] On top of this, the layering of garments had itself become fashionable in 2008.

Another tendency in mainstream fashion in the year of 2008 was the incorporation of headscarves on the catwalk. Galliano did a fashion show in homage to Edie Beale's imaginative headscarf creations. Watanbe's design of a doomsday in need of full covering of the face also evoked responses and discussions on blogs on Islamic fashion.[7] Mainstream chain stores such as Indiska and H&M also participated in this trend by displaying headscarves in their shop front windows and on billboards.

As one additional expression of this trend's dispersal, the spring 2008 edition of the H&M magazine had a model on the front page wearing a headscarf tied like a turban. Through labelling the issue 'exotica', the association of Islam with 'the Orient' was made explicit. But how were these associations understood by Muslim women in Sweden in search of fashion inspiration that spring? Asked for her thoughts on this, Maha shrugged her shoulders telling me that, for one, she didn't see the headscarf creations as wearable and, secondly, that she regarded them as beautifully taken photographs but with clothes that did not appeal to her personal style. She could see how they could be labelled as exotic, and she considered the images not orientated towards her eyes.

Mejsa, the 27-year-old hijab designer, on the other hand, was glowing with pleasure when these images were highlighted in the fashion scene since she felt them to be in accordance with her own personal style. She too considered the scarf creations decorating the models' heads to be somewhat non-functional but had another mode of looking at fashion imagery that she had developed through her work with styling hijabs. That is, she had cultivated a non-realist mode of looking in her search for inspirational abstractions to take away and deploy on clients.

Both of these women felt they could understand and to a certain extent appreciate the exotification of the headscarf in the magazine. Although deploying completely opposite strategies of relating to the images, they still managed to recognize the concept of exotica in this magazine as having some sort of Islamic connotation. This alliance did not seem to bother Maha and even less Mejsa. In fact, she felt this issue with represented her personal style as being exotic.

In order to comprehend these women's connotative understanding of this imagery, one needs to see how the notion of Islamic and the notion of exotica are connected. Even if H&M suggests such a connection, there still seems to be no good reason why these women should apply an exotifying gaze to their own personal styles. However, that is what seemed to be happening during our conversations. Seeing such representations as 'Islamic fashion gone Western' could be regarded as the internalization of an exotifying gaze. Here it is the aesthetic values connected to cultural, religious and ethnic categories that are being exotified. With subtitles such as 'Queen of Africa' accompanied by images of the desert and a model wearing a headscarf in patterns associated with 'Africa as a whole', one is left with a highly unmistakable yet ambiguous impression. The ambiguity in this particular spread has to do with the reification of notions of some sort of timeless Africa based on historical structures of colonialism and Orientalism.

At first glance, it might appear that due to the lack of representative images in the print media, these young women have been forced to identify with pop cultural depictions and had developed a self-exotifying gaze as an intermediate solution (hooks 1992; Fanon 2000). But this explanation is unsatisfactory as it relies on a simplistic understanding of media reception. In reality, the women were comparing the pictures to the authenticity of their own style. In terms of temporality, they were amused to note that these styles now visibly in fashion belonged to the past for them. A friend of Mejsa commented:

> It's so interesting! I wore these types of headscarves five years ago before they were even modern and photographed for fashion magazines.

The point here is that through their narrations of these images, their own style was experienced as more real and more modern than the contemporary fashions which drew on Islamic connotations. Employing the notion of modernity as the present (cf. Agamben 2009), they succeed in positioning themselves as more contemporary than contemporary fashions and therefore in a relation of superiority to them, challenging fashion's pretentions to modernity. Although this turned the table on dominant-subordinate positions, so to speak, the problem of self-exotification still remains, raising the question of whether the concept of 'exotic' still bears the implication of subjection.

SOME CONCLUSIONS

It would be wrong to imply that young Muslim women in Sweden share a particular way of reading fashion images. Their perspectives vary as my discussion of two particular women shows. However, there are certain recurring nodes of mediation in their ways of understanding fashion images. One such node is the dichotomy of modern/traditional and the way it is employed in the reading and valorization of different fashion images. Their understanding of modernity was often in line with conventional understandings of modern images in Sweden. This understanding was at times used to avoid the depiction of their own personal styles and tastes as traditional and thereby inferior according to the discourses of modernity.

In addition, some had developed an appreciation of the more connotatively driven fashion illustrations of haute couture. Others less invested in the world of fashion regarded these 'arty' depictions as less relevant to their lives.

These women also engaged with the convergence of the neo-liberal de-mands of individuality and the anti-Islamism of the day. Although both these structures could be seen as externally imposed, people experienced the quest for uniqueness in style as an internally embodied desire. External prejudices which perceived Muslim women as homogenous and lacking in personal style were combated through internal quests for uniqueness, a strategy of media-tion that Mejsa, for example, enjoys provoking.

My understanding of these women's interaction with images in glossy maga-zines is that they are both intimate and complex interactions that throughout my fieldwork have been employed with a processual mode of interpretation. This processual understanding is accordingly also applied on the issue of self-exotification. The women involved in this study are engaged in an act of me-diation that partly takes into consideration dominant imagery alleged to be modern. Simultaneously, they utilize connotations of an exotic Other. Mediating between those depictions of being modern/being in fashion, they also engage in an act of position reversal by employing the same fixed, linear and reifying mode of understanding fashion. They simply state that styles similar to that of exotica are not at all contemporary for them. In fact, those styles belong to a far flung past. In a way, they have actually successfully mediated themselves into a superior position in the fashion game of 'who is most contemporary'.

NOTES

1. The image of the garment is here referred to in a double sense. Image is meant to be regarded as both a consumable photograph of the clothes and as a social 'image', an aura that the garment carries.
2. See Bengtsson (2006) and Johansson (2007).
3. An example of this circular journey is certainly tourist advertisement imagery.
4. This awareness can be easily understood when considering her involve-ment in the world of fashion.
5. My translation.
6. This negligence of shape, coverage and size in dress is restricted to a pictorial reading of fashion and cannot be applied on the shop-ping moments that in their own right possess other modes of sensory regulation.
7. See Kirna (2008).

REFERENCES

Agamben, G. (2009), *What Is an Apparatus,* Stanford, CA: Stanford University Press.

Aspers, P. (2001), 'A Market in Vogue, Fashion Photography in Sweden', *European Societies* 3: 1–22.

Banks, M. (2001), *Visual Methods in Social Research,* London: Sage.

Barthes, R. (1993), *Mythologies,* London: Vintage.

Barthes, R. (2000), *Camera Lucida,* London: Vintage.

Barthes, R. (2006), *The Language of Fashion,* Oxford: Berg.

Baudrillard, J. (1975), *For a Critique of the Political Economy of the Sign,* St. Louis: Telos Press.

Bengtsson, A. (2006), 'Slöja mode som vill synas', *Aftonbladet.se* (16 March) <http://www.aftonbladet.se/sofi sode/article361684.ab>.

Berger, J. (1972), *Ways of Seeing,* London: BBC.

Bourdieu, P. (1984), *Distinction: A Social Critique of the Judgment of Taste.* Cambridge, MA: Harvard University Press.

El Guindi, F. (1999), *Veil: Modesty, Privacy, Resistance,* Oxford: Berg.

Fanon, F. (2000), *Black Skin, White Masks,* New York: Grove Weidenfeld.

Göthlund, A. (1997), *Bilder av tonårsflickor. Om estetik och identitetsarbete,* Motala: Kanaltryckeriet.

hooks, b. (1992), *Black Looks: Race and Representation,* London: Turnaround.

Hutnyk, J. (2000), *Critique of Exotica: Music, Politics, and the Culture Industry,* London: Pluto Press.

Johansson, N. (2007), 'Stolt over sin slöja', *Aftonbladet.se* (5 October) <http://www.aftonbladet.se/sofi smode/article943193.ab> accessed 11 November 2009.

Kirna (2008), 'Strange Hijab', *Preciousmodesty.blogspot.com* (1 February) <http://preciousmodesty.blogspot.com/2008_02_01_archive.html> accessed 16 November 2009.

Lewis, R. (1995), *Gendering Orientalism: Race, Femininity and Representation,* London: Routledge.

Massad, J. (2007), *Desiring Arabs,* Chicago: University of Chicago Press.

Mazeralla, W. (2004), 'Culture, Globalization, Mediation', *Annual Review of Anthropology* 33: 345–67.

McRobbie, A. (1998), *British Fashion Design: Rag Trade or Image Industry?,* London: Routledge.

Niessen, S., A. Leshkowich and C. Jones (2003), *Re-orienting Fashion: The Globalization of Asian Dress,* Oxford: Berg.

Said, E. (2000), *Orientalism,* New York: Pantheon.

Tarlo, E. (2010), *Visibly Muslim: Fashion, Politics, Faith,* Oxford: Berg.

13

Miss Headscarf: Islamic Fashion and the Danish Media

Connie Carøe Christiansen

In the spring of 2008, the Danish National Broadcasting Company, DR, launched a headscarf contest entitled 'Miss Headscarf' in its online youth section, called SKUM. The contest sparked considerable debate about Muslim appearances and raised the question of how far headscarves could or could not be considered as items of fashion. In this chapter, I explore representations of Muslim dress in the Danish media, showing the discrepancy between Muslim women's concerns about issues of self-presentation and those of the Danish and wider public. I begin with the public debate surrounding the Miss Headscarf Contest and then go on to explore some of the different ways Muslim women seek to challenge public perceptions through their modes of self-presentation in the Danish media.

What was interesting about the headscarf competition was both how it invited people to perceive the headscarf as an item of fashion and the way so much of the debate about the contest ignored this possibility. The debate which ensued went far beyond the online community of DR, reaching other national and international media. The timing of the contest was also significant. It was launched in the midst of media debates already taking place in the Danish news media during spring 2008 concerning headscarves in the workplace and their unsuitability for working in particular professions. Nevertheless, on the Web page DR announced that the intention of the contest was to raise further debate:

> Why has DR's 15–19-year-old online community launched this contest?
>
> It is one of our most important tasks to inspire debate and encourage young people to engage in society and its important issues. Lately, there has been some debate about headscarves both in the media and in the Danish parliament. We have launched the Miss Headscarf 2008 contest for several reasons: firstly, to inspire young Danes in general to engage in the debate and secondly, to encourage the young women who actually wear headscarves in particular to make themselves seen and heard in the debate.[1]

The idea, in other words, was also to encourage Muslim women, the objects of the headscarf debate, to step forward. On the DR Web page directed at youth, the purpose of the Miss Headscarf Contest was explained in terms of finding the most stylish wearer of a headscarf:

> What exactly is Miss Headscarf 2008?
> It is a fashion and style contest for girls and women who wear headscarves. Anyone may participate regardless of religion or ethnicity, but there is a minimum age limit of fifteen.

There were no requirements regarding the faith of participants. As mentioned, the context of the contest was already an ongoing national media debate about Muslim women's headscarves, and perhaps for this reason, debaters took for granted that the contest referred to *Muslim* women's scarves. In spite of this, a few of the forty-two contestants submitted photos in which scarves were worn in ways that suggested that they were unlikely to be Muslim.

Whilst editors were clear that this was a fashion contest, they were also clear that it was not a beauty contest:

> Is this a beauty contest?
> No. It is a fashion contest, not a beauty contest. The pictures we receive from the participants will be reviewed according to criteria such as style, aesthetics and fashion savvy. We do not take into consideration the physical appearance (i.e. face or body) or the beauty of the contestants.

In spite of the clarification that this was not a beauty contest and that it was not exclusively for Muslims, it raised protests both from secular and religious camps and was noted in other Danish and international media including Fox News, the BBC, the *Financial Times* and some Arab channels such as Al-Arabiya. The international media tended to connect this contest to the controversy over the cartoons of the Prophet Mohammed, originally published in 2006 by the Danish daily *JyllandsPosten*. The cartoons had placed Denmark in the headlines, sparking controversy and protest, a bomb attack against the Danish embassy in Pakistan and expressions of negative sentiments towards migrants in Denmark. In light of these events, the contest was presented as a countermove with the potential to balance out the negative view of Denmark among the world's Muslims.

In the Danish media, the most vociferous debaters, many of them politicians and members of parliament, insisted on discussing the pros and cons of Muslim women wearing a headscarf at all rather than issues of fashion and style. For instance, Vibeke Manniche, the president of the Danish organization Women for Freedom ignored, or perhaps was unaware of, the largely positive international attention the contest was generating when she wrote in her blog:

> One gets sick at heart—and feels sick, nothing less when one sees the sex-fascist contest initiated by DR. Beautiful headscarf-imprisoned girls! What about headscarf-imprisoned boys? No, I guess! It is chilling and very, very terrifying. It should stir a storm of protest.[2]

In fact, the political right wing along with politicians from the Liberal Party, the Social Democrats and the Socialists all claimed in unison that such a contest was condoning a sign of women's oppression. So too did Nasser Khader, who is from a Syrian/Palestinian background and at the time was a member of Parliament for the Conservatives:

> It's not the task of DR to spend license contributions [paid by the viewers] to produce commercials for the headscarf. Why don't they make a contest about who is able to produce the best arguments for Muslim women *not* to wear the headscarf?[3]

One politician was more positive: Asmaa Abdol-Hamid, a heavily exposed media figure, then candidate for the Danish Parliament and herself a hijab-wearer, defended the contest even though Miss Headscarf sounded a bit superficial to her:

> It's not about finding the most beautiful Muslim, but about showing the multiplicity of women with headscarves. As long as the girls submit decent and nice pictures, I see no problems.[4]

Abdol-Hamid found her own reasons for condoning the contest—showing the variety of headscarves and challenging resistance to Muslim women's headscarves. References to modesty were also included when she suggested that girls submit 'decent and nice pictures'. This was not a position shared in other quarters. Smain Benyrbah, the president of Islamisk Trossamfund (Society of the Islamic Faith) in the city of Odense told a daily newspaper reporter: 'I don't think that Muslim girls should be exposed in this manner, and I want to encourage the girls to stay away from the contest'.[5] The attempt to provoke aesthetic evaluations of the headscarf was, in other words, ignored both by secular politicians and by spokesmen of the Islamic community in Denmark.

A different objection was raised by the scholar of Middle Eastern studies Mehmet Necef, who pointed out that the 'covering styles' of Muslim women did not prevent them from being gazed upon and judged as sexual objects, since aestheticizing and sexualizing gazes are ubiquitous in current hyper-modern consumer society (Necef 2008). Such gazes penetrate everyday life as a consequence of commercialization, generating media-enticed readings of surfaces in everyday interactions.[6] In other words, there can be no escape from the aestheticizing gaze—not even through covering. Here it was the unavoidable aestheticization implicit in the contest that was under attack. However, such an interpretation fails to take into consideration the multi-dimensional nature of Islamic fashion which is not just concerned with appearances but also with religious, political and moral ideals (Sandikci and Ger 2007, 2010; Moors 2009; Moors and Salih 2009; Jouili 2009, 2011; Tarlo 2010; Christiansen 2011). For many women, aesthetic concerns go hand in hand with moral practices of self-cultivation (Mahmood 2005).

Necef was critical of the references to 'inner beauty' made by Helen Latifi, one of the judges of Miss Headscarf and herself a committed Muslim. He considered her suggestion that one could measure inner beauty from outward appearances 'far-fetched'. Yet for Latifi, ethical elements were built into the contest as she pointed out in her blog where she explained why she agreed to be a judge in the competition:

> As I understand the veil from my religious conviction, it symbolizes modesty, humility and grace. These are the elements through which I have judged the women. Furthermore, I don't think it would be ideal if only my co-judge, Uffe Buchardt, were to judge the women, as this would involve different criteria to those I emphasise as a Muslim woman.[7]

Helen Latifi suggested that as a religious Muslim woman she had a different and more profound basis for judging the contestants than her co-judge, who was a mainstream fashion stylist. Humility and modesty were personal qualities that Helen claimed could be perceived from the photos. Helen gave the following comments about the winning photo of eighteen-year-old Huda, who wore a light blue hijab tied with a lace band across the upper forehead:

> The royal blue headscarf stands in lovely contrast to her dark brown colour. She appears deep, reflective and strong. Her beauty is hidden and only her inner heart is left. The headscarf reveals reflection and inner tranquillity.[8]

Helen referred to the character of Huda from a reading of her outfit, suggesting that she was 'deep, reflective and strong'. She also pointed to the 'lovely contrast' between the colour of her skin and the 'royal blue' of the headscarf, undeniably also bringing in an aesthetic judgment of surfaces.

Uffe Burchardt, a leading fashion stylist in Denmark, who was also a judge in the contest commented:

> Fantastic and stunning colour (mega summer trend) which really shows attitude and impact. Beautiful draping covering the breast. Perfect style, looks almost like a small piece of art.[9]

This judge referred to 'attitude and impact' as well as to the look of the headscarf. In other words, although their emphasis was different, both judges read Huda's personal character from her appearance. Similarly, many Muslim women attribute moral values to covering practices, which they associate with modesty, just as Helen Latifi did in her judgement. Necef's argument that the aestheticizing gaze dominates perception in all interactions seems to fall flat in the light of reactions to the Miss Headscarf competition, where aesthetic judgments were often subordinated to judgements of morality and character or went hand in hand with them.

ATTITUDES OF MISS HEADSCARF CONTESTANTS

Whilst cultural commentators tended to downplay the aesthetic potential of the headscarf, contestants were generally more sensitive to its potential both as an item of fashion and self-cultivation. They were also conscious of the need to challenge perceptions of Muslim women through their appearance. In several of the Danish newspaper articles which featured the contest, young Muslim women in Denmark were given the opportunity to speak and to present another angle on the headscarf to that usually presented in discussions for or against it. One of the contestants interviewed for a newspaper article argued, 'I want to show people another side of being Muslim and what that is like. Not showing too much of myself actually makes me feel more feminine.'[10] Another contestant told a journalist, 'It's trying to suggest something different from the usual claim that headscarves are repressive. Here they are trying to look at the headscarf as something beautiful.'[11]

In a video sequence shown on the SKUM Web page, Khadije, at the time an actress and a student, presented herself by name and age. Standing before the camera in an accessories shop wearing a black headscarf with a white bonnet underneath it, she explains to the camera:

> I have my own style; it is rather conservative or dull, simple. I have been wearing the headscarf for four years now and in the beginning I was wearing wild colours, like yellow.

She goes on to point out that she is careful to match her headscarf with the rest of her clothes:

> I would most likely go shopping for headscarves if for instance I were going to go to a wedding, as I would want to make sure my headscarf matched my clothing. Last time I counted I had eighty headscarves and fifty bonnets. There is a kind of fashion in headscarves.

Khadije also explains that she no longer likes the colourful scarves, especially not the ones that imitate well-known and expensive brands. She grabs a scarf in white-and-black check: 'I love black and white and it looks a bit like a Palestinian scarf' (the *keffiyeh*). She demonstrates how she ties it with pins on the side of her head. She also shows different types of headscarves and points out what she does not like and asserts that it is quite possible to tell where people come from just by looking at their headscarves. Khadije characterizes her own current style as 'conservative'; she also explains that a *popgirl*[12] with a headscarf is a teenager wearing tight clothes and lots of glitter: 'They could be young girls from Nørrebro [a part of Copenhagen] who are interested in Gucci, Chanel, Louis Vuitton.' Khadije presents and valorizes the headscarf as a consumer item to be judged aesthetically. As a consumer item, it is also used to distinguish between different categories of wearer. 'Just, get it', she comments. 'Young Muslim women are interested in fashion!'

The self-cultivation (Mahmood 2005) and stylistic navigations (Tarlo 2010) of the Muslim women who responded to the contest showed concern both with covering and with fashion norms. Self-cultivation for Khadije involved the cultivation of a covered style rather than the view that style did not matter. She does not refer to notions of inner self or Islamic principles; she simply points to changed practices which imply a change of moral disposition. In interviews with women who have been central to the debate on Islamic clothing and fashion style in the Danish media, two assertions emerge: one is that the hijab brings about modesty; the other is that modesty leads to people wearing hijab. These variations, I argue, indicate the creativity with which Danish Muslim women using Islamic fashion draw both on Islamic ethics and moral conduct and on cultural elements not associated with Islam in their cultivation of a Muslim self. In this, they are similar to 'visibly Muslim' women in Britain (Tarlo 2010) and the Netherlands (Moors 2009).

HIJAB AS EMBODYING MODESTY— MODESTY AS EMBODIED BY HIJAB

When Helen Latifi referred to 'inner beauty' as a criterion for selecting the winner of the headscarf contest, she referred to an aesthetic which included ethical judgment and moral comportment as well as fashion savvy. I conducted an interview with her in late 2007 at the faculty of medicine of Copenhagen University where she was a 25-year-old student at the time and used to write a daily blog. Helen was attached to the organized (Sunni) group of Muslim students at Copenhagen University, although she explained that her Iranian family was affiliated to the Shia line of faith, but she had converted to Sunni Islam. This conversion had consequences for the way she dressed:

> It started with my clothes getting longer and the covering of the neck little by little. I became calmer; I used to be very aggressive. I became humbler, more tolerant towards all points of views.

Fig. 13.1 Helen Latifi, 2008. Photo: Birgitte Carol Heiberg

Helen's perception of what covering one's body and one's hair does to one's comportment comes very close to that found among Mahmood's participants in the Cairo mosque movement (Mahmood 2005); it is the wearing of the headscarf and long clothing that creates the changes in character, not the other way around. In her clothing style, Helen condones colourful and chic clothing and is explicit about rejecting 'dull' clothing such as dour colours and long and loose *jellebas*. A chic style which underlines your femininity, she argues, is important:

> I want it [my clothing style] to match and radiate strength, to reflect the person I am, to express grace, be a little classical, like the person I am inside. Femininity and at the same time strength are important, for instance when you wear trousers something masculine emerges. I often used to wear a velvet suit which for some-time was very in. Sometimes a skirt.

Helen also claims that God encourages women to reveal their femininity, and she rejects the idea that Islamic dress is about concealing women from men. For her clothing is about revealing the self:

> I don't feel that I need people's recognition, it's enough that I have God's. Actually I have been very influenced by wearing the veil. I feel that I value myself more, when I look at myself in the mirror now, I can really see how beautiful I am. Now I can really see my beauty, see my hair and how beautiful it is. That has come as

a surprise to me. The common Muslim argument that I am covering so as not to show myself to men is wrong if one really considers what covering does to you, and you don't know until you do it.

In Helen's understanding, the modesty she embraces by wearing the hijab gives her the opportunity to enjoy her own beauty, and it does not prevent her from enjoying different clothing styles:

[I like the] Latino look, long dresses, long in the back and short in the front—long, flowing, gypsy style skirts. I also like military jackets. Everybody wants to transmit something, so I think mixing in this way reflects my characteristics. Here at Panum [the faculty of medicine] one can wear it all. Mixing styles has always interested me.

The covering of hair, body and skin takes centre stage in Helen's arguments (see Figure 13.1). But she claims that it is a restriction she finds inspiring and which has had the effect of changing her conduct and her perception of self.

However, the choice of what to wear and the decision about how to be represented in the media varies considerably amongst different Muslim women in Denmark. In the final section of this chapter, I examine the sartorial strategies of two other women who, like Helen, have a significant public presence in the Danish media but who choose to present themselves in very different ways.

Sherin Khankan is a well-known media figure in the more intellectual parts of the Danish press, where she takes part from time to time in debates and writes features for newspapers. I interviewed Sherin in her home in early 2008. A few years previously, she had married a man of Pakistani descent and was on maternity leave, having recently given birth to their second child. Sherin has a master's degree in the history of religion and is a frequent contributor to public debates about Islam. She also gives talks to live audiences on such topics as Islam and women, Muslims in the West and radicalization. For Sherin, the guidance of shyness and modesty that she finds in her religion is expressed in the way she dresses. Her increased covering is a sign that her attention to modesty has increased over the years:[13]

But I can feel that my limits of modesty have moved. Now it's more a question of God watching me all the time, in other words it's not for others, but rather about my relationship with God.

Sherin describes the development in her perception of modesty as occurring almost without her noticing it—she just feels that her limits have moved. In contrast to Helen, she presents her faith as developing in congruence with her intellectual progress.

A few years ago, Sherin published a book, *Islam og forsoning—en offentlig sag* (Islam and Reconciliation—a Public Matter; Khankan 2007). The front cover of the book shows a photograph of a beautiful, slender woman in a purple *galabiya* with long, decorated sleeves; the headscarf accompanying this attire is light blue, long, transparent and loose, revealing the forehead, above which dark brown hair parted in a straight line is also visible (see Figure 13.2). Discussing the decision to feature 'herself' on the cover, she explains:

> Regarding the front cover of my book, my husband thought I should have a simple cover with text and some sort of splendid art related to Islam—he is very opposed to exposing the self. It has to be the cause that is important, not the person expressing it. He has influenced me very much from the moment I met him. I remember thinking right after I met him, he is very realistic. And then I thought, there is really something about it. And for a while after I met him, I refused to give interviews if they wanted a picture of me. I said, 'Now I have taken a new decision; I will only give interviews without photographs, since it's not my person or appearance that counts but the material, ideals, text and cause.' But the result was that no one really wanted to interview me because there needs to be a picture with an article, or people do not want to read it. So I have now abandoned that strategy. I have also come to the conclusion today that there needs to be a balance. It is important for me to be publically visual and visible because one of my missions has been to make Muslim women visible in public space and in the debate about Islam. So I have used myself actively in that way, and that is the point of my being on the front cover.

Fig. 13.2 Image from *Islam og forsoning—en offentlig sag* (Khankan 2007)

Self-cultivation is for Sherin an act of balancing different purposes against each other. In principle, Sherin ascribes to the argument that it is not the person but the subject matter which counts; in other words, her outer appearance is potentially a distraction away from the cause. However, she weighs this argument against other more important concerns and concludes that her photo needs to be there to bring attention to the message that she wants to convey. This reasoning is contextual—she takes the wider secular context, rather than her personal concerns about modesty and piety into consideration before she determines the kind of self-cultivation demanded of her. Put differently, Sherin's attempt to promote a different image for Muslim women takes shape through the style of clothing she wears, which is fully in accordance with her development as a Muslim or, in her own terms, her journey as a Muslim.

Sherin's classic, almost biblical image is in sharp contrast to that of Tesnim, who is equally concerned with trying to change perceptions of Muslim women in the Danish media. Tesnim is a 21-year-old student of design at Kolding in Denmark. In August 2010, she exhibited her designs of Muslim women's wear in an exhibition in Copenhagen (see Figure 13.3) and was interviewed for a radio program. In the interview, Tesnim explained that as a young Muslim woman she found punk style an inspiration. This inspiration emerged clearly in the designs exhibited. Most remarkable were the hijabs with cones of cotton-filled triangular spikes sewn onto them. 'The cone is made from a triangle of totally traditional headscarf in red chequered fabric, I have just made spikes from it and filled them with cotton,' she explained in a radio program, which gave a portrait of her style. Moreover the chequered fabrics in gray, black, bright yellow and bright red, along with accessories of heavy chains, safety pins and badges (one of them stating, 'I am not weird, I am gifted!'), an abundance of zippers and buckles, a kilt to be worn on top of trousers and a nose ring leave no doubt that the 1970s and 1980s punk style has found a new expression in these designs. Tesnim calls herself a Muslim Goth punk: 'I am tired of generalizations and prejudices about Muslim girls. That's why I am a Muslim Goth punk.'[14] The designs she makes cover the legs, the arms and the neck:

> 'When I was younger I found it difficult to find clothes that were chic and covering. The chic was much too revealing, and then it quickly became layer upon layer, and I came to look like an old granny. I wanted to change that', Tesnim explains, while eagerly gesticulating with her black mitts with skeleton prints, and chain bracelets which rattle.[15]

Tesnim bought her first rivet bracelet when she was eleven years old. In high school, she began to wear black clothing and continued with black all the way through school. She knew how to sew, and it came naturally to her to try to sew 'some weird punk clothes'.

A cone sewn onto a hijab is, according to Tesnim, something which provokes people, something they have not seen before:

Fig. 13.3 Tesnim's designs exhibited in the exhibition 'Denmark 2010—A Guide for the Nation of "The Happiest People in the World"', Ovengaden Nedenvandet, Copenhagen, 26 June–15 August 2010. Photo: Connie Carøe Christiansen

> The cone symbolizes me and provocation. It demonstrates my messages; that I am tired of people's prejudices concerning what a Muslim girl should be like. Wearing this made me more aware of myself, more myself.[16]

Tesnim is explicit about the proximity of aesthetics, self-cultivation and communication:

> I don't want to give up my headscarf. I am a Muslim, I like my religion, I like my headscarf. I pray five times a day and will go on pilgrimage. And at the same time I like this rebellious style. I cannot see any hindrance to combining Islam and punk.[17]

Muslim Goth punk became the solution for Tesnim, enabling her to combine norms about clothes that cover with her own sense of style. She recognizes that the style is provocative but provocation is not its key purpose:

> I wear it because I think it's cool and suits me. I did not design it to provoke. But my message is at the same time that one should not think that Muslim girls just sit at home and are boring.[18]

The Goth punk style introduces another image of Muslim women—one which combines provocation, self-consciousness and nerve. Like the female Muslim rappers of Poetic Pilgrimage in Britain, whose experiments with clothes have been described by Tarlo (2010: 81–92), Tesnim combines unexpected stylistic components which many would consider incompatible. She wants to convey that Muslim women are not boring and not restricted to the home. This message is not external to her style but integral to it.

What these examples suggest is that Muslims in the Danish media are creating alternative aesthetics in which they draw not only on principles inspired from Islam or the Quran but also on the notion that clothing reveals personality—an idea central to mainstream fashion discourses. The aesthetic choices made by women like Helen, Sherin and Tesnim include concerns not only about Islamic ethics and modesty but also secular concerns linked to fashion and to the place of Muslim women in Denmark. In a creative way, they take inspiration from the religious and the secular in different degrees with the result that each presents her own highly personal interpretation of Muslim women's dress.

CONCLUSION

The Miss Headscarf Contest introduced the Danish and international public to the idea that the headscarf could belong to the aesthetic realm of style and beauty and not just to the domains of morality, religion and politics. However, the emphasis on fashion and style, and on the hijab as a consumer item, was largely obscured by many who participated in public debates about the contest. They were unable to recognize the elements of moral and aesthetic self-cultivation found within Islamic fashion and failed more generally to recognize that Muslim women could be legitimate moral and political actors. The views of commentators stood in stark contrast to those of Muslim women in Denmark, many of whom expressed complex understandings of their own dress practices. Their discourses suggest that like the women of the mosque movement in Cairo described by Mahmood (2005), they seek constantly to improve themselves as Muslims. But at the same time, they are also highly conscious of the societal context in which they operate (Jouili 2008, 2011; Moors 2009). Consequently, their self-cultivation is aimed in part at establishing a certain image of Muslim women, whether as decent and beautiful, self-confident and provocative, or judicious and balanced. Such aesthetics are based on an evaluation of looks perceived as intimately connected to inner qualities; hence their different formulations concerning the correspondence between outward appearances and inner qualities in the cultivation of a Muslim self. Although care for one's outward appearance is sometimes presented as an obligation for Muslim women, this endeavour is presented by Muslim women who cover as an integral part of their development as a Muslim.

NOTES

1. See <http://community.dr.dk/default.ns?lngItemID=1402>. DR closed the Web page on 31 March 2011. These motivations of the SKUM editors were published in English.
2. <www.blog.kvinderforfrihed.dk>. Quotations from the Danish media and interviews conducted in Danish have all been translated by the author.
3. RITZAU, 'Khader beklager tørklædekonkurrence', *JyllandsPosten,* 27 May 2008.
4. SKUM <www.community.dr.dk> accessed June 2008.
5. Nanna Balslev and René Fredensborg, 'Huda er stolt af sit tørklæde', Nyhedsavisen, 10 June 2008.
6. The most prominent research carried out in Denmark developing and refining this line of sociology is conducted by Henning Bech, who has published primarily in the cross-fields of urban sociology and sexuality (e.g., 1998, 2003).
7. Helen Latifi's Smalltalk (blog), <helenlatifi.wordpress.com> accessed 10 June 2008.
8. SKUM <http://community.dr.dk> accessed June 2008.
9. Ibid.
10. Excerpts from Mette-Line Thorup, 'Vil du se min smukke tørklæde?', *Information,* 6 June 2008.
11. Ibid.
12. A *popgirl* as well as a *popboy* are emic youth categories—that is, a categorization (in line with *nerd* or *emo*) that Copenhagen youth apply to each other, and Khadije's point is that such a category also exists for those wearing a hijab.
13. Sherin was interviewed in Danish, and she referred to the Danish word *blufærdighed,* which covers the Arabic term *al-haya* more accurately than modesty, since it also has the meaning of *shyness.*
14. Evalina Gold and Kristina Gjelstrup Villadsen, 'Muslimsk punkertøs med hanekam', *Information* <http://www.information.dk/239251> accessed 18 July 2010.
15. Evalina Gold and Krtistina Gjelstrup Villadsen, 'Muslimsk pigepunker med hanekam', interview in *Gazette,* a Danish and Turkish language Turkish paper, published in Copenhagen <http://www.gazette.dk/?p=1081> accessed 18 July 2010.

16. Alicia Jordanova, Cedilie Kubert and Julie Aagaard, 'Islam er punk!' (radio programme), <http://www.dr.dk/P1/Klubvaerelset/Udsendelser/2010/02/23113958.htm> accessed 18 July 2010.
17. Ibid.
18. Gold and Villadsen, 'Muslimsk pigepunker med hanekam'.

REFERENCES

Bech, H. (1998), 'Citysex: Representing Lust in Public', *Theory, Culture and Society: Explorations in Critical Social Science* 15, 34: 215–41.

Bech, H. (2003), 'The Disappearance of the Modern Homosexual', in J. Weeks, J. Holland and M. Waites, eds., *Sexualities and Society,* Cambridge: Polity Press.

Christiansen, C. C. (2011), 'Contesting Visibilities: Sartorial Strategies among Muslim Women in Danish Media', *Journal of Intercultural Studies* 32, 4: 335–53.

Jouili, J. (2008), 'Re-fashioning the Self through Religious Knowledge: How Muslim Women Become Pious in the German Diaspora', in A. Al-Harmaneh and J. Thielmann, eds., *Islam and Muslims in Germany,* Leiden: Brill.

Jouili, J. (2009), 'Negotiating Secular Boundaries: Pious Micro-practices of Muslim Women in French and German Public Spheres', *Social Anthropology* 17, 4: 455–70.

Jouili, J. (2011), 'Beyond Emancipation: Subjectivities and Ethics among Women in Europe's Islamic Revival Communities', *Feminist Review* 98: 47–64.

Khankan, S. (2007), *Islam og forsoning—en offentlig sag,* Copenhagen: Lindhardt & Ringhof.

Mahmood, S. (2005), *Politics of Piety: The Islamic Revival and the Feminist Subject,* Princeton, NJ: Princeton University Press.

Moors, A. (2009), 'Islamic Fashion in Europe: Religious Conviction, Aesthetic Style, and Creative Consumption', *Encounters* 1: 175–99.

Moors, A., and R. Salih (2009), '"Muslim Women" in Europe: Secular Normativities, Bodily Performances and Multiple Publics', *Social Anthropology* 17, 4: 375–8.

Necef, M. (2008), *Tørklædets trekant: Æstetik, etik og politik,* Center for Mellemøststudier, February, <http://static.sdu.dk/mediafiles//Files/Om_SDU/Centre/C_Mellemoest/Videncenter/Nyheder/2009/100203MN.pdf> accessed 25 March 2013.

Sandikci, Ö., and G. Ger (2007), 'Constructing and Representing the Islamic Consumer in Turkey', *Fashion Theory* 11, 2–3: 189–210.

Sandikci, Ö., and G. Ger (2010), 'Veiling in Style: How Does a Stigmatized Practice Become Fashionable?', *Journal of Consumer Research* 37: 15–36.

Tarlo, E. (2010), *Visibly Muslim: Fashion, Politics, Faith,* Oxford: Berg.

Fashion designer Sarah Elenany, at work and play in London. Photos: Alessia Gammarota

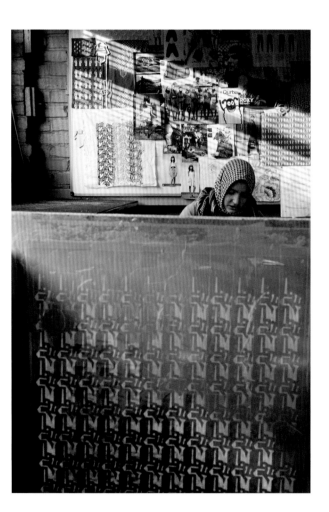

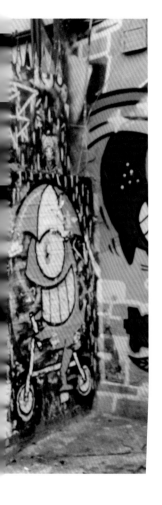

SECTION V

DYNAMICS OF FASHION AND ANTI-FASHION

Fashion and Its Discontents: The Aesthetics of Covering in the Netherlands

Annelies Moors

Since the later 1990s, a wide range of styles of Muslim dress has become visibly present on the streets of the Netherlands.[1] These vary from the layering of colourful, mainstream items that produce a highly fashionable yet recognizably Muslim outfit to the loose, full-length outerwear in subdued, dark colours that seems far removed from the world of fashion. This variety has also drawn the attention of journalists, politicians and the majority public, who not only discuss the presence of Muslim headscarves in public space but also evaluate and express expert opinions about the particular styles of dress Muslim women adopt. These opinions tend to be far more positive with respect to the rapidly growing number of young women who wear these more fashionable and often more revealing styles than in the case of the much smaller number of women who wear the more fully covering styles. With fashion strongly linked to modernity, fashionable styles become an indication of the willingness of these women to fit in and to adapt to a mainstream aesthetic.[2] For those wearing full-length, loose outerwear and large headscarves, fashion is not invested with similar levels of approbation. Are their styles of dress then to be considered a strong example of anti-fashion? Exploring how the women who have adopted more fully covering styles of Islamic dress engage with fashion and anti-fashion, this chapter investigates the ambiguities of their sartorial practices, which include alternative perceptions of the aesthetics of fashion and its place on the body and in public space.

THE BIFURCATION OF STYLES OF MUSLIM DRESS

A convenient starting point to discuss the fashion-Islam nexus is the eight-page article 'Hip with the Headscarf'. Appearing in 1999 in the weekend magazine of an upscale Dutch daily, *Volkskrant Magazine,* this article started with the observation that 'more and more women with headscarves wear fashionable styles of dress and lots of make-up' (Jungschleger and Riemersma 1999).

Fig. 14.1 Different styles of covering, with the woman on the right wearing a long khimar

Next to portraying a number of young women wearing such fashionable styles, it also presented the points of view of 'expert' commentators. Some, such as a Moroccan Dutch politician for the Labour Party, who wears a headscarf herself, emphasized the growing self-confidence of these young women. Including herself in the category, she made the comment, 'We are really stylish. We read *Cosmopolitan* and buy our clothing at Hennes & Mauritz.' Concerning the sartorial styles of these women, she added, 'They develop their own style, hip and attractive', 'they claim presence, they have guts' and 'they are saying, "I wear a headscarf because I am a Muslim, but I am living in the Netherlands"'. Others cited in the article pointed to contradictions and ambivalences. 'They show their Arabic or Islamic identity, but in such a way that it makes them more attractive', a Moroccan Dutch psychiatrist in training stated. 'It is very

creative what they are doing, but also ambivalent. The intention of the headscarf is to cover women's beauty. If you simultaneously accentuate this, what
are you then doing?'

The dress trajectories of the women I did research with also indicate that
by the later 1990s, more fashionable styles had started to appear on the
streets in the Netherlands.[3] The emergence of such sartorial practices indirectly goes back to the 1960s when the Dutch government invited labour
migrants from countries such as Turkey and Morocco, as a solution to labour
shortages. In the next decade, these mostly male workers started to bring
their families to the Netherlands.[4] But it was only in the later 1980s that the
Dutch public began to define these labour migrants, their offspring and refugees from Muslim-majority countries as Muslims. At the same time, women
inspired by the Islamic revival started to cover their hair more strictly with
larger headscarves knotted or pinned under the chin, which were worn in
combination with long and loose styles of dress, such as oversized raincoats
bought in the cheaper-end department stores and markets.

A decade later, as the article mentioned above indicates, recognizably Muslim styles of dress were not only more widely present, but these outfits had
also become more fashionable. By then, the daughters of these labour migrants were completing their education, and some of them had started to
work. These young women were far better educated than their mothers and
even if still in school, held jobs on the side and hence had more money to
spend on their appearance. Some of them also became more interested in
religion, especially after 9/11 and even more so after the murder of Theo
van Gogh in 2004, when they were regularly confronted with questions about
Islam. Those who took up covered dress often selected items from the same
stores where their peers were shopping but layered and matched them in
such a way that they turned into a fashionable yet Islamically licit (halal) outfit.
They also used under-scarves and bonnets, hijab pins and broaches to experiment with a wide range of styles to drape, knot and tie headscarves in more
sophisticated ways.

The 1999 article did not mention another style emerging at the turn of the
millennium that involved a much smaller number of young Muslim women.
Distancing themselves from the highly fashionable outfits some of their
peers had started to wear, these young women adopted a distinctively non-
fashionable style of covering. However, they neither wore the cheaper-end styles
of strictly covering dress of the 1980s nor the better-fitting and more sophisticated full-length coats that Islamic fashion companies, especially in Turkey,
had started to produce (see Ünal, this book). Instead, they turned to a different aesthetic. They adopted loose, full-length overgarments, usually in darker,
subdued, solid colours, garments they themselves referred to with terms such
as *abaya* or *jilbab*. They often combined these cloaks with larger veils, such as
the khimar (a round-cut, closed veil of various lengths that can easily be pulled

over the head) or, less often, a very large rectangular scarf draped around the head, shoulders, back and chest; in addition, an exceedingly small number of women added a face-veil (niqab) to their outfit. Such a style of dress looked rather similar to that commonly worn in the Gulf states, Yemen and parts of Egypt. The use of Arabic names for these garments further emphasized their Arab-Islamic connections.

The main question this contribution attempts to answer is whether wearing such apparently uniform and sober styles of dress can be considered as anti-fashion. As mentioned in the introduction to this book, fashion theorists deal in various ways with 'fashion' and 'anti-fashion'. Here I do not consider these concepts in terms of a contrast scheme but rather as part of a continuum

Fig. 14.2 Styles of fully covering in the Netherlands: the woman on the right wears a jacket over her khimar to produce a more acceptable appearance in the workplace

Fig. 14.3 Part of the wardrobe of a Moroccan Dutch woman in her mid-twenties: abayas and other full-length coverings of different muted colours

(see also Jouili 2009). Styles of dress may be considered as more fashion-able or less so in a double sense. In terms of temporality, the modalities of fashion refer to slower or more rapid changes of styles. In an aesthetic sense, labelling particular items of dress as fashionable or not depends on what is 'in fashion' at a particular historical moment.

At a first glance, the styles these women wear would appear to represent a strong case of anti-fashion. Indeed, in this chapter I will, to some extent, substantiate this argument. I start with a discussion about how these women position themselves with respect to those wearing 'fashion headscarves' in the Netherlands and then continue with their responses to the emergence of 'fashion abayas' in the Gulf states. In the next section, I then turn to how they discuss fashion and style in their own dress narratives. As it turns out, they have developed a particular alternative notion of aesthetics, which is closely intertwined with morality and comfort. At the same time and in spite of considerable changes in their outerwear, they also point to continuities with their earlier engagements with fashion. Their stance then is more ambivalent than simply rejecting fashion altogether.

CRITICIZING FASHIONABLE COVERING

It is not only the bareheaded Moroccan Dutch psychiatrist in training, cited in the 1999 article, who pointed to the ambivalences of fashionable covering. The more fully covering women who were my interlocutors also highlight what they consider inconsistencies of combining fashion and Muslim covered dress. Their criticism is, first of all, grounded in theological lines of argumentation. On the one hand, they take issue with the temporality of a fashion system that is characterized by continuous change, considering it as wasteful, superficial and mundane and hence in contradiction with such eternal and unchanging religious values as modesty and faith. Simultaneously, they also criticize how the fashion industry promotes styles of dress that are too revealing of the female body. Rather than hiding the shape of the body, these styles draw attention to it in undesirable, sexualized ways. In some cases, they also target particular styles of covering, such as the headscarf style that produces a particular shape of the head—very high in the back—by adding buns and other artificial elements.[5]

In their opinions about and sometimes approaches towards women who wear such fashion headscarves, more fully covering women hold a variety of positions. Some excuse them by stating that they may have only recently started their trajectory towards wearing covered dress, that they may not know the correct meaning of wearing hijab and that making an attempt is better than not covering at all. Others, in contrast, point out that they find it painful to see women wearing headscarves with skinny jeans and tight tops and consider it a disgrace. In their opinion, these girls are only playing with the headscarf, as there is enough information available for women to know what the correct hijab entails. For many, what matters most is a person's intentions, something only God can judge, while others point out that what is in the heart should also be publicly practiced. Some may even consider it their religious duty to provide others with 'friendly advice' about how to cover better. The addressee, however, may not perceive such advice as a friendly act but rather as undesirable interference in her private affairs.[6]

The Fashion Headscarf and Its Societal Effects

The more fully covered women did not only highlight theologically grounded forms of criticism of fashion headscarves in their narratives. Time and time again, they also stated that 'those wearing a fashion headscarf make it more difficult for us'. This was especially the case for those who were employed. In the words of one of them, a Dutch convert in her mid-twenties,

> Then the supervisor points to one of these girls with a fashion headscarf and tells you, look, she is also wearing a headscarf, but hers is smaller and more colourful, and looks much more pleasant and attractive, why do you need to wear something that is so big and dark? Can't you wear it the way she does? She is a Muslim, too!

It is true that such an argument is similar to when employers argue that it is not necessary to wear a headscarf at all because some Muslim women do not do so. But the women themselves find it easier to explain that they consider wearing a headscarf a religious duty than to go into great detail about the correct ways of wearing it.

That the ways in which women cover—and not only the fact that they cover their heads—are increasingly scrutinized and have become an employment issue is also substantiated through the opinions of the Commission for Equal Treatment (CGB).[7] Between 2006 and 2011, this commission dealt with at least six cases in which employers or school boards intended to take measures against employees and students not because they were wearing a headscarf but because of the kinds of headscarves they had adopted. These cases mainly concerned regulations that only allowed for headscarves that only covered the hair and that were tied at the nape of the neck rather than under the chin.[8] The employers concerned—a hospital, a library, a school and a catering agency—did not accept employees, interns or pupils who insisted on wearing a headscarf that also covered the upper back, the shoulders and the chest or even the neck and the throat.

In line with earlier jurisprudence, the commission explicitly stated in its opinions that wearing a headscarf may be an expression of religious conviction for Muslim women, even if there are differences of opinion amongst Muslims about whether covering the head is a religious obligation and, if so, how the headscarf needs to be worn. Hence, the commission usually considered regulations about styles of wearing the headscarf as indirect discrimination on the basis of religion. Whereas employers may present valid grounds for indirect discrimination, in most cases they did not succeed in convincing the commission that these regulations were both necessary and the only means possible to achieve aims such as maintaining standards of hygiene (a hospital), safety (a school), representativity (a catering company), an open appearance and communication (a library and a hospital). In the case of the library, for instance, women were requested to only wear headscarves that did not cover the eyes, ears, chin, throat and neck in order to facilitate communication. The commission agreed with the demand that the face needed to be visible but failed to see how covering the throat, neck and ears would a priori impair communication.[9]

In one particularly highly publicized case, the commission partly agreed with the arguments of the defendant.[10] This case concerned a secondary school that had developed new dress regulations, stating that the headscarf may only cover the hair and not the chin, eyebrows and the area above it, nor the sides of the face.[11] The school argued that it needed such a regulation to prevent headscarves from becoming larger and covering more of the face, as this would impede communication and make it harder to determine whether students were cheating during exams. Students interviewed for a local television station, mainly girls wearing rather fashionable styles that covered the forehead to a large extent, seemed to protest most of all against the fact that girls wearing headscarves were singled out, while girls with hairstyles that cover the forehead and the sides of the face were not targeted.[12] The commission ruled that such regulations needed to be clearly stated and could only be applied in the case of new pupils. In its regulations, the school then both referred to particular styles of wearing headscarves and to specific hairstyles, stating, 'Headscarves and hair may be worn so that good communication is possible. This means that at least the eyebrows and a space above them, the chin and the sides of the face need to remain uncovered.'[13]

Varieties of Fashion Abayas

Women who favour more fully covered forms of dress did not only distance themselves from fashion headscarves. They were also critical of the development in the Gulf states of 'fashion abayas', at least the more spectacular styles. In the course of the last decade, the abaya has been transformed from a non-distinct, all-enveloping black gown into something more akin to a fashion item, with seasonally changing cuts and models, materials and decorations (Al-Qasimi 2010; Lindholm 2010). A new group of Emirati women designers has emerged, often trained at fashion colleges in the United States and the United Kingdom. They have developed their own brands of designer abayas (high-end casual wear pieces that are available in limited numbers) and couture abayas (their more extravagant pieces).[14] Designer Web sites and Web stores, such as Rabia Z., promote such upscale abayas, which are also displayed at events such as the Islamic Fashion Festival or the Dubai Fashion Week.[15] These abayas have become part of an international fashion circuit. Not only have Emirati women been trained at fashion schools in London and New York, but French and Italian fashion houses, such as Dior, Nina Ricci and Alberta Ferretti have designed abayas as well, which were then sold at Saks Fifth Avenue stores in Saudi Arabia and elsewhere in the region, while fashion abayas are also sold in Harrods in London. Another example is how Swarovski collaborated with Sweet Lady, an abaya house in Abu Dhabi to launch Jawaher (jewels), with a range of abayas featuring the latest collection of Atelier Swarovski.

Fig. 14.4 Fashionable abaya designed by Rabia Z. as presented at her Web store

As the abaya is considered a quintessentially Islamic garment, many design-ers do not feel the need to highlight the Islamic nature of this style of dress; this seems to be taken for granted. Instead, they focus their efforts on how to turn the abaya into a highly fashionable garment (see Moors 2013). Also, their style of presenting these abayas is structured by the fashion discourse. Both during fashion shows and in the presentation of designer abayas online, there is little concern with discussions about Islamically correct ways of covering nor is there an engagement with debates about how to present the female body to the public, offline or online.[16] Some of the models appear bareheaded on the catwalks, and Web sites and Web stores present the models without religiously induced modi-fications. Whereas some Islamic Web stores are careful not to depict live mod-els at all—and if they do, they don't depict the full body but instead present the models from the neck down or waist up, sometimes also leaving out the facial features—this is not the case with these fashion-conscious abaya designers.

The more fully covered women in the Netherlands keep their distance from this world of designer abayas. Taking price into consideration, these outfits are considered far more wasteful than street fashion. Also, some of them do not cover the body up to their standards and may even be worn without a headcovering or with one that shows the hair and is worn very high in the back. However, also some of the abayas that cover the body and hair well have been influenced by fashion in terms of cut and decoration. In some parts of the world, these have been introduced as a new, more modern, style of full covering, such as in Yemen where they replaced existing styles of all-covering dress (Moors 2007), in South India where they are popular amongst migrants who have returned from the Gulf (Osella and Osella 2007) and in Indonesia (Amrullah 2008) where they have often been introduced by returning migrants and students. Fully covering women in the Netherlands are less critical of such styles and would consider wearing them in places like Dubai, where 'everyone wears those styles', but not in the Netherlands, as they feel they would stand out even more than they already do.[17] This does, however, not meant that they are not interested in beauty. When they discuss their own abayas, it is evident that their notion of aesthetics is different.

THE AESTHETICS OF FULLY COVERING

The types of Islamic styles available online are just as diverse as those available in shops, if not more so (see also Tarlo 2010). When fully covered women in the Netherlands look to Web stores, they steer away from those selling highly fashionable abayas in favour of those which present and sell abayas in ways that verbally and visually resonate with the aesthetics they admire and the values they adhere to. A good example of such a Web store is Sunnah Style, which operates from Toronto, Canada.[18]

Sunnah Style was launched as an online store in August 2007. Whereas most of its customers appear to come from Canada and the United States, the company also ships to the United Kingdom, Europe and South East Asia. Allowing for shopping by category, collection and colour, the focus in on a wide range of specifically Islamic items of dress, such as abayas, (long) dresses, hijabs and niqabs. As is the case with other Web stores, extensive information is provided about sizes, shipping and payments, and the Web store is well-connected to social media, including a blog, Facebook and Twitter.

Compared to many other Islamic dress or fashion sites operating from North America or Europe that provide customers with Western, yet Islamically licit, styles of dress, Sunnah Style does not elaborate extensively on the Islamic nature of the Web store.[19] This may be the case because such markedly Islamic styles such as abayas are so obviously intended to cover fully that the

Fig. 14.5   Butterfly abaya as presented at the Sunnah Style Web store

owners of these Web stores do not feel that they need to preach to the converted. Not only the items of dress available but also the ways the Web store
presents them—avoiding the use of live models and blanking out the faces in
drawings—highlight the Islamic nature of the site.

There is, however, one particular moment where Sunnah Style refers to religion; that is when it engages with the concept of fashion. Whereas this Web
store presents itself with the catchphrase 'Sunnah Style: Elegantly Modest', at
the bottom of the 'About' section, it includes a 'style' disclaimer that explicitly
engages with fashion and religion:

> Although we have chosen Sunnah Style as the name of our store we are by no
> means implying that it is legislated in the Qur'an or Sunnah to follow or keep up

with fashions and trends. Rather, the use of the word 'style' in our name represents the various styles or varieties of clothing that we offer.[20]

In other words, the owners of the Web store distance themselves from fashion, but they do use the concept of style. On the company blog, they further explain: 'We design and manufacture all of our own styles and put a strong emphasis on modesty. Our styles are simple yet sophisticated with both classic and trendy influences.'[21] Their engagement with style then mainly focuses on differences in the cut of the abaya (whether it is worn on the head or the shoulders, whether and how it is closed in the front and the kind of sleeves it has) and in the nature and quality of the fabrics and decorations used, as the following example indicates:

> [Our Starlight Closed Abaya] is made from high quality Maliki crepe that has slight ridges in the fabric weave, making it breathable. Maliki crepe is wrinkle-resistant and has a medium weight, allowing the abaya to drape beautifully.[22]

Although the 'look' of the abaya—that is, its visual effects—is addressed in this quotation, as in many similar ones, tactility, the 'feel' of wearing an abaya is at least as important. Highlighting the importance of experiential knowledge—as they stated, they regularly wear abayas, khimars and niqabs themselves—Sunnah Style foregrounds terms such as *comfort, practicality* and *breathability*:

> More importantly, our abayas (along with all of our other styles) are designed by women. We try to incorporate extra room into our styles for modesty and include practical features like pockets. We design most of our closed styles with a zipper or snaps at the neck to accommodate nursing mothers.
>   Again, all of our niqabs are designed by sisters who wear niqab on a daily basis and have corrected the problems that most manufacturers have with their niqabs.[23]

Against this background, Sunnah Style has developed a special face-veil, the 'no-pinch niqab':

> [It] features an eye-opening that is designed 3/4″ high with V-shaped corners for style. This design keeps the fabric away from the eyes and prevents the bottom piece from riding up and pinching the eyes. The result is a super-comfortable niqab that will not need to be pulled down to give the eyes more room. It also works very well for sisters that wear glasses and have trouble getting them in and out of a thin slit. Like our regular one piece niqabs, the niqab is made of soft, high quality chiffon that is comfortable and breathable.[24]

The ways in which Sunnah Style presents items of dress may be compared with Shusterman's notion of somaestethics. Building on an Aristotelian notion of aesthetics, which engages with sensorial experience (referring to aisthe-sis or sensory perception) rather than starting from a Kantian objective mea-sure of beauty, Shusterman uses this term to refer to both representational and experiential forms of aesthetics. The former emphasizes the body's ex-ternal appearance, a form of representation, while the latter focuses on the aesthetic quality of its inner, lived experience (Shusterman 1999: 305). The more fully covered women in the Netherlands discuss their styles of dress in analogous ways—that is, they underline that their styles of dress should not only 'look good' but also 'feel good'. The latter they deem important as their commitment to the willed, virtuous act of fully covering depends on somatic efficacy, which is facilitated if items of dress are breathable and do not pinch. Comfortable abayas make it easier for women to consistently adopt what they consider the correct hijab.

If their evaluation of such garments is based on the link between ethics, morality and aesthetics, the same is true when it comes to attitudes of the general public. Those who consider wearing covered dress as a sign of wom-en's oppression and the backwardness of Islam often describe such styles of dress as ugly or disgusting (Moors 2009a, 2012). A prime example is how Geert Wilders, a member of parliament and leader of a political party known for its anti-Islam stance, argued his proposal to implement a 'headrag tax' in 2009 by referring to the public presence of women wearing a headscarf as a form of pollution.[25] The dress narratives of the women themselves indicate that they do not only consider fully covering as a religious duty but also experi-ence it as aesthetically pleasing. Wearing more fully covered dress was for the women concerned first and foremost a highly desirable religious practice—an act of worship and a means to express their love for, and to get closer to, God—that demanded spiritual growth and self-discipline. At the same time, they loved the feel of the flow of the long and loose garments; some would refer to it as experiencing a sense of 'floating through the air'.[26] They appre-ciated the aesthetic simplicity, with everything in one or at most two colours, and experienced such an aesthetic style as embodying a pure, asexual form of beauty. Such a style of appearing in the public stands in strong contrast to a secular notion that considers the visibility of women's sexualized bodies as a measure for their freedom and gender equality.[27]

FASHION REVISITED

When women in the Netherlands wear abayas or other kinds of long, loose gowns, these are usually simple models with little decoration. Whereas they appreciate the particular qualities of the fabrics, the different cuts and some decorations, their engagements with fashion in their public dressing styles remain, in their own view, limited. Yet, they also underline that according to Islamic notions of propriety, the licitness of particular styles of dress is strongly contextual. The most meaningful distinction for them is whether they are or are not in the presence of non-*mahram* men.[28] This does not fully overlap with being indoors or outside, in the private or in the public; for instance, an all-women gathering may well be considered public, yet it does not require covered styles of dress. Moreover, in practice, women cannot always follow these rules strictly, as it may be unacceptable to close kin—such as cousins—whom they may have known all their lives, or too inconvenient if living together in cramped space. The need to compromise is particularly strongly felt by women who have converted to Islam and whose family is unfamiliar with gender segregation.

Wearing an overgarment that is full-length, loose and non-transparent affects an outfit differently than when the more fashionable layered 'mixing and matching' styles are adopted. The former, with its strong capacity for concealment, enables wearing a host of different styles of garments underneath. It can hide both clothing that carries the imprint of poverty and neglect (Ünal, this book) and highly fashionable, revealing outfits. In other words, it is a highly versatile form of outerwear. Some of the women wearing abayas and similar all-enveloping forms of outerwear would argue that they are not less involved in fashion than those not wearing such kinds of covering, with the major difference being that they wear their fashionable dress underneath and would only reveal it in the presence of women, their husband and, more generally, mahram men. Emphasizing that they wear fashion in such contexts enables them to connect with their 'former selves'.[29] They desire to look attractive for their husbands and dress up when they go to all-female gatherings, be those the sister groups they attend or more festive occasions such as weddings. A Dutch convert, for instance, highlighted that she likes to look good when her husband comes home, using the following, often-encountered line of argumentation:[30]

> Others try to look their best when they are outside, on the street, they comb their hair and put on make-up before they leave the house. As soon as they come home, they change into jogging pants and a sweat shirt...We do the opposite. We make an effort to look attractive for our husbands, family, and female friends, but when we go outside we cover up.

Yet, these women may also develop a corporeal habitus that is more at ease with longer and looser garments. The very same woman explained to me that she would change from the long dress she likes to wear at home into trousers and a form-fitting shirt when her husband comes home; yet as soon as it is prayer time, she would put her dress back on and not change back again. In her words, she did not only do so because it is more comfortable but also because 'if I wear a pair of jeans I feel less Muslim'.

More generally, women referred to fashion to connect with their 'previous selves', linking inner states of being and convictions with outward appearances in sometimes complicated ways. The case of a twenty-year-old Moroccan Dutch student is illustrative in the multiple connections she made. Reflecting on how her sartorial style had developed through time, she pointed out that her outerwear had changed substantially, as earlier she had been wearing highly revealing styles of dress. Yet at the same time, she also explained that she still liked to wear quality materials (as had been the case previously) and that she continued to wear some of the same items of dress underneath, especially designer jeans. She also argued that in spite of these visible changes in her outerwear, her personality had not changed: 'In the past I was extreme in uncovering, and now I am extreme in covering'. Moreover, she then connected interior states of being with exterior appearances by highlighting that in her heart she had always been a pious Muslim and that she had already been fulfilling the requirements of praying a long time before she had taken the step to adapt her outer appearances to her inner convictions.

TO END WITH

Whereas in the Netherlands, as elsewhere, a shift towards more fashionable styles of Islamic dress has occurred in the course of the last decade, a small number of women have adopted abayas, khimars and similar styles of covered dress that are sober and distinctively non-fashionable. In some respects, their styles of dress may indeed be considered anti-fashion. They distance themselves both from the highly fashionable layered styles of mixing and matching mainstream items and from the rather spectacular fashion abayas that have emerged in the Gulf states. Their main criticism of such styles is grounded in theological reasoning, but they also argue that the emergence of Islamic fashion affects them negatively, as it turns them into a strongly marked category. Still, labelling their sartorial style as anti-fashion does not do justice to the complexities of their position. Whereas they opt for abayas and other loose, long and flowing gowns because of Islamic normativities, they simultaneously talk extensively about the beauty of such forms of covering. This beauty is not restricted to a visual register but also includes the feel of the fabric and the comfort of the cut; aesthetic styles matter to them. Moreover, long, loose, all-covering forms of outerwear also enable them to wear a broad range of styles of dress underneath, including highly fashionable ones, which may be displayed in settings where this is deemed religiously licit. Although some would also be critical of the wastefulness of such an engagement with fashion, others enjoy this possibility.

NOTES

1. This chapter is part of a research project on the emergence of fashionable styles of Islamic dress in the Netherlands; it was first funded as part of a NORFACE (New Opportunities for Research Funding Agency Co-operation in Europe) project on the emergence of Islamic fashion in Europe and later as part of the Cultural Dynamics Programme of the Netherlands Organisation for Scientific Research (NWO).
2. For a more extensive discussion about the turn to 'Islamic fashion' in the Netherlands see Moors (2009b); for the most criticized style (women wearing face-veils), see Moors (2009a).
3. Since 2007, I have engaged in two ethnographic research projects: one on the emergence of Islamic fashion in Europe and the other on wearing face-veils in the Netherlands.
4. However, in those days the public did not yet label these women as Muslim. The women did not wear the kinds of headscarves that covered all hair; in fact, some did not wear headscarves at all. Instead, their styles of dress were considered traditionally Turkish or Moroccan but not Islamic.
5. They often use the term *camel hump* to describe this style. This term refers to a Hadith that considers 'scantily dressed women, the hair on the top of their heads like a camel's hump' as cursed. In contrast, others have used a particular Hadith ('Allah is beautiful and He loves beauty') to point out that appearing well-groomed and neat and presenting a pleasant, harmonious look are recommended in Islam (Sandıkçı and Ger 2005).
6. See also Tarlo (2010) for London and Bendixsen, this book, for Berlin.
7. This commission monitors compliance with the Dutch Equal Treatment Act, which prohibits discrimination in education and employment on grounds of religion, sex, race or political orientation. It does so by responding to complaints in the format of a non-binding opinion that is, however, taken seriously in court cases. On 2 October 2012 the Commission for Equal Treatment became part of The Netherlands Institute for Human Rights, *College voor de rechten van de mens*, <http://www.mensenrechten.nl> accessed 2 March 2013.
8. The case numbers are 2006–84 (catering agency), 2007–70 (library), 2008–73 (intern at a school), 2010–96 (hospital). In addition, there was also a case of a hospital prohibiting the wearing of a long skirt instead of trousers (2011–88). In all these cases, the opinion of the CGB was unlawful discrimination.
9. The arguments presented show the impact of earlier CGB opinions about face-coverings, which considered prohibiting face-coverings in educational settings lawful if the argument was phrased in terms of impeding communication. See CGB case number 2003–40.
10. The CGB agreed only in two cases (to some extent) with the arguments of defendants. The other case concerned an employment agency that did not

unlawfully discriminate against a cleaner who insisted on wearing a headscarf that covered the shoulders, back and chest when it stopped mediation for a job in the cleaning industry, as all potential employers refused to employ her on the grounds of safety and hygiene (CGB case no. 2011–19).

11. CGB case no. 2011–09.

12. *RTV Utrecht,* 25 January 2011, <http://www.rtvutrecht.nl/nieuws/322542/school-mag-eisen-stellen-aan-hoofddoek> accessed 2 July 2012.

13. Gerrit Rietveld College, <http://www.gerritrietveldcollege.nl/Home/Aanmeldinggroep8/Veelgesteldevragen/tabid/307/Default.aspx> accessed 2 July 2012. The Dutch original text is equally awkward. Obviously, such regulations are hard to enforce. As a pupil explained, 'If they ask me, I will pull up my headscarf for a few seconds and then push it down again.' For the emphasis on good communication, see also note 6.

14. See Al Hinai (2012).

15. Rabia Z., <http://www.rabiaz.com/collection?q=dubai%20fashion%20week> accessed 2 July 2012.

16. Such debates were reported in Turkey when the first Islamic fashion was presented on catwalks (Navaro-Yashin 2002), while Sandikçi and Ger (2007) point to the major shifts in conventions about how to present Islamic dress and fashion in advertisements.

17. In the United Kingdom, in contrast, where a far larger number of women wears fully covering dress, including a face-veil, there is more space for wearing more fashionable abayas (see Tarlo, this book).

18. This does not mean that they actually order from this Web store. As international shipping costs are high, they are more likely to order from Dutch Web stores, such as islamproducten.nl.

19. For such Web stores, see Akou (2007), Tarlo (2010: Chapter 7) and Moors 2013.

20. Sunnah Style, <http://www.sunnahstyle.com/about_us.php?osCsid=amok50mofkj5hpshvmrndin885> accessed 2 July 2012.

21. Sunnah Style, <http://blog.sunnahstyle.com/about/>; see also on Facebook,<http://www.facebook.com/sunnahstyledotcom/app_2374336051> accessed 2 July 2012.

22. Sunnah Style, <http://www.sunnahstyle.com/product_info.php?pName=starlight-closed-abaya-sapphire-collection&cName=abayas-all-abayas&osCsid= 7ubo60g8m61gpi13hktiddh561> accessed 2 July 2012.

23. Sunnah Style, <http://blog.sunnahstyle.com/about/> accessed 2 July 2012.

24. Sunnah Style <http://www.sunnahstyle.com/product_info.php?pName=nopinch-one-piece-tie-back-niqab-eggplant&cName=niqabs-1piece-niqabs&osCsid= iimeivijcfgglpm2aoh6o6pr70> accessed 2 July 2012.

25. Imposing a tax is then congruent with the environmental policy principle that 'the polluter pays'.

26. This is very similar to how Na'ima Roberts (2005: 189ff), a British convert, describes her experiences. Amongst the women wearing more fully

covering styles, there are a considerable number of converts, while also the women who are from Muslim background have also often gone through major shifts in dressing styles and forms of religious commitment. In most cases, their mothers did not wear such a style of dress, and quite often their families expressed strong hesitations and dislike.

27. See also Scott (2007), Moors (2013) and Karlsson Minganti, in this book.
28. The categories of *mahram* and non-mahram distinguish between Muslim men a woman is (non-mahram) or is not (mahram) allowed to marry according to Islamic law. For the fully covering women, gender segregation or covering are to be observed in the presence of non-mahram men.
29. See more generally Tarlo (2010: Chapter 4).
30. See also Stoica, this book.

REFERENCES

Akou, H. (2007), 'Building a New "World Fashion": Islamic Dress in the Twenty-first Century', *Fashion Theory* 11, 4: 403–21.

Al Hinai, M. (2012), 'Fashionistas Embrace the Abaya, Turning a Basic Garment into Couture', *The National* (17 March), <http://www.thenational.ae/lifestyle/fashion/fashionistas-embrace-the-abaya-turning-a-basic-garment-into-couture> accessed 2 July 2012.

Al-Qasimi, N. (2010), 'Immodest Modesty: Accommodating Dissent and the "Abaya-as-fashion" in the Arab Gulf States', *Journal of Middle East Women's Studies* 6, 1: 46–74.

Amrullah, E. (2008), 'Indonesian Muslim Fashion. Styles and Designs', *ISIM Review* 22: 22–3.

Jouili, J. S. (2009), 'Negotiating Secular Boundaries: Pious Micro-practices of Muslim Women in France and Germany', *Social Anthropology* 17, 4: 455–70.

Jungschleger, I., and G. Riemersma (1999), 'Hip met de hoofddoek. De dubbele cultuur van islamitische meisjes', *Volkskrant Magazine* 8 (23 October): 26–33.

Lindholm, C. (2010), 'Invisible No More. The Embellished Abaya in Qatar,' *Textile Society of America Symposium Proceedings,* <http://digitalcommons.unl.edu/cgi/viewcontent.cgi?article=1033&context=tsaconf> accessed 4 August 2012.

Moors, A. (2007), 'Fashionable Muslims: Notions of Self, Religion and Society in San'a', *Fashion Theory* 11, 2/3: 319–47.

Moors, A. (2009a), 'The Dutch and the Face Veil: The Politics of Discomfort', *Social Anthropology* 17, 4: 392–407.

Moors, A. (2009b), '"Islamic Fashion" in Europe: Religious Conviction, Aesthetic Style, and Creative Consumption', *Encounters* 1, 1: 175–201.

Moors, A. (2012a), 'The Affective Power of the Face-veil. Between Disgust and Fascination', in B. Meyer and D. Houtman, eds., *Things: Material Religion and the Topography of Divine Spaces,* New York: Fordham University Press, 282–95.

Moors, A. (2013), 'Discover the Beauty of Modesty: Islamic Fashion Online', in R. Lewis, ed., *Modest Fashion,* London: I.B. Tauris.

Moors, A., and E. Tarlo (2007), 'Introduction', *Fashion Theory* 11, 2–3: 133–43.

Navaro-Yashin, Y. (2002), 'The Market for Identities: Secularism, Islamism, Commodities', in D. Kandiyoti and A. Saktanber, eds., *Fragments of Culture: The Everyday of Modern Turkey,* New Brunswick, NJ: Rutgers University Press, 221–53.

Osella, C., and F. Osella (2007), 'Muslim Style in South India', *Fashion Theory* 11, 2/3: 233–52.

Robert, N. (2005), *From My Sisters' Lips,* London: Bantam.

Sandikçi, Ö., and G. Ger (2005), 'Aesthetics, Ethics and Politics of the Turkish Headscarf', in S. Küechler and D. Miller, eds., *Clothing as Material Culture,* Oxford: Berg, 61–82.

Sandikçi, Ö., and G. Ger (2007), 'Constructing and Representing the Islamic Consumer in Turkey', *Fashion Theory* 11, 2/3: 189–210.

Scott, J. (2007), *The Politics of the Veil,* Princeton, NJ: Princeton University Press.

Shusterman, R. (1999), 'Somaesthetics: A Disciplinary Proposal', *Journal of Aesthetics and Art Criticism* 57, 3: 299–313.

Tarlo, E. (2010), *Visibly Muslim: Integrating Fashion, Politics, Faith,* Oxford: Berg.

–15–

The Clothing Dilemmas of Transylvanian Muslim Converts

Daniela Stoica

CLUJ-NAPOCA AS AN URBAN SARTORIAL CONTEXT

The Transylvanian city of Cluj-Napoca has lost much of the visual uniformity that dominated it during the socialist and immediate post-socialist periods. With elegant or bohemian cafeterias, stylish dining rooms and clubs, it has become a setting that stands in sharp contrast to the uniform socialist neighbourhoods created under communism. At the beginning of the summer, when the Transylvania International Film Festival animates the city with a young and diverse public, and at the beginning of autumn, when students, both Romanian and foreign, come to attend the five state universities in the city, Cluj-Napoca becomes a lively, culturally diverse city.[1] Film-lovers, local inhabitants inspired by the festival's atmosphere and tourists, as well as university students from different backgrounds, display a wide variety of sartorial styles. These bring together a mix of designer label products, as well as combinations of branded items, and second-hand and vintage pieces. It is against this background of urban cosmopolitanism that I would like to consider the dress practices of Romanian converts to Islam.

Since 2007, when the first malls were opened in this city of three hundred thousand inhabitants, the field of consumption has rapidly expanded. Well-known clothing brands are now readily available in Cluj-Napoca, and the malls periodically organize shopping night events that draw a large number of customers. However, for many, these branded items still remain unaffordable. Outlet stores, where branded items from older collections are available at lower prices, and shops that sell low-price clothing imported from Turkey and China cater to the large number of customers who cannot afford the latest fashion items. Also, second-hand clothing shops, which emerged in the early 1990s to make famous brands that could not be purchased during the communist years available, are still popular, especially amongst students who look for original yet affordable outfits that are not necessarily inspired by current fashions. In addition, vintage fairs are held periodically in Cluj-Napoca during cultural events and festivals, while hand-made accessories, mainly produced by local artists, especially art students, are a favourite amongst young, educated people who want to adopt nonconformist looks.

This range of eclectic styles contrasts strongly with the more conservative and sober styles worn by the working classes, which have been strongly affected by the post-socialist process of privatization. While they had to adjust to the new context, in which they lack state-guaranteed job security, and are employed in lower-paying jobs or dependent on modest pensions, few of them engage with the new fashions on offer. Instead, used to the communist system in which the market offered a very limited selection of goods, they continue to wear sober styles of dark-coloured dress.

Some of the older women, especially those who moved to the city from rural areas during socialist industrialization, wear headscarves. Roma women also wear headscarves, but their scarves are more colourful, form part of a distinctive outfit and are worn with long, flower-patterned skirts which mark their ethnic background. Amongst this wide array of styles of dress, the Muslim headscarf (also referred to as hijab) has also made an appearance in the urban landscape.[2] This is largely due to the presence of Muslim students from Arab countries as well as some Romanian women converts. Focussing exclusively on the narratives of converts, this chapter reflects on their understandings of Islamic modest dress, their attitudes to fashion and the sartorial practices they have adopted.[3]

MUSLIMS IN ROMANIA: A HETEROGENEOUS COMMUNITY

During the last decades, the Muslim population in Romania has grown increasingly heterogeneous, consisting of both 'ethnic Muslims'—mostly Turks and Tatars—as well as Arab students and entrepreneurs and Romanian converts.[4] The ethnic Turkish and Tatar communities consolidated their presence in the south-eastern part of the country (the Dobrogea region) during five centuries of Ottoman presence. Arab migration, by contrast, has a much more recent history. In the 1970s and 1980s, the Romanian authorities decided to accept a few thousand students from the Middle East and North Africa in their efforts to expand the state's economic relations with Arab countries. This was the beginning of an approximately twenty-year collaboration in the field of university education (Chiriac and Robotin 2006).[5] After the revolution of 1989, these relations continued. According to the 2001 National Census, there were 67,257 Muslims in Romania, of whom 31,118 were Turks and 23,641 were Tatars.[6] Others have estimated the Muslim population at around 70,000 (Pew Research Centre 2011.[7] However, this number does not include temporary residents or Muslim converts. No statistics or estimates are available about the number of converts to Islam in Romania since conversion is not formally registered.

Many mosques where Romanian women convert to Islam operate under the aegis of Islamic non-governmental organizations (NGOs). These Islamic NGOs, which include converts' and women's associations, became a constituent part of the religious and cultural landscape after the 1989 revolution. Nowadays, they are active in the online environment, employing Web sites, social media affiliation, multimedia content, chat rooms, email listing, blogs and discussion fora promoting Islam. Some of these organizations also have their own publishing houses and are actively advertising online Islamic schools. They function independently from the Muftyat, which is the official denominational and cultural representative institution of the Muslim community.[8]

Muslims in Romania cannot be considered a homogeneous community. Contacts between 'ethnic Muslims' and Muslims coming from abroad are limited (Lederer 2001). The Romanian Turks and Tatars have their own state-funded mosques and live concentrated in the south-east, while in the main cities Arab Muslims have established houses of worship that function under the umbrella of Islamic NGOs. Disputes sometimes occur concerning the Muftyat's authority. This was, for instance, the case after 2007, when the Mufti officially contested the diplomas obtained by Romanian Muslims from Islamic theological institutes in Jordan, Saudi Arabia, Syria and Sudan (Vainovski-Mihai 2010), to which these Muslim organizations had provided access. Moreover, in statements in the media, the Mufti has openly criticized these institutions, claiming that they might be facilitating the spread of religious extremism and insisting that they should be more closely supervised by state authorities.[9]

MUSLIMS IN CLUJ-NAPOCA

In 1999, the Cultural Islamic League emerged from the Muslim Students' Association, which had been established in the early 1990s and had branches in the main university centres. Cluj-Napoca is one of the cities where the league has opened a mosque. Situated in close proximity to two university campuses, it vividly reflects the composition of the local Muslim community. Its users consist mainly of students and entrepreneurs from Arab countries, as well as Romanian converts, most of whom are young women, married or engaged to men from Muslim backgrounds.

Attracted by the university's medical school, foreign Muslim students have been a constant presence in the city since 1990. Through time, they have gained an increasingly visible presence both in public spaces and in the mosque. According to the 2009–10 university medical school report, 857 Tunisian students had been accepted at the bachelor level in that academic year alone, representing almost 40 per cent of the total number of foreign students frequenting this educational institution.[10] Other non-European students come from Morocco and in smaller numbers from Jordan, Nigeria, Palestine, Pakistan, Iran, Iraq and Turkey.

The Muslim community in Cluj-Napoca has an Arab imprint; the mosque is led by a Palestinian imam, while the Cultural Islamic League is coordinated by a Romanian convert who studied Islamic theology in Jordan. The mosque is predominantly frequented by Arab Muslim men and, to a lesser extent, by women, both born and converted Muslims. Although it does not have an explicitly radical agenda, the Cultural Islamic League and its members, including those from Cluj-Napoca, foreigners as well as Romanian citizens, have been the object of a series of investigations carried out in April 2011 by antiterrorist government departments.[11]

In the following, I focus on the narratives of seven Romanian women from Cluj-Napoca who have converted to Islam and whom I interviewed extensively in 2010.[12] Living in a context in which Islam is still a relatively new presence in public space, these women converts need to adjust their dressing styles. They feel that they need to both comply with the requirements of Islamic modest dress and to adapt it to the expectations of the dominant non-Muslim group, especially to those of their families. Their conversion to Islam is often particularly difficult to accept for their families when they wear headscarves, a practice that publicly displays their new religious affiliation.

As there are no Islamic clothing shops available in Cluj-Napoca, converts need to put together outfits by making use of what is locally accessible, combining various items of clothing to produce an overall modest appearance. In order to develop a suitably modest Islamic look, Muslim converts actively search for reliable sources of information and are continuously scrutinizing themselves and other Muslims. In her study of dress and the social construction of gender in two sororities, Arthur (1999) suggests that peers and women with authority evaluate women entering such groups in the light of the communities' norms, through processes of informal social control which engenders the development of a sense of 'gender role obligation' (1999: 84). Convert groups function in a similar manner, since their members are expected to produce a correct look. This sense of obligation is internalized by new Muslims through learning and gathering knowledge. They discipline themselves, and, in Foucault's terms, a process of 'self-formation' unfolds, which includes 'operations on (people's) own bodies, on their own souls, on their own thoughts, on their own conduct' (Foucault, in Rabinow 1984: 11). According to Foucault, self-discipline produces 'docile bodies' that are both the 'object and target of power' and 'may be subjected, used, transformed, and improved' (Foucault, in Rabinow 1984: 180). In the following, I reflect on how this occurs by asking, how do coverts conceptualize and embody Islamic modesty? What is their attitude towards fashion? What kinds of strategies do they employ to cope with societal ambivalence or hostility towards veiling?

DRESS STORIES: A MAJOR SARTORIAL SHIFT?

Carla is a 22-year-old medical student who converted to Islam when she was seventeen and was still living with her parents.[13] Married to a Tunisian man, she was the only respondent who sometimes wore a face-veil (niqab).[14] For her, the wearing of modest clothing and her later adoption of face-covering constituted major shifts in her appearance since in her rebellious teenage years she used to be a rocker with dyed hair and platform shoes.

When I visited her in her apartment—situated in the vicinity of the mosque—where medical books stood side by side with Islamic books, she was wearing a black tunic and had her hair covered with a black veil. Coming from a high status family with ample resources, Carla can afford to order Islamic clothing online, which is not an option for some of the other converts I interviewed. Her wardrobe consists of different types of abayas, tunics and sporty jilbabs, which she orders from the British Web site Islamicdesignhouse.com. Sometimes, when she is inspired by an item she finds online, she has it made by a seamstress.

Carla started to wear the hijab in response to the normative pressure she felt from other Muslim women and also as a natural step in her 'quest for religiously based recognition' (Tarlo 2010: 1). She was eager to visibly display her Muslim identity and her affiliation to the Muslim community:

> I used go to the mosque with my veil on, and one day, at school [at the university], I met this girl from the mosque. And she said, 'Where is your headscarf?' I was so ashamed, that I wanted to hide somewhere . . . I said to myself, 'It is clear that I have to do something.' And then I turned towards my colleagues—it was during a laboratory class—and I said, 'Tomorrow I will come with my hijab on. Please, no comment!'

Desiring to cover herself as much as possible, she rejects fashion which she feels exploits women's bodies and criticizes what she sees as the dominant understanding of Islamic modesty among other Romanian Muslim women:

> Most of the Muslim women do not wear clothes that are properly modest. They put on a longer blouse and a pair of pants, which unfortunately still reveals body shapes. And this is not Islam. You must dress in such a way that men are not able to distinguish your figure and shape . . . In Romania, people cannot afford to buy clothes from the Internet and there are no Islamic shops. So each of us is on her own; one may download a picture from the Internet and have clothes made by the seamstress. But this does not happen very often, because girls don't wear the abaya and would rather be fashionable, which is not the same thing as being modest.

For Carla, creating a properly modest look, adequate to the context, is the responsibility of each Muslim woman; thus, she explains how she tries to adjust her clothing to specific settings. For instance, when she is taking exams at the university, she puts on a robe, while when frequenting the mosque—an environment where there is a risk of mixing with men—she wears the face-veil. Nevertheless, in both contexts, she feels that she becomes the object of specific associations:

> I want my garments to be long enough to cover my shoes...During the exams they [the professors] tell me, 'You are not from Tunisia, you are from the Emirates'. Tunisian women do not wear these things.

She recognizes that it is difficult to wear the face-veil in Romania because it can 'scare people' and it attracts unwanted attention. Therefore she only wears it in public if her husband is accompanying her. However, Carla is determined to wear it whenever she visits the mosque, a site where she feels she becomes an object of curiosity for born Muslim men. In this context, she wears the face-veil to protect her from the male gaze. For the same reason, she transferred from one university department, where she was studying with predominantly male colleagues, to another, where most students were female:

> I realize that some Arab boys have a lot of nerve. They see me coming [at the mosque] and then they go to the window and stare at me. I cannot explain this: is this curiosity or what? And the Tunisians are asking 'Look, there is a Muslim girl. Where is she from?' Honestly, I feel so ashamed, that I immediately blush. So the niqab is a solution for me and believe me, the feeling is extraordinary. I love it!

Carla recalls her sartorial trajectory towards modesty as a gradual process of increased covering, a disciplining journey which she took her parents along on after they had first rejected her conversion and then her decision to marry a Muslim man.

> I gradually started to put on more clothes: a knee long blouse, and then this became longer and longer. And now I wear robes—my parents even like them better than the tunics. A robe is more elegant and people accept it...It is something long and simple. I wear an abaya only for prayers...I also have some sporty models.

EARLIER DRESSING STYLES AND FAMILY CONSIDERATIONS

Like some of the Muslim converts in London described by Tarlo (2010), some Romanian converts try to connect their new modest appearances with their dress histories in order to make their shift in appearance more acceptable in a non-Muslim environment and especially to their often Christian families. Relying on her intuition, Ella—a 29-year-old convert—employs 'subjective knowledge' (Field Belenky et al. 1986) in defining her modest clothing in order to make her transition to Islam as smooth as possible, not only for herself but, more importantly, also for her parents.

Ella embraced Islam at the end of an unsuccessful attempt to persuade her Muslim Tunisian husband to become a Christian. Her conversion was an unexpected outcome even for herself, an attractive young woman who used to receive attention from men and who enjoyed going out dancing with her friends or visiting the swimming pool with her family. As a Muslim, she attempts to fulfil the requirements of modest clothing by wearing colourful hijabs, long-sleeved blouses, polo necks with loose shirts and pants, garments that she considers as 'modern' rather than 'fashionable'. In the course of this gradual process of covering, 'the agency of hijab' (Tarlo 2010: 13)—that is, its effects both on the wearer and those she interacts with—was activated:

> I want to take Islam step by step and to make it simple for me as well...I want to make it easy, so that my family can understand it, too. I don't want to change. I am trying to wear more modern outfits, more or less similar to what I used to wear. I want my outfits to look modern for my family and those around me...This is how I see things. Maybe I am wrong, I don't know. I think there is a time for everything. The veil knew when to come.

In other cases, wearing covered dress was regarded as a natural continuation of existing sartorial practices. Lilly, another 29-year-old convert, related her pursuit of Islamic modesty through clothing with her long-standing interest in the Arab world. During the interview, she was wearing a long, black tunic and a brown hijab tightly wrapped around her face, a look that her Christian family had slowly started to accept as it related to her pre-conversion biography:

> I liked the veil even before I became a Muslim. I really liked veils...I generally liked the idea of being covered. And even my friends know I used to wear headscarves in all sorts of fashions before. I had become fascinated with the Arab world, when I was studying art and art history.

Irina, a 24-year-old convert, had to find another solution, as her parents did not accept her wearing hijab. She had already begun to wear longer and looser outfits, trying to cover her body, after her initial conversion from Orthodox Christianity to a neo-Protestant church. Her subsequent gradual shift to Muslim modest dress was not so easily tolerated by her parents, especially when she decided to wear the hijab, which they regarded as inappropriate for a young woman because of its associations with the headscarf worn by older women in the countryside:

> Sure, they were a bit reluctant when we discussed the hijab topic; [they insisted] I should not wear it, that I was not supposed to wear it because I was young and

things like that. I did not put it on while I was living at home and neither when I was a university student. I preferred to postpone it until after I graduated.

Another 24-year-old convert, Doris, was also already accustomed to covering her body but in a different way. Singing in a hip hop band before becoming a Muslim, she had avoided revealing her figure by wearing clothing that was typical to the urban culture to which she had adhered. Later on, as a Muslim, she adopted a different style of covering, wearing black tunics and black headscarves. Moreover, as a Muslim, she began to make a clear distinction between public and domestic dress, dismissing what she considers the common female practice of dressing up exclusively when outdoors:

> I am not interested in outside clothing, everything is reversed in my case. When I go home to my husband, I am not wearing my sport pants, smelling like the frying oil I used for cooking the day before. You should dress up only for your husband, for your family. And this is different: when I put on makeup and perfume, I am doing everything for him, for my husband. Why should I do everything for other people? This is how things are regarded in this society: you should be beautiful and dressed up when you are outside the house, in the office or I don't know where.

For Doris, who was already wearing clothing that did not show the shape of her body, her conversion to Islam also brought about a change in her style of dressing. It was only after her conversion to Islam that she began to be interested in more feminine clothing and in looking attractive, but only in private settings.

FACING THE PUBLIC, DESIRING ANONYMITY

For more Romanian converts, who had been Muslim for at least ten years, the biggest challenge was to avoid the high degree of unwanted attention they experienced when wearing the hijab in public places. They feel that they are continuously in the spotlight and have to develop ways of responding to the reactions their styles of dress evoke.

Sonia is a 42-year-old Romanian convert who lives in Dubai and periodically returns home to visit her family; here, she tries to adjust her clothing to the local setting, wearing pants, loose blouses and colourful hijabs instead of the black abaya and the *shayla* (large, black, rectangular headscarf) that she usually puts on when she is in the United Arab Emirates. For her, wearing the headscarf when she is in Romania is the most difficult aspect of her conversion to Islam:

> I had changed my religion and I was feeling very good, very happy. But it was difficult with the hijab. It is not difficult there [in Dubai], because everybody is alike.

Ever since I was young, I did not like to be in forefront and to have everyone look at me. And this is what I feel when I am outside wearing my hijab: everyone is looking at me and I don't like it...I just want to be an anonymous person, but with the hijab on I cannot be anonymous here.

For Sonia, who works as a sports trainer, the obligation of covering herself activated a disciplining process she undertook with difficulty:

I used to say, 'Dear God, please help me! I know I must put it on and I cannot do it. But I am doing my best.' And I would cry and put my hijab on, cry and put it on...Since I've been an active person my entire life, I enjoyed feeling the wind going through my hair when walking or doing no matter what.

Carmen, a 45-year-old dentist and another Romanian convert, also experienced veiling as being in tension with her professional profile and thus with her daily life and activities in her family's private dental practice:

I find it very difficult to work with my veil on, because I am also wearing the protection mask and the glasses. I cannot breathe...However, I accept this torment, I believe it is worthy.

Although she is pleased with her patients' attitudes, since they never reacted to her veiling, she declares herself strongly affected by the sometimes offensive reactions she receives in other social contexts, where she cannot enjoy what Goffman called 'civil inattention' (1972).

When driving, I have been shouted at many times: 'Are you hot?' or 'Are you cold?'...Once, it happened when I was in the street...It was in the very beginning; I was wearing a purple skirt, which was a bit tighter than what I would wear now and I had a headscarf on. And one guy looked at me and said, 'You are so hot!' Well, this really got on my nerves. I mean you see a woman with a veil: she does not want your attention; that's for sure.

Reflecting on what Islamic modest clothing means, Carmen relies both on liberal, authoritative voices within Islam—therefore, on 'received knowledge' (Field Belenky et al. 1986)—as well as on her intuition and personal taste—in other words, subjective knowledge. In her understanding, modesty involves moderation; it does not exclude the desire to look pleasant but should not be too attention-seeking either. Carmen is aware of the reductionist interpretations often made of the Muslim headscarf, which is frequently perceived as being imposed on women. This is how she justifies her interest in looking good:

There also these modern preachers in Islam saying that you are allowed to put make-up on or dress nicely, but you should not exaggerate. For instance, I don't wear make-up because it is my choice and not because Islam forbids it...When you are in your forties, when you wear make-up, you start feeling that your age is visible. And then I prefer to look younger...You need to do everything with common sense...You should not stand out. If you put on a pink or purple headscarf, you can no longer achieve what you wanted in the first place...And by putting on a headscarf that is too beautiful, you are again in the spotlight. Well, I have some nice veils as well, because you need to be happy when you see yourself covered like this, instead of having the others say, 'Oh, poor thing, look how miserable she is!'

As older converts, Sonia and Carmen no longer need to deal with their families' reluctance towards veiling, but they continue to be involved in self-disciplining endeavours in order to be able to cope with undesired forms of attention and with the sometimes disturbing reactions and comments they receive in response to their visibly Muslim appearance in everyday interactions.

CONCLUSION

Female converts are part of the small but increasingly active Muslim community in Cluj-Napoca. Their covered presence in public space raises a series of issues in terms of visibility, representation, perception and understanding of Islamic clothing. Although this is a young community in a central Transylvanian city, personal interpretations of Islamic dress among these Romanian converts and their sartorial practices are best understood, as Tarlo (2010) suggests for London, as occurring at the intersection of personal life experiences, religious background, education, personal aesthetics, taste, identity and faith.

Reflecting on the conversion narratives of Romanian converts, this chapter has discussed their understandings of Islamic dress and their embodiment of Islamic modesty. In some ways, these may be considered major ruptures with their previous dressing styles. Yet in many cases, there are also continuities with their pre-conversion clothing preferences. In their efforts to have their new modest Muslim appearance first understood and then accepted or at least tolerated by their Christian families, they develop strategies such as trying to cover gradually and to adjust to the local context. In the case of older converts for whom the reactions of their families were less an issue of concern, it was societal responses that they experienced as challenging and problematic. They tried to cope with these by conceptualizing covering as a form of personal sacrifice for which they disciplined themselves. While generally criticizing the notion of fashion and taking distance from it, some of the converts interviewed showed an interest in developing modern outfits to create a style that was more easily accepted by non-Muslims.

NOTES

1. The Transylvanian International Film Festival (TIFF) was founded in 2002 by the Romanian Film Promotion Association and is the first international feature film festival in Romania.
2. The dress diversity of this Transylvanian city has been innovatively displayed in a recent photo journalistic project, launched in 2010 on Facebook by the young photographer Andrei Niculescu, whose urban portraits are highly appreciated by the users of this social network service (see <www.facebook.com/#!/Cotropitor>).
3. Research for this contribution is part of the 'Investing in people!' PhD scholarship; the project was co-financed by the Sectoral Operational Program For Human Resources Development 2007–13, Priority Axis 1.
4. This is more extensively discussed in Stoica (2011).
5. See Ethnocultural Diversity Resource Center (2006).
6. See National Institute of Statistics (2002). A new national census was carried out in October 2011, so new figures are available.
7. See Pew Research Center (2010).
8. Based in Constanţa, a south-eastern city situated by the Black Sea, with a significant indigenous Muslim community. This institution is led by Mufti Iusuf Murat, who is of Turkish background and was appointed in 2005.
9. See România Liberă (2007).
10. See Universitatea de Medicină şi Farmacie 'Iuliu Haţieganu' (2010).
11. See Direcţia de Investigare a Infracţiunilor de Criminalitate Organizată şi Terorism (2011).
12. This contribution is part of a larger PhD research project about Romanian and Dutch women's conversion to Islam.
13. To protect the privacy of the women concerned, all names have been changed.
14. I interviewed the Cluj-Napoca coordinator of the league, who stated that the organization disapproves of the niqab and any form of face-concealing among women Muslims in Romania, claiming that the dominant non-Muslim population does not understand or tolerate it.

REFERENCES

Arthur, L. B. (1999), 'Dress and the Social Construction of Gender in Two Sororities', *Clothing and Textiles Research Journal* 17, 2: 84–93.

Chiriac, M., and M. Robotin (2006), *The Unknown Next Door Residents, Refugees, Asylum Solicitants, Illegal Migrants in Romania*, Cluj-Napoca: EDRC.

Direcţia de Investigare a Infracţiunilor de Criminalitate Organizată şi Terorism (2011), *Comunicate de Presă*, <http://www.diicot.ro/index.php?option=

com_content&view=article&id=510:comunicat-de-presa3–2004 2011&catid=38:mass-media&Itemid=81> accessed 5 May 2011.

Ethnocultural Diversity Resource Center (2006), *The Unknown Next Door Residents, Refugees, Asylum Solicitants, Illegal Migrants in Romania*, edrc.ro, <http://www.edrc.ro/resources_details.jsp?resource_id=14> accessed 5 April 2011.

Field Belenky, M., B. McVicker Clinchy, N. Rule Goldberger and J. Mattuck Tarule (1986), *Women's Way of Knowing. The Development of Self, Voice, and Mind,* New York: Basic Books.

Goffman, E. (1972), *Relations in Public: Microstudies of the Public Order,* Harmondsworth: Penguin.

Lederer, G. (2001) 'Islam in East Europe', *Central Asian Survey* 20, 1: 5–32.

National Institute of Statistics (2002), *Census of Population and Dwellings,* <http://www.insse.ro/cms/rw/pages/rpl2002.en.do> accessed 25 November 2010.

Pew Research Center (2010), *The Future of the Global Muslim Population*, Forum on Religion and Public Life, <http://features.pewforum.org/Future GlobalMuslimPopulation-WebPDF.pdf> accessed 27 January 2011.

Pew Research Center (2011), *The Future of the Global Muslim Population. Projections for 2010–2030,* Washington, DC: Pew Research Center's Forum on Religion & Public Life.

Rabinow, P. (1984), *The Foucault Reader,* New York: Pantheon Books.

România Liberă (2007), *Iusuuf Murat, muftiul-şef al cultului musulman din România. Libertatea de a te manifesta, condiţionată*, romanialibera.ro, <http://www.romanialibera.ro/opinii/interviuri/libertatea-de-a-temani festa-conditionata105554.html> accessed 15 May 2011.

Stoica, D. (2011), 'New Romanian Muslimas. Converted Women Sharing Knowledge in Online and Offline Communities', in K. Gorak-Sosnowska, ed., *Muslims in Poland and Eastern Europe: Widening the European Discourse on Islam,* Warsaw: University of Warsaw.

Tarlo, E. (2010), *Visibly Muslim: Fashion, Politics, Faith,* Oxford: Berg.

Universitatea de Medicină şi Farmacie 'Iuliu Haţieganu', Cluj-Napoca, Informaţii de Interes Public (2010), *Raport privind starea universităţii* 2009/2010, <http://umfcluj.ro/Detaliu.aspx?t=Informatii-de-interes-publicandeID= 287andc=0andm=0andy=0> accessed 3 October 2011.

Vainovski-Mihai, I. (2010), 'Romania', in J. S. Nielsen, S. Akgönül, A. Alibašić, B. Maréchal and C. Moe, eds., *Yearbook of Muslims in Europe*, vol. 2, Leiden: Brill.

–16–

'I Love My Prophet': Religious Taste, Consumption and Distinction in Berlin

Synnøve Bendixsen

If you stroll down the street in any of the three Berliner neighbourhoods of Neukölln, Wedding and Kreuzberg, it is common to see young women wearing the headscarf.[1] Looking closer, one notices that the shape, form, style and colours of their headscarves and their dress vary greatly. Walking through Oranienstrasse in Kreuzberg or Sonnenallee in Neukölln, one passes several veiled youth with sexy clothes and large amounts of make-up, some smoking cigarettes and going out to discos in the evenings. Other Muslim women in the same street wear long Turkish overcoats and headscarves or long, plain black garments (abayas) worn in several parts of the Middle East (Figure 16.1).

In contemporary Berlin, more than 25 per cent of the residents in the city districts of Neukölln, Wedding and Kreuzberg are non-German citizens, and the majority of mosques and Islamic organizations in Berlin are situated here. All three neighbourhoods have a high unemployment rate and a large percentage of inhabitants on social benefit programs. Today, Neukölln and Wedding are considered 'troubled' areas, associated with social issues such as gang violence and low educational and work achievement. Although sometimes called a 'Turkish ghetto' (Mandel 2008), Kreuzberg generally has a more positive reputation and is characterized as a mixed migrant, artist and student neighbourhood, attracting both ethnic Germans and people with migrant backgrounds, as well as international students and artists (Figure 16.2). Over the last couple of years, it has undergone a gentrification process, partly due to being centrally located once the city was restructured following the demolition of the Berlin Wall. Nicknamed 'Little Istanbul', this was the main district where Turkish and Kurdish immigrants settled from the 1970s onward following the bilateral working agreements signed between Germany and Turkey in the 1960s. Apparently, the assortment and prices of headscarves at what is commonly known as the Turkish market situated on Maybach-Üfer in Kreuzberg on Tuesdays and Fridays can compete with those found in Istanbul. The headscarves for sale at this market, now renamed to BiOriental, are typical Turkish-style headscarves in variously patterned dark and pastel colours and

Fig. 16.1 Young Muslim women in Kreuzberg. Photo: Synnøve
Bendixsen

fabric which is frequently polyester, as well as black-and-white cotton under-
scarves. The market is frequented by Muslim women of all ages and ethnic backgrounds seeking an additional and affordable headscarf for their
wardrobe.

Fashion is often a major concern for youth, and Muslim youth are no
exception (see Dwyer 1998; Sandikci and Ger 2005, 2010; Moors 2009;
Tarlo 2010).[2] In her research on Muslim women in London, Tarlo (2010) has
suggested how some young women are inventively creating their own ways
of 'looking Muslim', while others follow more austere dress practices, sometimes informed by minority radical political organizations. My focus here is on
examining how the dress styles of a group of young Muslim women in Berlin
are formed in relation both to spatial factors and to the dress politics of a

Fig. 16.2   Adalbertstrasse, Kreuzberg. Photo: Synnøve Bendixsen

moderate, but what may be considered as a conservative, religious organiza-tion. The youth in this study all participate in the religious youth organization Muslimische Jugend in Deutschland (Muslim Youth in Germany; MJD), whose Berlin group was located in the neighbourhood of Kreuzberg during my field-work.[3] The organization is attracting both males and females, although it has a significantly higher rate of female participation both at the local Berliner level and overall in Germany.

Different religious organizations have different understandings of the de-sirability of particular dress styles and forms. Examining the perspectives of female participants in one Muslim youth organization, I suggest how the de-veloping of a specific taste contributes to feelings of belonging within a faith community and mark internal distinctions amongst Muslim communities in Berlin. How has a particular Islamic form of fashion developed within this religious youth organization? How are the stylistic navigations of young women informed not only by religiously defined prescriptions but also by the attitudes of socially relevant others, such as parents, friends and other (Muslim) youth in Berlin?

MUSLIM YOUTH IN BERLIN

The majority of mosque associations and prayer rooms in Berlin were established by the so-called first-generation migrants who arrived as guest workers in Germany in the late 1960s and early 1970s. These religious organizations and places are mostly divided along ethno-national lines in terms of their participants, language of instruction and religious references. In contrast, the religious youth organization MJD was established in 1994 by eight young Muslims with various ethnic and national backgrounds. Starting with the simple idea of providing religious teaching and activities in the German language to youth born in Germany, it has today expanded to comprise approximately fifty branches across the country, making it the second largest Muslim youth organization in Germany, after the Islamische Gemeinschaft Milli Görüş (IGMG). The local MJD groups have gender-divided meetings with one day for the 'brothers' and another for the 'sisters'. The weekly MJD meetings in Berlin attract relatively few people—sometimes less than fifteen young Muslim women—but annual national meetings are popular, with an upper limit of approximately 1,200 participants (Figure 16.3).[4]

MJD appeals to young, well-educated and upwardly mobile Muslims, mostly from immigrant families of Turkish, Bosnian and Middle Eastern origin. The majority are educated in a Western intellectual tradition, are socially and politically well-informed and are active users of the media, including the Internet. Most of the youth I talked to had passed the *Abitur* (university qualifying examination). Some of them worked; others studied at university, in programs such as law, Islamic studies, social education, graphic design, teacher training, dentistry and medicine. The majority of them participate in MJD in order to acquire more knowledge of Islam and religious practices and to search for better ways to live an Islamic life in a non-Muslim society. Rejecting forms of Islam that they perceive to be traditional or cultural, the youth in this organization aspires to an Islam based on the acquisition of knowledge through which they situate their religiosity as part of 'modernity' (Bendixsen 2009; Fadil 2009; Jouili 2009; Moors 2009).

It is partly in light of the possible tension between being young and religiously active that MJD was constructed. As Fatima, who is thirty-one years old and has parents of Turkish origin, told me: 'One of the ideas behind MJD is to inform the young generation in German society that it is possible to be Muslim and German and at the same time cool'. The leaders of the multi-ethnic

Fig. 16.3 Public MJD event in Berlin. Photo: Synnøve Bendixsen

organization try to provide the youth with the emotional support and motivation to live a religious life and offer them increased understanding of who they
are and where they are going. They give them religiously informed guidance
about how to deal with challenges such as the pressure to take part in swimming and gymnastics in mixed-gender settings and the pressure to follow
mainstream Western fashions.

The organization does not promote ready-made religious instruction but
draws on a variety of authorities which they believe advocate an Islam of the
middle way, including Tariq Ramadan, Yusuf al-Qaradawi and the Egyptian television preacher Amr Khalid. The messages of these authorities are followed
selectively. For example, some aspects of al-Qaradawi's teachings, such as
the idea that women are allowed to travel alone, are pursued. Others such as
the recent call to jihad against Israel are rejected. Similarly, whereas some
members may be attracted to Khalid's profile, others will consider him too
populist.[5] While MJD rejects accusations from the German media and the
Federal Office for the Protection of the Constitution that they represent
the Muslim Brotherhood (MB) in Germany, elements of their vision do
resemble that of international Muslim revivalist movements, including the
Muslim Brotherhood.[6] For example, MJD embraces the concept of a culture-
less Islam around the world, which the Muslim Brotherhood, among others,
has also encouraged (Hermansen 2003: 309). Likewise, MJD incorporates a

form of identity politics, promoting the idea of 'Muslim and proud of it'.[7] The attendees at MJD are in this respect participants in what has been called the 'revival of Islam' in different contexts in Europe and globally (Eickelman 1992; Husain 1995; Mahmood 2005). Forming a specific dress style and taste is one element of this process of shaping the self as a religious, pious subject, through disciplinary and body practices (see Bendixsen 2013; Mahmood 2005; Jouili 2009; Fadil 2009, 2011).[8]

LEARNING TO COMBINE FASHION AND PIETY

During the meetings, the youth are provided with religiously defined ideas and ideals that should guide their everyday behaviour, thoughts, desires and actions. How to participate in youth activities and be fashionable without compromising their religious behaviour is a frequent theme of the weekly MJD presentations and friendship discussions. The importance of learning to dress 'correctly' but simultaneously present or keep one's modern youth style is something the leaders emphasize.[9] Through presentations, discussions and exemplary practices, including advice on where to buy what, and how to combine outfits with headscarves, young women are sensitized into becoming a modern religious youth.[10] They are part of the generation which, unlike their parents, seeks to combine Islamic authenticity and purification with fashionable understandings of Islamic dress.[11]

Few of the youth restrict themselves to the Muslim, Turkish or Arab clothing shops in Berlin or to the fashion of tesettür, which is popular in Turkey and amongst Turkish migrants in Germany (see Sandikci and Ger 2010). Instead, these youth make active use of the popular international Swedish chain store H&M and the international chain store C&A, which offer affordable, youthful and fashionable clothes.[12] These clothes, however, must be made to comply with certain religious rules and prescriptions. During meetings, leaders and peers recommend that the young women buy clothing one size larger than their bodies and likewise avoid wearing sweaters or dresses that look 'too tight'.[13] Through MJD meetings, Islamic events and regular discussions with peers, youth learn how a pair of jeans can be made respectable by covering one's thighs with a knee-length skirt or dress in the season's fashionable colours. Elbow-length, short tops can be made appropriate by being combined with loose arm-sleeves bought in Islamic shops. Some young women are keen to avoid wearing black for public discussions because they feel the colour creates a negative image or impression in relation to non-Muslims. At the same time, they suggest that red should be avoided as it is thought to attract too much attention. Ways through which ideas and ideals of dress comportment are promoted include various workshops, such as the one-time fashion show spontaneously called 'Walk of MJD'. This was directly inspired from the concept 'Walk of Islam'. The fashion gala 'Walk of Islam' was created in 2004 by four Berliner entrepreneurs mostly for Arabic and Turkish customers; it involved the young German fashion designer Catrin Weiland. Since then, 'Walk of Islam' has developed into a platform for fashion designers who create Islamic garments.

In contrast to most youth cultures, the value and taste authorities for these Muslim youth include knowledgeable elders such as imams and religious sources like the Quran, as well as younger modern authorities, such as Tariq Ramadan. Contributing to the development of Islamic fashion in Europe (Moors 2009), their points of reference are both German (European) styles and Islamic fashion from countries such as Turkey and Egypt, which they have picked up through cable TV and the Internet. The youth also shop extensively during the holidays in their parents' home countries and utilize online Muslim-branded clothes Web sites or German-based religiously ethical products, such as T-shirts with the motif 'I love my prophet'.[14]

If a young woman crosses the border of what is considered as proper—for example, wearing a belt around the waist and thus making an H&M dress too sexy—she is reproached explicitly or implicitly through remarks. For example, at one meeting, the leader said, 'When some of the girls wear a G-string, I can see that, you know. And that is not dressing for Allah.' She continued, 'When one of the sisters is not dressed properly, or not according to the Quran, one should talk to her about it.' Young women regularly correct each other when they are in the public sphere, such as approaching each other if their headscarves are out of order or asserting that the other's clothing is too sexy. Such corrections of imperfect practices have the effect of both controlling and integrating the individual subject, playing an essential part in the collectivization process within the group.

'MULTI-CULTI' ISLAMIC DRESS

Muslim women's fashions in this study do not conform to inherited traditions, yet neither do they merely represent individual or personal taste. Rather, Muslim women's dress style combines religiously defined ideas of Islamic fashion and images of the multicultural style in Berlin. For example, on our way to a picnic with a group of MJD youth, we were standing on a subway platform, waiting for other 'sisters' to arrive. Farah, a 23-year-old of Turkish origin, arrived and exclaimed, 'I was taken to be an Arab today!'; this resulted in the following dialogue:

Nawar (aged seventeen and of Egyptian origin):   You don't look Arab!

Synnøve (asking Fahra): Why?

Fahra: I don't know. Maybe 'cause I am wearing the headscarf like this. Most Turks wear their headscarves in a triangle behind and then up in the

> front, like Aysegül. And you know, 'cause we are multicultural and such,
> you get inspiration from the others, and then you learn other ways to
> wear it, and so I wear it like this.

Synnøve: What did the person say?

Fahra: Naja. It was like, I was buying these things in a shop, and the woman
behind the counter was Turkish. But I was talking to her in German the
whole time, and then I said goodbye in Turkish, and then she asked,
'Are you Turkish?' And I said yes. And she asked why I didn't talk to
her in Turkish then. And I said that I normally speak German...'cause
there were not very many Turks where I went to a school, and I am just
more used to talking in German. And she said that she had taken me
to be an Arab.

Fahra first refers to the headscarf as the marker of her collective identity
instead of making reference to language to explain why the shopkeeper
perceives her as Arab. The symbolic work of consumption is obvious here
(Willis 1990: 71). Patterns of consumption express who one is or seeks to
be. Dress is recognized as a marker of boundaries between different group
identities (Hebdige 1979; Dwyer 1998: 54). These boundary markers are
not, however, recognizable by the whole population. While few Berliner non-
Muslims would reflect upon whether a veiled woman is Turkish or from the
Middle East, within the Muslim population external signs like the style of the
headscarf provide additional signs of that person's identity. Taste and consumption not only mark Muslims from non-Muslims but also mark internal
differences within the Muslim population (Tarlo 2010).

Moreover, Fahra explains her style as different compared to other Turkish youth by referring to the multicultural characteristic of MJD. In Berlin, the term *multi-culti* is politically thick, mainly related to migration and
(failed) integration policies targeting youth with migrant backgrounds living
in Berlin and initiatives to integrate them. The youth make use of this term
among themselves, mostly in a positive manner and sometimes jokingly (see
Bendixsen 2013). Although the participants' emphasis on the fact that that
MJD is ethnically mixed is religiously motivated, they are simultaneously ap-
propriating the multi-culti characteristic of Berlin within this religious sphere.
Viewing themselves and their material practices and (re)presenting their religious organization as multi-culti, the youth are situating their Muslim faith
community as belonging in Berlin.[15]

Thus, while Muslim dress may be informed by the different regional backgrounds from which German Muslims come, whether Turkey, Egypt, Sudan,
Bosnia or Iraq, it would be insufficient to reduce the understanding of Berliner Muslim women's fashion to their geographic origins. The youth in this
research were mostly born in Germany, and their dress behaviour is shaped
by experiences which include their migration histories—as well as their life in

multicultural Berlin (see also Tarlo 2010 on London)—and the multicultural nature of the organization MJD.[16]

The city of Berlin offers a range of Islamic organizations, movements and mosques which Muslims can visit once in a while or more regularly. The religious focus, ethnic composition, style of teaching and expectations of each of these varies. The other big organization targeting Muslim youth in Berlin is Milli Görüş, which has youth groups all over the city.[17] The outlook of Milli Görüş is generally less multicultural and significantly more Turkish-oriented than MJD; the majority of the presentations and meetings of Milli Görüş take place in Turkish, and Ottoman history and culture are valued there.

When asking Aysegül, a 29-year-old of Turkish origin, whether she saw any differences between the clothing style of the MJD and Milli Görüş, she explained that she found the Turkish girls in Milli Görüş more consistent and believed they took more care with their outer appearance than those in other religious groups. A majority of the youth participating in Milli Görüş wear a long Turkish coat (*pardösü*), even in the summer, and they use a triangular style headscarf (*basörtü*) and flat shoes. Underneath the long coat, some wear dresses but others wear jeans and H&M clothes.[18] Aysegül points to how she is not always that consistent: she is always wearing make-up and sometimes wears tight clothes. Yet, she prefers the MJD style because she sees it as more easygoing.

RELIGIOUS TASTE AS A BOUNDARY MARKER

MJD youth, however, seldom discuss the youth dress style of members of other organizations. Instead, their perception of a legitimate dress takes form in relation to a 'triple articulation' vis-à-vis socially relevant others: first, in relation to their parent's culture; second, to the dominant German youth culture; and third, to incorrect Muslim youth.[19] First, young people stress that their headscarves are not similar to those of their mothers—which they often make fun of—since they consider their mothers' headscarves to be not only unfashionable but also worn without the correct intention and necessary religious self-reflection. The effort in MJD to make a separation between culture and religion and the search for a pure Islam, detached from ethno-national references, also becomes a point of departure for religious understandings of what is Islamic or un-Islamic. As already suggested, although regional styles may not necessarily be viewed as un-Islamic, they are not necessarily considered authentically Islamic either. Second, the dominant German youth culture is deemed too focussed on sexual emancipation, sexually explicit clothes and *haram* (illegal) activities, like drinking alcohol and going to discos. At the MJD meetings and discussions, it is often emphasized that women in Islam are better off than German women, as 'they don't have to focus on their outer appearance the whole time'. They distance themselves from a taste and aesthetic which they believe equates modernity with indecency (cf. Sandikci and Ger 2010: 28) and links freedom with sexiness and sex. Third, these young women's style and comportment is also distinguished from what they consider as incorrect Muslim youth who, although fashionably veiled, do not wear their clothes in a religiously correct manner and lack good comportment and appropriate religious intentionality (cf. Moors 2009).

The MJD youth regularly distance themselves from covered women they encounter on the streets whom they consider improperly dressed (i.e., wearing the headscarf with extensive make-up and sexy clothing) or who are dressed correctly but not behaving appropriately (i.e., holding hands with a male in public without being married). Practices such as using extra material to create a high and voluminous head shape, which gives the impression of having a lot of hair, is explicitly considered distasteful. Such female youth are characterized as insincere, or their appearance highlights their shallow understanding of religious norms.[20] The youth argue that these incorrectly veiled women are sending out the wrong signals, both to Muslims and non-Muslims, about what it means to be and what is involved in being a correctly dressed Muslim woman.

Through what they wear, young people construct boundaries and express 'what kind of Islam' they identify with. Consumption is one aspect of the 'broader cultural strategies of self-definition and self-maintenance' (Friedman 1994: 103) and the crafting of a young religious self. Frequently at stake is the representation of who and what Muslims are or should be in a non-Muslim society. These are internal struggles where an individual identifies, to some degree or not at all, with certain religious practices and moral standards, which are expressed through a certain religious aesthetic (style, values and behaviour) and taste. It suggests how 'putting on clothing is a form by which one exposes one's "self" to the outside world' (Woodward 2005: 22). In the crafting and presentation of the self, fashion becomes a 'technology of civility' or 'sanctioned codes of conduct' (Craik 1994: 5). On the street, bodily style forms an important part of everyday encounters and public debates in which people express their affiliations and identifications, thereby contributing to the drawing of distinctions and social boundaries between Muslims within Germany. For example, as fourteen-year-old Jamila, who is from an Egyptian background, commented as we were walking in Kreuzberg on our way back from the weekly MJD meeting: 'Many girls with headscarves are "chiki micki". They are not real Muslims.' When I asked her why, she told me that it was because they were 'only wearing it [the headscarf], but did so without the right intentions'.

It seems that young MJD women are provoked by the seeming ease and light-heartedness with which some other young women cover, whereas their own decision to cover the head is connected to religious effort. The combination of a headscarf with tight clothes does not reveal the level of modesty with which headscarves should be associated, according to Jamila. Many criticize Muslim youth who cover but dress incorrectly or have inappropriate comportment because they believe that these ways of covering are adopted purely for their symbolic value (fashion, political statement or marker of identity) rather than as a means to craft a virtuous religious self.[21] Additionally, by criticizing how other youths are veiling, identification is established with those who wear the same type of headscarf or conform to the same standards. This emphasis on correcting the comportment of others can also be understood in relation to the concept of *da'wa* (invitation to Islam); many believe that by behaving in a religiously correct way, this will make Islam more attractive to other people.[22] The following event exemplifies how struggles over Muslimness are played out in everyday situations:

> After meeting Ines, a twenty-year-old of Palestinian origin, at her work in a Turkish clothing shop in Kreuzberg, we are walking down Adalbertstrasse some meters from the infamous subway station KottbusserTor, which is often associated with gangs and drug dealers. Ines is complaining about how her work colleagues always speak together in Turkish, which she—as an Arabic speaker—cannot understand. Living in Wedding, she jokingly says, 'Being in Kreuzberg is like not really being in Germany.' We enter a small kiosk to buy ice cream and a conversation unfolds between Ines and the young woman behind the counter. The young Turkish-looking woman is in her early twenties, with long dark hair, make-up, a short T-shirt, tight jean trousers and 'evil-eye' jewellery. She asks Ines if she is visiting Berlin. Ines answers, 'No. I am not often here, at Kotti.' Ines laughs nervously (probably because she used the slang name for the area) and then asks, 'How is it to work here the whole day?' The young woman replies, 'How would you like to work here?' Ines exclaims, 'I could not work here, 'cause you sell alcohol.' A large part in the back of the kiosk is reserved for beverages, including alcohol. The young woman behind the counter quickly asserts, 'I am also a Muslim, you know. It's also difficult for me. But when the customers expect it [what can I do]?' Ines shrugs her shoulders, adding, 'But I couldn't do that, not even if it is just selling it.' The young woman insists, 'Like I said, I am also a Muslim. But it's like, religion and society is one thing and business is another. I just sell it; I don't drink it. Since I got married, I don't drink alcohol.' Ines adds, 'It's good that you can distinguish like that. [I couldn't have.]' Leaving the topic with which she seems uncomfortable the young woman asks Ines, 'Where do you come from?' Ines replies uneasily, 'Lebanon. And you?' The young woman, now with self-confidence, answers, 'Turkey.'

What is a Muslim or a Muslim youth, and who defines who is a Muslim? Such questions are asked not only by social scientists and politicians but also internally within the Muslim population. The situation above becomes framed around the question, what is a good Muslim and Muslim behaviour?

At the time of the encounter, Ines had struggled to find part-time work and had declined a job that would have involved her in haram activities (such as selling alcohol). During the conversation, the young girl emphasized twice that she too was Muslim, finding her religious identity being challenged indirectly by Ines, who explains that she (as a Muslim) could not have worked there. The two young women's different dress styles play an important factor in the framing and negotiation of the situation. While the shop woman is not veiled and wears tight clothes, Ines appears as a model for the correct young Muslim: she is dressed modestly with a long jacket over her skirt that hides her figure well. She does not wear any make-up and wears a tight headscarf completely covering her hair and neck. Ines's Muslim identification is stated in her whole physical appearance and cannot be disputed. It suggests how 'wearing covered dress is an embodied religious practice par excellence' (Moors 2009: 191). In the discussion, Ines challenges the other woman's Muslim identity while the latter seems to feel her Muslim credentials are being threatened or not taken seriously.[23]

Noticeably, the atmosphere of the conversation changed when the young woman working in the shop regained confidence and exclaimed that she was Turkish, compared to Ines who had hesitantly given her ethnic background.[24] The socio-geographical location of the encounter is significant: they are in a neighbourhood which is characterized by its Turkish migrants and their economic and social infrastructure. Kreuzberg has typically been described by researchers as an area where immigrants and their children 'feel at home' (Mandel 1996, 2008) and can capitalize on a social and cultural background (Caglar 2002) that is not valued in mainstream German society.[25] It is generally considered to be a place where Turkish immigrants can be proud and no longer feel out of place but, on the contrary, where they have managed to produce territoriality—developing a 'sense of place' (cf. Massey 1998).[26] Thus, while Ines feels confident in her Muslim identification and representation, she is less so when it comes to her ethnic origins, and particularly in a place like Kreuzberg, which is in sharp contrast to the young woman of Turkish background. This suggests also how local belonging, religious orientation and national identification are intertwined in complex ways.

CONCLUSION

For the MJD youth, the learning of a specific religious dress taste which combines elements of youthfulness, fashion and piety takes place at weekly religious meetings and in daily conversations with peers (Figure 16.4). The Islam taught in the religious organization also shapes the dress politics of the organization and the youth: the practice of distinguishing between culture

Fig. 16.4 The annual MJD summer camp meeting. This is the seminar tent were women enter on the left, and men enter on the right. Photo: Synnøve Bendixsen

and religion and the focus on living as a Muslim in Germany and on being multicultural informs their taste and perception of what is considered correct dress.

Youth frequently evaluate other youth according to their dress. Among young Muslim women, clothing styles combined with public behaviour are interpreted as clues of one's religious orientation—marking both distinctions within Muslim communities and creating feelings of belonging to a particular religious organization. While wearing the headscarf is a clear sign that the person is Muslim, the way the headscarf is shaped, the style and its colours, in combination with body comportment, communicates in more detail clues about one's ethnic/national background (Bendixsen 2010, 2013). Socially relevant others, such as their mothers and sexily dressed Muslim youth, present images against which they distinguish their own correct multicultural Islamic style. Through repeated discussions, youth acquire a disposition where they learn to differentiate between other Muslim youth's dress styles, some of which are considered as flawed or even un-Islamic. Thus, dress choice not only forms part of the path towards becoming a more correct or pious Muslim woman, it also forms an important part of one's credibility, signalling one's religious outlook and belonging and contributing to forming one's sense of place in Berlin.

NOTES

1. Kreuzberg is administratively structured into Kreuzberg-Friedrichhain. However, the local identification remains divided: few immigrants live in Friedrichhain, previously situated in East Berlin.
2. Consumption has been linked to youth cultures since the 1950s (Hebdige 1979). The early research on youth culture particularly emphasised the meanings of fashion and style in the establishment of subcultural identities and affiliations. In the mid 1970s, Clark, Hall, Jefferson and Roberts (1975) conducted research on subculture in England, investigating the construction of styles through the selection and transformation of objects and goods. Their empirical investigations of how youth actively convert and subvert objects from their initial meanings and applications influenced later youth studies, including this one.
3. MJD had to find a new place for their meetings after they closed down their bookshop, Greenpalace, in 2010. For a while during the summer of 2010, the 'sister' part of MJD met in the Bosnian mosque in Kreuzberg. Currently, they are meeting in the locales of Deutschsprachiger Muslimkreiz e.V. (a German-speaking Muslim group) in Wedding. MJD participants come from all over Berlin, in particular Neukölln, Wedding and Kreuzberg but also Spandau. I conducted ethnographic fieldwork with the organization and its female participants for long periods from 2004 to 2007 for my PhD thesis.
4. Similar Muslim youth organizations exist in Austria, France, Italy, Norway, Sweden and the United Kingdom, and MJD is represented at the European level by FEMYSO (Forum of European Muslim Youth and Student Organizations).
5. MJD has developed a particular organizational culture or content, which successive *shuras* (councils) uphold with only minor modifications. According to the leader of the shura, changes in what is religiously acceptable or not considered as religiously accurate (for instance, whether or not hip hop is acceptable at religious meetings) could be understood to be a result of a situation where the organizers have gained more and more experience. They have become adults and thus are less afraid of doing something that may be considered incorrect.
6. Since 2003, the organization has faced negative media attention and suspicion, and in 2005 the Federal Office for the Protection of the Constitution put MJD on its list of Islamist organizations in Baden-Württemberg (and since 2006 in Hessen, where the annual national MJD meeting takes place), partly due to suspicions that the organization has links to the Muslim Brotherhood, a fact the organization has publicly denounced (see Bendixsen 2010 for a longer discussion of this).
7. During some of the more intensive, closed meetings, MJD makes reference to the ideas of Egyptian ideologue Sayyid Qutb and the Pakistani

ideologue Mawdudi. These two form a basis for several of the ideas revised by Hizb ut-Tahrir (Tarlo 2010)—an international Sunni pan-Islamic political organization that works to create a unified, transnational Islamic state, and at times condones the use of violence. Yet, I was informed that the way MJD makes use of their ideas is by reading them in a critical manner and situating them in relation to other ideologues and ideas.

8. For Mahmood, piety is the perfection of virtuous behaviour akin to Foucauldian 'techniques of the self'. The 'techniques of the self' are particular practices which, when performed by the subject, allow her or him to take up certain subject-positions; in this case, that of the 'virtuous' Muslim woman (Mahmood 2005).

9. *Modern* is here used as an emic term; thus, the person's own understanding of the term.

10. Tarlo (2010: 8) points to how there are few references in the Quran to women's dress and that these are largely open for interpretation. Islamic scholars, consequently, are participating in much discussion concerning Islamic dress.

11. There are similarities here with some of the Muslim women in London discussed by Tarlo (2010). Yet, certain elements are specific to the Berlin scene.

12. This is similar to the young women in the Netherlands studied by Moors (2009). Tarlo (2010: 79) also mentions one woman for whom H&M became 'a real life saver' after she converted to a more pious dress style.

13. Certain public comportment, such as shouting or hanging around with boys, is also discouraged at the MJD meetings.

14. Such T-shirts can also be found elsewhere in Europe, such as in London (Tarlo 2010). Popular online sites are www.MuslimGear.com, www.styleislam.com, TheHijabShop.com, TheNasheedShop.com, and www.myumma.de. See Bunt (2005) for a discussion of the increase in 'Islamic cyberspace' after 9/11.

15. In their free time, the youth also make efforts to 'get to know' Berlin by attending not only religious happenings (such as visiting mosques, religious events and celebrations) but also organizing more typical youth activities, such as bowling, ice skating and picnics. Through these events, which are conducted with other religiously devoted youth, they appropriate Berlin spaces as their own. At the same time, some of the difficulties they face in living out Islam in Berlin may well be a consequence of Berlin's overall secular character, compared to other cities in southern Germany in which religion plays a more important role in everyday life.

16. A person's attire is, of course, also made up through experiences of racism and marginalization, encounters with various expressions of identity politics and Islamic revivalism, as well as personal interests. More global

flows such as the Internet, cable TV and international travel also inform styles of dress (Tarlo 2010).

17. Milli Görüş apparently has more than 500 mosque associations in Germany. The Islamische Gemeinschaft Milli Görüş (IGMG) is closely linked with political Islam in Turkey, including the Refah Partisi (Welfare party) and its predecessors (Henkel 2004). The exact nature and quality of this relationship is disputed. The Federal Office for the Protection of the Constitution (1999: 164; 2000: 207) argues that Milli Görüş is an extremist Islamist organization aiming to hinder the social and cultural integration of youth into the German society. What is clear is that the IGMG represents a more politicized version of Islam, endorsing Muslim activism in the public sphere and asserting that in order to secure an Islamic life Muslims must be politically represented. See, for example, Şen and Aydin (2002). For a critical discussion on the regular accusations against the Milli Görüş as 'threatening' the German national identity, see Ewing (2003). See also Schiffauer (2008) for a discussion on the relation between the Federal Office for the Protection of the Constitution and Islamic organizations and Schiffauer (2004) for a discussion on Milli Görüş in Germany.

18. A youth with a different dress style underneath her long coat can thus appear very different in a separated female space, compared to those who do not wear a long coat but a religiously 'proper' outfit. One may question whether this different dress style creates a distinction in how the two different youth groups come to perceive the public and private.

19. The term *triple articulation* is influenced by the term *double articulation* coined by Clark, Hall, Jefferson and Roberts (1975: 15).

20. In contrast, the youth seldom discuss women who wear the niqab, face-veil or *tesettür*. This might be because the youth would seldom dispute the religiousness of these women (although in one instance, it was suggested that a sixteen-year-old who wore the niqab was doing it more as a performance than for religious purposes as she was apparently not wearing it consistently). At the same time, they may not affiliate with women who wear the niqab or face-veil since it would be difficult to categorize their appearance either as modern or as religiously incorrect. The youth mainly discuss 'German immorally dressed women'.

21. Tarlo found similar perceptions among pious Muslim women in London. She argues likewise that some of the pious women she interviewed consider that many women 'wear the hijab as a fashion accessory and that, in doing so, they misunderstand its true meaning' (Tarlo 2010: 65).

22. *Da'wa* is a religious duty, which today is directed both to non-Muslims and Muslims who are considered to be living Islam incorrectly. The practice of da'wa among the youth may take the form of urging one's fellow Muslims to perform Islam with greater vigour (Mahmood 2005: 57) by pointing

out their failings—such as irreligious outfits or comportment or that they fail to fulfil certain religious duties.

23. This situation also draws attention to the fact that 'clothes have important social and material effects which go beyond the intentions of the wearer' (Tarlo 2010: 12).

24. Additionally, the discussion on Turks in Kreuzberg some minutes before between Ines and me perhaps reflect Ines's perception of being in a neighbourhood belonging to Turks, a space she does not completely fit in, even if she is a Muslim.

25. This social and cultural capital can also be transformed into economic capital—that is, by establishing halal butchers or ethnic/religious supermarkets.

26. More than in Wedding, in Kreuzberg there is a feeling that everyone knows each other, although this resembles the 'imagined community' of Anderson (1983) rather than being a social fact. Yet, this creates both a form of belonging and a form of social control or social policing in the streets of these neighbourhoods, which is not necessarily dependent upon whether the family is religiously oriented. Ideas of family honour where the social behaviour of the daughter is in focus are often tied to tradition and the socio-economic situation of the family and its social network.

REFERENCES

Anderson, B. (1983), *Imagined Communities: Reflections on the Origins and Spread of Nationalism,* London: Verso.

Bendixsen, S. (2009), 'Being Muslim *or* Being "German"?: Islam as a New Urban Identity', in G. Tibe Bonifacio and V. Angeles, eds., *Gender, Religion and Migration: Pathways of Integration,* Lanham: Lexington Books.

Bendixsen, S. (2010), '"It's Like Doing SMS to Allah": Young Female Muslims Crafting a Religious Self in Berlin', PhD thesis, Berlin, Humboldt Universität; Paris, Ecole des Hautes Etudes en Sciences Sociales.

Bendixsen, S. (2013), *The Religious Identity of Young Muslim Women in Berlin. An Ethnographic Study,* Leiden: Brill.

Bunt, G. (2005), 'Defining Islamic Interconnectivity', in M. Cooke and B. Lawrence, eds., *Muslim Networks from Hajj to Hip Hop,* Chapel Hill: University of North Carolina Press, 235–51.

Caglar, A. (2002), 'A Table in Two Hands', in D. Kandiyoti and A. Saktanber, eds., *Fragments of Culture,* London: I.B. Tauris.

Clark, J., S. Hall, T. Jefferson and B. Roberts (1975), 'Subcultures, Cultures and Class: A Theoretical Overview', in S. Hall and T. Jefferson, eds., *Resistance Through Rituals,* London: Routledge.

Craik, J. (1994), *The Face of Fashion. Cultural Studies in Fashion,* London: Routledge.

Dwyer, C. (1998), 'Contested Identities: Challenging Dominant Representations of Young British Muslim Women', in T. Skelton and G. Valentine, eds., *Cool Places: Geographies of Youth Cultures,* London: Routledge.

Eickelman, D. F. (1992), 'Mass Higher Education and the Religious Imagination in Contemporary Arab Society', *American Ethnologist* 19, 4: 643–55.

Ewing, K. P. (2003), 'Living Islam in the Diaspora: Between Turkey and Germany', *South Atlantic Quarterly* 102, 2/3: 405–31.

Fadil, N. (2009), 'Managing Affects and Sensibilities: The Case of Not-hand-shaking and Not Fasting', *Social Anthropology/Anthropologie Sociale* 17, 4: 439–54.

Fadil, N. (2011), 'Not-/unveiling as an Ethical Practice', *Feminist Review* 98, 1: 83–109.

Federal Office for the Protection of the Constitution (1999), 'Bundesministerium des Innern, Verfassungsschutzbericht 1999', report, Berlin, <http://www.verfassungsschutz.de/de/publikationen> accessed 3 February 2007.

Federal Office for the Protection of the Constitution (2000), 'Bundesministerium des Innern, Verfassungsschutzbericht 2000', report, Berlin, <http://www.verfassungsschutz.de/de/publikationen> accessed 3 February 2007.

Friedman, J. (1994), *Cultural Identity and Global Process,* London: Sage.

Hebdige, D. (1979), *Subculture: The Meaning of Style,* London: Routledge.

Henkel, H. (2004), 'Rethinking the dâr al-harb: Social Change and Changing Perceptions of the West in Turkish Islam', *Journal of Ethnic and Migration Studies* 30, 5: 961–77.

Hermansen, M. (2003), 'How to Put the Genie Back in the Bottle? "Identity" Islam Muslim Youth Cultures in America', in O. Safi, ed., *Progressive Muslims: On Justice, Gender, and Pluralism,* Oxford: Oneworld Publications.

Husain, M. Z. (1995), *Global Islamic Politics,* New York: Harper Collins.

Jouili, J. S. (2009), 'Negotiating Secular Boundaries: Pious Micro-practices of Muslim Women in French and German Public Spheres', *Social Anthropology/Anthropologie Sociale* 17, 4: 455–70.

Mahmood, S. (2005), *Politics of Piety: The Islamic Revival and the Feminist Subject,* Princeton, NJ: Princeton University Press.

Mandel, R. (1996), 'A Place of Their Own: Contesting Spaces and Defining Places in Berlin's Migrant Community', in B. D. Metcalf, ed., *Making Muslim Space in North America and Europe,* Berkeley: University of California Press.

Mandel, R. (2008), *Cosmopolitan Anxieties: Turkish Challenges to Citizenship and Belonging in Germany,* Durham, NC: Duke University Press.

Massey, D. (1998), 'The Spatial Construction of Youth Cultures', in T. Skelton and G. Valentine, eds., *Cool Places: Geographies of Youth Cultures,* London: Routledge.

Moors, A. (2009), 'Islamic Fashion in Europe: Religious Conviction, Aesthetic Style, and Creative Consumption', *Encounters* 1, 1: 175–201.

Sandikcil, Ö., and G. Ger (2005), 'Aesthetics, Ethics and Politics of the Turkish Headscarf', in S. Kuechler and D. Miller, eds., *Clothing as Material Culture,* Oxford: Berg.

Sandikci, Ö., and G. Ger (2010), 'Veiling in Style: How Does a Stigmatized Practice Become Fashionable?', *Journal of Consumer Research* 37: 15–36.

Schiffauer, W. (2004), 'Die Islamische Gemeinschaft Milli Görüs—ein Lehrstück zum verwickelten Zusammenhang von Migration, Religion und sozialer Integration', in K. J. Bade, M. Bommes and R. Münz, eds., *Migrationsreport 2004. Fakten—Analysen–Perspektiven,* New York: Campus, 67–97.

Schiffauer, W. (2008), 'Suspect Subjects: Muslim Migrants and the Security Agencies in Germany', in J. M. Eckert, ed., *The Social Life of Anti-terrorism Laws. The War on Terror and the Classification of the 'Dangerous Other',* Bielefeld: transcript, 55–78.

Şen, F., and H. Aydin (2002), *Islam in Deutschland,* Munich: Beck'sche Reihe.

Tarlo, E. (2010), *Visibly Muslim: Fashion, Politics, Faith,* Oxford: Berg.

Willis, P. (1990), *Common Culture: Symbolic Work at Play in the Everyday Cultures of the Young,* Boulder, CO: Westview Press.

Woodward, S. (2005), 'Looking Good: Feeling Right—Aesthetics of the Self', in S. Kuechler and D. Miller, eds., *Clothing as Material Culture,* Oxford: Berg.

Index